Exporting the American Model

EXPORTING THE AMERICAN MODEL

The Postwar Transformation
of European Business

MARIE-LAURE DJELIC

Oxford University Press

1998

Oxford University Press, Great Clarendon Street, Oxford OX2 6DP

Oxford New York

*Athens Auckland Bangkok Bogota Bombay Buenos Aires
Calcutta Cape Town Dar es Salaam Delhi Florence Hong Kong Istanbul
Karachi Kuala Lumpur Madras Madrid Melbourne Mexico City
Nairobi Paris Singapore Taipei Tokyo Toronto Warsaw*

and associated companies in

Berlin Ibadan

Oxford is a registered trade mark of Oxford University Press

*Published in the United States
by Oxford University Press Inc., New York*

© Marie-Laure Djelic 1998

*The moral rights of the author have been asserted
First published 1998*

British Library Cataloguing in Publication Data

Data available

Library of Congress Cataloging in Publication Data
Djelic, Marie-Laure.
Exporting the American model: the post-war transformation of
European business/Marie-Laure Djelic.
p.   cm.
Includes bibliographical references and index.
1. Industrial organization—Europe, Western—Case studies.
2. Industrial organization—United States.   3. Industrial productivity—
Europe, Western—Case studies.   4. Industrial productivity—United States.
5. Reconstruction (1939–1951)—Europe, Western.   6. Economic assistance,
American—Europe, Western.   7. Technology transfer—Europe, Western.
8. Technology transfer—United States.   I. Title.
HD2844.D53   1998   338.94–dc21   98–2541
CIP

ISBN 0–19–829317–8

1 3 5 7 9 10 8 6 4 2

*Typeset by J&L Composition Ltd, Filey, North Yorkshire
Printed in Great Britain on acid-free paper by
Biddles Ltd, Guildford and King's Lynn*

Nothing is possible without human beings,
Nothing can last without institutions.

Jean Monnet (1976)

CONTENTS

ACKNOWLEDGMENTS

I have incurred, throughout the process of writing this book, numerous debts of gratitude. I alone, though, am responsible for any remaining errors of fact or judgment.

My greatest debt, undeniably, is to Theda Skocpol, who provided direction and support from the outset. Her work for me is a model and an inspiration. I also wish to express special thanks to John Campbell, Peter Marsden, Mauro Guillén, and David Frank, who read the manuscript from beginning to end at an earlier stage. While in the Sociology Department at Harvard, I benefited from fruitful exchanges with professors and graduate students, many of whom became friends: Victoria Alexander, Liah Greenfeld, John Hall, Francie Ostrower, Yasemin Soysal, Cynthia Cook, John Glenn III, Meyer Kestnbaum, and Mark Warren. At the Harvard Business School, I wish to thank not only Nitin Nohria and Paul Lawrence but also Thomas McCraw, who invited me to attend the Business History seminar. I learnt a lot, in this seminar, from Alfred Chandler, William Lazonick, and Richard Tedlow amongst others.

Elsewhere in the USA and in Europe, I have accrued debts to many other scholars and colleagues, who gave me invaluable advice, commented on my work, shared their own work, or were highly supportive: Antti Ainamo, Kàroly Balaton, Andrew Creighton, Michael Creswell, Daniel Dayan, Chiarella Esposito, Richard Farnetti, Marc Flandreau, Neil Fligstein, Regina Gramer, Mark Granovetter, Gary Hamilton, Wade Jacoby, Bruce Kogut, Jessica Korn, Richard Kuisel, Maurice Lévy-Leboyer, Charles Maier, Rachel Parker, William Roy, Gerald Salancik, Raymond Saner, Yehouda Shenhav, Marc Ventresca, Richard Whitley, Richard Whittington and Martha Zuber. I would also like to thank, collectively, the Economic History seminar at the OFCE (Organisation Française pour le Commerce Extérieur) in Paris and members of the CEREM (Centre d'Etudes et de Recherche sur les Enterprises Multinationales) at Paris University, Nanterre, for valuable feedback.

Work for this book would never have been possible without the support of a number of institutions. Harvard University has provided me with a congenial environment, a profusion of resources, and funding. The Krupp Foundation in Essen, Germany, has offered me fellowships for research, through the Center for European Studies at Harvard. The staff at the Archives Nationales de France in Paris, at the Monnet Foundation in Lausanne, Switzerland, and at the German Bundesarchiv in Koblenz were particularly helpful, guiding me through their holdings.

At the Ecole Supérieure des Sciences Economiques et Commerciales (ESSEC) in Paris, I wish to thank my colleagues for their unfailing support and in particular Alain Bernard, Laurent Bibard, Alan Jenkins, Jane Salk, Maurice Thévenet, Radu Vranceanu.

At Oxford University Press, I am first of all indebted to David Musson, who believed in this project from the beginning and helped me see it through. I also wish to thank Leonie Hayler and Kim Allen who were of great help throughout the last stages.

Last but not least, nothing would have been possible without my friends and family. My very special thanks and warmest feelings go to Milena my daughter, Bozidar my husband, and to my parents, to whom this book is dedicated.

FIGURES

TABLES

ABBREVIATIONS

AFL	American Federation of Labor
AMA	American Management Association
BAC	Business Advisory Council
BIDEC	Bipartite Decartelization Commission
CED	Committee for Economic Development
CIA	Central Intelligence Agency
CIO	Congress of Industrial Organization
CPRB	Combined Production and Resources Board
ECA	Economic Cooperation Administration
ERP	European Recovery Program
GARIOA	Government Account for Relief in Occupied Areas
HICOG	American High Commission in Germany
MSA	Mutual Security Agency
NAM	National Association of Manufacturers
NBER	National Bureau for Economic Research
OMGUS	Office of Military Government, United States
SAM	Society for the Advancement of Management
WPB	War Production Board

AFAP	Association Française pour l'Accroissement de la Productivité
BIC	Bénéfices Industriels et Commerciaux
BNCI	Banque Nationale du Commerce et de l'Industrie
BTE	Bureau des Temps Elémentaires
CEGOS	Centre d'Etudes Générales d'Organisation Scientifique
CFA	Comité Français pour l'Approvisionnement
CFDT	Confédération Française Démocratique du Travail
CFTC	Confédération Française des Travailleurs Chrétiens
CGC	Confédération Générale des Cadres
CGP	Commissariat Général à la Productivité
CGPF	Confédération Générale du Patronat Français
CGPME	Confédération Générale des Petites et Moyennes Entreprises
CGT	Confédération Générale du Travail
CGT-FO	Confédération Générale du Travail-Force Ouvrière
CIERP	Centre Intersyndical d'Etudes et de Recherches de Productivité
CNOF	Comité National de l'Organisation Française

CNP   Comité National de la Productivité
CNPF   Conseil National du Patronat Français
CNR   Conseil National de la Résistance
CRC   Centre de Recherche et d'Etudes des Chefs d'Entreprise
ENA   Ecole Nationale d'Administration
ESSEC   Ecole Supérieure des Sciences Economiques et Commerciales
FME   Fonds de Modernisation et d'Equipement
HEC   Ecole des Hautes Etudes Commerciales
IAE   Instituts d'Administration des Entreprises
INSEE   Institut National de Statistiques et d'Etudes Economiques
ISEA   Institut Supérieur d'Economie Appliquée
MRP   Mouvement Républicain Populaire
PCF   Parti Communiste Français
PME   Petites et Moyennes Entreprises
SADEP   Société Auxiliaire de Diffusion des Editions de Productivité
SARL   Société à Responsabilité Limitée
SEEF   Service des Etudes Economiques et Financières
SFIO   Section française de l'Internationale Ouvrière
SGCI   Secrétariat Général du Comité Interministériel

GERMANY

AG   Aktiengesellschaft
AsU   Arbeitsgemeinschaft selbständiger Unternehmer
BDI   Bundesverband der Deutschen Industrie
CDU   Christlich Demokratische Union
CSU   Christlich Soziale Union
DGB   Deutscher Gewerkschaftsbund
DKV   Deutscher Kohlen Verkauf
GEDEC   German Decartelization Commission
GEDAG   German Decartelization Agencies
GmbH   Gesellschaft mit beschränkter Haftung
KFW   Kreditanstalt für Wiederaufbau
KPD   Kommunistische Partei Deutschland
NSDAP   Nationalsozialistische Deutsche Arbeitspartei
RDI   Reichsverband der Deutschen Industrie
RKW   Rationalisierungs Kuratorium der Wirtschaft
RWK   Rheinisch Westfälische Kohlensyndicat
SPD   Sozialdemokratische Partei Deutschland

ITALY

CGIL	Confederazione Generale Italiana del Lavoro
DC	Democrazia Cristiana
CIR-ERP	Comitato Interministeriale per la Ricostruzione
CISL	Confederazione Italiana Sindicati Lavoratori
ENI	Ente Nazionale Idrocarburi
IMI	Istituto Mobiliare Italiano
IRI	Istituto per la Ricostruzione Industriale
LCGIL	Libera Confederazione Generale Italiana del Lavoro
PCI	Partito Communista Italiano

COMMON

CEEC	Committee for European Economic Cooperation
ECSC	European Coal and Steel Community
EEC	European Economic Community
EPA	European Productivity Agency
EPU	European Payments Union
EU	European Union
GATT	General Agreement on Tariffs and Trade
IMF	International Monetary Fund
INSEAD	Institut Européen d'Administration des Affaires
NATO	North Atlantic Treaty Organization
OECD	Organization for Economic Cooperation and Development
OEEC	Organization for European Economic Cooperation
OSR	Office of the Special Representative

Introduction

National systems of industrial production have undeniably converged over the second half of the twentieth century. The world has turned into a 'global village' and similarities have increased across national units. In spite of strong isomorphic pressures, though, differences have persisted that set apart, to this day, national sytems of industrial production. Local peculiarities are sufficiently significant and resilient that one can still identify and contrast national models and point to distinctly German, French, Italian, or American features. In fact, both trends—convergence and persistent differentiation—are key to understanding our contemporary industrial world and the evolution of national systems of industrial production, particularly since 1945. This book developed from the belief that the very coexistence of these two trends was in itself a paradox worth studying. The main puzzle seemed to be the fact that differences had persisted while, at the very same time, similarities had been increasing. The challenge was thus to propose an account of the evolution of national systems of industrial production after 1945 that would take in those two apparently contradictory trends.

The gap between existing accounts or theoretical arguments and empirical reality prompted me to define the research agenda along those lines. Indeed, the literature has focused either on convergence or on national specificities, rarely on their coexistence. As a consequence, accounts have always been partial. A focus on convergence has led researchers to disregard differences between national systems of industrial production or to dismiss them as merely transitory. A focus on national specificities, on the other hand, has generally meant forgetting isomorphic pressures, which as a matter of fact worked their way into the real world despite or around local peculiarities. Empirical territories, furthermore, rarely overlapped. Studies of convergence have tended to target countries such as the USA, the UK, or Germany. France, Italy, Sweden, or Japan have repeatedly been used, on the other hand, to illustrate the argument that national systems of industrial production were unique. Convergence and differences were thus made intellectually incompatible while, on the ground, they remained stubbornly intertwined. In contrast, I propose to study in this book three Western European countries taken from both types of empirical territories—France, West Germany, and Italy—and to account for the balance, in each national system of industrial production, between the impact of isomorphic pressures and the long-term persistence of peculiar, local features.

Beyond the fundamental differences that set them apart, arguments focusing on convergence and those accounting for national specificities make a common mistake. They both rely on the assumption that national systems of industrial production can ultimately be treated as discrete entities, independent from each other. I argue in the following pages that national systems of industrial production did not evolve in a discrete or independent fashion, particularly after 1945. It will be shown, as a matter of fact, that the American system of industrial production which emerged in a specific national context, was constructed after 1945 as a universal model for the Western world. I will argue that the attempt at a cross-national diffusion or transfer of this one and single model, on a large scale after the Second World War, accounts for the partial convergence of national systems of industrial production. A key actor behind this attempt at a cross-national transfer was the Marshall plan administration, at least throughout the first period. Differences, on the other hand, in the degree to which national peculiarities have persisted, can be explained to a significant extent by more or less efficient channels of transfer and more or less powerful and organized movements of resistance or opposition at the national level.

This overall argument will be documented and further developed in the following pages. It can be articulated, in summary form, around four main stages. First of all, a radically new system of industrial production emerged at the turn of the twentieth century in the USA. Large corporations, using mass production techniques and competing on oligopolistic markets policed by antitrust regulation, became an alternative on the new continent to small-scale, family-owned and -run industrial units linked together through cartels and other types of loose agreements. The emergence of this new system of industrial production was a complex and sometimes messy process, deeply embedded within a peculiar historical and institutional context and reflecting, beyond economic and technological evolution, social and political confrontations. By the end of the Second World War, this model of industrial organization had become dominant in the USA, which was then taking on the economic and political leadership of the Western world. In a second stage, a parallel was thus easily drawn between American geopolitical and economic power on the one hand and the peculiar system of industrial production characteristic of that country on the other hand. Legitimated during its early years through a discourse on efficiency, the American model of industrial production would be constructed right after the Second World War as superior and universal. Thus, in a third stage, the American system of industrial production became a model for a number of Western European countries. A peculiar geopolitical and economic situation had created the conditions for American involvement in Western European affairs. Cross-national mechanisms of transfer were devised, institutionalized, and operated; American military governments in defeated countries and the Marshall plan administration playing there a significant role. But the American model was not accepted nor adopted to the same extent in all Western European economies. National peculiarities remained and they were more or less significant in each case. Indeed, for each country, the transfer process was embedded in different economic, political, cultural, and institutional environments. In turn, those national differences had an impact not only on transfer mechanisms and their efficiency but also on the nature and degree of resistance and opposition that was to emerge, nationally, to the cross-national transfer process.

NATIONAL SYSTEMS OF INDUSTRIAL PRODUCTION: DEFINITION AND COMPARISON

National systems of industrial production are understood to be the dominant structural frameworks shaping conditions of industrial production in given countries.[1] Those structural frameworks are believed to be social constructions where technology and economic factors play a role without being entirely determining. As defined here, national systems of industrial production have four key dimensions, brought together in Table 1.

A national system of industrial production is characterized by the size of its production units—physical structures and by the legal identity of its firms. Organizational structures or, in other words, dominant modes of production and institutionalized patterns of action and interaction within legal entities are also defining elements. Finally, governance structures or institutionalized patterns of interaction across and between legal entities are another important dimension of national systems of industrial production.[2]

As outlined earlier, the central argument of this book rests on a set of empirical observations with respect to national systems of industrial production and their evolution in post Second World War Western Europe. While economic expansion and rapid industrial development were common to a number of countries in the 1950s and 1960s, national 'miracles' each had their own peculiar features. There clearly were different paths to prosperity and economic growth seemed compatible with various types of structural arrangements. In those countries where economic and industrial development came along with a rapid and significant transformation of the national system of industrial production, the evolution was unmistakably towards the structural model originally pioneered by the USA. The number and role of large firms increased a great deal in those countries during the two decades that followed the end of the war (Cassis, 1997). Corporate ownership structures became increasingly popular and an alternative to sole proprietorships or family ownership and management. Forms of internal organization such as the multi-divisional structure, unknown until then in Europe, were adopted fairly

Table 1. National systems of industrial production: a definition

Physical structures	Ownership structures	Organizational structures	Governance structures

rapidly, particularly by the new large firms. Cartels and loose interfirm agreements, characteristic of Western European economies before the war, were on
the other hand declared illegal. Markets came to be regulated through antitrust
legislation in the American tradition. Both France and West Germany bear
witness to such an evolution although, in each case, structural arrangements
have in the end retained some of their own specific features.

   In other Western European countries, economic expansion and industrial
growth marked the postwar decades but without such a radical evolution of
national systems of industrial production. Transformations in the structural
arrangements of Italian industry, for example, never took place on such a
scale and the Italian system of industrial production seemed to resist
systematic and large-scale 'Americanization'. By the 1970s, small-scale or
medium-sized family firms still dominated Italian industry. Those family
firms worked together within locally embedded networks and this was particularly true in the most dynamic parts of Italy, in the industrial districts of
the center and the northeast. The choice of those three Western European
countries—France, West Germany, and Italy—as empirical cases for the
book can thus be justified. Taken together, they provide a convincing illustration of the fact that economic expansion and industrial growth were
compatible, in the postwar Western European environment, with different
types of structural arrangements. As documented in the following pages, both
increasing similarities and persistent differences emerge from a systematic
study of those three national systems of industrial production and of their
evolution after 1945.

Physical Structures

As shown in Figure 1, the twenty years following the end of the Second
World War have been characterized in West Germany and also in France by
rapid and radical changes in the physical structures of national industries.
The relative stability of Italian industry with respect to its size distribution,
also documented in Figure 1, appears all the more striking in comparison.
Over those twenty years, West German and French firms became increasingly similar to their American counterparts at least as far as size and
physical boundaries were concerned. Units of medium or large size multiplied in the industrial sectors of both countries, displacing to a significant
extent smaller entities. Meanwhile in Italy, small units retained their predominant role in the national industry.

Ownership Structures

Together with variations in the size of production units and in the physical
boundaries of firms came an evolution of their legal identities and of owner-

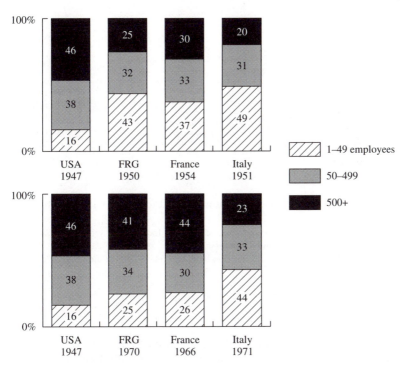

Figure 1. Distribution of industrial labor force by size of establishment
Note: Those figures are for manufacturing industry only. Utilities, energy, and construction are not included.
Sources: Bureau of the Census (1951, 1971), Statistisches Bundesamt (1954, 1974), INSEE (1956, 1974), Istituto Centrale di Statistica (1955, 1976).

ship structures. From 1950 to 1970, ownership structures characterized by a dispersion of ownership and limited liability—defining elements of the corporate structure—became increasingly popular in France and in West Germany as Figure 2 underscores. In the meantime, in Italy, the number of firms adopting corporate structures also increased but to a less significant extent.

An overall common trend is thus unmistakable, with some variation in scope across the three countries. In France and in West Germany, the widespread adoption of corporate ownership structures between 1950 and 1970 came with a sharp decrease in the total number of sole proprietorships. This was not the case in Italy where that number remained relatively stable.[3] There were, on the other hand, national specificities with respect to the types of corporate ownership structures adopted in each country. In France and in Italy, the preference went to joint stock companies. In West Germany, limited liability companies and limited partnerships were clearly favored over the public joint stock corporation.[4]

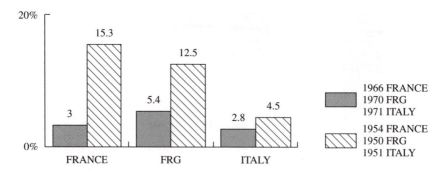

Figure 2. Corporate ownership structures and mixed forms after 1945. Percentage of industrial firms

Note: Those figures are for manufacturing industries only. Included are joint stock companies, limited liability companies, and limited partnerships.

Sources: INSEE (1956, 1974), Statistisches Bundesamt (1953, 1973), Istituto Centrale di Statistica (1955, 1976).

Organizational Structures

The postwar period also witnessed the adoption of new modes of internal organization in Western European industries. The multidivisional structure, in particular, pioneered in the 1920s by a few American corporations, spread at a quick pace amongst large French and West German firms. The multidivisional structure, or M-form, was characterized by decentralization and a reorganization of the firm's activities along product lines, a general office being in charge of coordination and long-range planning (Drucker, 1946; Chandler, 1962; Sloan, 1963). Figure 3 shows clearly that the multidivisional

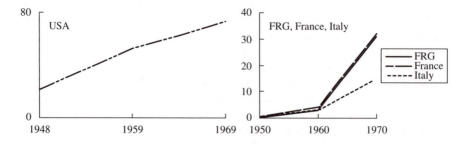

Figure 3. Multidivisional structure in large manufacturing firms after 1945

Sources: Fligstein (1990: 336). USA = 100 largest companies. Dyas and Thanheiser (1976: 29). FRG = 78 largest German-owned companies. France = 79 French-owned companies. Italy = 61 Italian-owned companies.

structure was unknown in Europe in 1950. Twenty years later, around 40 per cent of the largest French- and German-owned manufacturing concerns had adopted the M-form.[5] Italian firms, on the other hand, were more reluctant and by 1970 only 25 per cent of the largest firms in that country had settled for the M-form.[6]

Governance Structures

While governance structures did also undergo changes in the postwar period, particularly in France and in West Germany, measuring such an evolution is much more difficult. The size of West German and French industrial entities increased significantly over the period, which can be taken as a fairly good indication that 'hierarchies' were in the process of being created in these two countries. Those new large firms or 'hierarchies', often the products of mergers and acquisitions, internalized many formerly inter-unit relationships thus redefining governance structures within each industrial sector. This was not so much the case in Italy, naturally, where small- or medium-sized family-owned firms had remained predominant.[7] While industrial concentration was increasing both in France and in West Germany, legislative bodies were at the same time crafting and adopting acts outlawing cartels and most forms of loose agreements. Organized markets as a form of governance structure thus became illegal in most industrial sectors. In part under American pressure, the American antitrust tradition was transferred to France, West Germany, and to the emerging European space as Table 2 documents. Exact figures on cartels and loose agreements are not available for the period. It is nevertheless undeniable that the new legislation often deterred the informal organization of markets. It also stimulated the re-definition of many French and West German industrial sectors into competitive oligopolies, following the model pioneered by American industry.

Table 2. Anticartel legislation in Western Europe

	Antitrust or Anticartel Acts
France	Décret relatif au maintien et au rétablissement de la libre concurrence industrielle et commerciale. August 9, 1953.
West Germany	Law #56—Prohibition of excessive concentration of German economic power. February 12, 1947. Gesetz gegen Wettbewerbsbeschrankungen. July 1957.
European Community	Articles 60–61, European Coal and Steel Community Treaty. April 1951. Articles 85–86, European Community Treaty. July 1957.

GEOPOLITICAL EMBEDDEDNESS: A NEGLECTED DIMENSION

The picture that has emerged of Western European industries and of their
evolution from 1950 to 1970 is a fairly complex one. The systematic comparison, at a macro level, of French, West German, and Italian systems of
industrial production has shown both significant convergence and strikingly
resilient differences over the period. Existing theoretical arguments have
rarely been articulated around the empirical complexity that is revealing of
the coexistence of both trends. On the one hand, evolutionary theories have
focused on convergence and similarities. Identifying a universal and unavoidable logic of change, those theories have put forward the argument that it
ultimately impacted national systems of industrial production in a parallel but
independent fashion. The universal logic of change might be of an essentially
technological and economic nature (Chandler, 1962, 1977, 1990; Williamson,
1975, 1985). It could also be understood as a set of global cultural rules
leading towards increasing rationalization (Scott, Meyer *et al.*, 1994). National
specificity theories, on the other hand, have tried to account for resilient
national differences, disregarding or underplaying signs of convergence. The
structural patterns characteristic of national industries have been traced, within
this latter perspective, back to the peculiar features of national environments.
Embedding national environments might be identified as being of a cultural
nature (Dobbin, 1994; Hofstede, 1980; Hickson, 1993); they might also be
defined as essentially institutional (Campbell *et al.*, 1991; Fligstein, 1990;
Hamilton and Biggart, 1988).

Despite significant differences with respect to working hypotheses, objectives and claims, evolutionary and national specificity theories have common
shortcomings. They tend, in particular, to provide a determinist picture of
national industries and of the evolution through time of their structural
arrangements. For evolutionary theories, the future determines the present
and a universal logic of change implies parallel convergence towards a unique
and possibly superior set of structural arrangements. National specificity
theories, on the other hand, claim that contemporary systems of industrial
production are shaped and determined by constraining national legacies,
whether of a cultural or of an institutional kind. Both types of determinism
singularly fail to do justice to the empirical complexity underscored above.
They ultimately reveal, I argue, a common mistake over the level of analysis.
Existing theoretical frameworks, in the end, all treat national systems of
industrial production as discrete entities, self-contained and independent
from each other. If taken into consideration at all, the international environment is being identified merely as the disembodied source of global trends,
whether economic or cultural, shaping each national economy in a parallel but
unrelated fashion.

In reality, the international environment is a concrete political and geopolitical arena, characterized by multiple, multilateral, and context dependent

cross-national interactions. The nature of those interactions has been such, particularly since the end of the Second World War, that they came to have a significant impact not only on the political and military balance of a given country but also on its social and economic make-up. As national industries are embedded within a specific geopolitical space, cross-national relationships have to be taken into consideration when trying to account for the transformation of structural arrangements. I argue, in fact, that the partial convergence of national systems of industrial production after 1945 cannot be understood outside of a peculiar geopolitical context. Increasing similarities across national industries have followed the attempt at a cross-national transfer or diffusion of a particular system of industrial production that was originally American. This large-scale attempt at a cross-national transfer was made possible by a redefinition of the geopolitical balance of power after the Second World War and by the consequent creation and institutionalization of channels and mechanisms of transfer under the leadership of a small group of actors. The keystone and main agent behind this process, undeniably, was the administration of the Marshall plan. Meanwhile, the persistence of differences across national industries can be accounted for by the fact that the transfer did not take place in a vacuum. Each European country had a given position within the geopolitical constellation. Channels and mechanisms of transfer thus differed in part and proved more or less efficient in each case. Moreover, Western European countries were all characterized by their own peculiar national legacies and institutional make-up that generally turned out to be sources of diffraction. Each country, finally, had its own key actors with preferences and value orientations that could not be entirely accounted for by the surrounding frame of institutional constraints and legacies. The same system of industrial production was thus diffused or transferred but also diffracted, which implied in each case a greater or lesser degree of adaptation, interpretation, or 'translation' of the original model.

INSTITUTIONAL CONSTRAINTS, ACTORS, AND NETWORKS:
A THEORETICAL FRAMEWORK

The complexity underscored above emerged in an inductive manner from systematic empirical work. A comparative study of national industrial censuses revealed, in particular, the coexistence of two *a priori* contradictory trends in the evolution of national systems of industrial production. Accounting for the unmistakable structural convergence of a number of national industries in the second half of our century and for the persistence, at the very same time, of significant national peculiarities thus became the main research objective. The multifaceted character of industrial stories in the post Second World War period clearly called for a theoretical framework that would take on complexities, including *a priori* conflicting developments. A revised version of the neo-institutional argument, combining a 'theory of constraint' with a 'theory of action' and enlarging the embedding environment to its geopolitical dimension appeared to fit the historical and empirical material best.[8] The choice of an institutional approach did not mean that economic and cultural factors were considered unimportant and that they would thus be disregarded. Such a choice merely followed from the realization that economic and cultural factors are always embedded and that, in a given context, they are defined by and sifted through a specific institutional framework (Polanyi, 1944; Granovetter, 1985). At the same time empirical complexity implied that the theory of constraint characteristic of neo-institutional arguments had to be articulated with a theory of action, where the individual agent was defined as a complex set of motivations and value-orientations at the crossroads of various networks and not entirely reducible to the constraining environment. The failure to systematically articulate systems of constraints with actors and networks has in fact, together with the leaving-out of geopolitical embeddedness, been a theoretical flaw common to all existing arguments, both in evolutionary and national specificity literatures.

Evolutionary Theories

Whether in their efficiency or rationalization variants, evolutionary theories have identified a universal and unavoidable logic of change believed ultimately to impact on all national systems of industrial production in a parallel but independent fashion. National transformations have been understood to take place along a predetermined trend or continuum, implying parallel convergence towards a unique and possibly superior set of structural arrangements. Meanwhile, national peculiarities have generally been explained away by the stage of evolution of a given country, or attributed to contingent obstacles set along the evolutionary path. Differences, in other words, have been treated in evolutionary accounts as temporary and bound to disappear.

The efficiency variant of evolutionary theories has traced structural transformations back to a universal logic of economic and technological change (Chandler, 1962, 1977, 1990; Williamson 1975, 1985). A defining claim of efficiency arguments has been that new structural arrangements emerge as efficient answers to changes in the economic and technological environment. Those arguments have presented the large modern corporation, for example, as the most efficient and rational response to a rapid development of technology, of the railway network, and to a significant extension of markets (Chandler, 1962, 1977). While the American economy was historically the first to undergo transformations on such a scale, the trend has been presented as unavoidable and as bound to affect, in turn, other national industries (Chandler, 1990). The efficiency account has thus set up the American system of industrial production as a superior and universal model, most advanced on the evolutionary continuum. The functionalist nature of the argument and its tendency to turn outcomes—efficiency or more exactly perceived efficiency—into causes has often been criticized (DuBoff and Herman, 1980; Fligstein, 1990; Roy, 1990). On the other hand, the explicit assumption that pioneers of the modern industrial corporation were rational actors, motivated only by a benign desire for efficiency, has also been seriously challenged (DuBoff and Herman, 1980; Perrow, 1981; Fligstein, 1990). Finally, the orderly picture of the evolutionary process, brought out by efficiency accounts, has contradicted historical records that have told of turbulence, conflicts, and violence in the USA during the early years of the new system of industrial production (Kolko, 1963; Edwards, 1979; Fligstein, 1990).

Similar criticisms apply to the account, which is either proposed or suggested by efficiency arguments, of structural transformations in other national industries. Those arguments do not convincingly explain national differences with respect to the timing and span of structural transformations. They tend to neglect processes, disregarding in particular the multiplicity of actors and the complexity of their motives. They reduce mechanisms to predetermined evolution or rational individual decision making. They say nothing about obstacles and resistance, although a large-scale process of structural transformation is bound to be conflict ridden. Reconciling the account provided by efficiency arguments with the long-term persistence of structural differences across nations—and this despite increasingly convergent economic environments and conditions—would also be fairly difficult. The theoretical setting up, finally, of a single most efficient, superior, and universal model can be shown to contradict the reality of a relative decoupling between structural arrangements and industrial growth or performance.

On the other hand, the rationalization variant of evolutionary theories has identified global and universal cultural rules as being the source and the instrument of cross-national structural convergence (Scott, Meyer, *et al.*, 1994). National economies have been described, within this perspective, as emergent social constructions embedded in larger institutional environments understood as sets of cultural rules. Those sets of cultural rules, it has been further argued, have had a tendency to grow increasingly similar across national boundaries, evolving towards greater rationalization the world over. The homogenization of cultural rules has been understood to lead in turn to a worldwide isomorphism of structural arrangements and behaviors. Indeed, rationalization arguments claim that structures and actors are not only enmeshed within surrounding sets of cultural rules but that they are also shaped and acted by them (Scott, Meyer *et al.*, 1994: 18).

The evolution of national systems of industrial production and of structural arrangements is thus, within this theoretical framework, guided and bounded by a strict and predetermined system of constraints of a cultural nature. The determinist and quasi-functionalist character of this type of argument clearly echoes that of efficiency arguments discussed earlier. In both cases, systems of industrial production appear to be necessary responses to unavoidable demands stemming from the environment, the latter being understood either in its economic and technological dimension or as a set of cultural rules. The logic of change and transformation, in rationalization arguments, is once more evolutionary, predetermined, and universal. Those arguments can undeniably account for increasing similarities, the mechanism being a parallel diffusion, to each country, of global and rationalizing rules or values. They have a tendency, though, to remain blind to timing, historical embeddedness, actors and obstacles, to the persistence of differences, and to the multiplicity of national structural arrangements in a manner that is quite reminiscent of efficiency arguments. The question of the origins of global rules and rationalizing tendencies is not even taken up, betraying an ahistorical and functionalist logic also characteristic of the efficiency literature.

National Specificity Theories

In striking contrast to evolutionary arguments, national specificity theories have generally set out to account for the peculiarities of a given national system of industrial production and for persistent structural differences across national boundaries. National specificity arguments all start from the hypothesis that systems of industrial production are embedded within national environments, identified as either cultural or institutional. Those arguments then trace structural arrangements back to specific features of the embedding national environment. By restricting the environment to its national dimension, though, national specificity arguments have tended to forget or disregard cross-national isomorphic trends that work their way despite or around peculiar national features.

A variant of national specificity arguments has underscored the cultural nature of the embedding national environment (Dobbin, 1994; Hofstede, 1980; Hickson, 1993). National culture has been defined in this case as an historically constructed system of reference embodied in a set of basic practices. Within this perspective, national cultures are set up as ultimate explanatory variables. Beyond transformations in the economic environment or in political institutions, stable cultural features at the national level are believed to account, ultimately, for structural arrangements or industrial policies. National cultures are thus understood to be the source of persistent differences across countries with respect to institutions, structures, customs, or methods. In fact, by postulating stable and permanent cultural features as ultimate explanatory variables, cultural arguments dismiss or significantly reduce the possibility of change. Structural convergence appears difficult, nay impossible, since cultural isomorphism is hardly conceivable. By all means, reconciling those arguments with the unmistakable historical trends documented earlier would prove quite difficult. Structural change, as we have shown, is not only possible; it did take place on a significant scale and in a rapid manner, in some of those countries where cultural arguments have precisely pointed to the permanence, through time, of a peculiar logic of management and economic organization. While structural convergence did not happen to the degree that evolutionary arguments had predicted, increasing structural similarities have nevertheless become unmistakable. In fact, partly contradicting the claims of cultural arguments, structural similarities have increased despite the persistence of cultural differences. In some circumstances, structural transformations have even brought about the evolution of cultural schemes of reference, which would seem to call into question the definition of national cultures as sets of permanent features and their use as ultimate explanatory variables.[9]

Institutional or neo-institutional arguments describe, on the other hand, economies and industries as being deeply embedded within national institutional environments, understood as constraining frameworks of an essentially structural nature. Within this perspective, the state and political institutions are key elements of the constraining framework (Skocpol, 1979; Fligstein, 1990; Campbell *et al.*, 1991). Institutional legacies are sets of constraints, creating path dependencies at each historical moment and significantly limiting opportunities for change (Whitley, 1992, 1994). Structural arrangements within national industries are shaped to a significant extent by the national institutional framework and are thus essentially social constructions (Polanyi, 1944; Granovetter, 1985). Neo-institutional arguments, though, have generally not pictured this system of constraint as entirely determining. They have allowed for unexpected turning points and unforeseen events. In late nineteenth-century America, for example, political and legal institutions created path dependencies and limited the possibility of structural change. None the less, institutional arguments have pictured the evolution of the American system of industrial production within this constraining framework as being partly unexpected and accidental (Fligstein, 1990). The strength of those arguments has lain in their capacity to integrate complexities and the multiple dimensions of an historical reality that was altogether economic, social, and political.

By limiting the relevant institutional environment to the national level, though, they have tended to neglect one important element of empirical complexity that was identified above. Tracing cross-national differences in systems of industrial production to country specific institutional constraints, those accounts have failed to take in the geopolitical environment as a potential source and engine of change or of partly unexpected evolution. The structural convergence of national systems of industrial production observed empirically cannot, as a consequence, be easily reconciled with the existing neo-institutional literature. Furthermore, while institutional accounts have proposed sophisticated theories of constraints, they have failed to articulate them with theories of action (Campbell, 1994). Individual actors, as sets of complex motivations belonging to a number of networks and only partially

constrained by the institutional environment, have rarely been brought into
neo-institutional frameworks.

The main theoretical ambition of this book is in effect to articulate a system
of institutional constraints, enlarged to include the geopolitical environment,
with individual choices and actions. The original contribution, on a theoretical
level, will be to propose a framework reconciling partial determination with
the possibility of unexpected change and unforeseen evolution. Networks, both
at the national and at the international level, will be identified throughout the
book as essential mechanisms of such a reconciliation. Fitting more or less
tightly into the surrounding system of institutional constraints, those networks
may be, for individual members, the source of more or less significant leverage. Individuals, as will be shown throughout this book, may indeed have a
strong impact on systems of institutional constraints if they belong to or weave
networks that can amplify their decisions, increase their capacity to implement
those decisions, and widen the span of their action. It is argued here that the
intervention of individual actors through such mechanisms undeniably represents one potential source of unexpected change and unforeseen evolution. The
geopolitical dimension of the institutional environment, too often neglected in
the existing literature, was underscored earlier as being another such potential
source of change.

COMPARATIVE HISTORICAL ANALYSIS: A METHODOLOGICAL PROGRAM

The formulation of the research question and the nature of the empirical data
called for a methodological approach that would capture both the general
patterns of causalities or regularities across countries and the historical and
contextual singularities. Considering those constraints, comparative historical
analysis stood out as the most appropriate.[10] This approach, indeed, is particularly well adapted to studies focusing on macrosociological phenomena, of
which there are only a small number of cases (Skocpol, 1979). It combines
detailed case studies with systematic comparison. Detailed accounts, building
on primary and secondary material, ensure that historical and contextual
singularities are not being disregarded and find their way into the analysis.
A systematic comparison of well chosen cases, on the other hand, allows for
significant theoretical leverage and represents a powerful tool, thus making
generalization possible.

For comparison to play its role as a theoretical lever, however, it should
amount to more than a mere collection of unrelated cases, treated in an
independent fashion. John Stuart Mill's two-sided comparative method allows
us precisely to turn comparison into a key tool of analysis (Skocpol, 1979).
Through the method of agreement or positive comparison, several cases characterized by similar outcomes can be compared. The objective there is to track
down regularities and similarities in patterns of conditions. Those regularities

Table 3. Methods of agreement and of difference in comparative analysis

	Case I	Case II	Case III	Case IV
Outcome	X	X	Non-X	Non-X
Bundles of conditions	a	d	a	a
	b	e	b	b
	c	f	c	c
	L	L	L	—
	M	M	—	M

Note: It can be read, from this table, that the bundle of conditions (L,M) is likely to account, at least in part, for the outcome X. The negative cases, seem to confirm, that conditions L or M alone are not sufficient to bring about the outcome X.

are likely to account, at least in part, for the common outcome. Then, the method of difference makes it possible to compare cases with fairly different outcomes. A negative comparison of this sort leads to the identification of those conditions or patterns of conditions which may be responsible for variation in outcomes. Table 3 brings together in a synthetic manner the double logic of the comparative method.[11]

Sets of theoretical tools proposed and developed in the following pages have thus emerged, inductively, from a methodological approach combining historical case studies with systematic comparison, both positive and negative. Primary historical work and archival research have supplied, for each country, the material which was systematically compared. Methodological requirements have also oriented the choice of empirical cases. This choice, indeed, was crucial and cases had to be carefully selected so that their systematic comparison could lead to the identification of similarities as well as differences, both in bundles of conditions and in outcomes. France and West Germany were selected as two positive cases, where outcomes proved sufficiently similar and systems of industrial production have tended to converge towards the American model although to a different extent. Italy was included as a negative case, where the national system of industrial production appeared relatively unaffected by isomorphic trends.

The outline of the book reflects those methodological choices as well as the theoretical framework that has emerged from historically grounded comparisons. Each part of the book corresponds to a particular stage in the cross-national transfer process. For each of those stages, a number of theoretical generalizations are proposed, emerging directly from the confrontation and comparison of the three empirical cases—France, West Germany, and Italy. Part I proposes an historical account of the emergence of the American system of industrial production that was later to be transferred. It also provides a description of those European systems of industrial production which came to be displaced, to a greater or lesser extent, after the Second World War. In Part

II, the focus is on conditions—geopolitical and national—most favorable to a cross-national transfer, on the channels of transfer, and on the strategies of actors involved. Part III identifies different types of mechanisms through which the cross-national transfer process took place. Finally, Part IV points to obstacles to the process, of a national and institutional kind. Theoretical generalizations are proposed, at that point, on the diffraction that necessarily comes with processes of cross-national transfer or diffusion and on what amounts, in the end, to an institutionally embedded national adaptation, translation, or interpretation of the original model.

Notes

1. A number of scholars have focused on quite similar dependent variables. Labels, though, have changed. Chandler (1990) used the term 'forms of capitalism', Piore and Sabel (1984) 'industrial divides', and Whitley (1992) 'business systems'. Although the focus, in the following pages, will be on structures, it is undeniable that national industries are also characterized by bodies of ideas, organizational and economic ideologies, 'models of management' (Guillén, 1994), or 'industrial cultures' (Dobbin, 1994).
2. This definition of 'governance structures' builds upon those provided by Williamson (1981) and Campbell *et al.* (1991).
3. In fact, amongst Italian manufacturing firms employing over 50 people, 1,249 were sole proprietorships in 1951 and 1,781 in 1971. In France, this number had gone down from 1,408 in 1954 to 901 in 1966 (INSEE (1956, 1974), Istituto Centrale di Statistica (1955, 1976), Statistisches Bundesamt (1953, 1973)).
4. Ibid.
5. For figures showing that the M-form spread even further in Europe in the 1970s and 1980s, see Whittington *et al.* (1997).
6. Since over half of this same sample had already chosen diversification as a strategy by 1950, slow adoption of the M-form in Italy could not be accounted for, as traditional arguments would have it, by a failure to diversify (Chandler, 1962). Neither could Italian reluctance to the M-form be accounted for by peculiarities of the Italian economic environment since, by 1970, most foreign-owned subsidiaries in Italy (33 out of 39) had adopted the multidivisional structure.
7. Both in France and in West Germany, the total number of industrial units decreased sharply from around 700,000 in 1950 to around 400,000 twenty years later. The firms that disappeared were mostly smaller entities. In Italy, on the other hand, the number of industrial units remained stable during that period at around 600,000. Some very small firms (less than 10 employees) disappeared but they were replaced, for the most part, by small or medium-sized entities (between 10 and 500). See Statistisches Bundesamt (1953, 1954, 1973, 1974), INSEE (1956, 1974), Istituto Centrale di Statistica (1955, 1976).
8. See Campbell (1994) for a review of neo-institutional theories and for the terms 'theory of constraint' and 'theory of action'.
9. For a criticism along similar lines of cultural arguments, see Hamilton and Biggart (1988), pp. S69–S74.
10. The origins of comparative historical analysis can be traced to John Stuart Mill

(1843) and Max Weber (1996). Later, Bendix (1956), Moore (1966), Skocpol (1979), or Ragin (1987) formalized and established it as a valid methodological program for the social sciences. Recent studies building on this methodological tradition are Guillén (1994) or Soysal (1994).

11. This table has been elaborated, building essentially on Skocpol (1979).

PART I

CROSS-NATIONAL TRANSFER: STRUCTURAL TYPES

National systems of industrial production were defined earlier as those structural frameworks shaping conditions of industrial production in a particular country. A systematic historical comparison of several national economies revealed, in fact, the existence of a number of broad types of national systems of industrial production that could easily be differentiated. It also underscored the possibility, through time, of one type replacing another within a given national environment. In a number of Western European industries, for example, the post Second World War period has witnessed a significant transformation of national structural frameworks. When it took place, the evolution was unmistakably towards the model or type originally pioneered by the USA and labelled below 'corporate capitalism'. The four key dimensions identified earlier as constitutive of national systems of industrial production—physical, ownership, organizational, and governance structures—are used in Table 4 to frame a typology of national industries and structural arrangements.

The purposes of this study and its historical scope have limited the number of relevant ideal types (Weber, 1978). In particular, only capitalist contexts

Table 4. National systems of industrial production: a typology

	Laissez faire capitalism	Family capitalism	Organized capitalism	Corporate capitalism
Physical structures	small firms	small/medium firms	small/medium firms	large firms
Ownership structures	personal ownership	personal ownership or partnership	partnership or mixed forms*	joint stock, public ownership
Organizational structures	not formalized	not formalized	not formalized or functional	functional or multidivisional
Governance structures	free markets	loosely organized markets	formally organized markets	markets superseded, hierarchies

* By 'mixed forms', we understand here all those legal structures which are essentially crossbreeds of 'partnerships' and 'joint stock companies', such as for example the German GmbH, the French SARL, or the *société en commandite*. Those forms are located somewhere in between personal and public ownership.

have been considered, where a significant part of the economic scene was characterized by private ownership of the means of production. Moreover, recent trends in the structural evolution of national industries have not been taken into account for the elaboration of the typology, the validity of which, as a consequence, is historically bounded.

Laissez faire capitalism, characterized by a predominance of small, privately held and run family firms, competing in essentially free markets, belongs in the typology mostly because of its particular significance for classical and neo-classical economic theory. More than the other three systems of industrial production identified in Table 4, *laissez faire* capitalism is an ideal type and it is rarely to be found as such. There are very few national industries, in real life, where all firms are equally marginal actors and can be treated as black boxes, the structure and organization of which matters little. There are very few real life markets where many such small family firms engage in totally free and unhampered competition. In real economic life, in fact, small industrial entities generally tend to coexist, in the same industry, with somewhat bigger units. This means, in turn, a relative imbalance in the competitive game. At the same time, decision makers in both small and bigger units, try to reduce the uncer-tainties stemming from a competitive situation and to avoid the potentially disruptive effects of free competition. A widespread tendency, in fact, is for markets to become organized, through more or less formal agreements between firms—cartels, *ententes*, or trusts for example. Family capitalism and organized capitalism, as outlined in Table 4, are therefore two variants of the same broad type of arrangements, and they have characterized at some stage of their history most national industries. Differences between those two variants can mostly be explained by the fact that medium-sized firms tend to be bigger and more numerous in organized capitalism than in family capitalism. As a consequence, forms of ownership allowing an increase in capital while still preserving family or individual control tend to become much more wide-spread under organized capitalism. New solutions may also be proposed to problems of internal organization which are naturally becoming more acute within bigger units. The increased size of the main players, finally, combining with a reduction in the total number of players, may lead to a more formal organization of markets, particularly when political institutions and national legislation remain indifferent to—or even tend to favor—the generalization of such forms of market regulation.

The system of industrial production labeled in Table 4 as 'corporate capit-alism' is of an entirely different nature. The increase in size, on an unprece-dented scale, of production units calls for a radical redefinition of internal modes of organization and communication. At the same time, corporate capit-alism is characterized by the generalization of corporate ownership structures and by a widespread decoupling of ownership and management. The increased size of individual industrial entities also implies a significant reduction in the total number of players, leading in many industrial sectors to a situation of oligopoly. Before the end of the Second World War, the corporate system of industrial production could be identified as essentially American, while variants of the family or organized types characterized the industry of most other capitalist powers. In fact, corporate capitalism had been an American innova- tion. It was invented and pioneered in the USA around the turn of the twentieth century. The very process of the emergence of the corporate type was deeply embedded not only within a given economic context, but also within a peculiar social and political context. Economic and technological environments were then extremely turbulent. This was a time when science and technology were starting to expand the range of the possible, creating various options and opportunities that would or would not be seized upon. However, economic and technological disruptions were first of all begging questions, engendering problems, and pointing towards general trends. They were not, in any kind of absolute way, defining nor shaping structural answers. Structural answers were in part constrained by the institutional environment and in part shaped by individual and collective actors, characterized by value-orientations and con- victions not entirely reducible to the surrounding systems of constraints. This left some space for partly unexpected developments and the emergence of the American system of industrial production was, thus, to an extent, the conse- quence of a series of contingent encounters between actors, constraints, and potential solutions, as will be shown below.

On the other side of the Atlantic, structural transformations when they took place at all in the period before the Second World War, were much less radical, most of the time incremental. In particular, French, German, and Italian indust- ries remained, during those years, relatively close to the ideal types of family or organized capitalism. Most industrial sectors, in those three countries, were dominated by small or medium-sized industrial units, family-owned and run. Ownership structures allowing increased flows of capital, while still safe- guarding family or individual ownership and control, were being devised and adopted in a fairly rapid manner. Markets had become increasingly organized through the end of the nineteenth and the first part of the twentieth centuries, with slight differences in the extent to which national legislations and political institutions fostered such a systematic organization of markets. The object of this first Part is to set the historical scene and to provide snapshots of national industries before the beginning of the cross-national diffusion process. Chapter 1 tells of the emergence of the corporate type in the USA at the turn of the twentieth century and of its unique features immediately singling it out as a radical innovation. Chapter 2 contrasts the evolution taking place in the USA with the relative stability characteristic of Western European industries until the Second World War. It also underscores the early mistrust on the old continent towards the emerging American system of industrial production which was perceived as a threatening oddity rather than as a model.

1

The American Structural Revolution
Inventing the Corporate System of Industrial Production

If the Lord had intended things to be big, he would have made man bigger—in brains and in character . . . . I have considered and do consider that the proposition that mere bigness cannot be an offense against society is false, because I believe that our society, which rests upon democracy cannot endure under such conditions.

Louis D. Brandeis[1]

Fathers of the American Constitution and Thomas Jefferson in particular had identified freedom as a constitutive element of the future American social and economic space. In sparsely populated and essentially rural territories, the ideal typical situation of many individual and independent entrepreneurs, competing healthily in a mostly unregulated environment, seemed a legitimate ambition. Such a 'proprietary-competitive' type of capitalism appeared to embody freedom, the very spirit of the new Nation.[2] The small firm, through which the individual acquired the means—essentially independence, wealth, and social status—of his freedom, was an economic but also a moral entity. The small firm, like motherhood and apple pie, was the stuff of the American dream. In a short period of time, though, during those years bridging the nineteenth and twentieth centuries, the economic component of the American dream would come to be radically redefined. By the 1920s, 'big' was undeniably becoming 'efficient', if not always 'beautiful', in American industry. A corporate version of capitalism, increasingly regulated at the federal level, was pushing the small producer republic to the periphery of the national economy. Emerging within the context of significant economic and technological disruptions, corporate capitalism had also been shaped within particular historical and institutional conditions. The reconstruction of American capitalism, or the invention of the corporate system of industrial production, was in fact a fairly messy process, revealing social and political confrontations as much as it was reflecting economic and technological evolutions. The institutional environment, particularly in its political and legislative dimensions, set significant constraints. Still, the multiplicity of actors, characterized by bounded rationalities as well as divergent and complex motives, meant that unintended and contingent developments were not rare.

There were three main stages to the emergence of corporate capitalism in the

USA. The competitive environment, first of all, was significantly redefined. This redefinition was soon associated with a large-scale and revolutionary transformation of ownership structures. Then, once the make-up of industrial sectors had been significantly altered and the boundaries of individual firms redrawn, solutions came to be devised to acute problems of internal organization. The corporate system of industrial production that emerged was peculiarly American and undeniably an innovation. Its fate would be closely related to that of the new Nation as a whole and, as it turned out, glorious days lay ahead.

Good
Paper

⇢ REDEFINING THE COMPETITIVE ENVIRONMENT: THE 'TRUST QUESTION'

By the 1870s and 1880s, the 'trust question' had come to occupy center stage in the American national debate. Definitions were hardly clear and the term 'trust' was used to refer to all types of business cooperation and aggregates, loose agreements as well as tight combinations.[3] The public concern with the 'trust question' could be traced back to an undeniable evolution of business conditions in the aftermath of the American civil war. It stemmed, in particular, from the growing power of large business aggregates and from their use of ruthless practices in what came to resemble economic warfare (Lloyd, 1894; Josephson, 1932; Chernow, 1990). In a mostly unregulated and fairly turbulent environment, business arrangements and agreements had multiplied. Attempts were made at organizing industries in order to bridle competition and to achieve a certain measure of control over markets, prices, and eventually profits. Until 1890, cooperation within American industry mostly took the form of loose agreements (McCraw, 1984; Chandler, 1990; Fligstein, 1990). Those gentlemen's agreements or cartels shared markets in an informal manner, defined production quotas, or set price levels. In contrast to the situation that would come to prevail in Germany, American cartels had neither legal nor administrative backing and were therefore quite vulnerable constructions. The 'trust' form in the narrow sense of the term emerged in this context, in the 1880s, as an alternative to fragile cartel agreements and as an attempt to formalize cooperation. The stock of companies that were part of the agreement was entrusted to a central board. While there was no transfer of ownership and each company retained its own legal identity and management structure, the board of trustees was empowered to make operating and investment decisions at the aggregate level (Chandler, 1977; McCraw, 1984). Still, despite the somewhat more formal nature of the trust device, both American cartels and trusts were then loose forms of business cooperation. Loose cooperation, in fact, allowed industrial units to combine the best of two worlds. A welcome alternative to destructive competition, it brought relative stability to turbulent environments. While markets and prices were controlled and bankruptcies limited, the loose quality of the agreements ensured on the other hand that each firm preserved its legal autonomy, each business owner his prestige, privileges, and at least the appearance of power. In fact, cooperation within loose agreements was certainly perceived by many industrial leaders at the time as a lesser evil than falling prey to outright merger. Had the legislation not banned loose agreements in the USA, the chances are that they would have remained a dominant way of organizing in many industrial sectors.[4]

The Sherman Act: Legislative Intent and Institutional Constraints

Despite their lack of formal structure, some of those cartels or trusts, had, by the late 1880s, become formidable industrial aggregates, wielding unprecedented power. The control they exercised in many industries was often ruthless and predatory, devastating to those smaller interests which remained outside the boundaries of the agreements or which had to deal with them from a position of powerlessness. The growing uproar and discontent amidst, in particular, small independent business owners and western or southern farmers indicated that the 'trust question' could indeed have destabilizing effects on the American social and political scene. The unrest of small America brought the issue of the power of trusts onto the agenda of politicians and Congressmen. The pressure was such that Congress did enact first a legislation regulating railroads and, a few years later, a general antitrust act.[5]

A careful study of the legislative process shows that a number of Congressmen had their own ideological reasons to push for the legislative regulation of anti-competitive practices. For conservative members of the Republican party, competition was a key value, closely related to freedom, and one that should be preserved at any cost (Thorelli, 1954). American conservatism at the end of the nineteenth century was a surprising mix of classical economic theory, social Darwinism, and puritan doctrine. The invisible hand of the market, natural selection, or divine election had the common characteristic of being regulative forces beyond human and social reach. Economic and social equilibrium, it was understood, could and should be reached without human or institutional intervention. Intervention, in fact, could only bring about disturbances and have disastrous consequences. Within this ideological framework, competition was a *sine qua non* condition to the free play of regulative forces and the sole guarantee of a healthy economy and society. The preservation of a competitive environment thus had to be the central concern of a federal legislation. The curbing of trusts, called for by farmers and small business owners, would be a mere side-effect of the fight for competition and freedom.

This general intent was reflected in Congressional debates and in the initial version of the draft bill proposed by Senator John Sherman (a Republican from Ohio) in August 1888, which provided 'that all arrangements, contracts, agreements, trusts or combinations between persons or corporations *made with a view or which tend to prevent full and free competition* . . . are declared to be against public policy, unlawful and void'.[6] Big business or, more exactly, business owners and managers involved in the cartelization and trust move-ment at the time were well represented in the 51st Congress, which discussed and passed the Sherman bill. In his systematic study of Congressional debates, Thorelli (1954) has nevertheless found no evidence of powerful and organized opposition to the bill, which can be explained in different ways. The bill may have appeared to be unavoidable in order to quieten the uproar occurring in some parts of the country. It may also have appeared to be relatively innoc-uous, since so little was provided for in terms of enforcement (Thorelli, 1954: 220). More importantly, perhaps, it could be argued that big business was by then calling for a federal regulation of business conditions and thus welcomed any form of Congress intervention. A significant part of the American business class, which had tried to gain control over troubled environments through cartels or trusts, was greatly disturbed by its relative failure. Competition did not seem to subside and agreements were rarely fully respected. The confusion was only compounded by differing if not diverging legislation across the various states of the Union and by a lack of consistent ground rules. It had become clear, at least to some key industrial and financial leaders, that a chaotic industry and the absence of regulation through legislation would in the long run be dreadfully destructive of their interests and profits, if not of firms, cartels, and trusts themselves. As a consequence, a number of those business leaders came to advocate and expect a degree of legislative regulation of business conditions, particularly at the federal level (Thorelli, 1954; Kolko, 1963; Sklar, 1988).

Favorable conditions thus existed for the enactment of a general legislation prohibiting all forms of anti-competitive behavior. However, the version of the Sherman Act that was eventually signed by President Harrison on July 2, 1890, differed from the initial wording of the bill in a way that would prove to be significant. Section I declared illegal 'every contract, combination in the form of trust or otherwise, or conspiracy, *in restraint of trade or commerce*'. Section II declared criminal 'every person who shall monopolize or attempt to mono-polize or combine or conspire with any other person or persons, to monopolize any part *of the trade or commerce among the several states* or with foreign nations'.[7] Such rewording had not come about by chance. It reflected a number of constitutional legacies and institutional constraints that weighed on the legislator. First, the federal origin of the Sherman Act clearly set limits to its scope and potential reach. The very nature of American political institutions and the existence of two levels of jurisdiction, federal and state, constrained the legislative freedom of Congress. Congress could only work within the boundaries of its competencies—federal level legislation, interstate or foreign relationships. It could not meddle into the affairs of individual states of the Union. As a consequence, the Sherman Act could only regulate 'trade or commerce among the several states or with foreign Nations'. It apparently could not deal with anti-competitive behavior taking place within the borders of any given state. The limits set by the 'commerce clause'—as the excerpt quoted above came to be known—would prove of great significance in the following years, significantly narrowing the domain where the law could apply.[8]

One of the first landmark antitrust cases, US vs E. C. Knight (1895), illustrated the significant impact of the commerce clause on the interpretation that was to be made of antitrust legislation. In the Anglo-Saxon tradition of common law, statutes are essentially empty shells, which are given meaning through successive decisions. Early court cases are thus of particular significance for the later interpretation and enforcement of the law. In 1892, a suit was filed against the 'sugar trust', which despite its name, had just reorganized as a holding company. In fact, the American Sugar Refining Company had gained control, through the holding device, of four large Philadelphia sugar refining companies. Altogether, the sugar trust controlled more than 90 per cent of the sugar refining capacity of the entire USA, and it was charged by the Federal Government with monopoly and attempt to monopolize. In January 1895, the Supreme Court dismissed the case. Supreme Court Justices had made a distinction between manufacturing and production on the one hand, interstate and foreign commerce on the other. As it turned out, all production sites of the five sugar refining companies had been located within the state of Philadelphia. Since all production was taking place in one single state, the Supreme Court argued, the Sherman Antitrust Act could not apply. Competency lay with state judiciaries.

US vs E. C. Knight was to become a building case for American antitrust tradition. The reading made by the Supreme Court of the commerce clause would be used by lower courts and by the Supreme Court itself in many cases to follow. It appeared, from such a reading, that tight combinations and mergers in general were forms of cooperation at the production level and, as such, could escape the reach of the Sherman Antitrust Act, which could only prosecute cooperation at the level of trade. While institutional constraints weighing on the legislator had undeniably been reflected in the Sherman Act, the wording still left some room for interpretation and the Supreme Court could have construed the act somewhat differently. It could have argued, for example, that monopolies or attempts to monopolize at the level of production had a direct and negative impact on the freedom of trade and commerce.[9] This alternative interpretation of the commerce clause would have meant a fairly different construction of the Sherman Act and possibly a different definition of competition in the USA. In turn, this would certainly have had an impact on the process of reconstruction of the American system of industrial production.

The signal given by the Supreme Court to the business community through its decision in the E. C. Knight case was thus contingent and in part unpredictable. It can reasonably be argued, to all intents and purposes, that it differed significantly from what the legislator had expected when writing the Sherman Act. Corporate lawyers immediately drew conclusions from the E. C. Knight decision. Tight combinations and mergers seemed to escape regulation under the Sherman Act since they did not fall under the commerce clause at least in the interpretation chosen by the Court. Lawyers thus immediately started to advise their clients to enter mergers rather than cooperate informally through cartels and trusts across state boundaries (Thorelli, 1954; Sklar, 1988; Fligstein, 1990). In a clearly related development, the first American merger wave started in 1895, immediately after the Supreme Court had rendered its decision in the E. C. Knight case. Between 1895 and 1904, an average of 300 firms disappeared annually through mergers.[10]

The Federal Government and the office of the Attorney General, on the other hand, also rapidly drew conclusions from the Supreme Court decision. Loose combinations in restraint of trade were more likely to be successfully prosecuted than tight combinations or merged entities. Considering the scarcity of funds and the lack of enforcement means, it is naturally not surprising that the Government would target, first of all, those cases that could be more easily won.[11] And the Sherman Antitrust Act, indeed, was primarily used against loose combinations. Out of a total of 322 cases brought to court on antitrust grounds between 1890 and 1930, more than 85 per cent were against loose combinations of small or medium-sized firms (McCraw, 1986). Antitrust legislation in the USA and its early interpretation thus clearly limited the number and types of solutions available for American businessmen in search of stability and control over their environments. The solution which finally emerged and which came to dominate—tight combinations into single legal entities—was, ironically, the partially unintended and contingent consequence of a legislation that had been originally enacted under pressure from advocates of small-scale, competitive capitalism (Thorelli, 1954; Bittlingmayer, 1985; Fligstein, 1990).

Political Construction of the Sherman Act: The 'Rule of Reason'

While the legislator had been constrained by institutional legacies to limit the reach of the antitrust act, his clear objective was to strike at the intent to restrain trade. The Sherman Act declared unlawful all restrictive practices and restraints on trade, regardless of the form they took. Congressmen had acknowledged that restrictive practices could vary in type through time. A certain amount of flexibility was thus written into the Sherman Act and the courts were given the responsibility of interpreting and reinterpreting the legislation, as customary in a country with a common law tradition. The debate in the years following the enactment of the Sherman Act thus naturally centered on the exact nature of those practices that should be prosecuted. In common law tradition, a distinction was made between 'reasonable' restraints of trade, that were deemed lawful, and 'unreasonable' ones, that were outlawed. In legal terms, the debate after 1890 in fact bore on the cogency of a common law construction of the Sherman Act. Should the Sherman Antitrust Act be read in light of common law or should it be interpreted, on the contrary, as superseding common law? The main puzzle, in other words, was whether all combinations in restraint of trade should be outlawed, or whether only unlawful or unreasonable combinations in restraint of trade, as defined through common law, should be declared illegal. Justices were divided and fought over the issue from 1890 to 1911.

This was much more than a mere disagreement on legal interpretations. The debate, indeed, had significant economic, political, and social implications. It pitted against each other two Americas, two ways of life, two types of capitalist organizations and models. Justice John Marshall Harlan led the group in the Supreme Court which argued that the Sherman Act superseded common law and that all combinations in restraint of trade, whether reasonable or unreasonable, were to be outlawed. To those men, the ultimate values were competition and freedom. They defended the small producer republic and the competitive market. Champions of proprietary–competitive capitalism underscored its moral superiority and its significance for the American dream. Under the lead of White and Holmes, a second group of Justices argued that the Sherman Act should be read in light of common law and that the rule of reason should be used, systematically, to differentiate good from bad combinations. Beyond a common law interpretation of the Sherman Act lay the argument that competition should sometimes be sacrificed to the benefit of efficiency which was increasingly being equated with large size. Supreme Court decisions around the turn of the century reflected the confrontation between those radically different points of view. By 1911, though, the second group of Justices had clearly become dominant within the court and the rule of reason had lastingly been built into the American antitrust tradition. In direct contradiction with the very words of the Sherman Act, not all combinations in restraint of trade would be from then on declared illegal, only those deemed 'unreasonable'.

This particular interpretation of the Sherman Act was formalized through the 1911 Supreme Court decisions on two cases, Standard Oil and American Tobacco. Calling for a dissolution of defendant combinations, those decisions provoked an uproar in the business community. In reality, though, they were institutionalizing a common law reading of the Sherman Act and were as such quite favorable to big business. The Court ruled, in both cases, that the unreasonable character of restrictions to competition did not stem from size or market power in themselves but from the intent and purpose to exclude others that had characterized the combinations. Those decisions were thus serving the interests of corporate America, as President Taft attempted to show in a message to Congress on December 5, 1911:

In the recent decisions the Supreme Court makes clear that there is nothing in the statute which condemns combinations of capital or mere bigness of plant organized to secure economy in production and a reduction of its cost. It is only when the purpose or necessary effect of the organization and maintenance of the combination or aggregation of immense size are a stifling of competition, actual or potential, the enhancing of prices and establishing of a monopoly, that the statute is violated. Mere size is no sin against the law.[12]

Dissolution proceedings following the 1911 decisions only confirmed that the corporate revolution was strengthened and institutionalized rather than threatened by this interpretation of the antitrust statute. The objective of the dissolution was not to create many small and competing firms. Each emerging unit, in fact, was to be relatively large and the result in both sectors turned out to be an oligopoly.[13]

By the 1910s in the USA, the antitrust debate had thus been settled. The logic behind this settlement had been essentially political. The emerging social compromise, which reflected the increasing power exerted by big business representatives over political institutions, was packaged under the allegedly neutral notion of efficiency.[14] This compromise would define for years to come American economic thinking or competition policy and it would shape industrial structures in a partly unexpected manner. Through an essentially political process characterized by a number of contingent developments, the Sherman Act came to be constructed in the light of common law and the rule of reason was institutionalized in American antitrust tradition. Cartels and loose agreements were denounced as unreasonable restraints of trade and therefore outlawed in principle. While the Sherman Act clearly became a prohibition law as far as cartels and loose agreements were concerned, it would only be used to target abuse when it came to mergers. Only extreme forms of concentration, unreasonable mergers that created or attempted to create outright monopolies, were to be prohibited. In fact, the label 'anticartel legislation' would have more clearly described the nature of American competition regulation as it had come to be interpreted by the beginning of the twentieth century.

REINVENTING CAPITALIST OWNERSHIP: THE CORPORATE REVOLUTION

The enactment of the Sherman Act and its partly contingent interpretation had in turn a significant impact on the nature of American capitalism. The average size of firms and production units, the definition of competition, but also governance structures were all radically transformed by the first merger wave that followed legislative activity on the issue of competition at the federal level. The most revolutionary transformation, though, was certainly the redefinition of property rights or ownership structures and the re-allocation of capitalist power taking place at the very same time. Property rights are legal provisions enforced by political institutions and defining the nature, extent, and limits of property relations. They determine conditions of economic production and exchange and set the institutional framework for many interactions. As a consequence, they help to shape not only the economic but also the social and political balance of power within a given country (Campbell and Lindberg, 1990).

The first merger wave in the USA coincided with a rapid redefinition of property rights and with the spread, in particular, of corporate ownership to large parts of the American manufacturing sector. In 1890, less than ten manufacturing firms had been corporations and listed on regional stock exchanges. At the time, most large aggregations of economic power were limited partnerships or trusts. By 1905, however, the number of large corporations was increasing exponentially. There were already 316 manufacturing corporations listed on major stock exchanges, comprising altogether more than 5,000 plants or industrial establishments, and the corporate revolution was still in progress. The upward trend with respect to incorporations undeniably paralleled both in time and magnitude the first merger wave.[15] In fact, this merger wave might have been impossible or short-lived—and in any case would not have had the same impact—without the concomitant corporate revolution. Indeed, in the peculiar American context of the time, mergers implied and required incorporation. In their search for lawful strategies to organize markets and control competition after 1890, a few representatives of the 'big business' community stumbled on the corporate legal status as a potential solution—at least in the version that was being proposed by New Jersey legislation.

Corporate Form: Origins and Evolution

In English law, the corporate form goes back to the fourteenth century when it was exclusively used by the church and professional guilds. By the sixteenth and seventeenth centuries, most European monarchies had adopted the corporation as a tool of their mercantilist ambitions, thus extending the form to the commercial, productive, and financial sectors. Corporate status became a privilege granted by the King for the undertaking of economic tasks which were to increase the crown's glory. An important feature of the corporate form was that the entity it created could survive even after the disappearance of its creators or members and that this entity as a whole could hold property. Monarchies also granted corporations a number of privileges to make up for the costly and risky nature of the proposed undertakings, which generally required sizeable capital well beyond the reach of a lone investor. Those privileges included the right to a monopoly over a market or over the production of an object, the exemption from a number of taxes, and the limited liability of individual members and investors (Chayes, 1969).

Throughout the nineteenth century, conditions of incorporation were progressively relaxed. Most American states, in particular, passed legislation that made the corporate form more widely and easily accessible. The corporation thus became a contract at law between several individuals, legitimated by incorporation legislation at the state level. By the late 1880s, the corporate form had become available to almost any interested party in the USA, but it was still rarely adopted.[16] At the same time, the democratization of the corporate status had led to the elimination of a number of privileges, such as exemption from taxes, and product or market monopolies. Other privileges, though, were preserved and the modern corporation still enjoyed limited liability, the right to hold property, and recognition as a legal *personae*. Furthermore, starting with the landmark Santa Clara case in 1866, individual rights as defined in the Fifth and Fourteenth Amendments of the American constitution were to be extended to the corporation. Treating corporations as individuals with respect to property and its protection, the United States Supreme Court prepared the way for inter-corporate stock ownership. In 1888, the state of New Jersey was the first to include, in its corporate law, provisions granting corporations the right to own and hold stock in other corporations, provisions which it further liberalized in 1889 and 1893.[17]

The features characteristic of the corporate form—limited liability and inter-corporate stock ownership in particular—have generally been identified as the source of its efficiency in modern business conditions. They have been presented in the literature as legal adaptations to changing economic conditions, allowing capital accumulation of the magnitude required by technological progress and by the expansion of markets (Chandler, 1977; Williamson, 1985). Those distinctive features, in fact, pre-existed changes in the economic and technological environment and the logic of their emergence had clearly been more political and legal than economic. The corporate form had been available in the USA for a number of years before it suddenly became an important element of the structural reconstruction of American capitalism at the turn of the twentieth century. The key puzzle is thus not so much the emergence of the form as its diffusion to large sectors of the American manufacturing industry, a process that started relatively late but then was extremely rapid.

Diffusion of the Corporate Form within American Industry

In fact, the diffusion of the corporate form within American industry was a partly unintended consequence of the search for stable and lawful governance structures within a particular institutional and legal context. The passing of the Sherman Act and its early interpretation by the Supreme Court triggered, within the business community, a frenetic search for governance structures that would be lawful while still fulfilling the role played earlier by cartels and loose agreements.[18] The search process was bounded by resource and information constraints and stopped, unsurprisingly, at already existing and available options. Corporate status *per se* was not particularly interesting for a business community hoping to regulate interfirm relations and to control competition. The provisions added to its corporate law by the state of New Jersey in 1888 and 1889 seemed, on the other hand, to create opportunities. These provisions allowed unrestricted inter-corporate stock ownership and sketched out the holding company device. The process leading to the enactment of the New Jersey Holding Company Act had been highly contingent but, by 1890, the legal device was available.[19] In their search for lawful means of market control and business cooperation, members of the 'big business' community stumbled upon it. The holding company allowed the combination of several firms into a single legal entity and the decision of the Supreme Court in the E. C. Knight case appeared to validate this as lawful. Consequently the form spread rapidly within American industry.

Until 1888, corporations, like all other types of companies, had only been allowed to hold physical property. They could not own other firms nor stock in other corporations. Under New Jersey legislation, the corporate form became the only legal status making it possible for a firm as an entity to own another or parts of another. Not all state corporate laws were as liberal with respect to inter-corporate stock ownership. The state of Virginia, for example, had confirmed in 1887 that it prohibited firms incorporating on its territory from owning stock in other corporations. Ohio, Maine, or Massachussets had put very strict limits on the type and amount of stock that could be owned by corporations on their respective territories (Parker-Gwin and Roy, 1996). After 1889, however there were no limits or restrictions in New Jersey to the ownership by one corporation of stock in others. A corporation could thus easily be created in that state for the sole purpose of owning stock in other corporations. The holding company, as this device came to be known, turned out to be a powerful and lawful tool through which industries could organize and check competition.

There was a dramatic rush towards that device in the American business community after the Supreme Court had rendered its decision in the E. C. Knight case. Between 1895 and 1905, the number of incorporations increased exponentially. Those new corporations combined several formerly independent firms and represented large aggregations of capital. Many were registered in New Jersey, although production facilities might be located in other states.[20] By 1901, 66 per cent of American companies with US$10 million capital or more were incorporated in New Jersey and the success of that state in attracting incorporations soon gave rise to competition amongst the states of the Union (Parker-Gwin and Roy, 1996). New York and Delaware, in particular, liberalized their corporate laws in 1892 and 1899 respectively to allow unrestricted inter-corporate stock ownership. They rapidly became serious challengers to the dominant position of New Jersey and their rates of incorporation increased dramatically.[21]

A comparison of incorporation rates at the state level around the turn of the twentieth century thus clearly shows that incorporation was not sought *per se* within American industry (Parker-Gwin and Roy, 1996). Furthermore, during those early years, the choice of the corporate form was rarely motivated by a search for internal efficiencies.[22] Individual firms within the holding company often went on for some time, operating as they always had before. As the success of the New Jersey legislation seemed to indicate, the rush was much more towards a device—unrestricted inter-corporate stock ownership—that made interfirm cooperation possible and provided a lawful framework for market control. The main problem of the time was the creation of stable governance structures and the harnessing of competition. The holding company device, combined with mergers, appeared to represent a solution to that problem. Incorporation was necessary, to the extent that holding companies were corporations and that mergers could only take place amongst corporations. The possibility to incorporate, though, was not sufficient to allow mergers. Without unrestricted stock ownership attached to their corporate laws, most states registered only few, if any, incorporations. Those states, on the other hand, which had adopted liberal provisions with respect to inter-corporate stock ownership were characterized by an exponential increase of incorporations.

The corporate revolution, coinciding as it did with a large-scale merger movement, led to a radical redefinition of property rights. Ownership structures changed drastically in most sectors of American industry and the very meaning of capitalist ownership was deeply altered. In turn, conditions of production and distribution, organizational structures and work methods were to change significantly in the USA. We argue here that those changes were much more the consequence than the cause of both the American merger movement and the corporate revolution.

REORGANIZING CORPORATIONS: MASS PRODUCTION AND FORMALIZATION

At the turn of the twentieth century, individual companies in most sectors of American industry were being merged at a frenzied pace into large corporate entities. Dominant accounts have tended to explain mergers and incorporations in that period as the result of a rational quest for increased efficiency.[23] This explanation, though, does not seem to be compatible with an historically faithful account. As underscored earlier, the first and main motive behind the simultaneous consolidation and incorporation movements had been the control of competition and the creation of a relatively stable business environment. Rather than being their cause, the rationalization of production and the formalization of organizational structures were the consequences of mergers and incorporations, following them by a few years when they took place at all. Indeed, a significant number of emerging industrial entities remained relatively decentralized federations. Others were reorganized internally and came to be formally structured more or less rapidly. The objective was at least as much to increase efficiency as to establish a measure of control over what were then large, chaotic aggregates (Edwards, 1979; Fligstein, 1990). By the early years of the twentieth century, the corporate form, large firms, and oligopolistic markets regulated by antitrust legislation had become characteristic features of the American system of industrial production in most sectors. Before the start of the 1930s, this system would be further defined by a rationalization of the productive process and by the formalization of organizational structures.

Mass Production, Rationalization, and Control

The main motive behind the first wave of mergers had been the control of direct competition and the establishment of market power—if not dominance—over a particular industrial sector. Many of the emerging holding companies, as a consequence, were horizontal combinations of previously independent units.[24] A number of those horizontal combinations were associations of peers. They brought together several firms of similar weight and power. In other cases, a dominant concern had led the way towards market organization, dragging along, whether they liked it or not, formerly independent smaller firms. Power struggles and conflicts of interests, which had until then been articulated on the market or within loose associations made up of independent companies, were therefore and to a varying extent internalized in the newly created legal entities.

A systematic comparison of the experience of several industries showed a correlation between the nature of the merger—'association of peers' or 'strongly dominated'—and its capacity to survive and transform itself into a single operating entity.[25] Mergers that attempted to combine a number of individual concerns of relatively similar weight and strength were generally slow to move beyond mere federation and towards a systematic internal reorganization and a rationalization of production. They had obvious difficulties overcoming internal power struggles and transforming themselves into single operating—and not simply legal—entities. This was the case particularly in the textile, apparel, lumber, and paper industries and also in rubber and steel. The rubber industry provides an interesting example. By the late 1880s, there was no clear leader in that industry. Two holding companies were created in 1892, each bringing together several units of similar weight. Although the rubber industry has been identified as having 'particularly powerful cost advantages of scale', it took more than ten years before an attempt was made to turn the companies into 'centrally administered, integrated enterprises' or to rationalize production.[26] Conversely, most holding companies dominated by a leading concern were successful in harnessing internal power struggles and therefore were able to proceed with a reorganization and a rationalization of production. They rapidly became single operating companies. This was the case in the oil industry under the lead of Standard Oil, in the glass industry with Pittsburg Plate Glass, in the sugar industry following the American Sugar Refining Company, and in chemicals with DuPont.

It has often been argued that the move from a holding to a single operating company allowed the corporate entity to benefit from economies of scale and scope, increased its efficiency, and ultimately ensured profits and success (Chandler, 1977, 1990; Williamson, 1985). Without denying the fact that rationalized production facilities and formalized organizational structures ultimately and eventually increased the efficiency of holding companies, I propose that the search for efficiency was not, in most cases, the main motive behind internal reorganization. The shutting down of certain plants, the enlarging of others, or the building of newer and larger factories were undeniable attempts to cash in on the new situation of market control or dominance. To the leading concern of a newly created holding company, these choices were also means to secure control within the combination, to eliminate disturbing conflicts of interests and destructive power struggles between the representatives of previously independent units. The centralization of administrative processes, the reorganization of productive facilities, and their rationalization unmistakably benefited the leading concern, if there was one, within a holding company. They established its control on solid ground, institutionalized its power, further weakening other members who had earlier been competitors. Internal reorganization, it is argued here, was thus more likely and more rapid in those holding companies where a dominant concern was able to impose transformations, sometimes against the interests of other members.[27]

In those holding companies that successfully launched a process of internal reorganization, the rationalization of productive facilities and administrative centralization created the right conditions for the adoption, or the spread, of techniques of mass production. Internal reorganization led to the concentration of production in fewer and larger facilities (Thorelli, 1954; Chandler, 1990). Those larger facilities, in turn, stimulated the adoption and the diffusion of machines and techniques that would allow production on a larger scale. In nineteenth-century USA, technological developments had made standardized production a possibility. Nevertheless, by the end of the century, the use made of those technologies within American industry had remained limited (Hounshell, 1984; Kogut and Parkinson, 1994). The newly created holding companies took hold of those available technologies at the beginning of the twentieth century during the process of reorganization into single operating firms. In combination with the increased size of production facilities, such technological choices led to the development of American mass production systems and to continuous flow production on the assembly line.[28] At least as much as economies of scale and scope, the adoption and the diffusion of mass production systems and standardization methods was to ensure a systematic control of the shop floor and of workers within the newly enlarged production facilities. Scientific management methods, elaborated by Frederick Winslow Taylor with such a control objective in mind, reinforced the overall trend. Through 'time and motion' studies of work processes, Taylor and his engineers proposed to appropriate the accumulated knowledge and *savoir faire* of the workers and to transfer them to management (Taylor, 1947; Braverman, 1974; Edwards, 1979). The diffusion of Taylor's system was relatively slow, due in particular to the violent opposition of labor and trade unions. Nevertheless, by the 1930s and 1940s, the 'spirit of Taylorism' had become deeply ingrained within the American system of industrial production. A strict control of labor through a rationalization of the production process, an emphasis on productivity and productivity measures, or time and motion constraints set by the machinery and assembly line, were its unmistakable expressions (Kogut and Parkinson, 1994; Guillén, 1994; Rupert, 1995).

Formalizing Internal Structures, Building Managerial Hierarchies

The increased size and complexity of firms combined with new ownership patterns to bring about a redefinition of leadership in American industry. A separation between ownership and control meant, in particular, an increased role for salaried employees and professional managers at the top of the firm. Internal reorganization, on the other hand, and emerging administrative and coordination problems made middle managers and clerks necessary. The 'visible hand' of managerial hierarchies thus soon became the main regulating principle within the new corporate giants.[29] Managerial hierarchies were initially built so as to handle the coordination and control problems created by the new mergers and to try and turn an aggregate of formerly independent units into a single operating entity. This early objective of greater centralization came to be reflected in organizational structures. Central offices were divided along functional lines—production, sales, accounting, and then marketing—all directly reporting to the President or Chief Executive. Bureaucratization and specialization increasingly turned management into a profession characterized by a set of specific tools. This evolution was confirmed and reinforced, within society at large, by the development of management education, by the multiplication and spread of management literature, and by the emergence, in the 1920s and 1930s, of professional associations and consulting firms.

In the late 1910s and early 1920s, reorganized giants turned to new strategies in their search for a stable environment. Vertical integration and diversification created, in their turn, new organizational problems. DuPont and General Motors were the first companies to propose, in close succession, a solution to those problems in the form of a new internal structure.[30] The diversification strategy, chosen after the First World War by the top management at DuPont had backfired in part and the company was soon faced with serious losses. Problems were being blamed on organizational shortcomings and, in the early 1920s, the board of directors adopted a plan which proposed a radical restructuring. The company was to decentralize and reorganization was to take place along the main product lines. Each department or product division was to be fairly independent, operating almost as a self-contained unit. Managing directors at the divisional level ran their own functional departments—accounting, sales, production, or purchasing. An executive committee or general office was to concentrate on strategic decision making and long-range planning for the company as a whole. No chairman of an operating division could sit on the executive committee and no member of the committee could run the affairs of a division (Chandler, 1962). Although at first sight fairly different, the situation at General Motors could in fact be handled in a similar way. General Motors had been much less successful than DuPont at turning an aggregate of formerly independent firms into a single operating entity. By 1920, General Motors was still a loose federation, a hodgepodge of fairly independent units. The multidivisional structure in this case represented a means of bringing about a form of administrative coherence while still preserving the multiplicity and diversity of product lines. The economic success of those two corporations in the years following the adoption of the M-form would in time, albeit slowly, reflect on the structure itself and the multidivisional structure would come to spread. It was sometimes adopted in direct imitation of a successful competitor as in the case of Ford, taking the organizational structure of General Motors as a model at the end of the Second World War. After 1945, the adoption of the M-form was also recommended by strategy and organization consultants in a process that had the characteristics of a large-scale diffusion of professional norms (DiMaggio and Powell, 1983). By 1948, 20 out of the 100 largest firms in the USA had adopted a multi-divisional structure; 73 had done so by 1969 (Fligstein, 1990; Rumelt, 1974). Those firms were for the most part industrial champions and as such highly visible on foreign markets. The M-form thus naturally came to be identified, after the Second World War, as being a key and striking feature of the American system of industrial production (Drucker, 1946; Chandler, 1962).

During the years bridging the nineteenth and twentieth centuries, the American system of industrial production had clearly undergone a radical and large-scale transformation. A new paradigm of industrial organization, a new form of capitalism emerged from a process which comprised three stages: a restructuring of the competitive environment; a redefinition of ownership structures; and a reshaping of organizational structures and modes of production. In the same period of time, the situation had remained fairly stable on the other side of the Atlantic. The American structural revolution had no equivalent before the Second World War on the western side of the old continent. Changes, when they took place in Western European industries during that period, were relatively marginal and tended in fact to reinforce those features characteristic of the more traditional types of family or organized capitalisms.

Notes

1. Clapp Committee Testimony (1911), p. 1167, quoted by McCraw (1984: 109). Before becoming Supreme Court Justice in 1916, Louis D. Brandeis had embodied, as the 'people's lawyer' of the Progressive Era, the fight against big business and trusts.

2. The term 'proprietary–competitive' was coined by Sklar (1988) to identify *laissez faire* capitalism or more exactly its family and organized variants, which he contrasted to the 'corporate–administered' type that was emerging at the turn of the century.

3. Conceptual vagueness was still obvious in the definition of the term proposed in 1904 by John Moody. 'The term "trust" is applicable to any act, agreement or combination believed to possess the intention, power or tendency to monopolize business, interfere with trade, fix prices . . . . A "trust" is characterized by its largeness' (Moody, 1904: xiv).

4. McCraw (1984: 47) confirms this, indicating that in this case 'American business history may have taken a very different path'. For more on counterfactual reasoning in historical analysis, see Roy (1990).

5. Interstate Commerce Act (1887), Sherman Antitrust Act (1890). One should underscore, at this point, the role of the Populist Movement, which federated those small interests, playing on their fears and calling for the break-up of large aggregates (Goodwyn, 1976).

6. Quoted in Bork (1966: 15). I believe, with Thorelli (1954), that ultimately the cause for the enactment of the Sherman Act was the pressure brought to bear by farmers and small producers on Congress. Without such an organized movement, antitrust legislation may have never been enacted despite a sincere desire on the part of many Congressmen to protect competition and freedom.

7. The Sherman Antitrust Act of July 2, 1890, is reprinted in Thorelli (1954), appendix I.

8. A number of Congressmen had anticipated the potentially disturbing consequences of the 'commerce clause'. Senator Wilson (Democrat, West Virginia) believed that 'the inability to control what corporations were doing in individual states might prove a hindrance to an effective regulation of competitive conditions' (Thorelli, 1954: 203).

9. This was what Justice Harlan attempted to do in his dissent opinion on the E. C. Knight case, but he was the only one to dissent.

10. Nelson (1959). See also Thorelli (1954), Kolko (1963), Lamoreaux (1985), Sklar (1988), or Fligstein (1990).

11. Kolko (1963) and Sklar (1988) go further, arguing that the office of the Attorney General and other Federal agencies were influenced in part by big business actors, particularly during the McKinley and Theodore Roosevelt administrations. Prosecution was thus selective, often sparing the new corporations.

12. Taft (1911: 11). Taft became President of the USA in 1909. As Supreme Court Justice, he had been a champion of the rule of reason and of a common law interpretation of antitrust. See Sklar (1988: 130–1).

13. 'Objection was made by certain independent tobacco companies that this settlement was unjust because it left companies with very large capital in active business . . . . This contention results from a misunderstanding of the antitrust law and its purpose. It is not intended thereby to prevent the accumulation of large capital in business enterprises in which such a combination can secure reduced cost of production, sale and distribution' (Taft, 1911: 9).

14. A 'social compromise' is understood here to be the result of a confrontation where parties can be significantly unequal and to which they bring all their respective resources, economic or non-economic. The power balance in a society, itself partly

dependent on the social division of resources, thus largely shapes the final compromise. I do not want to imply here, therefore, that all social groups in the USA
agreed on the solution that was finally proposed to the 'trust question'. I merely
wish to say that this solution had become clearly dominant by the end of the decade
and that this certainly reflected the increasingly significant impact of corporate
business leaders on the national debate.

15. A comparison between Roy's (1991) figures on incorporations and Nelson's (1959)
    account of the merger wave shows clearly that both trends were parallel with a
    slightly later start for the incorporation movement.

16. Limited liability, hailed since then as the most interesting feature of the corporate
    form, was certainly, in the nineteenth century, the main cause for its lack of
    success. Investors were distrustful of a form which seemed to foster irresponsible
    behavior (Chayes, 1969).

17. Parker-Gwin and Roy (1996). Traditionally, corporations had been able to hold
    only physical assets and property. Until corporations came to be treated as indivi-
    duals, courts had tended to rule that corporations could not hold other firms nor
    their stocks.

18. For more on the idea of search and on how it relates to the definition and redefini-
    tion of property rights, see Campbell and Lindberg (1990). They underscore the
    significance of political institutions, if not for the search process itself, at least for
    setting its boundaries.

19. Parker-Gwin and Roy (1996) show that the new legal device had been tailored to
    solve the problem of a particular group of private interests in the cotton oil
    industry.

20. New Jersey law did not require holding companies to produce in the state. Their
    duties were to own and manage stock, elect officers, and pay dividends (Thorelli,
    1954: 256).

21. Obviously, large-scale incorporation could increase state income quite significantly
    (Thorelli, 1954; Nelson, 1959).

22. That internal reorganization and a rationalization of production took place later is
    another story, and one that will be told below.

23. Chandler (1990: 73) has argued that 'legal combinations were a prerequisite for
    centralizing the administration of constituent companies. The new legal form
    permitted a rationalization of facilities.' The danger of transforming outcomes
    into causes has been well articulated by Perrow (1981) and Roy (1990).

24. Livermore (1935) differentiated consolidations from mergers, keeping the latter
    term for transformations taking place between 1890 and 1905. Its very 'purpose
    distinguished the merger', he argued, that is 'gaining more power by the elimina-
    tion of active competitors'.

25. I have used, for this comparison, the data provided by Chandler (1990), particularly
    in his chapter IV. Chandler has told the stories of a large number of American
    industries, providing information both on the nature of the new holding companies
    (information which I translated in two main categories—'association of peers' and
    'strongly dominated') and on the speed of adoption of a rationalization strategy.
    Naturally, Chandler himself did not point to a potential correlation between those
    two dimensions.

26. Chandler (1990), chapter IV. Some of those holding companies, created from an

association of peers, never made the move and ultimately had to disband. See in particular the cut glass and paper industries.

27. Chandler (1990: 73) argued that, in trade associations, cartels, or trusts, 'rationalization was difficult' because 'members were rarely willing to vote to shut down their own plants, to enlarge those of others or to build factories in which they had no direct interests'. I argue that this was also the case within holding companies where there was a certain balance of power between individual concerns. On the other hand, clear and uncontested dominance made it much easier to take and impose such decisions.

28. The argument, here, is that technological developments are important to the extent that they create opportunities and options. The adoption, though, of a given technology is always problematic and not unavoidable. It is in reality often driven by a complex set of motives, amongst which the quest for efficiency may be just one, sometimes not the most important (Edwards, 1979; Piore and Sabel, 1984).

29. This process led in turn to the emergence of an American 'middle class' with its own lifestyle and values (Berle and Means, 1932; Burnham, 1941).

30. In fact, the same man, Pierre DuPont, was involved in both reorganizations. Running the family firm with two of his cousins, he became President of General Motors in 1921 because DuPont had a significant stake in the car maker (Chandler, 1962; Sloan, 1963).

2

Stability of European Industries
Preserving Structural Arrangements before 1939

And so is Europe, gaping in astonishment, if not horror, in between two experiences which are going on, one in Russia, the other in America.

Georges Duhamel (1930: 240)

West European systems of industrial production were characterized before the beginning of the Second World War by overall stability and they shared a number of key structural features. French, German, and Italian systems of industrial production, in particular, all ranged somewhere between family and organized types of capitalism. And the general evolution in that part of the world, during the first years of the twentieth century, was unmistakably towards increasingly organized markets and structured forms of interfirm cooperation.

With respect to the structural revolution taking place on the other side of the Atlantic, West Europeans had, on the whole, mixed feelings. In France, the transformation of American industry brought mostly dismay and fear of contagion. The German industrial community, on the other hand, had become much more familiar than its French counterpart with American industrial reality throughout the first part of the twentieth century. Indeed, economic relationships between Germany and the USA had increased in density following the Dawes plan, which after 1924 brought vast quantities of American capital to Germany. Nevertheless, despite this greater familiarity with the new American industrial model, there was no systematic attempt before the Second World War to transfer to Germany, on a large scale, the corporate system of industrial production. German industrial leaders—not any different in that from their European neighbors—resisted mergers, incorporation, and internal reorganization. They feared that an evolution in this direction would weaken or even destroy the control each private owner wanted to retain over his particular concern.

FAMILY CAPITALISM IN FRANCE: STABILITY OF THE SOCIAL ORDER

The picture which emerges from an historical study of French industry before the Second World War is one of moderate growth combined with great structural stability (Clough, 1946; Clapham, 1968; Caron, 1981). In fact, during the first part of the twentieth century, French industrialization took place within the boundaries set by nineteenth-century economic and industrial structures. Changes on the French industrial scene were therefore merely incremental. The picture becomes all the more striking when comparisons are made with the transformations taking place in the USA at the very same time. French industry remained, until the Second World War, dominated by small or medium-sized family firms. While intent on preserving their identity and independence, those family units were trying to control markets and bridle competition by entering more or less formal interfirm agreements, cartels, or *ententes*.

The French System of Industrial Production before 1939

French firms remained small well into the twentieth century. There was no discernible trend, before the Second World War, towards an increase in the average size of industrial establishments (Cassis, 1997). Table 5 clearly shows that a small number of larger establishments and firms could be found but only in coal mining, iron, or steel.

In fact, a significant share of French industry would have been more accurately classified as craft and a large number of French industrial firms were no more than workshops. By 1950, 85 per cent of all industrial establishments still had no more than five employees (INSEE, 1953). Large firms or establishments remained rare and were concentrated in a few industrial sectors. From 1906 to 1936, the number of industrial establishments employing more than 1,000 persons had gone up but only from 215 to 296 (Trotignon, 1986: 180). The stability of the size structure within French industry was all the more striking and surprising given the fact that American industry was undergoing radical transformations in that respect. Figure 4 shows that small or medium-

Table 5. Average number of workers per industrial establishment, France in 1926 and 1946

	1926	1936
Mining	953	995
Iron and steel	502	586
Rubber, paper	45	44
Chemicals	35	37
Textiles	31	39
Metal industry	12	11
Leather	6	7
Food	4	5
Apparel	4	5
Woodworking	5	4

Source: INSEE (1953).

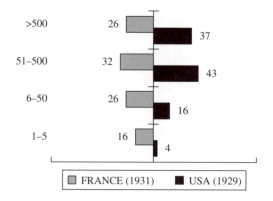

Figure 4. Labor force per size of industrial establishments, USA and France around 1930 (%)
Source: Trotignon (1976: 110).

sized concerns were still predominant in France when medium-sized or large establishments had already begun to define American industry.

Those small or medium-sized French firms, with often a single factory or productive establishment, belonged in general to individuals or families. Ownership in France thus remained coupled with control, the head of the family both owning and ruling the industrial unit. Until the Second World War, industrial undertakings involving more than one investor tended to be partnerships or limited partnerships. The French limited partnership or *société en commandite* was an interesting legal device, created in 1808 by the administration of the First Empire. A number of sleeping partners were involved merely as purveyors of capital and enjoyed limited liability. Active partners who were running and managing the business worked, on the other hand, under conditions of unlimited liability. This legal form had rapidly become popular amongst owners of medium-sized or larger concerns, because it allowed them to bring in the necessary capital while still preserving the family or individual nature of the firm. Sleeping partners often belonged to the family or to the first circle of friends and acquaintances.

After 1863, the liberalization of the joint stock company status, granted until then only through political fiat, somewhat stimulated its adoption within the French industrial community. The preference, though, for ownership structures protecting family or individual control remained undisputed and was to be further illustrated by the striking success of the private limited liability form (*société à responsabilité limitée* or SARL). The SARL, directly modeled on a German legal structure—*Gesellschaft mit beschränkter Haftung* or GmbH— became available in France in 1925. All partners involved in a SARL, whether sleeping or active, enjoyed limited liability. The private nature of the firm, however, was protected since shares were not freely transferable. French industrial leaders rapidly seized upon an ownership structure that combined the advantages of limited liability with the stability and control that characterized partnerships.[1]

The difference between France and the USA, with respect to ownership structures, was therefore quite significant. By 1936, the American corporate revolution was already well under way and around 70 per cent of industrial firms in the USA were corporations. French industry, in the meantime, had remained dominated by family-owned and run industrial units with only 22 per cent of firms being SA or SARL (Landes, 1964). Little trace could be found in France of the managerial revolution which had, for some years by then, been disrupting the organization of work in the USA and redefining the social make-up of that country. Neither were there any signs, within French industrial firms, of a large-scale internal reorganization and of a systematic formalization of organizational structures.

Those small, family-owned and run French firms were often linked together through more or less formal agreements. French firms entered horizontal or vertical cartels and *ententes* in order to regulate buying or selling, to agree on prices, and to share markets. Cartels and *ententes* were prompted, in France as in the USA or in Germany, by a desire to control the environment and limit competition (Magondeaux, 1937). A somewhat more formal type of collective agreement existed in France and represented an alternative way to organize markets. The French *holding* was created with a view to enlarging, through financial cooperation, the capital base of member firms without endangering individual or family control. French holdings had a central administrative office and cooperation was thus more structured and formalized than within cartels or *ententes*. Nevertheless, the agreement preserved the legal and functional independence of participating entities and allowed individual owners to retain control, prestige, and a significant amount of power.[2]

The First World War gave a significant impetus to the organization of markets in France and the cartelization movement continued to gain ground, thereafter, at a swift pace. On the eve of the Second World War, there were somewhere between one thousand and three thousand cartel agreements or *ententes* in France. In those industrial sectors that were organized, around 85 per cent of the total production was regulated.[3] There were no legal or official means, though, to impose and enforce those agreements. In the 1930s, the peak French business association, the Confédération Générale du Patronat Français or CGPF, was calling loudly for legislation granting cartels and *ententes* legitimacy and possibly making them compulsory. In 1935, the French business community came close to obtaining such a legislation but the Flandin–Marchandeau bill was finally rejected by the second chamber of the French Parliament. The preference for organized and stabilized markets, characteristic of French industry, would finally be institutionalized during the Second World War. Corporatist policies of the Vichy regime made business cooperation lawful and even compulsory, placing business agreements under the protection and control of the state. Overall, this particular feature of corporatism was welcomed by the French business community (Ehrmann, 1957; Paxton, 1973; Vinen, 1991; Rochebrune and Hazera, 1995). Industrial sectors were organized through centralized committees or *comités d'organisation*, placed under the direct supervision of the Ministry of Industrial Production. Each committee agreed on production quotas, set prices, and shared markets. Voluntary and informal cartels or *ententes* had thus been institutionalized and transformed into rigid and compulsory organizations. Whereas prewar French cartels had been loose agreements, difficult to enforce, the Vichy committees had significant power, organizing production within members firms, defining quotas and norms, and imposing specialization and an internal division of labor.

The Social Embeddedness of French Industry

Small-scale units, family ownership, and organized markets were three constitutive features of the French system of industrial production before the Second World War. The great stability and permanence of those features throughout the first part of the twentieth century undeniably deserves scrutiny. Economists and historians have tended to identify, in the French case, economic, demographic, and technological peculiarities as accounting for stability.[4] The argument, within this perspective, is as follows. A lack of productivity in the French agricultural sector limited the transfer of labor from farms to factories, thus thwarting industrialization and the growth of industrial units. The transformation of industrial structures was further hindered by low rates of population growth, a lack of market dynamism, and a very segmented distribution system. French industry, it has been argued, was therefore not subject to a sufficient degree of market pressure (Clough, 1946). On the other hand, France was undeniably a technologically advanced country and produced its fair share of scientists and inventors. A national preference, though, for non-productive and international investments drastically limited the funds available as venture capital and thus prevented large-scale transfers of technology to the national industry (Clough, 1946; Lévy-Leboyer, 1976). It has been argued, finally, that in the context of an international division of industrial labor, the comparative advantage of French industry and its particular output mix essentially explained the stability of structures in that country (O'Brien and Keyder, 1978; Cameron and Freedeman, 1983). The French system of industrial production, in other words, was well adapted to craft-like, high quality industrial production.

Without questioning the value of these arguments, we should nevertheless underscore the fact that economic, demographic, and technological features are not themselves independent variables. They also have to be accounted for. In the French case, the failure of markets to expand or the peculiar nature of investment patterns for example are puzzling characteristics worth investigating. The development of a dense railway network in nineteenth-century France had apparently created favorable conditions for an expansion and integration of markets.[5] But in contrast to what happened in the USA, French industry failed to seize the opportunities created by the new railway network. Industrial dynamism was triggered in France during the Second Empire by the Péreire brothers and encouraged by the regime. It was quickly brought to a halt, though, under pressure from powerful and well entrenched interests striving for stability and *status quo* within the national economy and society.[6] In the end, French markets remained fragmented and production essentially small-scale. Economic and technological arguments, in the French case, thus fall short of providing satisfying answers. The strength of conservative interests and their success in imposing stability have to be accounted for in a context where the development of infrastructure could theoretically have led to industrial dynamism. In fact, systems of industrial production are embedded in a much wider social environment (Polanyi, 1944; Granovetter, 1985). Industrial structures are institutions and they not only have economic objectives but also social functions. The search for potentially relevant explanatory variables should thus be extended beyond the economic, demographic, and technological spheres. It will be argued that in the case of France before the Second World War, the stability of industrial structures essentially reflected the rigidity of the social order.

Before 1945, firms and workshops in France were obviously economic and production units. More importantly, though, they were a source of financial independence for families and represented the material basis of their prestige and status. Workers and employees dreamt of becoming their own masters, of opening their own workshops or stores, of running their own farms or small firms which they would then pass on to their sons. Property more than wealth conferred social status and low birth rates in France could in part be explained by a wish to avoid breaking up the estate (Rowley, 1982). Bankruptcy, as a consequence, meant not only economic but also social downfall, a stain on the family name and honor.[7] In this context, risky managerial decision making and daring choices that could lead to rapid success and wealth or alternatively to disastrous failures and bankruptcies were considered irresponsible and proved to be, in fact, extremely rare.

Considering the important social function of the firm, management had to be fairly conservative and its main priorities were the survival of the firm and the protection of family control. The firm was kept small so that the family could retain control—both financial and managerial—and thus preserve its independence. Most investments were self-financed and projects requiring outside capital were often forsaken through fear of a partial loss of control.[8] Since industrial firms in France tended to favor self-financing, potential outlets for capital in the productive sector were limited. Savings were thus naturally funneled into foreign investments, state bonds, or gold. The peculiar nature of investment patterns in France thus appeared to be a consequence rather than a cause of the relative stability of industrial structures. Within a risk adverse community such as French industry before the Second World War, even technological innovation seemed fraught with danger. Its cost could lead to financial dependence. The complexity of new machines and techniques might imply a partial transfer of control and power from business owners to engineers and professional managers. Technological innovation was likely, in the end, to disturb the existing balance within a given industry. Even though it might increase productive capacity, reduce costs, and create growth opportunities, it therefore had to be shunned. In a context where stability was the highest of priorities, all firms could stand to lose by a disruption of the *status quo*, including the largest. Eugène Schneider—who was running a large French steel company—was clear about the fact that 'what is essential and comes before all other things is stability'. Between 'exceptionally favorable but unstable general conditions and others, less brilliant but assured of great stability', he claimed that he would 'not hesitate to choose the latter'.[9] René-Paul Duchemin, chairman of the peak business association—the Confédération Générale du Patronat Français—praised the caution and wisdom of French businessmen who did not rush towards technological innovation. The 'ransom for the meritorious modesty of modernization efforts' had been the high price of French goods but, according to him, economic and social stability were worth it.[10]

Cartels and *ententes*, which French business associations hoped to make compulsory, were precisely the means to stabilize industrial sectors further and to institutionalize the existing balance within those sectors. Through industry-wide agreements, prices were kept at a level where less efficient firms could survive while more efficient ones prospered. Auguste Detoeuf, who was running a large electrical company, argued that 'agreements and cartels allowed small and medium-sized firms to survive' because they offered protection against industrial concentration. And for him as for many other French business leaders small or medium-sized firms were a guarantee that 'economic and social relations (would not become) unbearable and inhuman'.[11] In the end, economic *malthusianism* and a lack of industrial dynamism were thus justified on the grounds that they were conditions not only of economic, but also of social, stability.[12] In France, the protection of property clearly took priority over growth. This was true across all propertied classes, with large or small assets, of high or low status. The permanence of French industrial structures thus essentially reflected the rigidity of the social order, where fear of failure or bankruptcy, and of the social stigma associated with them, tended to dwarf ambitions, to eliminate risk taking behaviors, and to prevent change.

Political actors played a further stabilizing role, the period of the Second Empire representing a partial exception. They adopted a *laissez faire* attitude on the national territory, allowing free rein to cartels and *ententes*, while protecting national markets against foreign competition. The harmony and compatibility that undeniably existed, during the Third Republic, between the policies of the French state, on the one hand, and the interests of the national business community, on the other, was no mere coincidence. It was, to a significant extent, a consequence of the relatively homogeneous character of the French élite. Civil servants in charge of economic and financial policy, the famous *Inspecteurs des Finances*, were often the gifted sons of the *bourgeoisie*, linked to industrial élites through social networks and marriage. As a consequence, political institutions only had a limited and conservative impact on the French industrial landscape, essentially creating the right conditions for the stability the industrial community desired.[13]

The American Nightmare

While stability was the key word within French industry, an increasingly powerful national economy on the other side of the Atlantic was undergoing a radical transformation. The type of capitalism that emerged in the USA, so peculiar in many ways, became for a few individuals in France a source of inspiration, a model for imitation. For most Frenchmen, though, it represented a threat, an economic and social inferno, all the more frightening in that it appeared to be efficient. The group echoing American models in France before the Second World War, was small and lacked institutional power. While positivism had come close to being official ideology during the Second Empire, by the beginning of the twentieth century its appeal was limited to a few engineering schools and communities. French positivists equated progress with economic and technological developments, advocating industrial growth (Comte, 1907, 1943). Unsurprisingly, a few of them were quite fascinated by the emerging American system of industrial production. But French engineers trained within the positivist tradition had, in reality, little institutional power within an economic order where family firms were still being run by their owners and where stability and security remained dominant objectives. The relative failure of their attempt to diffuse Taylor's ideas and system of management to French industry was a clear illustration of this lack of institutional power.[14] Ultimately, positivist engineers were not decision makers at the time, neither in the economy nor in the polity. And their ideological convictions were very much at odds with the conservatism which was then pervasive in French economy and society.

In fact, the dominant reaction in France to the American system of industrial production was one of dismay and fear. Corporate capitalism and the social and cultural transformations it brought with it did not appear compatible with the existing French economic and social order. They seemed to threaten, in fact, a certain idea of French 'civilization'. Anti-Americanism in France reached a peak in the 1920s and 1930s, not only within the *intelligentsia* but also within political and business communities (Strauss, 1978). The main targets for criticism were the new American system of industrial production and its social, cultural, or political consequences. Descriptions were apocalyptic and the rejection of the model was often violent. Two books, in this respect, had a key impact: *Les Etats Unis d'aujourd'hui* and *Scènes de la Vie Future*, written respectively by André Siegfried and Georges Duhamel. Those two books rapidly became works of reference and significantly contributed to shaping the image of the USA in France before the Second World War.[15] Both Siegfried and Duhamel were at the time important actors on the French intellectual and political scene. Siegfried, moreover, held a strategic institutional position as dean of a school that trained civil servants and politicians, the Ecole Libre des Sciences Politiques.

A particularly striking feature for the French observer of the USA was the primacy of the economy in that country. Economic relations and institutions seemed to be shaping American social institutions and cultural values and not the other way round. Within the 'cathedral of commerce', the religion was 'materialism' and 'materialism' was identified as the most dangerous threat to a French definition of 'civilization' (Siegfried, 1927). This 'materialist religion' was embodied, in the USA, in mass production and mass consumption. Production on a large scale, within huge industrial units where machines were setting a frantic pace, led in turn to standardization. This evolution was seen to contrast sharply with the spirit of French industrial production where 'the value is in the originality and finish of the article, and competition requires not the standardization of a few types, but a higher level of perfection and a greater variety of models' (Siegfried, 1927: 180–1). In the process of mass production, the French observer claimed, quality was sacrificed for quantity. The object as a unique product, the expression of the worker's craft and *savoir faire*, the object as a work of art, was turned into the standardized unit of a production batch. The worker was demoted from the rank of skilled craftsman, rich in knowledge and experience, to that of obedient and submissive underling, a cog in the productive process, who could be as easily trained as he could be replaced.

Standardization was not only a characteristic of mass production, the observer went on, it also defined its corollary, mass consumption. In this case, the standardization bore on values, individual tastes, men and women themselves. Advertising was the powerful tool through which this frightening process of human homogenization was taking place. Advertising, indeed, 'by accustoming people to a small number of brands, facilitate[d] the mass production of an article'. The American, Siegfried claimed, was 'molded as easily as clay' but 'standardizing the individual', he added, 'in order to standardize the things he [would] buy [was] to lose sight of the fact that goods were made for man and not man for goods'.[16] In the process, the individual was in danger of disappearing. The French observer believed he was witnessing, on the other side of the Atlantic, the triumph of the mass and the dawn of its dictatorship, already predicted and feared by Alexis de Tocqueville.[17]

The image of the USA thus dominating in France at the time was that of a country where uniform men lived in standardized towns, worked in huge, mass producing factories, produced and bought standardized goods, and shared the same values.[18] To Frenchmen across the entire political spectrum, similarities between this system and the Soviet version of communism were simply striking. In fact, both the USA and the USSR appeared to be as far removed as possible from a French model of civilization.[19] The increasing role of those two countries, though, on the world scene and their undeniable achievements with respect to economic growth and industrial production were such that many in France feared they were becoming dominating powers of unparalleled strength. This evolution was a source of dismay for Frenchmen who, caught in between, dreaded contagion.

Such a fear was not yet justified though. Before the Second World War, an americanization or for that matter a bolshevization of the French economy and society were only remote nightmares. The characteristic features of the French system of industrial production were still strikingly different from those of the emerging American model. There was, moreover, absolutely no indication that the French system of industrial production was changing and even less that it was evolving towards the American corporate type of capitalism. The French definition of civilization had managed to survive, despite significant transformations in other parts of the world. The stability of the French economic and social order was ensured by its deep institutional embeddedness and by a relatively widespread consensus around it within French society. It would take a significant crisis for the internal debate to evolve and for structural change to become not only likely, but desirable. It would take significant questioning and reshuffling within the French élite before the 'American nightmare' was to become a positive model for the national economy.

ORGANIZED CAPITALISM IN GERMANY: CHECKING COMPETITION

For German kingdoms, the nineteenth century was a period of crucial change. Two developments of great consequence prepared the way for the economic expansion and for the rapid industrialization that marked the end of the century. The first was an agrarian reform in the eastern kingdoms and the abolition of serfdom. Combining with demographic dynamism, it led to the release of a surplus population that would both fuel German industrialization and produce waves of emigration, particularly towards North America. The second major development was the process of unification, that went from economic cooperation between German kingdoms through the *Zollverein* of 1834 to political integration around Prussia in January 1871. The new German Empire or *Reich* was founded on military victory in the Franco-Prussian war. An unprecedented industrial boom followed unification in the early 1870s, setting those years apart as crucial to the economic and industrial development of the new *Reich*.[20]

The German System of Industrial Production before 1939

The industrialization of Germany before the Second World War was not an homogeneous process. In particular, there was a significant difference between the dynamism of German heavy industry and the more sluggish performance of the consumer goods sector. This was translated at the level of structures. Firms and productive establishments tended to grow larger in capital goods industries while remaining small was the rule in other industries. At the same time, both a predominance of family control and patterns of interfirm relations unmistakably tied the German system of industrial production to a European tradition. In fact, the German system of industrial production before the Second World War closely fit the type that was earlier labeled 'organized capitalism'.

After 1870, the size structure of German industry changed rapidly and significantly. Very small firms tended to disappear while larger units were growing (Pietri, 1982: 365). As Table 6 shows, though, this general trend concealed differences between sectors, with larger establishments dominating in coal and steel while most consumer goods or the metals industries remained overwhelmingly defined by smaller firms. In fact this undeniable evolution of German industry around the turn of the twentieth century could in no way compare with the contemporary disruption of American industrial structures.[21] In the first part of the twentieth century, the largest German firms were still surprisingly small when compared to their American counterparts. A comparison of assets values of the 200 largest firms in Germany and in the USA before the Second World War clearly shows this.[22] Results of this comparison are summarized in Table 7.

When assets values are compared, the largest American firm in 1914, US Steel, proved to be seventeen times bigger than the largest German firm that year. Both in 1914 and 1930, 90 per cent of the largest 200 German firms were smaller than the last firm on the American list of 200.[23] Clearly, large size did not mean the same thing in Germany as it did in the USA. As documented in

Table 6. Labor force per size of establishments, Germany in 1907 (%)

	1–50	51–200	201–1000	> 1000
Coal and steel	3.3	10.7	33.5	52.5
Machinery	19.8	31.1	29.4	19.7
Chemicals	24.4	30.7	26.7	18.2
Textile	32.5	29.2	33.9	4.4
Metals	53.0	23.4	28.5	4.1
Construction	59.5	26.4	12.8	1.3
Foods	78.2	14.4	6.2	1.2
Apparel	87.7	8.4	3.3	0.6
Wood	77.7	16.8	5.2	0.3

Source: Pietri (1982: 365).

Table 7. Comparing assets values; the 200 largest firms in Germany and the USA before 1939

	First World War		1930		
Germany	number 1 Friedrich Krupp = Value V1	number 17 Bergmann Elektricitäts = Value W1	number 1 Vereignite Stahlwerke = V2	number 3 Allgemeine Elektricitäts = W2	number 16 Guttehofnungshütte Oberhausen = X2
USA	number 1 US Steel = 17*V1	number 200 E. W. Bliss around W1	number 1 US Steel = 5*V2	number 3 General Motors = 10*W2	number 200 International Agricultural around X2

Source: Compiled from Chandler (1990), appendices A and C.

the introduction, small and medium-sized firms still represented the foundations of German industry in the early 1950s. With respect to the size of industrial firms and establishments, Germany was thus, until the end of the Second World War, much closer to a European than to an American model.[24]

Whatever their size, German firms remained generally, and throughout the first part of the twentieth century, the property of individuals or families who were also running and managing them. Before German unification, anonymous stock ownership and limited liability had been rare privileges granted only through political fiat. The number of joint stock companies— *Aktiengesellschaften* or AG—increased rapidly after conditions for incorporation were liberalized in 1870. The increase was particularly significant in heavy industry.[25] In fact, the joint stock form proved to be a success amongst the largest industrial entities in Germany while it remained a marginal ownership structure when German industry was considered as a whole. But the German AG was quite different from the American joint stock corporation. In Germany, adoption of the joint stock form rarely led to a loss of control for founders and their families as was the case in the USA (Chandler, 1990). In the USA, since the turn of the century, incorporations had been legal prerequisites to large-scale mergers, and they had often implied a dispersion of ownership and a decoupling of ownership and control. In Germany, on the other hand, capital development had tended to remain an internal process, controlled by founders and their families. Mergers and acquisitions had been rare (Tilly, 1982). Incorporation, in Germany, represented an interesting tool to enlarge the capital base but in no circumstances was it to lead to a loss of control.[26]

A transformation of ownership structures thus rarely came with a redefinition of the identity and integrity of the firms that were going through it. The meaning of capitalist property and ownership, as a consequence, would remain much more concrete and much less disembodied in Germany than in the USA, and this so until the end of the Second World War. The creation of the *Gesellschaft mit beschränkter Haftung* (GmbH) in 1892 was perfectly consistent with the needs and preferences of German industrial leaders.[27] The GmbH was a peculiar ownership structure, a crossbreed between joint stock company and private partnership. Stocks were issued, thus allowing a capital increase. The liability of stockholders was limited but stocks were not freely transferable so as to protect the main property holder who was also most of the time running the business. The GmbH was perfectly well adapted to medium-sized or even larger German firms, the owners of which needed funds and capital while striving to retain full control and power.[28]

Organization of Markets and the Role of the German State

As was also the case in France, the stability of business conditions before the Second World War was a key concern of the German industrial community. Both within the more sluggish consumer goods sector or in the fast growing and dynamic heavy industries, German business leaders strove first and foremost to preserve the integrity of their firms and the interests of their families. This search for stability and security translated, in particular, into a large-scale cartelization movement. A severe but relatively short slump following the industrial boom of the 1870s undeniably provided the impetus for cooperation and for the organization of markets.[29] The cartelization movement, though, lasted well beyond those difficult years, increasing in scale and in scope in buoyant times as much as in more difficult ones. The need for stability and security apparently remained acute, even in periods of economic expansion. A government inquiry showed that, by 1905, there were somewhere around 385 cartels and interfirm agreements in Germany.[30] In 1923, the Federation of German Industry, Reichsverband der Deutschen Industrie, or RDI, estimated the total number of cartels at 1,500.[31] Those cartels and interfirm agreements were to be found in many sectors of German industry and Table 8 offers a partial sample.

As early as 1907, 50 per cent of the production of raw steel, 82 per cent of

Table 8. Number of cartels in German industrial sectors, 1923

Iron and steel goods	234
Textiles	201
Machinery	147
Paper	107
Chemicals	91
Iron and steel	73
Mining	51
Sugar and foodstuff	24

Source: Compiled from Liefmann (1938: 30–1).

coal, and 90 per cent of paper had been regulated through cartels or other types of interfirm agreements (Pietri, 1982). Numbers, naturally, do not tell the whole story. Interfirm agreements clearly differed in power and strength. A large number of cartels in the textile sector reflected in part the structure of the industry, with its numerous small or medium-sized units. The mining sector, on the other hand, characterized by a smaller number of larger firms, did not need so many cartels or interfirm agreements to regulate markets in an effective way.

From 1870 to the end of the Second World War, there were also significant variations in the nature of dominant types of interfirm agreements and in their degree of formalization. Most early agreements between German firms were of a horizontal type and relatively loose. *Kartelle*, as Liefmann (1938) defined them, were 'voluntary agreements between independent enterprises of a similar type to secure a monopoly of the market'. Those loose agreements allowed a sharing of markets (zonal or regional cartels), the stability of prices (price-fixing cartels), or the setting of production quotas (production cartels). Towards the end of the nineteenth century, more formal associations in charge of distribution and sales started to appear, the first one being the Rhenisch–Westphalian Coal Syndicate in 1893. This sales office, common to a large number of mining concerns, had its own administrative machinery. It could thus control production levels and prices amongst its members in a much more effective way than looser types of agreements. All orders first went through the syndicate, which then re-allocated them to individual firms according to pre-determined quotas. The coal syndicate soon had its imitators in steel and other industries.

By the end of the nineteenth century, horizontal cooperation was also supplemented by vertical cooperation within the emerging *Konzerne*. Beyond the traditional goal of market control and stability, *Konzerne* played the role of financial centers. They were a source of capital funds to member firms that were able, at the same time, to retain their legal identity and operating integrity.[32] The immediate post-First World War period, characterized by hyperinflation and financial instability, saw a multiplication of *Konzerne*. This period also stimulated the emergence of profit pooling agreements, *Interessengemeinschaften* or IG. Profit pooling agreements were created to smooth out variations in profit levels stemming from an unstable economic environment while preserving the integrity of member firms.[33] Individual firms often came to belong to several of these interfirm agreements, which spun a dense web across German industry. By the end of the 1930s, competition had all but disappeared in Germany as a mechanism for regulating markets and interfirm relations. German industry and markets had become highly structured. The intervention of the national state only further institutionalized this structure.

The movement towards organized markets in Germany took place in an institutional, political, and cultural context that was highly conducive to such an evolution. German political and legal institutions generally adopted a hands-off policy towards cartels when they did not show them outright support. Within the German intellectual tradition of historicism, then dominant amongst economists, lawyers, and politicians, this choice of policy was perfectly legitimate. In the philosophy of this tradition, indeed, economic policy making and legislation absolutely should not attempt to mold business conditions. They should simply reflect and smooth the way for 'natural' evolution. Within this perspective, competition and price wars were seen as being potentially disruptive both of the national economy and of the social order. And 'natural' evolution unmistakably seemed to mean increasingly organized markets and the disappearance of competition. The evolution, as a consequence, from free markets or family capitalism to organized capitalism was to be accepted and welcomed as a progress for society at large and not only for members of interfirm agreements.

Immediately after the First World War, however, public concern about cartel abuses increased significantly in Germany. Retailers, organized in the Reichsverband Deutscher Konsumerverein, were particularly vocal and, in December 1921, petitioned the Parliament of the new Weimar Republic for legislation regulating cartels and setting limits to the cartelization movement. Discontent increased further in 1923, during the dark period of hyperinflation, when interfirm agreements were being used by member firms as a means to externalize risk and pass on the costs of inflation to retailers and consumers.[34] When Gustav Stresemann, who was closely connected with German heavy industry, came to power in 1923, he could not but yield to public pressure. A 'decree against abuses of economic power' was adopted in November and the government created a cartel court. As stated in its preamble, though, the purpose of the decree was not to abolish cartel organization 'as this would, in the long run, not favor freedom of markets'. The abolition of cartels, the decree went on, 'would probably leave small and medium-sized firms under the domination of big concerns'.[35] The cartel decree provided that agreements and cartels should be made in writing (section 1) and that they could be voided if 'they endangered the common welfare' (section 4). Section 8 granted individual members the right to withdraw without prior notice, 'for reasons of weight', while section 9 declared legal pressure on outsiders to join the cartel, provided the cartel court had been notified. Through its section 4, the decree had the potential to become a real cartel abuse law. In the 1920s, though, out of more than 1,700 cases, only 22 were brought to court under that section. The bulk of cases were brought under section 8, while section 9, which could in fact be interpreted as a step towards compulsory cartelization, was applied in 60 instances.[36]

The tendency towards organized markets and cooperation through interfirm agreements was to be asserted further in Nazi Germany, during the 1930s. The leading German business association, the RDI, urged Hitler's new government in 1933 to make cartelization and industrial cooperation compulsory. It would help protect smaller firms, they argued, from the power of larger concerns and prevent their disappearance through failure or merger. A systematic and centrally-controlled organization of markets had, in any event, been part of Hitler's program. So the Nazi government acted rapidly and, in July 1933, passed a law giving the Ministry of Economic Affairs the power to 'federate enterprises into syndicates, cartels, conventions or similar agreements or affiliate them to already existing organizations of this kind in order to regulate market conditions, if such combinations seem desirable with regard to the demands of the enterprises in question'.[37] By the end of the 1930s, the German cartel movement had thus come close to reaching its ultimate stage, with the government being able to enforce or impose all types of interfirm agreements. Cartelization and systematic market organization tended to stabilize market shares and interfirm relations. They also had a significant impact on firms themselves, allowing small and medium-sized firms to flourish or survive in a number of industrial sectors and making the large-scale transformation of ownership and organizational structures highly unlikely.

German Industry and the American Model before the Second World War

While the German system of industrial production undeniably shared important features with the structural arrangements of other European industries before the Second World War, it was also characterized by a number of peculiarities. From the end of the nineteenth century until the 1930s, Germany was subjected much more than any other continental European country to American influences, particularly in the industrial field. The impact of American models, in fact, could often explain those characteristics that made it possible to differentiate German industry from its European neighbors.

Starting in the 1860s and 1870s, a number of German manufacturers or would-be manufacturers were travelling to the USA in search of ideas, training, and technologies.[38] Ludwig Loewe, who was to become one of Germany's most successful machinery makers, had started by producing sewing machines. Around 1870, following a trip to the USA, he hired some American engineers who helped him to adapt American technology and organize his plants more efficiently. In 1902, Heinrich Lanz, later to become the most successful German producer of farm equipment machinery, went to the USA where he spent some time studying production processes and distribution methods (Chandler, 1990: 492–3). Carl Duisberg, a successful executive in the German chemicals firm of Bayer, arrived in the USA in 1903, at a time when the merger movement was in full swing. He visited a number of the new American industrial giants—Standard Oil, US Steel, Corn Products Refining, or Westinghouse. He then went back to Germany with the idea of federating the chemicals industry into a single entity, on the American model. The idea, though, did not arouse enthusiasm within the German chemicals industry and late in 1904 the industry was reorganized in the form of a profit pooling agreement or

Interessengemeinschaft. The great advantage manufacturers had seen in the IG form was that overall it preserved the autonomy of individual member firms. By 1910, according to Duisberg, the IG formed between Bayer, BASF, and AGFA had not been successful in increasing production or lowering costs and was 'little more than an organization for mutually safeguarding profits'.[39] When, in 1905, August Thyssen was calling for a merger in the German steel industry, he also had an American model in mind, US Steel. Once again, though, most German steel makers disliked the idea, preferring instead informal cartels and sales syndicates as a means to police interfirm relationships and regulate markets within the industry (Chandler, 1990: 492–3). Many examples could be cited of the direct impact the American system of industrial production had on some German industrial leaders. Until the First World War, however, American models reached German industry through one-on-one, random, and partly accidental relationships, in a process that remained patchy and limited.[40] German industrial leaders who became familiar with the American system of industrial production and saw it as a model were only a very small minority within their communities at this time.

However, the networks spun between both countries in the early years of the twentieth century would last in spite of a temporary breakdown during the First World War. Industrial cooperation, in fact, between Germany and the USA increased significantly in the 1920s, following the financial stabilization plan of 1924. Named after the American banker, Charles Dawes, who chaired negotiations at the international level, this plan was designed to deal with a worsening economic situation in Germany. The total amount of war reparations owed by that country was significantly reduced and a loan was raised, essentially in the USA, so that the German government could face its short-term financial commitments. The Dawes plan launched, in fact, a large-scale capital flow from the USA to Germany which would last until the Great Depression. Capital flowed, most of the time, directly from an American company to its German contact or ally. Relationships of dependence were created in this way and the American sponsor often made its assistance conditional on technological adaptation or internal reorganization, as the following examples illustrate.

The German steel industry had been badly in need of funds by the end of the First World War. And funds could then come only from the USA, German banks playing at best the role of intermediaries. Around 1924, the idea of an industry-wide merger in the German steel sector was once again put forward by a few steel makers and bankers who were convinced that 'fusion was a more likely course than any other to bring rationalization and lower costs and thereby to increase the possibility of obtaining funds abroad, particularly in the United States' (Chandler: 1990: 552). Despite the refusal of Krupp and Mannesmann to participate, the Vereignite Stahlwerke (VSt) was finally formed in 1926. The internal reorganization and rationalization that followed was financed by a substantial loan, underwritten essentially by the American investment banker,

Dillon Read. Following the American model, rationalization meant a concentration of production facilities and the introduction of modern machines that made possible an integrated production process and significant economies of scale. The German rubber company, on the other hand, Continental Caoutchouc und Gutta Percha, received significant assistance in the 1920s from its prewar American ally, Goodrich. Goodrich helped Continental obtain rubber supplies and provided funds for the modernization of its plant. But the American impact on the German rubber industry was not only technological. The industry-wide merger that took place in 1928 and led to the creation of an incorporated firm, Continental Gummi Werke, was unmistakably the direct consequence of strong American involvement in that industry and of German dependence.[41]

Until the 1930s, American presence and influence were undeniably quite significant in German industry and relatively well accepted. The German business community overall had a much more positive attitude towards the USA and the American model than its counterpart in other European countries and particularly in France. Nevertheless, even within this more favorable context, the fact remains that technological innovations and management methods were accepted much more easily and readily than the structural peculiarities of the American system of industrial production. Before the Second World War, a very large proportion of German business leaders still remained highly reluctant to enter mergers, to risk their independence and control by incorporating, or to compete with each other in non-organized markets. It would take a major disruption of the German economy and society before this reluctant majority would be outrun by a small group who viewed the American system of industrial production as a desirable model for German industry.

The presentation of European systems of industrial production will end with a discussion of the Italian case and a rapid overview of its most striking features. Italy was a late modernizer and industrial dynamism in the period from 1848 to the Second World War was financed through foreign capital or was due to the direct involvement of the Italian state. By 1938, the Italian share in world industrial production was 2.7 per cent, somewhat less than France's 4.5 per cent.[42] When compared to a German or British 10 per cent or to an American 32 per cent, however, the overall contributions of France and Italy to world industrial production appeared to lie within a similar range. Furthermore, industry in both countries employed around 30 per cent of the national labor force while, by the beginning of the Second World War, the equivalent German figure was closer to 40 per cent.[43] In fact, the Italian system of industrial production had, around that time, many common features with the type of family capitalism that could be found in France. As the figures presented in the introduction clearly showed, small and medium-sized firms were dominant within the Italian industrial landscape, with 80 per cent of the industrial labor force still working in units employing less than 500 persons by the end of the Second World War. In most sectors of Italian industry, those small and medium-sized firms were family-owned and run and they were cooperating with each other through relatively loose agreements in a pattern that was common to many continental European countries. Nevertheless, the process of Italian industrialization in the pre-Second World War period exhibited certain peculiarities that deserve to be mentioned here.

Starting in the 1870s, Italian industrialization was first of all characterized by its geographic imbalance. The process was concentrated in the north, and the Mezzogiorno region was all but left out. Remaining mostly rural, the southern part of Italy lacked infrastructural equipment. The population, for the most part, did not have access to education and often lived in dreadful conditions. The Mezzogiorno region suffered, in addition, from a political life corrupted by the local Mafia and from non-democratic institutions. All this could account for regular emigration flows from the south of Italy to the northern regions, to France, or to the USA. In the north, in the meantime, budding industrialization centered around the three cities of Genoa, Milan, and Turin. A second peculiarity of Italian industrialization was its significant dependence on foreign capital during those early years. British, German, Swiss, or French investments essentially launched the process, particularly in the textiles industry that came to be significantly developed around the turn of the twentieth century. Other sectors also went through a period of expansion, partly benefiting from foreign capital. In the steel, machinery, or automobile industries, a small number of somewhat larger entities emerged and imposed themselves. During the first part of the twentieth century, and particularly after Mussolini came to power in 1923, the Italian state tried to shake off the dependence of its national industry on foreign actors. The significant involvement of the state in the economy, and more particularly in the national industry, was indeed another specificity of Italian development in the period before the Second World War. By nationalizing the banking sector and creating a few very large state-owned holding companies, the fascist government hoped to take over as a provider of capital for Italian industry. Through its holding companies, such as the Istituto Mobiliare Italiano (IMI) or the Istituto per la Ricostruzione Industriale (IRI), the Italian state in fact controlled a fairly significant share of the national industry. State-owned entities produced, by the beginning of the Second World War, close to 80 per cent of national iron and 50 per cent of steel. The state controlled 50 per cent of armament production and 80 per cent of the shipbuilding industry. In the pre-Second World War period, Italy was undeniably the capitalist country in Europe with the largest and strongest state-owned sector. Although the German Nazi government could intervene in the definition of markets and in the organization of production, industrial firms had predominantly remained private entities in Germany. In Italy, the fascist state had gone one step further, taking over productive units in some key industrial sectors. Throughout the first part of the twentieth century, those large state holdings remained aggregates of many different and formerly independent units, brought together following a logic which was more political than economic. No attempt was ever made, however, during that period to rationalize those aggregates and to reorganize them internally (Romano, 1977).

By way of conclusion, let us repeat once more that in 1939, French, German, and Italian systems of industrial production were more similar to each other than to the corporate model then characteristic of the USA. For all three countries, albeit to a different extent in each case, the period of the war would represent a rupture and the years immediately following the war would prove to be critical. Prewar economic, social, and political arrangements were then questioned, albeit more or less radically, in each of these three countries. When change was considered, choices as to its direction were made quite rapidly. A number of institutional, political, and geopolitical developments turned out to have a significant impact on those processes in each of the three countries.

Notes

1. Between 1926 and 1944, around 20,000 new SARL were registered in France but only 3,000 SA and 3,000 partnerships, *société en nom collectif* or SNC (Caron, 1981: 215).
2. French *holdings* were thus peculiar business groups. Standing, with respect to formality, somewhere in between American cartels and American trusts, they had, in spite of the name, nothing in common with the American holding company.
3. Ehrmann (1957: 370) and Paxton (1973). Getting more precise figures is naturally impossible since those agreements were neither legal nor official.
4. Clough (1946), Lévy-Leboyer (1974), Roehl (1976), O'Brien and Keyder (1978), Cameron and Freedeman (1983), Nye (1987).
5. By the 1860s, the French railway network reached down to the remotest parts of the territory (Autin, 1984). Chandler (1977) has argued that the expansion and integration of markets depended to a significant extent on the development of a dense railway network.
6. According to Girard (1952), 'traditional financial interests got rid of the Péreire brothers. This fall had long been sought after . . . . It was essentially a revenge of the forces of order and of well entrenched interests.' See also Landes (1949) and Bouvier (1992).
7. French literature abounds in paintings of downfall and social disgrace following bankruptcies—see in particular Honoré de Balzac's *César Birotteau*. The conception of bankruptcy as a stain on family honor differed markedly from the American perception. Duhamel (1930) underscored this contrast: 'You [French businessmen] still think about César Birotteau. Yes, but the sense of honor changes very rapidly. When Smith [American businessman] goes bankrupt, he is not dishonored. He will just start all over again . . . .'
8. In the period before the First World War, close to 80 per cent of total investments had been self-financed and self-financing remained predominant in the interwar period (Landes, 1949, 1964; Caron, 1981; Rowley, 1982).

9. Eugène Schneider, quoted in Ehrmann (1957: 328).

10. René-Paul Duchemin, quoted in Ehrmann (1957: 329).

11. Auguste Detoeuf, quoted in Dussauze (1938: 110).

12. The expression 'economic *malthusianism*' was coined by socialist members of the French Parliament after the First World War who were blaming the steel *entente* for limited productive capacities during the prewar years (Journal Officiel (February 1, 1919)).

13. The limited role of the French state during this period can be contrasted with the active and creative impact it had on the national economy after the Second World War, but also during the war, under the Vichy regime. In fact, the French state was not always interventionist and its impact on the national economy has varied significantly throughout history.

14. This story has been told by Moutet (1975). See also Maier (1970) and Kogut and Parkinson (1994).

15. Siegfried (1927) and Duhamel (1930). Strauss (1978) underscores the key role of these books.

16. Siegfried (1927: 168–9). See also Duhamel (1930: 153).

17. 'What strikes the European traveller when he visits the USA is a disappearance of the individual, a progressive rarefaction of social types' (Duhamel, 1930: 224).

18. These stereotypes found an echo in American literature. Siegfried and Duhamel were constantly referring to the novels by Sinclair Lewis, *Babbit* or *Main Street*, for example.

19. Strauss (1978: 89) claimed that 'despite the fear of Bolshevism among conservative critics neither they nor their liberal counterparts were prepared to defend the American way'.

20. The new *Reich* had levied on France 5 billion gold francs as war reparations. The German industrial boom after unification was thus in part financed through French contributions. Pietri (1982), Droz (1970).

21. Cassis (1997) also documents the qualitative gap existing between German and American firms before the Second World War, particularly with respect to size.

22. Chandler (1990) compiled lists of the 200 largest firms in those two countries but he valued assets in local currencies of the period. Exchange rates found in Cameron (1989) and Kindleberger (1984) made an effective comparison of those lists possible. In 1914, the exchange rate was 4.2 marks to a dollar. The comparison for 1930 proved more difficult due to the instability of currencies. To avoid the traps of the currency problem, the exchange rate of December 1926 was chosen, 1 mark to 23.80 US cents.

23. By 1936, the exchange rate had become 1 mark to 40.30 US cents. Even with such a higher value for the mark, differences remained striking. In this case, the last American firm on the list of 200 ranked in 1930 with Germany's number 38, Singer Nähmaschinen.

24. It is undeniable still that, within this European framework, German industry had its own peculiarities, the least of which was certainly not the dynamism of its capital goods sector.

25. The total number of AG went from 200 in 1870 to 5,500 in 1900. In 1850, those AG had extracted 0.12 per cent of Westphalian coal and by 1876, 41.3 per cent (Pietri, 1982: 235–9).

26. The story of the electrical firm, Siemens and Halske, is revealing in this respect.

The firm was created and run for years by Werner Siemens. In 1897, Georg Siemens, a nephew who was also Chairman of the Deutsche Bank managed to convince Werner to incorporate. Georg, however, could not prevent his uncle from adding to the incorporation act a clause that secured full control for the family (Chandler, 1990).

27. The GmbH is equivalent to the private limited liability company in English. The German legislator was the first to create such a structure, which was later adopted in France and in Italy.

28. By 1950, 0.2 per cent of all industrial firms in Germany were AG and 1.2 per cent were GmbH.

29. This slump, sometimes labeled foundation slump or *Gründerkrise* lasted from 1874 until around 1879 (Pietri, 1982: 209 ff.).

30. 'Kartellenquete des Reichsamt des Innern' as quoted by Michels (1928: 171). Kocka (1978: vii. 563) estimated that there had been only four cartels in 1875.

31. The German government counted around 2,500 cartels in 1925 (Michels, 1928: 172; Liefman, 1938: 30). The gap is due in part to a different definition of cartels.

32. Liefmann (1938: 225 ff.). The German *Konzern* was thus, with respect to its financial aims, fairly similar to the French *holding*. A partial exchange of shares between members of the *Konzern* created a situation of mutual dependence.

33. Liefmann (1938: 238) underscored the peculiar nature of the IG, in which 'there is a disproportion between the drastic nature of the contract, making the profits of the firms depend on one another, and the great degree of independence of management which the individual undertakings still retain'.

34. Michels (1928: 28) describes the workings of those *Konditionenkartelle* in great detail.

35. 'Verordnung gegen Mißbrauch wirtschaftlicher Machtßtellungen vom 3 November 1923' (Levy, 1966: 143).

36. Michels (1928: ch. IV) and Liefmann (1938: ch. VII).

37. 'Gesetz über die Errichtung von Zwangskartellen', July 17, 1933 (Levy, 1966: 159).

38. German migration to the USA, then already in full swing, had undeniably prepared the way for such moves.

39. Duisberg, quoted by Chandler (1990: 480).

40. Chandler (1990), ch. 11 and ch. 12, provides many more examples of such one-on-one relationships. The main German firm in the tobacco industry was bought by American Tobacco in 1901. Close ties existed between one of the main German producers of rubber and the American firm Goodrich. A number of American companies were not only present in Germany through subsidiaries, they were also dominant on the markets of that country: National Cash Register, Otis Elevator, United Shoe Machinery. German firms, in machinery and also in textiles, had subsidiaries in America or developed close ties with American companies. Deutsche Grammophon was the subsidiary of the American managed Gramophone Company. Bergmann-Elektricitäts-Werke, a manufacturer of insulating and wiring conduits, was created by a close associate of Thomas Edison upon his return to Germany. There were close links between Emil Rathenau's Allgemeine Elektricitäts Gesellschaft (AEG) and American General Electric.

41. Those stories and many others are told by Chandler (1990), ch. 13 and ch. 14.

42. League of Nations (1945: 13).

43. Maddison (1991) and Romano (1977).

PART II

CROSS-NATIONAL TRANSFER: CONDITIONS, CHANNELS, AND ACTORS

The Second World War represented a turning point for France, Germany, and Italy, with more or less radical consequences in each case. The sense of national crisis at the end of the war and the questioning of prewar structural and institutional arrangements were of a quite different intensity in each of the three countries. The questioning took place within national contexts, strongly influenced by a redefined geopolitical environment. The war had bled European countries white. It had also confirmed the dominant position, on the world scene, of both the USA and the USSR, two countries where geopolitical and military might appeared to rest on a powerful industrial base. After 1947, the Soviet sphere of influence was contained behind the iron curtain and the USA became, for needy Western European countries, the sole provider and military shield. Relationships of asymmetrical dependence, more or less pronounced in each case, thus came to link the USA on the one hand, and France, the western territories of Germany, or Italy on the other.

The power of the USA and the direct dependence of Western European countries combined with a sense of national crisis to create the right conditions for the American system of industrial production to become a model for reconstruction. In France and West Germany, a small group of actors holding key positions of institutional power turned likelihood into process. These modernizing élites, minorities within their own national environment, worked closely with a group of American 'missionaries' out to convert the Western world to the 'miracle of mass production'. Dense webs of personal and institutional relationships were then spun between the USA, and France or West Germany. Channels of exchange and interaction were set up and institutionalized, particularly during the Marshall plan years, but also throughout the period of American military administration in the western parts of Germany. They would become, in fact, powerful tools for the large-scale transfer to France and West Germany of the American system of industrial production. In Italy, the modernizing network broke down. Despite geopolitical conditions favorable to a cross-national transfer, the national élite who had come to hold key positions of institutional power in Italy strongly resisted cooperation with the American end of the network. This Italian élite, in fact, did not intend to radically question the existing national industrial model.

For a large-scale, cross-national transfer of industrial structural arrangements to be at least possible and in order to increase its likelihood, it appears, therefore, that three main conditions are necessary prerequisites. First of all, a traumatic disruption should bring, on the national level, an acute sense of crisis and a questioning of the legitimacy of preexisting institutional and structural arrangements. Then, a redefinition of the geopolitical environment, and in particular the emergence of relationships of asymmetrical dependence, should turn a foreign system of industrial production into an available model that can appear both relatively familiar and superior. Finally, a binational 'modernizing' network, sharing similar and compatible if not common objectives, should create a bridge between both countries. Those modernizing individuals may be a minority within their respective national environments as long as they hold and control key positions of institutional power. Cross-national organizations and institutions and also those national institutions located at the articulation of state and economy within the receiving country are, in this respect, particularly important. Figure 5 brings together, in summary form, these three main preconditions. When these preconditions are met, they make a large-scale, cross-national transfer more likely. They are necessary for the launch of the process. They are not sufficient, however, to account for its mechanisms nor to ensure that the transfer will last or succeed, as will be shown in Parts III and IV. With respect to these preconditions, the systematic comparison of our three empirical cases has generated some theoretical conclusions, which are outlined below.

In conditions of relative stability, those actors with strong vested interests in the existing social, economic, and political order, will generally manage to prevent drastic change from taking place. Periods of major disruption, however, while they do not necessarily imply radical change, certainly increase the likelihood that it be contemplated by at least some groups within society. Defeat in war, military occupation, colonization, the collapse of a regime and of its dominant ideology, or deep economic crises are all examples of

Figure 5. Conditions of a large-scale, cross-national structural transfer

traumatic disruptions. A major upheaval of this type will often lead to the displacement of the former political élite and to a questioning, more or less radical, of preexisting social, political, or economic structures. An élite group taking over after disruption and defining itself in opposition to the group it displaced, will tend to emphasize the extent of the national crisis and to advocate significant transformations. The proposed reform could be in the military, political, or administrative spheres. After 1945, however, the dominant tendency was to point to industry as the main source of national power, the USA and the USSR providing here the model. National crises have since then generally been accounted for in economic and industrial terms. The large-scale transformation of the national system of industrial production was increasingly likely, as a consequence, to become a solution to a perceived national crisis.

The large-scale, cross-national transfer or diffusion of a system of industrial production does not only necessitate that the local political élite be ready for change, it also requires that a foreign model be available. A model is not necessarily available for a given country when it exists somewhere else. It should also be relatively familiar, at least to the élite in power, and it should appear to be superior. The availability of a model is in fact a function of the geopolitical environment in which the country in need of change is embedded. Geopolitical relationships characterized by asymmetrical dependence increase the likelihood that a model be available and that a cross-national transfer take place. Relationships of dependence in the geopolitical sphere imply proximity and interaction. Multiple contacts in turn create conditions for greater familiarity between countries. At the same time, an asymmetry in the dependence relationship will make it more likely that a familiar model be also perceived as superior. There are varying degrees of asymmetry in geopolitical relationships. In situations of military occupation or colonization, the imbalance in the relationship can be extreme. In less exceptional circumstances, dependence may still be so acute that ending the relationship would threaten the internal social, political, or economic order of the dependent country. Access to resources and markets vital to the survival of a given country may for example be entirely controlled by another. In certain situations, finally, the dependent country may hold a degree of bargaining power if alternatives or partial alternatives to the relationship exist and the dependent country can turn elsewhere to obtain what it needs. Figure 6 presents, in summary form, the argument linking the availability of a model to the nature of geopolitical relationships.

A disruption of the *status quo* at the national level or geopolitical dependence are not the only preconditions to large-scale cross-national transfer. A third precondition has to do with the actors themselves, who come to play a role within the redefined structural environments. The existence of a binational 'modernizing' network, linking individuals on both sides of the geopolitical relationship, appears to increase the likelihood that a process of large-scale

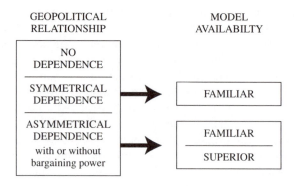

Figure 6. Geopolitical dependence and availability of a model

structural transfer will be contemplated and launched. Members of this binational network should have compatible objectives and work in close synergy.
The overall size of the network may be less important than the institutional
power of its members. The control of cross-national organizations or institutions appears particularly important, direct channels of communication and
cooperation increasing the chance for synergy in action. Those institutions at
the border between state and economy within the dependent country also seem
to be essential to the extent that they can have an influence on structural
arrangements of the economy or industry as a whole. A national system of
industrial production can be deeply transformed through legislation, credit, or
tax policies, and through other more or less powerful control tools available to
a given national state. A cross-national structural transfer will thus be all the
more likely to succeed if political institutions of the dependent country are
directly involved in the process. This involvement, in turn, will hinge upon the
identity, values, and objectives of the actors controlling political institutions
and in particular those at the border between state and economy. Were state
actors not involved, the cross-national transfer process might still take place
but on a more limited scale, through bilateral relationships linking economic
actors from both countries.

Ever since the end of the Second World War, new institutions have emerged
which are multinational in nature. The International Monetary Fund (IMF), the
General Agreement on Tariffs and Trade (now World Trade Organization), the
Bank for Reconstruction and Development (now World Bank) or the European
Economic Community (now European Union) have played an increasingly
significant role during the second part of the twentieth century. By defining
and formalizing common norms and by imposing them across national borders,
these multinational institutions have prepared the ground for and stimulated
cross-national processes of transfer and homogenization. They have, by the
time of writing, become key elements of the international institutional

environment and they certainly are major actors in the more recent cross-national transfer processes. However, their direct role during the historical period corresponding to the empirical cases under study was still relatively marginal and they rarely appear, as a consequence, in our stories.

3

Crisis Inside, Dependence Outside
Preconditions of a Cross-National Transfer

There is nothing more dangerous than victory . . . . Crises are opportunities.
Jean Monnet[1]

In France, Germany, and Italy, the end of the Second World War brought about the collapse of the national order. Germany had lost a war for which it was mostly held responsible. In the case of France and Italy, the situation was somewhat more complex. Those two countries had neither clearly won nor clearly lost the war but military defeat and occupation of the national territory had been common traumatic events.[2] Allied victory prompted self-questioning in all three European countries, more or less radical in each case. Although the end of the war led to the displacement of those regimes responsible for defeat and for a traumatic period, the sense of national crisis and emergency was not the same in each case. While a new political beginning seemed unavoidable everywhere, a redefinition of social and economic arrangements appeared more or less necessary and urgent in each country.

The war had left all three countries destitute. It had also confirmed a reshaping of the geopolitical balance of power to the clear benefit of both the USA and the USSR. In the early postwar years, all three countries were highly dependent on both superpowers merely to ensure survival. The division of the world in two spheres, crystallizing after 1947, significantly redefined the rules of the geopolitical game. France, Italy, and the western territories of Germany were to become unambiguously and solidly anchored to the American sphere of influence. The launching of the Marshall plan in 1947 and 1948 only institutionalized further the asymmetrical relationship of dependence between the USA on the one hand, and France, West Germany, and Italy on the other. By the late 1940s, the conditions seemed to have been created for the USA to have become a model for all three countries in their process of national reconstruction. A large-scale, cross-national transfer of American structural arrangements had become possible, even though such a transfer would turn out to be more or less likely in each of the three countries.

FRANCE: IN SEARCH OF A 'GREAT POWER' MODEL

Formally, France had won the Second World War and it would be sitting on the United Nations Security Council with other Allied powers. In reality,

France had emerged from the war a weak, divided, and humiliated nation. In the meantime, the USA and the USSR had unquestionably come to dominate the world. The contrast was sharp. French powerlessness was all the more striking in that it could be compared to the prestige and might of both super-powers. The geopolitical environment, in other words, gave the measure of the French national crisis. Partially redefined in the early postwar years, the geopolitical environment, had a direct impact on the way in which the national crisis was to be accounted for and explained in France. It also limited the number of solutions from which France could choose in an attempt to deal with the national crisis.

Identifying the National Crisis

The Second World War proved to be a particularly traumatic episode of French history. Military collapse, German occupation, and collaboration not only on the part of the Vichy regime but also of a significant proportion of the French population, challenged a glorious image of France. The myth of a 'Great Nation' ready to sacrifice itself in the fight for basic and universal rights of mankind it had helped to define, had undeniably been shaken by the end of the war, both inside and outside national borders.[3] Members of the French resistance coalition, led by General de Gaulle and fighting for legitimacy on the national scene as well as recognition in the world, were the first to denounce the 'un-French' character of the Vichy regime and of its politics of collaboration. They claimed to embody the essential French identity which they had seen it as their role to preserve throughout the war. The war had thus inflicted deep moral wounds on the French body social, creating deep and long-term internal divisions. Obviously this was in addition to physical destruction and material destitution. France would face difficult times in the short term, this was apparent. A significant amount of rubble had to be cleared, the infra-structure was crippled, and emergency services had to be secured merely for the population to survive. Beyond these short-term difficulties, the resistance coalition that came to power in 1945 also pointed out deep structural issues. A mere 'patching up' would not do. Members of the coalition argued in parti-cular that, with respect to the economy, a reconstruction following prewar patterns would not be enough.

The war had thus acted as a catalyst for members of the resistance move-ment. Within this movement, an acute sense of national crisis crossed over ideological differences. In striking contrast to what had happened after the First World War, the year of 1945 would be a turning point. In 1919, a conservative coalition, easily winning postwar elections, had opted for continuity and stability.[4] In 1945, the resistance coalition as a whole defined itself, despite internal divisions, in opposition to the previous regime and to the former holders of power. Members of the resistance movement outright rejected those systems of political, social, and economic organization prevailing before and during the Second World War. They were ready to propose a radical redefinition of national problems and to search for new solutions. They believed that healing the deep physical and moral wounds scarring the country would necessitate nothing less than a questioning of structures, institutions, even values. They called for a radical break from a past that was essentially associated with stagnation and economic crisis, shame, and defeat. As General de Gaulle put it in a speech to the national consultative assembly in 1945:

The events which nearly destroyed France have underscored the absolute necessity for a national rebirth. Not only is it obvious that to go back to the situation in which disaster fell on us would be to condemn ourselves to disappear should similar events occur again. It is also clear that what we are and what we are worth wouldn't be much and anyway not for long in the tough and changing world which can be guessed for tomorrow. We need to undertake once again in our history the ascent towards Power. In that respect, it is trivial to say that an important economic and social rebirth is a *sine qua non* condition.[5]

France had to turn itself decidedly towards the future and the future of France, in 1945, could not be constructed without taking into account the world around it. The geopolitical environment set the framework for the identification and definition of the national crisis. By 1945, the USA and the USSR had come to dominate the world scene and this was interpreted as heralding a new age when the greatness of a nation would lie in economic and industrial might rather than in the number of foreign colonies, in the prestige of its monarchs, or in the quality of its cultural production. In both countries, the economic sphere appeared to be pre-eminent.[6] Military and geopolitical power rested on a strong economy and on a dynamic national industry. This fact had not escaped members of the French resistance coalition. De Gaulle himself, who personally despised what he termed 'supply problems' was nevertheless convinced that, after 1945, 'the power of nations would directly depend on the economy' (De Gaulle, 1964: 777).

The coalition that came to power in France in 1945—essentially drawn from the national resistance movement—thus proposed an interpretation of the national crisis where economic factors loomed large. Only a few years before, the perceived national crisis in France had been accounted for in a strikingly different manner. Marshal Pétain and members of the Vichy government had found demographic and moral explanations for the military collapse of 1940 and for France's ensuing loss of prestige on the international scene.[7] In 1945, French defeat and national humiliation were traced back to a military and geopolitical weakness, that was blamed in turn on the failure of the prewar economic system. Members of the resistance coalition argued that the French economy, and more particularly French industry, had not been equal, before the war, to the historical prestige of the nation and had not served its ambitions. They claimed that economic backwardness and industrial *malthusianism* were to blame for national humiliation, fall in status, and a loss of prestige on the international scene. In turn, economic backwardness and industrial *malthusianism* had themselves been the consequences of rigid structures and of a conservative attitude on the part of business communities. Members of the resistance coalition pointed to the fear of innovation that had characterized French industrial leaders in the interwar period and denounced low levels of industrial investment. They strongly criticized the industrial community for clinging to old structures and values without taking into consideration the potential consequences of this choice for the nation as a whole.[8] Most members of the resistance coalition saw in the Vichy regime the triumph of French conservatism, the natural climax of this old and static order, which they were thus all the more intent on destroying.[9]

Searching for Solutions

The break away from the past which de Gaulle and the resistance coalition were advocating thus entailed, first of all, a radical questioning of economic and industrial structures. This would have to be accompanied by a significant renewal of the French élite, particularly within the industrial community. Both steps seemed necessary in order for the resistance coalition to achieve its main goal, which was to regain for France the status of a 'Great Power'.[10] In 1945, the positions of power of the USA and of the USSR highlighted the extent of French geopolitical weakness. That both countries had come to dominate the world scene narrowed significantly the range of options for a nation whose ultimate goal was to become a 'Great Power'. Both the American and the Soviet examples tended to suggest that a powerful economy and a highly productive industry were essential prerequisites to geopolitical greatness. Most members of the French resistance coalition thus believed that a redefinition of economic and industrial systems or structures was necessary if only as a means to higher geopolitical ends. Economic and industrial transformation or modernization became, as a consequence, priority objectives. The question still remained, though, of the meaning of modernization and of what transformation or redefinition entailed. The French resistance coalition covered the entire political spectrum and not surprisingly there were different answers to that question, reflecting the internal divisions of that coalition. The umbrella organization, the National Council of Resistance or CNR, had brought together communists, socialists, and more conservative elements. With respect to modernization and its definition, however, the resistance coalition could essentially be divided into two groups. One looked to the USSR for inspiration; the other had chosen the American economy as a model for France.[11] The evolution, since the prewar period, was striking.

Which of those two models would come to prevail remained relatively unclear until 1947. France seemed to hover between two systems of industrial production which had laid the foundations—each in its own way despite striking similarities—of geopolitical power. This French hesitation was in fact perfectly consistent with the position of the country on the geopolitical scene at the time, oscillating somewhere between the USA and the USSR. It also reflected the political balance of power on the national scene where the communist group had significant influence, both within the resistance coalition and in the country as a whole. Despite an acute dependence on foreign assistance, France enjoyed a degree of bargaining power from 1945 to 1947. At the point of intersection between the American and Soviet spheres of influence, French decision makers had quickly appreciated that they could gain a relative amount of freedom by playing off the two superpowers against each other. De Gaulle, in particular, was quite aware of the use he could make of the situation. As the following account by Jefferson Caffery, American Ambassador in France, illustrates, he obviously did not hesitate to take advantage of it:

[De Gaulle] said that after the war, there would be only two real forces in the world: the United States and the Soviet Union. He then said: 'I would much rather work with the United States than with any other country . . . . If I cannot work with you, I must work with the Soviets in order to survive, even if it is only for a while and even if, in the long run, they gobble us up too.'[12]

'Neutralism', as this type of behavior came to be called, would be fairly widespread in France during the months following the end of the war. Politicians and civil servants chose neutralism as a strategy which allowed them to make the most of the situation of double dependence in which France found itself. Intellectuals and journalists, on the other hand, tended to favor neutralist positions mostly because of the fit with their own values and beliefs. Building on ideological legacies from the interwar period, many intellectuals were convinced that both the American and Soviet models of society threatened the French definition of civilization.[13]

A 'neutralist' attitude on the world scene was also justified by the peculiar balance of power that characterized national politics in France at the time. Three main parties were clearly dominant from 1945 to 1947, in parallel with the structure of the resistance movement. More than 75 per cent of all seats in early French national assemblies were shared between the Communist party (PCF), the Socialist party (SFIO), and a center-left movement (MRP). When de Gaulle resigned in January 1946, these three parties formed a coalition government. Since the three parties differed markedly in many respects and particularly in terms of geopolitical preferences, the coalition government could survive only for as long as it continued to adopt a relatively neutral position in its official dealings with both superpowers.[14] The French government could therefore not afford, in this period, to take sides in the emerging geopolitical confrontation. The context was particularly unfavorable to a clear and decisive choice between the two economic and industrial models then dominant in the world. Partly due to pressure from the communist element of the coalition, a significant share of French industry and of the service sector was nationalized. Workers' councils (or *comités d'entreprise*) were also created in firms with more than 50 employees while a nation-wide welfare program was institutionalized. Social and economic arrangements were thus a patchwork and France seemed to lie somewhere between two worlds.

The French tripartite coalition was to be one of the first casualties of the breaking off of relationships between the USA and the USSR in 1947. Even during the early period, though, from 1945 to 1947, it always was fragile, as the episode of the Blum-Byrnes agreement in March 1946 illustrated. The coalition government had sent a small team to Washington to negotiate financial assistance. Led by the socialist Léon Blum from the SFIO, talks with the American Secretary of State James Byrnes turned out to be relatively disappointing for the French. Asking for a gift of US$4 billion over four years, they got only US$650 millions in loans, the cancellation of war debts, and they had, as a counterpart, to open their borders to Hollywood movies and Coca-Cola.[15] While Blum officially denied that the talks had had any political content, it seems that the refusal of the French delegation to pledge clear allegiance to the USA partly explained the lack of generosity on the American side.[16] Notwithstanding his respect of the terms of the geopolitical neutrality pact, Léon Blum was violently criticized by communists upon his return to Paris for selling out his country to the USA. The incident unmistakably heralded the future disintegration of the tripartite coalition.

Coming Down in Favor of One Side

The Americans took French wavering and indecision very seriously. They represented for the American administration a major challenge and a clear geopolitical threat.[17] The year of 1947, however, was undeniably a turning point in this respect. Significant changes on the geopolitical scene led to a redefinition of the rules of the national political game in France and prompted a clarification of geopolitical allegiance. France had to come down clearly in favor of one side and the communists lost all hopes of controlling the French government, to the great relief of the Americans.[18] The geopolitical upheaval of 1947, leading to the watertight division of the world into two spheres, created conditions in which the American economy and system of industrial production became the only legitimate models for French modernization. Two episodes proved particularly significant as far as the reshaping of the geopolitical environment was concerned—the definition of the Truman doctrine and the launching of the Marshall plan.

On March 12, 1947, the President of the USA, Harry Truman, asked Congress to grant Greece and Turkey the assistance both countries needed to resist communist takeover. In a speech that was to become famous, he put forth what would be known as the 'Truman doctrine'. He pledged to help all 'free people' in their fight against 'outside pressure'. Needless to say, Truman's speech had a significant impact on Soviet–American relations. It was undeniably a step towards the separation of the world into two spheres.[19] Truman's speech would also have an indirect impact on the internal political balance of power within a number of European countries. Parties across the political spectrum reacted by adopting increasingly rigid and uncompromising positions. In France, for example, the communist party and the communist trade union (CGT) had, from 1945 to 1947, been on the forefront of the national fight for production. They had created the conditions for a lasting social peace by advising against conflict and defusing social movements. A few weeks after Truman's speech, communist ministers reacted to a wide social movement by taking sides with strikers against the government to which they belonged (Rioux, 1980: 171). In early May, they were asked to resign. This put an end to the 'tripartite coalition'. The communist party was thus relegated to many years in opposition although it still represented, until the late 1950s, around 25 per cent of the French electorate.

This episode in French political affairs cannot be interpreted only as the consequence of internal developments.[20] The timing, in particular, only makes sense in the context of the emerging confrontation on the geopolitical scene. In the spring of 1947, American policy planners were already thinking about a program of assistance for Europe.[21] The rumor that such a program was in the making spread rapidly, all the more since official statements and speeches made by American politicians tended to provide indirect confirmation. A number of French decision makers started to wonder, particularly after Truman's speech, whether an American program of assistance would include a country where there were communist ministers in the government. Breaking up the 'tripartite coalition' thus made particular sense in the light of such a redefinition of the geopolitical context and in anticipation of further developments.

Indeed, the geopolitical divide between East and West was destined to get wider. On June 5, 1947, Secretary of State George Marshall proposed, during commencement ceremonies at Harvard University, a plan to help Europe economically and financially. In early July, the USSR flatly refused to participate in the Marshall plan or even to let Eastern and Central European countries participate. Officially, the USA had offered assistance to all European countries, East and West, including the USSR. Americans claimed that their 'policy [was] directed not against any country or doctrine but against hunger, poverty, desperation and chaos'. The purpose of the Marshall plan was to be the 'revival of a working economy in the world so as to permit the emergence of political and social conditions in which free institutions can exist'.[22] In reality, and this had clearly not escaped Soviet decision makers, behind the plan of economic assistance there were stringent political conditions and communist countries would not qualify. A discourse on 'freedom' in effect excluded the communist world and attacks against communism, albeit hidden, were nevertheless unmistakable.[23] The Marshall plan was a political and geopolitical weapon. This was rarely officially acknowledged in the USA but it was admitted behind the scenes in Washington as the following comment by Dean Acheson, Secretary of State from January 1949, clearly shows:

If General Marshall believed, which I am sure he did not, that the American people would be moved to so great an effort as he contemplated by as platonic a purpose as combating 'hunger, poverty, desperation and chaos', he was mistaken . . . What citizens and the representatives in Congress alike always wanted to learn in the last analysis was how Marshall aid operated to block the extension of Soviet power.[24]

The Marshall weapon proved all the more powerful in that it did not intend to confront the communist regime and communist ideology in a direct fashion. The strategy was to bring about significant economic and social transformations in participating countries in order to remove all danger not only of communist or Soviet influence but also of other types of totalitarian influences. The diagnosis of American decision makers was that a number of economic and industrial weaknesses, dysfunctions, and maladjustments were responsible for the great vulnerability of European societies to communism and other totalitarian ideologies.[25] Marshall planners did not intend to engage in a direct battle of ideas, nor in a confrontation of world views. Instead of opposing one ideology to another ideology, they proposed a form of economic organization and a system of industrial production that implied and carried with them a set of political and cultural values. Paul Hoffman, who from 1948 led the Marshall plan administration, summed up this strategy very clearly by opposing the 'American assembly line' to the 'communist party line' (Hoffman, 1951: 87). In Washington, throughout the period of drafting of a program for Europe, geopolitical and political questions were given mostly economic and industrial answers, in keeping with well-entrenched American tradition (Sutton *et al.*, 1956). The basic assumption behind policy making at the time in Washington was that a political and cultural transformation of European countries could best be achieved by first reshaping economic arrangements and industrial structures. The creation of a new economic and industrial world order—or more exactly the spread of the American economic and industrial order to the rest of the 'free' world—would, in the end, be the surest means to geopolitical ends, essentially containment of communist influence and peace. A bloc of wealthy, interdependent countries sharing similar structures and, later, values, would be the best stronghold against the spread of communism or against the return of other types of totalitarian movements.[26]

Clearly, the Marshall plan cannot be understood outside the peculiar geopolitical context it helped crystallize. Its launching in 1947–8 radically transformed the geopolitical environment for a country like France. It also brought about, together with the Truman doctrine, a redefinition of the rules of the game on the national political scene. It was, indeed, a partial and indirect cause behind the dismissal of communist ministers from the French government. By the end of 1947, France had been thrust into and solidly anchored within the Western camp. Its economic and geopolitical dependence on the USA had increased significantly and it had lost most of its bargaining power. All these conditions combined, in the end, to make the American economy and system of industrial production the only available and acceptable model for the modernization of French structures; the only possible answer to the national crisis as it had come to be defined after the end of the Second World War.

OCCUPIED GERMANY: CONDITIONS FOR A CONTROLLED EXPERIMENT

On May 8, 1945, Germany surrendered unconditionally.[27] A few days earlier, Hitler had committed suicide. Military defeat, he understood, was total. By April 25, Allied armies were occupying most of German territory and the Third *Reich* was crumbling. Members of the Nazi party who had held high ranking positions of power were soon arrested, although some managed to flee and a few committed suicide. Military defeat brought to Germany a disintegration of the government and a collapse of the state apparatus (Shirer, 1959; Grosser, 1985). The power vacuum that followed was unparalleled in its extent, but did not last. Soon after surrender, the four victorious Allied powers, the USA, the UK, the USSR, and France, were exercising complete political and administrative control, each in its own zone of occupation. They were following a plan prepared during the Yalta Conference in February 1945. Although not invited to Yalta, France had been granted during the Conference the status of fourth occupying power and its zone of occupation had been carved out of the British and American zones. In each zone of occupation, military governments with supreme legislative, executive, and judicial authorities were set up. An Allied Control Council, made up of the four Allied Commanders-in-Chief acting jointly, was created to allow for coordinated policy making.[28] As it turned out, however, supreme authority rested mostly with military governments in each individual zone of occupation. Coordinated policies across the four zones proved to be extremely rare. From the very beginning, the Allied Control Council was a poor forum for collective decision making. Agreement required unanimity between all four Commanders-in-Chief and was thus rarely possible. For General Lucius Clay, Commander-in-Chief of the American military government (Office of Military Government, United States or OMGUS), attempts at collective decision making in that context were always frustrating experiences.[29]

Towards American Hegemony in Western Zones of Occupation

The failure of the Allied Control Council to propose and pursue policies common to Germany as a whole led to the merging in December 1946 of the British and American zones. For American and British military governments, the Bizone was the first step towards German economic unity. While open, officially, to an agreement with other occupying powers they were in reality only ready to accept such agreement on their own terms, 'with a view to the extension of [the] arrangements [agreed on for the Bizone] to [other] zones of occupation'.[30] On paper, the Bizone was an association between partners on equal terms. The British, though, were soon unable to pay for their share and, by December 1947, the USA had taken on most of the financial burden. The role of Americans, as a consequence, and their relative power within the partnership increased significantly to the point where they had 'the right of final decision in financial and economic matters'.[31]

While fearing an extension of American control to their own zone of occupation, the French had little choice but to accept a degree of collaboration with the Bizone. This was all the more unavoidable as French dependence relative to the USA was increasing significantly at the same time with the launching of the Marshall plan. Furthermore, from 1948, Marshall plan authorities treated all western zones of Germany, including the French, as one single economic entity. Even if somewhat reluctantly at first, the UK and France thus had to acknowledge and accept that the USA was to play a dominant role in all three western zones of occupation. The Americans were soon clearly in charge, particularly with respect to economic policy making. In December 1946, American occupation authorities launched a reform of the banking system within the American zone of occupation. General Lucius Clay's Financial Adviser, Joseph Dodge, who had been chairman of the Detroit National Bank in the USA, proposed a decentralized banking system largely inspired by the American model. The rapid implementation and success of the reform soon convinced the French to extend it to their zone of occupation, while the British strongly resisted the idea of decentralization. After the creation of the Bizone and under strong American pressure, the British finally had to comply and to accept the banking reform prepared by the Americans (Clay, 1950: 204 ff.).

The British also had to reconsider their position on the double issue of decartelization and deconcentration that turned out to be at the core of American economic policies for Germany. In 1946, the British had bluntly rejected the American decartelization and deconcentration program and as a consequence 'the economic unification of the British and US zones (was raising) an acute problem in decartelization'.[32] A few months later, however, in February 1947, the British had to accept the enactment and implementation of joint antitrust laws in the American and British zones of occupation, respectively US Military Government Law #56 and British Military Government Ordinance #78.[33] The French soon followed suit with their own version of antitrust legislation, Ordinance #96. From a position of weakness, the British Labour government also had to give up its project of a large-scale nationalization of coal and steel industries in the Ruhr region. The Americans would simply not let the British authorities implement such a plan.[34]

Once the geopolitical confrontation between East and West had reached the point of no return, American influence over all three western zones of occupation was bound to increase further. In March 1948, the Soviet Commander-in-Chief, Marshal Sokolovsky, walked out of a meeting of the Allied Control Council. Once more, the four Allied powers had been unable to agree on a common policy for Germany. Relationships between both superpowers were by then already tense and compromise was less likely than ever. One month after this failed meeting, the three Western powers met in London and decided to merge their zones of occupation into a single economic and political German entity (Gatzke, 1980: 160). The Allied Control Council disintegrated altogether. This episode was clearly the expression in German affairs of the geopolitical confrontation that was splitting the world in two. The front line of the Cold War cut right across German territory. The western zones of Germany, as a consequence, later to become the Federal Republic of Germany, turned out to be of vital interest to the USA.

The sham of a three-sided sharing of power was definitely and officially given up in 1948, the UK and France being in even less of a position to challenge American hegemony after the launching of the Marshall plan. The replacement of military governments in 1949 by a tripartite civil High Commission institutionalized in fact the predominant role of the USA. The American High Commissioner, John McCloy, also head of the Marshall plan administration in Germany, would undeniably come to have a great deal of control over German affairs.[35] While the military were handing over to the civilian administration, the ground was also being prepared for a partial transfer of authority to German institutions and German decision makers. A German constitution, 'Grundgesetz' or Basic Law, was crafted in May 1949 and the Federal Republic of Germany was created in September 1949.[36] The Occupation Statute, signed in April 1949, defined the extent of power to be retained by occupying authorities and set aside a number of 'reserved fields', amongst which were decartelization and foreign trade over which the High Commission kept full control.[37] With the Marshall plan as an additional lever, the USA were thus in a position to exert significant influence over West Germany and its economy and this remained true until the end of the occupation regime in 1954.

American Debate on a Program for West Germany

It had taken some time for the USA to secure full power and control over all three western zones of Germany. Time would also be necessary to settle the debate, within the American administration, on a program for Germany. By the end of the Second World War, the Washington administration had been unanimous in its condemnation of the Nazi regime and of those men who had institutionalized genocide, turning it into state policy. The Americans denounced, in particular, close relationships between the Nazi regime and German economic actors, blaming such a collusion for the length of the war and for its most horrendous features. There was disagreement, however, in Washington, as to how this analysis should impact upon American and Allied postwar policies in Germany. To put it simply, three main programs were being confronted—championed respectively by the Treasury Department, the Justice Department, and an alliance between the War and State Departments.

Henry Morgenthau, Roosevelt's Secretary of the Treasury, had denounced with particular violence the collusion between German industrial power and the Nazi regime. According to him, this collusion revealed a natural affinity and the eradication of Nazism should come with a destruction of German industrial power. The Morgenthau plan, that was signed in Quebec by Roosevelt and Churchill in September 1944, provided for a dismantling of German industrial capacities and for the transformation of the Ruhr and the Saar—the very core of German industrial power—into rural regions. Roosevelt was to disavow the plan only a few weeks later. Parts of this plan, though, were integrated into the official directives elaborated for the American military government in Germany. The proceedings of the Potsdam Conference and the 'Directive to the Commander-in-Chief of the US Forces of Occupation Regarding Military Government in Germany', better known as JCS1067, both gave priority, for example, to the development of agriculture, allowing only marginal small-scale industry in a few peaceful sectors.[38]

The Justice Department and in particular the Antitrust Division around Assistant Attorney General, Thurman Arnold, had also vehemently criticized the role of German industry before and during the war and its support of the Nazi regime. Members of the Antitrust Division, however, came to conclusions that differed somewhat from those of the Treasury Department. They saw no need to destroy German industry. Bringing about the decentralization of that industry and weakening each firm through a systematic decartelization and deconcentration program would certainly be enough. As Francis Biddle, the Attorney General, argued 'the purpose of such a program would not be to destroy German economic life in its entirety, but to put industries into a form where they will no longer constitute a danger to the civilized world'.[39] In 1942, Thurman Arnold had created, within the Antitrust Division, an Economic Warfare Unit responsible for monitoring the activities of German firms involved in international cartels. This unit had had to assess, in particular, the impact of international cartels on the American war effort. Accusations made by its members in 1942 and 1943 proved very serious. German firms had apparently used international cartels, before Pearl Harbor, as powerful tools to obtain information on American production capacity and technological know-how. German members of international cartels had apparently even managed to limit the American output of some strategic products and materials. The Economic Warfare Unit accused a number of American firms of passivity and even, in a few cases, of outright complicity.[40] Those accusations were so disturbing, for the administration and for the American public as a whole, that the decartelization and deconcentration of German industry became an

American priority by the end of the war and a key objective of the military government. Official directives thus indicated that 'the German economy [was to] be decentralized for the purpose of eliminating the present excessive concentration of economic power as exemplified in particular by cartels, syndicates, trusts and other monopolistic arrangements'.[41]

Finally, the War Department around Secretary of War Henry Stimson had, together with the State Department, another program for Germany. A systematic denazification, they argued, was both necessary and sufficient to prevent Germany from becoming a threat once again. Structures were not a problem as long as the dangerous ideology that had manipulated them was systematically destroyed. Members of the War and State Departments emphasized at the same time that a weak and dependent German economy could be a source of disruption in Europe and a major financial burden for occupying powers. From such a perspective, rapid industrial recovery should be given priority if only to prevent communist contagion. Structural reforms of significant scope were criticized precisely because they would slow down economic recovery and it was argued that an American economic program for occupied Germany should not be suggesting nor encouraging reforms of that sort (Dorn, 1957; Backer, 1971).

The debate taking place in Washington at the end of the war was transferred to the German arena through the American military government in Germany (OMGUS) straight after the Allied victory. Members of the Decartelization and Deconcentration Branch in OMGUS, many of whom had previously been with the Economic Warfare Unit, wanted to impose those structural reforms provided for by Directive JCS1067 and by the Potsdam Agreements. The Economics Division of OMGUS and the American Commander-in-Chief, General Lucius Clay, were in the meantime working to speed up German economic recovery. Their key priority was to prevent chaos, hunger, and certainly communism from taking hold in Germany. They also hoped to relieve the American taxpayer fairly rapidly from the financial burden represented by a weak and dependent Germany. This group had a difficult time, in the beginning, reconciling its decisions and actions with official American policy. Indeed, fostering German economic recovery was far from being an official objective of the American military government in 1945 and 1946. Both Directive JCS1067 and the Potsdam Agreements forbade all actions and decisions that would lead to the 'economic rehabilitation of Germany' or were 'designed to maintain and strengthen' the German economy.[42]

General Clay and members of the Economics Division still managed to find a loophole in official directives allowing them to legitimate their actions and decisions. A partial amendment to JCS1067 provided that, in situations where 'starvation, disease or unrest' threatened, action could be taken to stimulate industrial production and to speed up economic recovery.[43] Not surprisingly, members of the Economics Division were soon considering the decartelization and deconcentration program as an obstacle to German economic recovery.

They saw it essentially as a set of constraints, preventing the increase in industrial production they were advocating. Members of the Decartelization and Deconcentration Branch, however, firmly criticized their colleagues from the Economics Division for reinterpreting official policy. Throughout 1946 and 1947, confrontation and conflicts became more and more violent. A climax was reached in early 1948, when 19 out of 25 lawyers and economists from the Decartelization and Deconcentration Branch drew up a petition to General‧ Clay. They were protesting against the watering down and significant reinterpretation of decartelization and deconcentration measures.[44]

An *ad hoc* group was set up in Washington to investigate the affair and a report was published in April 1949. This group, otherwise known as the Ferguson Committee, identified a number of obstacles put in the way of the Decartelization and Deconcentration Branch. It deplored the behavior of members of the Economics Division and their systematic undermining of decartelization and deconcentration policies. It disapproved, finally, of a tendency dominant within the Economics Division to oppose economic recovery and structural reforms as incompatible:

Economic Advisers to General Clay generally took the position that deconcentration would interfere with German economic recovery . . . . We have found no support for the proposition that deconcentration procedures would interfere when carried along the lines of a sound policy . . . . The Committee has carefully considered United States policy respecting cartels, restrictive practices, and excessive economic concentration in Germany . . . and recommends that the United States basic policies remain unchanged . . . that they should have been and should be, energetically enforced.[45]

Settling the Debate

At first reading, the Ferguson report seemed to vindicate the claims of the Decartelization and Deconcentration Branch. The conclusions of the report appeared merely to restate policy objectives as defined by Directive JCS1067 and the Potsdam Agreements. A second and closer reading, however, showed that the Ferguson Committee and the early Decartelization and Deconcentration Branch did not have quite the same view on the decartelization and deconcentration program. The Ferguson report, first of all, did not mention the punitive role of the program, particularly important to former members of the Economic Warfare Unit. Of greater significance, the report did not question at all the necessity for economic and industrial recovery in West Germany. In reality, the Ferguson report testified to a major, albeit subtle, redefinition of American policies towards Germany, taking place around 1947 and 1948 with a geopolitical confrontation in the background. Labels had not changed, but contents were evolving. The replacement of one team by another in the Decartelization and Deconcentration Branch at the beginning of 1948, was symbolic of this subtle and nevertheless real redefinition of official policy.

In 1947 and 1948, Germany was being divided in a process that ran parallel to the geopolitical confrontation between East and West. West Germany, in that context, became central to the geopolitical strategy of the USA. As the front line bulwark of the Western world against communism in the American scheme, West Germany was to become an advanced post of prosperity and of Western capitalism, a 'stronghold of the American economic concept' in Europe.[46] The economic recovery of West Germany thus became a prime objective for the American administration. Directive JCS1779 replaced JCS1067 in July 1947 as a set of instructions to military government. It confirmed such a policy shift:

It is an objective of the United States government that there should arise in Germany . . . a manner of political life which, resting on a substantial basis of economic well being, will lead to tranquillity within Germany and will contribute to the spirit of peace among nations . . . . An orderly and prosperous Europe requires the economic contributions of a stable and productive Germany.[47]

In conformity with this redefined policy, the USA were to include western parts of Germany within the Marshall scheme, treating them as an economic and very soon a political entity. It could thus be argued that official policy in Washington was in fact catching up, around 1947 and 1948, with the work already done by the Economics Division in Germany. Fostering the economic and industrial recovery of the western parts of Germany became an official American objective.

Recovery, however, was not to be fostered at any cost, in contrast to what members of the Economics Division had tended to think and do. The Ferguson report set limits within which this recovery could take place. The German economy should thrive, industrial production and productivity should increase. According to the Ferguson Committee, however, the best way to achieve those ambitious results was certainly not to preserve existing structural arrangements. Preventing structural reforms, as the Economics Division had tried to do, was a mistake. Structural reforms on the one hand, and economic and industrial recovery on the other, far from being incompatible, should be seen as reinforcing each other in a pattern that was to be common to all European partners to the Marshall scheme. The West German economy was to become the engine of reconstruction in Western Europe and a showpiece of Western—that is American-type—capitalism.[48]

A structural transformation of the West German economy following an American model was therefore necessary and the decartelization program could help achieve this. According to Charles Dilley, Assistant Chief of the Decartelization and Deconcentration Branch, 'the decartelization program [was] not intended to be an instrument for the punishment of the German people, German businessmen, or German business firms'. On the contrary, Dilley went on, 'the decartelization law [had been] designed to promote in Germany the same standards of business conduct that have been enforced vigorously in the US business community since the passage of the Sherman antitrust law in 1890'.[49] A redefinition of the objectives of the decartelization and deconcentration program had thus taken place. Starting in 1947, the label 'decartelization and deconcentration' would come to refer, in West Germany, to nothing more than an antitrust policy, in the American tradition. The revamped decartelization and deconcentration program was to stimulate the structural transformation of West German industry along the lines of the American model. The ultimate goal was a powerful and productive West German economy and industry, able to withstand communist onslaughts, a key weapon in other words for the Cold War. The model for such a powerful economy was obviously American, as Philips Hawkins, who would head the Decartelization and Deconcentration Branch from 1948, underscored:

The US cannot be in a position of taking a totally negative position and saying to the Germans that their former system of economy is not acceptable and that communism is not acceptable without offering them an alternative. The decartelization program attempts to offer the Germans a positive program for a sound and workable economy; that is the type of free competitive economy which has been so successful in the US. It is believed that this type of economy can and will work in Germany and that the German people can be taught to understand and want such an economy.[50]

In the context, naturally, a 'free competitive economy' did not mean the 'free market' of economists but the American economy, as it had come to be defined by the late 1940s. An economy, in other words, dominated by large-scale, mass producing firms, competing on oligopolistic markets, and policed by antitrust legislation in the American tradition.

By the end of 1947, the stage was therefore set. American occupation authorities had secured a fair amount of control over economic and political institutions in the western territories of Germany. They had clearly defined, albeit after some hesitation, their objectives for West Germany particularly with respect to its economy. In the years to come, they would attempt to reform and transform the economic and industrial structures of that country in order to create a wealthy bulwark against communism and a faithful ally in Western Europe. A large-scale transfer of the American system of industrial production was in order and everything seemed ready for the experiment to start.

ITALY: DEPENDENCE AND INDIFFERENCE

Like many other countries in Europe at the time, after the Second World War Italy was in a state of utter destitution. The country had been highly dependent on the USA ever since September 1943 when the fascist government had surrendered. Some organized groups, particularly in the north of the country had then sided with Allied powers, who had provided them with arms and supplies until the end of the war. The USA kept delivering emergency relief after the peace had been signed. They also guaranteed a relative stability around the contested border with Yugoslavia. While the USA were undeniably playing a key role on the Italian scene, the strength of the Communist party was the source of bargaining power for that country at least from 1945 to 1947 (Hughes, 1965; Romano, 1977; Miller, 1981). The year of 1947 represented a turning point for Italy as it did for France. Italians could not postpone taking sides in the Cold War anymore. In the months before the launching of the Marshall plan, Italian political leaders had already seen their freedom to maneuver sharply reduced. During a trip to the USA, early in 1947, the Italian Premier Alcide de Gasperi tried to secure renewed American economic assistance. He was told in no uncertain terms that financial and economic aid would be much more forthcoming if communist ministers left the Italian government.

Clear advice of that sort combined with rumors that Washington was preparing a large-scale aid package for Europe to speed up action on the Italian national scene. In May 1947, Alcide de Gasperi set up a new government without communist or left-wing socialist ministers (Hughes, 1965: 146). When Marshall dollars started to flow in, by 1948, Italy was well and truly anchored to the West and most of its bargaining power in the relationship with the USA had been lost. The American system of industrial production was therefore, and from that point on, available as a model for Italy as much as it was for France. Contacts between Italy and the USA became increasingly numerous throughout the Marshall plan period, multiplying the opportunities for the Italian population to become familiar with American economic and industrial structures. Those structural arrangements characterized a Great Power that also happened to be, for Italy, the main provider and the sole protector. Conditions thus seemed to have been fulfilled for the American system of industrial production to become a model, both familiar and superior, for Italian reconstruction.

It rapidly became obvious, however, that the American model was much less likely to be considered in Italy than it was in France. Indeed, the Italian power élite lacked, after the war, the sense of crisis and urgency that characterized its French counterpart. The group controlling political and institutional positions of power in Italy did not define itself in radical opposition to the former regime and system, nor did it declare a state of national emergency and crisis that would call for radical structural transformations. In Italy, the rejection of fascism had taken place during the war and had been, as a consequence, relatively short-lived. After the surrender of the fascist government in 1943, a number of Italians had shared in the Allied war effort. Allied powers themselves, in fact, encouraged oblivion to serve their short-term strategic interests. The fascist past, as a consequence, was rapidly dealt with and put aside in Italy (Miller, 1986: 147).

When the war came to an end in 1945, Italy was in a relatively ambiguous situation. That special status, neither winner nor loser, clearly had to be preserved in order to prevent issues such as military occupation or reparations to surface. Italians, therefore, were better off forgetting their fascist past at the time than loudly rejecting it. For the American government, on the other hand, the main danger in Italy, after the war, was not so much a return to the past as the strength of the Communist party. The USA, since 1943, had exercised a significant amount of control over Italian political affairs.[51] Washington came to believe, after the war, that the best way to limit the role of the Communist party, and thus Soviet influence in Italy, was to ask the Italian King Victor Emanuel III to abdicate and to let Italians choose their own political regime through a national referendum. The King and his Prime Minister, Pietro Badoglio, had brought discredit upon themselves by their attitude towards fascism before and after 1943. That they stayed in power after the end of the war could only strengthen, according to Americans, the more radical anti-fascist groups, in other words the communists.[52]

American decision makers were also suspicious of the Italian Socialist party, which they believed could be tempted at some point to collaborate with a Communist party representing 25 per cent of the Italian electorate. Political and geopolitical stability being their key priority in Italy, the USA thus ended up sponsoring the Italian Christian Democratic party (Democrazia Cristiana), certainly one of the least reform-minded Italian parties at the time. The *petite bourgeoisie* and small business represented a significant share of the consti-tuency of the Democrazia Cristiana which, not surprisingly, proved to be a quite conservative party. Its leaders, holding the reins of power in postwar Italy, were highly reluctant and often strongly opposed to any kind of sig-nificant change, particularly with respect to the economic and industrial struc-ture of the country. The Christian Democratic élite, championed by the USA, proved not at all ready to propose or accept large-scale disruptions of the Italian social, economic, and industrial order. The Italian group in power never questioned the legitimacy of this order nor did it link it with fascism. Christian democrats in Italy did not declare a state of national crisis and emergency. Since they were not calling for radical transformations, they did not have to look outside their national borders for a potential model.

By the end of the 1940s, two essential conditions were fulfilled in France and in West Germany, making a large-scale, cross-national structural transfer from the USA to those countries highly likely. The élites in power, first of all, were characterized in both cases by a sense of national crisis and emergency. A group of nationals in France defined themselves in radical opposition to the former regime and system. Foreigners in the western territories of Germany, and American occupation authorities in particular, believed in the necessity of bringing about a radical transformation of German economic and industrial structures with, ultimately, geopolitical aims in mind. In both cases, the problems of the country and the national state of emergency had been inter-preted in economic, industrial, and structural terms. Both France and West Germany, furthermore, were, by the late 1940s, in a relationship of asymmetrical dependence with the USA. The Western superpower was becoming, through the Marshall plan, a generous and regular provider of not only economic and financial but also technical assistance. In a divided world, where the threat from the East seemed real, the USA also appeared to be the only protectors of a weak Western Europe. The American system of industrial production was therefore highly likely, in those conditions, to become a model for those two countries and to represent a solution to their perceived national crisis. In Italy, on the other hand, while the geopolitical situation was also characterized by significant and asymmetrical dependence on the USA, the national condition was not fulfilled. The élite in power in Italy did not define itself in opposition to a preexisting social, economic, and political order and it lacked a sense of national crisis. It did not call, as a consequence, for radical transformations on the social, economic, and industrial scene, nor was it in search of a foreign model.

The combination of both conditions, the national and the geopolitical, significantly increased in the French and West German cases the likelihood of a large-scale, cross-national structural transfer. In both countries, the will of a small group of actors, holding key positions of institutional power, would turn likelihood into process. A cross-national network, made up of American and national modernizers, would come to share compatible if not similar objectives and would work together from strategically located positions of institutional power. In the Italian case, on the other hand, no such network emerged, further reducing the chance of a large-scale, cross-national transfer process.

Notes

1. Quoted in Duchêne (1994: 23).
2. German occupation in France and American occupation in parts of Italy after 1943.
3. This period has left deep psychological scars in France as contemporary debates keep illustrating (Paxton, 1973; Girault, 1986; Péan, 1994).
4. See Milza (1979: ch. 4) and Hoffmann (1962: 32). France had won the First World War and victory tends to vindicate existing systems and structures rather than bring about a sense of national crisis and a radical questioning.
5. De Gaulle (1970), 'Speech, March 2nd, 1945'.
6. See Sutton *et al.* (1956), Kogut and Parkinson (1994). Polanyi (1949) has argued that societies granting such a central role to the economy are rare historical occurrences.
7. See Barbas (1989). The internal French situation had not changed so radically from 1940 to 1945. The fact that groups in power proposed very different diagnoses in 1940 and in 1945 can be explained in two ways. Those groups, first of all, were characterized by different sets of values and ideological beliefs. The geopolitical environment in which France was embedded, on the other hand, changed radically between 1940 and 1945, from being shaped by Germany to being dominated by both the USA and the USSR. Reference schemes and dominant foreign models were thus bound to be different.

8. For criticisms and accusations of this type, see Michel and Mirkine-Guetzevitch (1954), de Gaulle (1964), Monnet (1976), or Bloch-Lainé and Bouvier (1986).

9. Lefaucheux (1945), Langer (1947: 65–72). In contrast to actors of the period, scholars do not so readily associate the prewar economic system with Vichy (Ehrmann, 1957; Paxton, 1973; Vinen, 1991; Rochebrune and Hazéra, 1995).

10. The National Council of Resistance (CNR) uniting all members of the resistance movement around de Gaulle clearly spelled out in its program what was understood by regaining 'Great Power' status: (1) restore France's sovereignty to the frontiers of 1939 and also over the Empire; (2) impose France's presence in important international negotiations and institutions as a winner of the war; (3) weaken the position of Germany in Europe and the world (Michel and Mirkine-Guetzevitch 1954).

11. Economic programs of various groups in the resistance coalition are in Michel and Mirkine-Guetzevitch (1954). See also Bloch-Lainé and Bouvier (1986).

12. 'Conversation between de Gaulle and Caffery, May 5, 1945', FRUS (1945: iv. 686). Some French officials may have gone too far in drawing their own conclusions. Georges Pâques, a member of the resistance movement who would represent France in NATO was convicted of high treason in 1964. He had apparently supplied the USSR with strategic and military information. In a letter to de Gaulle, published for the first time in *Le Monde,* January 8, 1994, he justified his action: 'I have tried all along to follow your own lessons. The independence of France, which should be our main goal, requires an alliance with Russia as counterweight to Anglo-Saxon ambitions . . . . I chose to remain faithful to you in spirit, even if it meant behaving in an undisciplined manner on a day-to-day basis.'

13. *Le Monde,* daily headed by Hubert Beuve-Meury, was a forum for neutralist positions of this second type.

14. The 'tripartite coalition' was sometimes described by Americans, in an interesting parallel, as a 'pact of non-aggression' (FRUS, 1946: v. 405).

15. Wall (1991: 48), Bossuat (1992: 90–7), Kuisel (1993: 19).

16. According to Robert Blum, who had assisted his father during the talks, the refusal of the French delegation to take sides 'on the problem which [for the Americans] is more important than anything, i.e. the rivalry between the United States and the Soviet Union' proved to have significant consequences. Quoted in Bossuat (1992: 92).

17. FRUS (1946: v).

18. 'Letter from Caffery to James Byrnes, Secretary of State, March 31, 1947', FRUS (1947: iii). By 1947, de Gaulle himself had to take sides: '[De Gaulle] has burned all bridges with Moscow and the French communist party and is their sworn enemy. As such, his orientation is now and at long last definitely towards the United States, for he believes that we are the only country which has the material resources and the will to prevent Soviet world domination.' 'Letter from Caffery, October 10, 1947', FRUS (1947: iii).

19. A summary of the scholarly debate on the origins of the Cold War can be found in Kaspi (1986: 400–1). There is no need to take sides in a debate that has pitted against each other scholars blaming the Soviet Union for the Cold War and a revisionist group underscoring American responsibility. Truman's speech was in any case significant because it marked the official beginning of the Cold War.

20. I agree here with Maier (1978) and Rioux (1980) against Milward (1984).

21. FRUS (1947: iii. 197–237). Key ideas to be found in the Marshall speech are already in working papers of the Policy Planning Staff and of the State–War–Navy Coordinating Committee, dated March, April, and May.

22. 'Remarks by the Honorable George C. Marshall, Secretary of State, at Harvard University on June 5, 1947', FRUS (1947: iii. 237–9).

23. It seems that making a general offer, including to the USSR, was only a strategic move on the part of Americans and that they did not really mean it. In a State Department meeting, on May 28, 'there was general agreement that the plan should be drawn with such conditions that Eastern Europe could participate provided the countries would abandon near-exclusive Soviet orientation of their economies' FRUS (1947: iii. 235).

24. Acheson (1950: 233).

25. FRUS (1947: iii. 225). See in particular 'Working Paper from George Kennan, Policy Planning Staff, to Dean Acheson, Under Secretary of State, May 23, 1947.' Other 'totalitarian' influences were naturally fascism, Nazism, or various types of corporatism, dominant in Europe for many years.

26. The existence of such a bloc of countries would also increase the influence of the USA worldwide, while providing markets for American goods. The objectives of the Marshall plan were in fact multiple. Early studies have tended to underscore the humanitarian and political objectives of the Marshall plan (Price, 1955) or the short-term economic aim of financing bankrupt European clients to avoid a recession in the USA and to create markets for American exports (Kolko and Kolko, 1972). More recently, historians have pointed to a longer-term goal— reshaping the Western economic and industrial world along essentially three lines: economic integration, enhanced productivity, and increased competition. See Hogan (1985, 1987), Milward (1984), Van der Pijl (1984), and Carew (1987). Although we have seen that this longer term goal was itself in part means to geopolitical ends, the 'missionary' dimension of the Marshall plan should not be overlooked. For Marshall planners, American economic and industrial structures were not only the surest bulwark against commmunism, they were also the best and most efficient structures available.

27. The 'Act of Surrender by Germany' was signed in Berlin on May 8, 1945. It is reprinted in Office of the Historian (1986: 14).

28. See 'Protocol of the Proceedings of the Berlin (Postdam) Conference, August 1, 1945' in Office of the Historian (1986: 56). Agreement had also been reached at Postdam that 'during the period of occupation, Germany (would) be treated as a single economic unit'.

29. Clay's frustration led him to take impulsive decisions, for example when he stopped, in May 1946, the dismantling of German plants earmarked for reparations. 'Further dismantling, he argued, would result in disaster if we are unable to obtain economic unity' (Clay, 1950).

30. 'Memorandum of Agreement between the United States and the United Kingdom on Economic Fusion of their Respective Zones of Occupation in Germany, December 2, 1946' in Office of the Historian (1986: 110–13).

31. Clay (1950: 178). See also Stokes (1988: 122).

32. 'Letter from James Martin to General Clay, Deputy Military Governor, August 2, 1946', OMGUS Rds, Bd40, #3/122-2/14.

33. 'Decartelization in the US Zone of Germany, Background and Policy', OMGUS Rds, Bd17, #3/225-10, no date.
34. In a letter to the Secretary of State, James Patterson then Secretary of War, insisted that Washington had every right to forbid the British program of nationalization 'since the load of carrying the two zones in Germany, particularly in the vital matter of food is falling more and more on our shoulders' 'Letter, June 13, 1947', FRUS (1947: ii. 1151).
35. McCloy had accepted the High Commissioner position on the condition that he could also control Marshall plan activities in West Germany. Schwartz (1991*a*: 41): 'McCloy recognized that control over Marshall plan funds was critical to the prestige and authority of the High Commissioner. As the Allies turned over more authority to the Germans, Marshall plan funds would become a major lever with which to exercise influence.'
36. Both the *Grundgesetz* and the Federal and decentralized structure of the Bundesrepublik Deutschland were inspired in part by American models, and elaborated with the assistance of American advisers (Clay, 1984; Zink, 1957; Peterson, 1977).
37. 'Occupation Statute, April 8, 1949' in Office of the Historian (1986: 212).
38. 'Protocol of the Proceedings of the Berlin (Potsdam) Conference, August 1, 1945' in Office of the Historian (1986: 58). 'Directive JCS1067, May 10, 1945' in Office of the Historian (1986: 15).
39. Quoted in Martin (1950: 16).
40. The case of Standard Oil was particularly striking. The Economic Warfare Unit claimed that agreements between Standard Oil and IGFarben in Germany had led the American company to stop the production of synthetic rubber and had thus caused a shortage, in the USA, of this strategic material. See Borkin and Welsh (1943), Martin (1950), and OMGUS Rds, Bd18, #11/11-3/6.
41. 'Protocol of the Proceedings of the Berlin (Potsdam) Conference' and 'Directive JCS1067' in Office of the Historian (1986).
42. Ibid.
43. Clay (1984) would later say: 'from the very beginning, I realized that we had to do something in the economic field in spite of JCS1067.'
44. See Taylor (1979). Seven of them later resigned, while the others changed divisions.
45. 'Report of Ferguson Committee, April 1949', OMGUS Rds, Bd41, #3/142-1/9.
46. Ludwig Erhard, Economics Minister in the Federal Republic of Germany, quoted in Schwartz (1991*b*: 192). See also Acheson (1950) and Kennan (1967).
47. 'Directive from the Joint Chiefs of Staff to the Commander-in-Chief of the United States Forces of Occupation, JCS1779, July 11, 1947' in Office of the Historian (1986: 124).
48. Hogan (1985) has called this process the 'search by American Marshall planners' for a 'European neo-capitalism'. See also Maier (1978).
49. 'Charles Dilley, Objectives of the Decartelization Program, November 1947', OMGUS Rds, Bd18, #11/11-3/7.
50. 'Phillips Hawkins, Acting Chief of the Decartelization Branch—Report on Progress of the Decartelization Branch since the Passage of the Decartelization Law on February 12, 1947 to General Draper, Chief of the Economics Division, June 14, 1947', OMGUS Rds, Bd18, #11/23-2/1.
51. See Hughes (1965) and Miller (1986). The USA had much more direct influence on political affairs in Italy than in France. The lack of a charismatic and legitimate

figure in Italy, who could compare with de Gaulle, can at least partly account for that.

52. After a trip to Washington in April 1944, Robert Murphy, then Political Adviser to the Supreme Allied Commander, reported that 'the President wanted the King out. Italian Americans disliked the Monarch and Roosevelt needed their votes in the fall presidential elections. In addition, Roosevelt was convinced that the King's continued political activities aided the growth of the communist party' (Miller, 1986: 95).

4

Actors and Institutional Channels
Emergence of a Cross-National Modernizing Network

*As of today, the one great area where the drive of the Kremlin has been
stopped cold is in Western Europe. Here we find it stopped not by bullets or
oratorical outbursts but by the force of an idea . . . the idea behind the
Marshall plan.*

Paul G. Hoffman[1]

By the late 1940s, cross-national networks were in place linking small groups
of French or West German actors with a number of progressive Americans, all
in key institutional positions of power. Such a network did not emerge in Italy
where the national élite and the American group involved in Italian affairs
turned out to have little in common, both in terms of ideology or of objectives.
In France, a small number of modernizing actors took over or created, immediately after the Second World War, key institutions at the border between
state and economy and at the point of articulation of Franco-American relationships. Originating from the public sphere and from the civil service, they
soon spun a dense web. Planning and preparing the large-scale transformation
of national economic, industrial, and even social structures, French modernizers looked towards the USA for models they could borrow. On the other side
of the Atlantic, in the meantime, a group of progressive businessmen, civil
servants, and economists was taking control of the Economic Cooperation
Administration (ECA), a newly created institution in charge of managing the
Marshall plan. The synergy between this American group and the modernizing
élite in France proved significant. They had compatible objectives and shared a
common ideology, a mixture of Keynesianism, productivism, and fordism.
They also came to be institutionally contiguous, in particular through the
French planning board and the ECA Mission in Paris, thus increasing the
likelihood of collaboration. In the western territories of Germany, however,
the situation was somewhat different. Until the creation of the Federal Republic in 1949, power ultimately rested with a non-local élite. American occupation authorities and representatives of the ECA played a particularly significant
role, designing a program for the large-scale transformation of German
economic and industrial structures. Those foreign actors soon realized, however, that reforms would not last if they were merely being imposed on the
Germans. By 1948, Americans thus started to co-opt a group of German

decision makers sympathetic to their modernization objectives. Institutional contiguity between the American and the German sides of the network was essentially provided through the American Military Government in Germany (OMGUS) and the American High Commission on one side, with the German Ministry of Economic Affairs and the German Ministry of the Marshall plan on the other.

FRENCH TECHNOCRATS AND THE MODERNIZATION IMPERATIVE

By the end of 1947, a small group of men who believed that the American model was a solution to French problems, had gained control of key institutions in France. Those institutions were a significant source of leverage and the actors controlling them were to play an instrumental role in the modernization process of French industry. Spreading from the public sphere and reaching the private sector only later, the French modernization drive had three main centers. The planning board around Jean Monnet played a key role. It developed close links with another center, the new civil service school (Ecole Nationale d'Administration or ENA) in charge of training top civil servants. Finally, a third center was located at the border between politics and civil society. Its figurehead, the politician Pierre Mendès-France, had the support of a dynamic group of journalists around Jean-Jacques Servan-Schreiber from the new weekly *L'Express*.

Jean Monnet and the Planning Board

Jean Monnet was an exceptional character and undeniably the keystone of early French modernization.[2] Belonging to both worlds, French and American, he was particularly instrumental in the cross-national transfer process. He created and ran a new institution, the French planning board, that was to serve his ambitious projects for the French economy. He was able, at the same time, to co-opt within the more traditional French administration a number of strategic decision making centers that were to provide crucial support to the modernization drive. Jean Monnet was a man of great vision, 'the specialist of general ideas', utterly pragmatic, though, when it came to implementation (Gravier, 1953: 23). Throughout his life, he strove to create conditions for coordination whether on the French scene or across national borders. He also believed in the necessity to institutionalize actions and decisions in order to ensure impact in the long term. The common thread of all his undertakings was an attempt to design institutions making coordination possible, whether during the First World War or the Second World War, when crafting the French plan, or when setting up the European Coal and Steel Community.

The personal history of Jean Monnet and his professional career help shed some light on his role in France after 1945. Without formal education, he started by working in the family business, a small Cognac trading company. A few months into the First World War, he managed to get access to the French Premier, René Viviani, and to the Minister of War, Alexandre Millerand. Voicing his concern about the lack of coordination between Allied countries in matters of supply and trade, he recommended and obtained the creation of Allied coordination committees. In the fall of 1914, when he had just turned 26, Jean Monnet was appointed French representative to those committees, based in London.

During the Second World War, he built on this early experience. The only foreign member of the British Supply Council, he was in Washington in 1941, negotiating supplies and equipment for the war effort. As such, he was soon working in close collaboration with members of the American War Production Board. He was also instrumental in bringing about the creation of a committee for the coordination of British and American war production programs, the Combined Production and Resources Board.[3] While working in the USA, during the Second World War but also in the interwar period as an investment banker, Jean Monnet came to greatly admire the economic power and industrial efficiency of that country, its productive capacities, and its dynamism. His stay in Washington also allowed him to nurture privileged relationships with American politicians, civil servants, lawyers, and businessmen that would prove particularly important after the war.[4] During the second half of the war, Monnet increasingly turned his energies towards French problems. After a short mission to Algiers, he was back in Washington but this time as representative of the French national liberation committee, in charge of supply issues.[5] Head of the French Supply Council (Comité Français pour l'Approvisionnement or CFA), he was in fact working on longer-term projects for the French industry and economy.

In 1944 and 1945, Monnet was busy sketching out the general features of what would become the French or Monnet plan, together with some of his American friends. Robert Nathan, chairman of the planning committee in the American War Production Board, was closely involved in this process. Monnet apparently used the CFA in Washington as an institutional cover to hire American statistical and planning experts, who in reality helped him with the design of the future French plan. George Ball, an American lawyer officially employed by the CFA in 1945, confirmed that 'it was during that period that [Monnet] was evolving in his mind the general direction and approach of the French plan' and that '[Monnet's] basic interest in having [him] around was that he wanted a kind of [intellectual] punching bag'.[6] Another American lawyer, Eugen Rostow, also played a significant role. In a letter to Jean Monnet at the end of July 1945, he set the financial conditions for his collaboration and chose a neutral title, 'consultant on supply problems', in order to avoid 'the notion of a foreigner meddling with basic French economic policy'.[7]

Jean Monnet and his American friends or consultants believed that conditions in postwar France would not be too different from those that had prevailed in the USA during the war. A common problem was to allocate scarce resources and deal with shortages while needs and demand were increasing. The proposed solution, in both cases, was to elaborate an investment program at the national level in order to avoid waste and duplication. A few key sectors with a potential multiplier effect on the whole economy should be given priority for the allocation of scarce resources. The national plan should be flexible enough to allow for adaptation in changing circumstances.[8] Undeniably, American Keynesianism was the tradition from which Jean Monnet drew in order to define French postwar planning. He had acquired first hand knowledge of this type of economic regulation by the state through his direct involvement in the second American New Deal. He credited flexible planning and high levels of government spending for increased production levels, high civilian demand, and full employment in the USA during the war. Jean Monnet believed that such success could be and should be replicated in France. His American friends, on the other hand, realized in 1945 that national planning was doomed in the USA. Under the more conservative Truman administration, they were bound to lose influence and power. They bitterly deplored the 'drift towards an unplanned economy' in their own country and may have seen in France, through Jean Monnet's planning board, a testing ground for some of their ideas.

On January 3, 1946, a few days before his resignation, General de Gaulle announced the creation of a planning board or Commissariat Général du Plan. Jean Monnet was appointed Commissaire Général du Plan and the set of directives he received followed word for word the proposal he had himself sent de Gaulle.[9] The structure, mechanics, and objectives of the French plan had been entirely defined by Jean Monnet and his team. The experience of Monnet during the Second World War proved of utmost significance in this case. The interpretation of French postwar planning that is proposed here underscores the significance of American influences.[10] The French planning board, it is argued, was the first attempt at institutionalizing in France an American interpretation of Keynesian thought.[11] The French Commissariat Général du Plan was clearly modeled on the American War Production Board. The War Production Board had been located on the fringe of American administration, which made its coordinating role much easier. A small group of experts—the planning committee led by Robert Nathan—had been defining the general direction, providing continuity for, and coordinating the production programs of, twenty-four industry branches that brought together representatives from business, labor, and government.[12]

Following this model, the French planning board was designed as a small and flexible institution. In order to facilitate its coordinating role, it was located outside the boundaries of traditional French administration and answered directly to the office of the French Prime Minister.[13] A task force of around twenty experts defined general trends for the evolution of the national economy, with respect, for example, to production and productivity levels, investment priorities, or restructuring. Detailed sectorial plans were the responsibility of eighteen modernization commissions bringing together representatives of business, labor, ministries, and the Commissariat. Members of the planning board were officially in charge of coordination but they were also responsible for overseeing the work of each modernization commission.

The small French team of experts was made up of hand-picked individuals. Amongst them was Pierre Uri, a young and brilliant economist who came to the planning board from the Institut Supérieur d'Economie Appliquée (ISEA).[14] The ISEA was a research institute created in 1944 by François Perroux. A Keynesian economist, François Perroux was an oddity within the French academic community where Keynesian ideas were all but unknown.[15] So was Robert Marjolin, another member of the planning board and one of the rare French Keynesian economists. He had first met Jean Monnet in London in 1940 and worked with him again in Washington, in the French supply council. Paul Delouvrier, Jean Vergeot, Jean Ripert, Alfred Sauvy, and Etienne Hirsch, other key collaborators of Jean Monnet in the planning board, had all been carefully selected and hand-picked in the same way for their intellectual capacity, a relatively non-conformist attitude, a deep belief in the necessity of economic and industrial modernization, but equally importantly also for their familiarity with American models (Fourquet, 1980; Rosanvallon, 1989).

The first plan elaborated by the French Commissariat had two main objectives. The *plan de modernisation et d'équipement* should before anything else ensure the coordination of national reconstruction particularly with respect to infrastructure and industry. Even more importantly for members of the planning board, the plan should also establish a road map for the modernization of French economic and industrial structures as well as steer the process along. By modernization, Jean Monnet and his team in fact understood the transformation of the national economy following their own definition and interpretation—albeit somewhat partial—of the American model.[16] While industry was identified as a sector of the national economy to be developed as a high priority, two features of the American system of industrial production seemed particularly striking to members of the French planning team. The large, mass-producing industrial corporation on the one hand and high levels of labor productivity on the other would frame the French modernization project. Harold Lubell, an American scholar who spent a few months studying the mechanics of the French planning board, confirmed that for its members it appeared obvious that 'the strength of America [lay] in the size of its industrial giants'. 'Any combination of French industrial firms', he indicated, '[was] almost automatically approved as a step in the right direction'.[17] Increased labor productivity was the other key objective of the French plan. As indicated in official directives, the priority granted to levels of productivity should translate into a systematic benchmarking of French industry against its foreign counterparts and in particular against American industry. It was specified that 'when the gap [was] too important, the planning board should account for it and propose strategies to bridge it'.[18]

Members of the French planning board had chosen the American system of industrial production as a model for national reconstruction but they clearly had their own understanding of what this model was all about. Large size corporations and labor productivity were not the only features of the American model as Jean Monnet's American friends were already reminding him in 1944 and 1945. 'Free trade', 'competition' or 'antitrust legislation', 'improvement of social relations' had all been mentioned at one point or another.[19] Although most of those features would become part of the national debate in France a few years later, partly due to American pressure, they would never fundamentally come to define or frame the French modernization project, while productivity and the large mass-producing corporation undeniably did.

Ecole Nationale d'Aministration: Training a New Technocracy

As an institution, the French planning board came to have a significant amount of power over the national economy and industry. The modernization project, however, would certainly have run into many more obstacles, had the planning board remained the only modernizing actor in France. But the modernizing drive found a number of routes: within the French administration, the new civil service school, the Ecole Nationale d'Administration (ENA), had in particular a key role. Soon after the end of the Second World War, a new generation of civil servants spread throughout the French administration and took over recently created public institutions, such as the national statistics institute (INSEE) or the national balance-sheet commission within the French Treasury (SEEF).[20] The key figure in this second group of modernizers was undeniably François Bloch-Lainé. Appointed in 1947 chairman of the Treasury, within the French Ministry of Finance, he set out to radically transform this institution which had traditionally been characterized by very conservative policy choices. The French Ministry of Finance and in particular the Treasury had indeed been, throughout the first half of the twentieth century, zealous champions of financial and budgetary orthodoxy, systematically striving to balance state accounts. The main objective of François Bloch-Lainé was to steer the Treasury towards a more positive and progressive role with respect to the rebuilding and restructuring of French industry. Consequently, Bloch-Lainé advocated close collaboration between this traditional administrative body and the otherwise unconventional and somewhat marginal planning board.[21] Those institutions soon shared common objectives and both groups of modernizers worked together, generally in agreement and synergy. The web they came to spin thickened rapidly, first across French administration and later across civil society. To implement such a 'trojan horse' strategy, the new civil service school, the ENA, proved to be a powerful institutional tool.[22]

The ENA was created in 1945 as a breeding-ground for high ranking civil servants. Most members of the resistance coalition had indeed denounced, by the end of the war, recruiting and training within the French civil service as being utterly inadequate. Birth rights and co-optation, they argued, should give way to meritocracy. The training of future high ranking civil servants, on the other hand, should take into account the greater role the state was bound to play in economic and industrial spheres. While future civil servants should be trained to value and respect their public service mission, the curriculum should also include economics and the pedagogy should be innovative, once again on the model of what was done in the USA—study groups, case studies, research and surveys, seminars.[23] The French provisional government thus proposed the creation of a school, the Ecole Nationale d'Administration, which was to train state technocrats, twentieth-century French *mandarins* sharing common values and objectives. This new technocracy was to guarantee an independence of state action relative to private interests, which, according to members of the resistance coalition, had been lacking until then.

Soon after its creation, the ENA was all but taken over by a small group of modernizers from the planning board and the Treasury.[24] Keynesian economics thus came to frame the ideological background within ENA while the writings of Schumpeter and Galbraith also had significant influence. Keynes was taught by Pierre Uri, amongst others, and François Perroux's *Histoire des Doctrines Economiques*, published in 1947, became a reference textbook. ENA students soon became champions of economic growth and efficiency, advocates of industrial society, managerial capitalism, and productivity. They clearly favored large bureaucratic and mass-producing hierarchies, feeling closer to professional managers than to small business owners.[25] The most impressive achievement of the ENA was thus the rapid creation of a new generation of civil servants, a professional group of modernizing state employees, who believed that the state was a necessary motor of economic or industrial transformation and economic expansion. The new civil servants were experts and not politicians. They were characterized by their pragmatism and their strong belief, unmistakably of Keynesian origin, that a rational, 'scientific' intervention of the state in the economy could only have positive effects. The planning board and the Treasury, in other words, had managed to diffuse their modernization project through the ENA. The new civil service school would prove to be a powerful instrument for the institutionalization within the French administration of those ideas, objectives, and values originally defined by the early group of modernizers.

The project of a modernization of the French economy and industry along the lines indicated earlier was thus, at the beginning, essentially a technocratic and civil service undertaking.[26] Consequently, it would endure, despite the climate of great political instability that characterized the Fourth Republic in France. The fragility of political actors increased, to some extent, the power of the French administration and the role of the planning board which came to embody a certain stability and policy continuity. The modernization impetus initially came from a small group of men who managed to turn institutional and administrative bodies, old or new, into powerful tools to diffuse their ideas and achieve their objectives. This strategy of top-down diffusion was justified and made possible by the increasing infrastructural power of the French state. The nationalization of basic industries and credit institutions in 1945 and 1946 created conditions in which the French state could have a direct influence on the economy and could even shape the national industry.[27] It was thus particularly significant in this context that those institutions in the French administrative apparatus most closely involved in economic and industrial affairs were controlled by the new modernizing élite.

Pierre Mendès-France or 'PMF' and the New Press

Although the first circle of early French modernizers had been civil servants and high ranking administrative agents, another center of influence should be mentioned, one at the intersection between administration, politics, and journalism. A key figure here was the politician Pierre Mendès-France, who found strong support in a dynamic group of journalists around Jean-Jacques Servan-Schreiber. The political career of Pierre Mendès-France had started when he was appointed, in March 1938, Under-Secretary of the Treasury by the socialist Premier Léon Blum. A young member of the national assembly, Mendès-France belonged to the Parti Radical Socialiste, a center party somewhat on the right of Léon Blum's SFIO.[28] Pierre Mendès-France had some understanding of economic problems and found them interesting, a rather rare quality at the time on the French political scene. Working with Georges Boris, his head of staff and one of the first Frenchmen to have studied and admired the New Deal experiment, Mendès-France proposed an economic program with some mild reflationary overtones.[29] But his experience in office was cut short one month later when Léon Blum's government was overturned in a pattern fairly characteristic of the unstable Third Republic.

After the military defeat of May–June 1940, Pierre Mendès-France was one of those who believed that France should not surrender and that its government should be transferred to North Africa. He thus boarded the *Massilia* in June 1940 and was later arrested and brought back to France to be tried under the charge of desertion by the Vichy regime.[30] Managing to escape, he joined the French resistance in London in 1942. He was appointed, in 1945, Minister of Economic Affairs within the provisional government led by de Gaulle. By then, Pierre Mendès-France had sharpened his views on the role of the state in the economy and his main project was a national plan. Once again, however, his experience would be cut short and he had to resign following a disagreement with de Gaulle and the Finance Minister, René Pleven, on postwar financial reform.[31]

By the end of the Second World War, Pierre Mendès-France was an oddity on the French political scene. He seemed to herald a redefinition of the role of the politician. He was the prototype of the 'technocrat-politician', a political actor interested in economic issues and characterized by a capacity to understand them. He believed that state intervention in the economic sphere should increase significantly and that politicians ought to become technicians and experts, just like civil servants. Although his language and his references had unmistakable Keynesian overtones, the short periods when he was in charge revealed a somewhat rigid and bureaucratic understanding of interventionism. His definition of national planning, in particular, owed more to a French tradition than to Keynes' writings. The national plan launched by Mendès-France in 1944 and 1945, while Minister in charge of Economic Affairs within the Provisional Government, built on a project for a ten-year plan elaborated during the war by the administration of the Vichy regime.[32] The traditional French administrative apparatus was to be in charge of managing this national plan, which was much more rigid and constraining in its design than the future Monnet plan. Jean Monnet and Pierre Mendès-France, in fact, disagreed on national planning and its definition. Monnet disapproved of Mendès-France's interventionism and Mendès-France described Monnet as 'a champion of the free market', arguing that Monnet's plan 'did not provide enough direction and discipline'.[33]

In spite of this partial disagreement over the definition of national planning, Pierre Mendès-France was, by the end of the 1940s and the beginning of the 1950s, the French politician who came closest to sharing the ideals of modernizing civil servants. He exemplified the modernizing politician with a progressive view on economic and industrial issues. This image crystallized after 1953 when two journalists, Jean-Jacques Servan-Schreiber and Françoise Giroud created *L'Express*, a weekly publication, with the stated purpose of bringing Pierre Mendès-France to power. Jean-Jacques Servan-Schreiber, a bright young man aged 25, was fascinated by the USA and by the American model. He also saw the need for economic and industrial modernization in France. He believed, in particular, that the emergence of a new breed of economic leaders, professional managers, technicians, and experts, should be stimulated. The emergence of this new status group, the *cadres*, with a peculiar lifestyle and specific patterns of consumption, would be symbolic of French modernization (Boltanski, 1982). The editorial board of *L'Express* set out to turn Pierre Mendès-France into the political symbol of this new France, which was in fact still to emerge. With this objective in mind, it found references and models on the other side of the Atlantic. Pierre Mendès-France was called PMF in *L'Express*, just as Franklin Delano Roosevelt had been called FDR by Walter Lippmann.[34] The purpose was not so much to highlight the interventionist nature of Mendès-France's platform as to suggest dynamism, technical expertise, and efficiency, all qualities identified at the time as very American. In 1954, one year after the launching of *L'Express*, Pierre Mendès-France finally became Prime Minister but his government lasted only a few months. A constitutional regime breeding government instability was thus partly responsible for defeating the political objectives of *L'Express*. However, the magazine emerged, throughout the 1950s and 1960s, as the mouthpiece of the modernizing drive, helping to institutionalize a new mode of industrial organization and a new style of leadership.[35]

In short, the drive to transform and restructure the French economy and industry after 1945 originated from the public sphere and particularly from within the civil service and the high administration. A group of men, often young and able to stand back somewhat from their own country and its institutional and intellectual legacies, defined a modernization project that centered around large-scale industrialization. This project was undeniably inspired by the American model, but French modernizers were selective and did not retain all the features of the American system of industrial production. Modernizing agents in France were originally a fairly small group, but they managed to take over key institutional positions that would allow them to spread their ideas widely throughout the French administration and later on throughout civil society. Following an increase in the infrastructural power of the French state, some of those institutional positions would eventually provide, for those individuals who held them, significant leverage over the national economy and industry.

AMERICANS IN WEST GERMANY AND THE STRATEGY OF CO-OPTATION

In the western territories of Germany, in the meantime, American occupation authorities were finally agreeing on a program for economic recovery and industrial restructuring. Members of the American military government in Germany (OMGUS) were aware that military occupation of Germany was only temporary. They understood that reforms should be embedded within the local institutional context and taken over at some point by a local élite if they were to last beyond the occupation period. Members of OMGUS were thus soon looking to co-opt a German group that would be sympathetic to their program for the West German economy. Ludwig Erhard, future Minister of Economic Affairs and future Chancellor of the Federal Republic of Germany, was to be the focal point of this German group. The economic program he elaborated and set out to implement proved to be perfectly compatible with American projects for the West German economy and industry. Members of OMGUS thus succeeded in the end in creating the conditions for American-imposed economic and industrial reforms to become integrated within a West German modernization project.

American Military Government in Germany (OMGUS)

As already mentioned, changes on the geopolitical scene around 1947 had brought about, both within the American administration in Washington and within OMGUS, a new balance of power in favor of those groups who were calling for the rebuilding of a strong German economy and industry. On the American map, the western territories of Germany had become a central ally in the war against communism. The American military government thus set itself the task of restructuring the German economy and industry following the American model. Members of OMGUS saw it as their key duty to try and 'give the German people an opportunity to learn of the principles and advantages of free enterprise'.[36] They had secured, through victory, institutional power in West Germany and they were ready to make use of it for their ambitious project. They were naturally familiar with the model they had chosen and they considered it superior and highly efficient.

By American model, in fact, they meant an economy centering around an industry where large, mass-producing corporations competed on oligopolistic markets. From the perspective of OMGUS members, it seemed that two features of this model of reference were particularly important for the projected restructuring of the West German economy and industry. They pointed, first of all, to the large size of American production units and firms, allowing rationalization, economies of scale and scope, and mass production. They also pointed out the regulation of anti-competitive behavior through antitrust legislation, identifying such regulation as a necessary step towards a redefinition of the West German economy and industry. In the immediate postwar period, American occupation authorities were all but almighty in West Germany. The Americans were writing law and setting new legal boundaries. They made economic policy choices which were to redefine the rules of the West German economic game and alter the structural features of the national industry. As OMGUS members acknowledged, they could 'do anything [they] want[ed], within some limits, to the German economy'.[37] In that context, antitrust legislation was understood as much more than a mere regulator of anti-competitive behavior. It was defined as a powerful instrument for large-scale industrial restructuring.[38] Once the Decartelization and Deconcentration Branch had renounced its punitive objectives, it became the institutional basis for the transfer to West Germany of antitrust legislation.

During the first two years of its existence, the Decartelization and Deconcentration Branch had been dominated by former members of the Economic Warfare Unit from the American Justice Department. James Martin, who became chief of the branch at the end of 1945, but also Johnston Avery, Charles Baldwin, Creighton Coleman, and Alexander Sacks were all American lawyers who had hunted down, from 1942 to 1945, German-dominated international cartels, denouncing their role as 'weapons of economic warfare'. Not surprisingly, in 1945 they pushed for the dismantling of German and international cartels and advocated the promulgation of legislation that would prohibit their re-emergence. They also planned to break up the largest German firms through deconcentration measures. This double objective and its essentially punitive character were reflected in the wording of the decartelization and deconcentration law that was enacted in February 1947:

This law is enacted 1) to prevent Germany from endangering the safety of her neighbors and again constituting a threat to international peace, 2) to destroy Germany's economic potential to wage war, 3) to insure that measures taken for Germany's reconstruction are consistent with peaceful and democratic purposes, 4) to lay the groundwork for building a healthy and democratic German economy.[39]

Article I outlawed 'monopolistic or restrictive practices' *per se*, be they cartels, combines, or trusts and the law set a limit to the size of economic and industrial units.[40] During this early period, members of the Decartelization and Deconcentration Branch were in overt conflict with the Economics Division in OMGUS. General William Draper, then chief of the Economics Division, had been vice-president of Dillon, Read, and Company before the war, an investment firm active in Germany following the 1924 Dawes plan. Draper had recruited most of his staff within the New York business community and the Economics Division soon had the support of those American business leaders with prewar links to German industry. Members of the Economics Division argued that the punitive character of American policy was responsible for the slow pace of economic recovery in Germany. Criticisms bore mostly on the deconcentration aspect of the program and on the policy of breaking up larger units.[41] Once it had become clear that official American policy in West Germany was changing, members of the Economics Division denounced even more loudly than before what they believed were self-defeating measures, '[OMGUS] pull[ing] on the hand of a man lying on the floor and wonder[ing] why he did not get to his feet in spite of the fact that [it] had one foot on his neck'.[42]

The conflict within OMGUS climaxed with the resignation of James Martin and of most members of his team. General Draper's son-in-law, Phillips Hawkins, took over the Decartelization and Deconcentration Branch and proposed a significant redefinition of its agenda.[43] The program was revised and made more constructive. Identified as essentially punitive, deconcentration measures were difficult to justify particularly in the light of American experience. Decartelization, on the other hand, was easily replaced within a long-standing antitrust tradition going back to the Sherman Act and the Branch could therefore easily argue that it was sound policy.[44] The decartelization and deconcentration program thus became the basis of antitrust legislation in the American tradition—nothing more, nothing less. As mentioned earlier, the Ferguson Committee confirmed this evolution. In its revised version, the decartelization and deconcentration program gained wide support within the American administration and business community, as it did in fact across the wider American public. Moreover, the redefined program was perfectly compatible with the larger American project of creating a 'new economic world order', that found institutional expression in the Marshall plan, the World Trade Organization, or the Bretton Woods agreements.[45]

The revamped Decartelization and Deconcentration Branch was thus intent on transferring to West Germany the characteristically American fight against cartels and other restrictive practices which aimed at a limitation of competition. At the same time, however, the new team was not striving for 'the ideal of perfect competition [with] hundreds of firms competing in the production of each product'. Following the model set by American industry, it was advocating 'an oligopolistic structure policed by the vigorous enforcement of antitrust or anticartel laws'.[46] Only a few months earlier, General Clay had been praising another version of the 'American model', a Jeffersonian free market made up of competing small family firms.[47] In a pattern strikingly reminiscent of what had taken place at the turn of the twentieth century in the USA, two radically different definitions of the 'American model' had thus confronted each other within OMGUS for a period of time. In both cases, the champions of corporate capitalism had finally gained the upper hand and those victories were not unrelated. That the corporate type of capitalism had come to dominate American industry by the late 1940s naturally increased the likelihood that it would be chosen, in the end, as the model to be transferred to West Germany. By 1948, OMGUS members claimed that large corporations competing in oligopolistic markets were the surest way to combine, in West Germany, 'technical efficiency' and 'economies of scale' with competition.[48] The Decartelization and Deconcentration Branch had given up most of its deconcentration program because deconcentration measures seemed to create obstacles for such an evolution. Members of the American military government were undeniably paving the way for Marshall planners and their politics of productivity.

As military occupation was turning into a constructive undertaking, members of OMGUS were becoming convinced that their intervention would only have a lasting impact if German institutions and the Germans themselves were drawn into the process. So that reforms would not be dropped or policies reversed as soon as the occupation period ended, it appeared to be necessary to try and co-opt at least a small group of Germans. Making the right choice was naturally crucial. The co-opted German group should come as close as possible to accepting the American project for West Germany and endorsing American reforms. With this objective in mind, in 1947, the occupation authorities in the Bizone started transferring some of their responsibilities and powers in the economic field to a set of German institutions they had themselves created. In particular, the enforcement of the decartelization law was entrusted to Germans under close control of Allied decartelization and deconcentration institutions. Decartelization and deconcentration were declared reserved fields of the Allied High Commission in the occupation statute of 1949. In reality, however, most of the decartelization program had by then been turned over to the administration of the new Federal Republic of Germany.

Deconcentration, on the other hand, 'as distinguished from fair trade practices and combinations in restraint of trade' remained the sole responsibility of occupation authorities in their civilian form. In 1950, the Allied High Commission formally demanded that the German Federal Government start working on a national trade practice law that would in time replace law #56. The demand specified that future German legislation should 'forbid cartels and similar restrictive practices and all limitation of competition', building on principles put forth in Chapter V of the Havana Charter that outlined an International Trade Organization.[49] Transferring responsibilities to West German institutions and actors, American occupation authorities thus once again made a distinction between decartelization and deconcentration. The decartelization and deconcentration program was being embedded in the West German context after its redefinition as an antitrust or anticartel policy. The German trade practice law that was to replace law #56 would deal mostly with cartels, agreements, and restrictive trade practices, not at all with the size of German firms. Deconcentration measures were allowed to disappear in this manner from West German legislation.

While American occupation authorities understood the necessity of co-opting a group of Germans if they wanted their antitrust revolution to be successful and long-lasting in West Germany, they were also aware that antitrust in the American sense was entirely foreign to German legal and economic traditions. They would have to push the process along and they were careful, as a consequence, to retain at all times a power of last resort over decartelization and its enforcement.[50] Practices prohibited by law #56 were, for the most part, similar to those prohibited by the Sherman Act and those Germans responsible for enforcement had difficulties understanding what they were exactly. OMGUS thus launched a large-scale training and 'indoctrination' program, the ultimate purpose of which was to ensure proper enforcement of the anticartel act. An enforcement manual was prepared using American antitrust cases and it was widely circulated. The Department of Justice in Washington provided human resources and material. Through the Technical Assistance program, after 1950, the High Commission and the Marshall plan administration sent teams of German lawyers to the USA to study antitrust and enforcement policy in that country. Most importantly maybe, American lawyers and in particular Robert Bowie, General Counsel to the High Commission, closely followed the drafting of the West German anticartel act, intervening in the process whenever it seemed necessary.

Ludwig Erhard and the Freiburg School

The partial transfer of responsibilities, beginning in 1947, benefited West German actors who were sympathetic enough to the American project for their country. Instead of imposing mere puppets, American occupation authorities co-opted a small group of men who had, on their own, proposed and developed a program compatible with American objectives. The group around Ludwig Erhard had until that time been relatively powerless in Germany and the chances are that, without American support, this would have remained so in the postwar period. American occupation authorities placed the West Germans they were co-opting at key institutional locations. This proved to be an interesting strategy. In the medium to long term, West German actors gained a legitimacy of their own and economic reforms were, in time, appropriated locally.

The small group around Ludwig Erhard was mostly made up of economists and lawyers from the Freiburg school.[51] From the interwar years, there had been criticism in Germany of dominant economic thought and policy making. A handful of lawyers and economists, who would come to be known as the Freiburg school, claimed that there was a direct relationship between lack of economic freedom and competition on the one hand, and political authoritarianism on the other (Wallich, 1955; Nicholls, 1984; Peacock and Willgerodt, 1989). They were blaming collectivism, state intervention, cartelization and protectionism for the dire straits of the German economy in the 1930s and ultimately for the rise to power of the Nazi party.

Franz Böhm, Walter Eucken, and Hans Grossman-Doerth published the manifesto of the Freiburg school in 1936, in which they distanced themselves from dominant economic theory and practice in Germany while proposing at the same time a program for a revival of the German economy.[52] According to the authors, the German tradition of historicism was to blame for the shortcomings of economic theory and practice in that country. Most German lawyers and economists, working within the tradition of historicism, were not even trying to shape legal and economic systems anymore: economic and legal conditions reflecting, in the historicist tradition, the spirit of the time, they could not and should not be manipulated. According to members of the Freiburg school, however, German lawyers and economists had in reality cleared the way for private and vested interests to assert themselves on the pretence that historical developments were driving legal and economic practice. In a radical departure from dominant thinking, members of the Freiburg school thus called for a constructive involvement of lawyers and economists who alone, they argued, could have a relatively objective grasp of legal and economic issues as long as they remained independent of private interests.

Their own 'objective and scientific' approach led them to claim that free markets and a competitive economy were necessary conditions for political democracy. Since history had shown, in Germany, that a *laissez faire* policy brought about collusion of private interests and thus a curtailment of competition, they believed that free markets had to be created and protected by enlightened political authorities.[53] The competitive economy as envisioned by members of the Freiburg school had undeniably neoclassical features. German neo-liberals had a romantic vision of a multitude of productive units, each one more or less corresponding to a private household. Their fight for economic freedom was also a fight for individual freedom and against prole-tarianization (Peacock and Willgerodt, 1989; Berghahn, 1984). Throughout the Nazi period, the Freiburg school was one of the main centers of German intellectual resistance. Franz Böhm, a lawyer, was dismissed in 1938 for political reasons from his joint appointment at the Universities of Freiburg and Jena. Wilhelm Röpke, Professor of Economics at the University of Marburg was also dismissed after the Nazis came to power and ultimately had to leave the country. A leading theorist of the school, Walter Eucken was an exception, managing to keep, until his death in 1950, his appointment as Professor of Economics at the University of Freiburg.[54]

Himself an economist, Ludwig Erhard had not been a member of the Freiburg school during the 1930s and early 1940s despite undeniable intellectual proxi-mity. Ludwig Erhard was convinced that, ultimately, the most efficient social policy was a healthy market and a truly competitive environment. Competition indeed meant higher productivity, lower prices, and better living standards. The 'social market economy' he wanted to create in West Germany was, according to him, 'the economic basis for a democratic form of government, which regards human freedom as an inalienable right'. This social market economy centered around 'the principle of freedom and liberalism' and the state had a 'duty to see to it that this basic right [was] not made inoperative by private collective agreements and obligations'.[55] Similarities between Ludwig Erhard's social market economy and the program of the Freiburg school have often been emphasized to the point of blurring differences of significant consequence. In particular, the peculiarity of Ludwig Erhard's position with respect to competi-tion and economic concentration deserves to be mentioned here.[56]

From 1948, when American occupation authorities placed him in control of the new German economic council (Wirtschaftsrat des Vereigniten Wirtschaftsgebiet), Ludwig Erhard strove to create a competitive economic environment in West Germany. His objective, however, was not the romantic ideal of perfect competition and individual or family ownership. He signifi-cantly differed in that from members of the Freiburg school. As a matter of fact, Ludwig Erhard was highly sympathetic to the American project for Germany as it came to be redefined in 1947 and 1948. His arguments in favor of competition often de-emphasized the ultimate neo-liberal aim of individual freedom to the benefit of growth, efficiency, and productivity.[57] Competition, according to him, should lead to an increase in production and productivity levels. He identified large-scale industrial units as allowing greater efficiency, increases in production and productivity, and ultimately mass consumption, which he clearly advocated.[58] Ludwig Erhard envisioned for West Germany an economic and industrial system where mass production and mass consumption would combine with competition. References to the American model were obvious even when he had to pretend that this was pure coincidence. He acknowledged that 'it [was] a very similar kind of thinking and feeling which ha[d] led the American economy to such obvious successes, and which, besides considerable detailed research, ha[d] strengthened [his] conviction about the damaging effects of limitations of competition'.[59]

Erhard was undeniably an 'American invention' as he once put it himself (Berghahn, 1984; Nicholls, 1984). Before the occupation of Germany by Allied forces, Ludwig Erhard and members of the Freiburg school had been virtual outcasts in their own country, both intellectually and institutionally (Wallich, 1955; Nicholls, 1984; Peacock and Willgerodt, 1989). They were propelled to the forefront and placed in positions of power by American occupation authorities essentially because of the relatively close fit between their program and the American project for the West German economy.[60] In 1946, the American military government appointed Ludwig Erhard Minister of Economic Affairs in his home state of Bavaria. After the merging of the British and American zones of occupation in 1947, a number of new German institutions were created. In particular, a German economic council (Wirtschaftsrat des Vereigniten Wirtschaftsgebiets) was granted some responsibility over Bizonal economic issues. The chairman, who was to act as a Minister of Economic Affairs with limited powers, was a member of the council and was to be elected by his peers. This election had been defined by the occupying powers as a political process, a first step towards democracy and it was to reflect the balance of power between German parties. Johannes Semler, a member of the Bavarian christian democratic party (CSU) was elected in July 1947 and became the first chairman of the German economic council. His public speeches, highly critical of American military government, and some of his actions as chairman soon attracted a lot of attention. In January 1948, members of the American military government decided unilaterally to dismiss him. In a process that was not quite democratic this time, they imposed Ludwig Erhard in his place (Peterson, 1977). This was the beginning, for Ludwig Erhard, of a long career, first as Minister of Economic Affairs until 1963 and from 1963 to 1966 as Chancellor of the Federal Republic of Germany. Throughout this career, he consistently received the full support of the American government and administration whether in West Germany or in Washington (Van der Pijl, 1984). As soon as he was in charge, Ludwig Erhard surrounded himself with members of the Freiburg school. In January 1948, he created an academic think-tank to advise the German economic council, most members of which were neo-liberal economists or lawyers: Böhm, Eucken, and Müller-Armack were all members. Throughout the 1950s, Franz Böhm was closely involved in the crafting of the German anticartel act while Alfred Müller-Armack was in charge of economic policy, after 1952, in the Federal Ministry of Economic Affairs.

In the West German case, economic and industrial restructuring were thus initiated by American occupation authorities. Choosing a smart strategy, the Americans progressively granted a carefully selected group of Germans increasing responsibilities in the economic and industrial fields. Such co-optation proved to be a success. The group around Ludwig Erhard, future

Minister of Economic Affairs in the new Federal Republic, worked towards a set of objectives that closely fitted American projects for the West German economy and industry. A binational, modernizing network had thus been institutionalized. Both elements of this network would work, throughout the years, in close synergy and in the same direction. Structural reforms, initially launched by American occupation authorities, were lastingly embedded in the West German context and most came to be appropriated by a small group of locals who were to gain, through time, their own legitimacy.

AMERICAN MARSHALL PLANNERS AND THE MISSIONARY SPIRIT

By the late 1940s, therefore, both in France and in West Germany, small groups of nationals were getting ready to launch or to take over restructuring programs of considerable scope. The American system of industrial production was the model of reference in both cases and a dense web of relationships linked those European groups to a number of Americans, in particular within the federal administration. The American government, in the meantime, was in the process of institutionalizing its intervention in foreign economic affairs. Through the launching of the Marshall plan and the creation of a special administrative machinery in charge of running it, the American administration significantly increased its capacity to have a direct impact on Western European economies and industries.

The European Recovery Program (ERP) or Marshall plan began officially in April 1948, less than a year after Secretary of State George Marshall had delivered his memorable Harvard speech. The American Congress adopted the Foreign Assistance Act, appropriated funds for Marshall assistance and created an Economic Cooperation Administration (ECA) responsible for running the program of assistance. ECA headquarters were located in Washington and the administration had local offices or national Missions in each country receiving Marshall assistance. Those countries participating in the Marshall scheme signed bilateral treaties with the USA, but cooperation at a European level was a condition of assistance. Sixteen Western European countries were to work together to draw common recovery plans and to divide up American aid, within the framework of the Organization for European Economic Cooperation (OEEC). The ECA was soon much more than an administrative machinery in charge of managing and controlling the flow of aid. It turned out that American Marshall planners had ambitious visions for Europe and the ECA consequently became an institution with a mission.

Structures and Men: Legacies from a Recent Past

The American Congress had demanded that the ECA be a relatively independent institution and it had refused to allow the new agency to be integrated within the State Department. The Republican Senator, Arthur Vandenberg, was particularly adamant that the administration of foreign assistance should be treated as a business undertaking and not as a federal program. He called, as a consequence, for the participation of the American business community and insisted 'that the European Recovery Program administrator shall come from the outside business world with strong industrial credentials and not via the State Department'.[61] The new institution was thus created outside traditional federal and administrative departments.

The ECA was a planning agency, the main objective of which was to manage aid allocation and to control its use. This meant reconciling, in the most efficient way possible, complex and often competing needs with limited resources. Lessons in flexible planning dating back to the New Deal and to the war therefore proved to be quite useful. In fact, the very structure of the ECA was apparently modeled after the structure of American planning boards from the New Deal or war periods. The central office in Washington was a coordinating agency located on the fringe of the federal administration. Since it could, whenever necessary, cooperate with various federal agencies and draw on their resources, it remained relatively modest in size (Price, 1955: 233). The decentralization of the ECA machinery, on the other hand, meant more flexibility, greater responsibility, and rapidity of action for each Mission at the national level. In the end, the administrator in Washington had to approve all important decisions but national Missions came to play a central role, managing the aid program on a daily basis and elaborating country programs together with local authorities.

The tripartite character of the ECA was another legacy from the New Deal and war periods. The agency brought together labor, business, and government representatives. Each national Mission had labor advisers who generally belonged to the major American trade unions, the American Federation of Labor (AFL) or the Congress of Industrial Organization (CIO). Paul Hoffman, chief administrator of the ECA in Washington, worked with a team of labor advisers headed by Bert Jewell from the AFL and Clinton Golden from the CIO (Carew, 1987; Wall, 1991). Golden had worked at Harvard for a while with Elton Mayo, a founding figure of the Human Relations school. During the war, he had been vice-president of the War Production Board. He was generally convinced that higher productivity meant better living standards for workers and was bound to have a positive impact on industrial relations. Most labor advisers to the ECA shared this belief and therefore gave their full support to the 'politics of productivity' of the administration.[62] In fact, the role of American labor representatives proved particularly significant in the attempt to co-opt local work forces. All members of the ECA were convinced that the Marshall project required the cooperation of European labor. And it appeared that trade unions were the most likely of American actors to have some influence on European workers.

While the role of labor advisers was undeniably significant, in the end business representatives all but controlled the ECA.[63] Most of the businessmen who joined the ECA already had some experience at tripartite cooperation and national planning. Many had been members of the Committee for Economic Development (CED).[64] The CED had been created in 1942 by a group of progressive businessmen together with the American Secretary of Commerce, Jesse Jones. Paul Hoffman, Chairman of the Studebaker Corporation, William Benton from the advertising firm of Benton and Bowles, and Marion Folsom, treasurer of Eastman Kodak Company, had all been, amongst others, founding members. The agenda of the CED was to involve the American business community in national planning for the postwar period and to determine the conditions necessary to preserve full employment.

The CED prided itself on being a technical and not a political committee, using and incorporating expert advice and rejecting ideologically tainted solutions (Schrieftgiesser, 1967; Jones, 1972; Collins, 1981). The group of progressive businessmen who made up the CED had come to terms with the New Deal and with the Keynesian revolution and they accepted a degree of government intervention in the economy. They believed that high levels of employment were necessary after the war to ensure economic and social stability. According to them, government had a significant role to play and it could use fiscal or monetary policies, and if necessary budget deficits, to keep employment levels high. Members of the CED believed that a smooth transition into the postwar economy demanded collaboration between government and business in the context of a flexible and pragmatic national plan. In 1948, American progressive businessmen and in particular members of the CED took over the ECA. Paul Hoffman became chief administrator and drew upon the CED to staff the new agency. Averell Harriman, partner in the Wall Street firm of Brown Brothers, Harriman, became the ECA Special Representative to Europe, located in Paris.[65] William Foster, Harriman's deputy, had been president of a steel products company and a member of the CED. Howard Bruce, deputy administrator in Washington had been director and board member of several large business firms. The man who headed the French Mission, David Bruce, was a Baltimore businessman. James Zellerbach, in Italy, had been board chairman of the Crown Zellerbach Corporation and also member of the CED.[66]

Through its control of the ECA, the progressive element of the American business community had acquired a capacity to influence foreign economic policy making much beyond what its size as a group would have predicted. In reality, only a very small minority of American businessmen shared the values embodied by the CED. A large share of the American business community, represented by the National Association of Manufacturers (NAM) or by the Chamber of Commerce, defended more classical free market and *laissez faire* values. The position of the CED on tax issues, budget deficits, or government intervention was considered, in those business circles, pure heresy. After the exceptional circumstances of the war, this more conservative majority rapidly reasserted its predominance over the national economy.[67] In the meantime, progressive businessmen were joining Keynesian economists and civil servants in the new foreign challenge. Together with productivist labor representatives, they rushed to take over the only niche that remained available to them. This can explain why a return to more conservative economic policy making on the American national scene coincided after the Second World War with American proselytism in foreign countries in favour of Keynesian economics, reflationary measures, planning, and limited government intervention.

The Missionary Spirit

From the very beginning, the ECA was much more than an administration for the allocation and control of foreign assistance. It was an agency with a mission, and a particularly ambitious one. The ultimate objective of Marshall planners was to bring about a radical structural transformation of European economies and industries and to redefine trade patterns on the old continent, using the American economic space as the model of reference.[68] Running an assistance program of that scale gave Marshall planners significant leverage, which they intended to use towards their objective. The transfer of American structural arrangements, they believed, would in the long run bring prosperity, stability, and peace to the western parts of the European continent and strengthen the foundations of an Atlantic community that essentially defined itself in opposition to the communist world. American Marshall planners saw it as their mission to transfer to Europe the 'miracle of mass production'.[69] According to them, however, mass production was only possible in sizeable markets. Corporatist traditions, tariffs, quotas, or agreements were described as so many obstacles in Europe, preventing local industries from taking full advantage of modern techniques of large-scale, low cost production that had made American industry a success. And indeed, American Marshall planners launched a fight against economic nationalism, protectionism, and restrictive trade practices. They believed that national economic borders had to be redefined, at least in part, so that mass-produced goods could move freely and increasingly cheaply throughout Western Europe.

Creating the conditions for mass production and freer trade had significant implications not only for the structure of national economies and industries but also for social and political frameworks in Western Europe. As a matter of fact, American Marshall planners were advocating changes in the ways of life and in the values of citizens across Western Europe. Mass production required a radical redefinition of European techniques and modes of production, through the adoption in particular of the assembly line and of scientific management methods. It also meant the transformation of physical and ownership structures characteristic of Western European capitalism. Indeed, large-scale companies and professional management appeared more conducive to production in large batches, at least they did if the American model was the reference. The ECA project for Western Europe was therefore bound to lead to a decoupling between ownership and control and ultimately to a managerial revolution. At the same time, the 'miracle of mass production' could only operate if conditions for mass consumption were also being created. Members of the ECA tended to believe that trade barriers should be lifted within Western Europe, allowing the emergence of a 'market big enough to justify modern methods of cheap production for mass consumption'.[70] In the late 1940s, economic cooperation on a European level was in fact essentially an American-sponsored idea. Marshall planners championed union in Europe, with the objective of bringing about a 'wide, free, competitive market to lower costs, to increase efficiency and to raise the standards of living'.[71] In the end, competition, free trade, and the adoption of mass-production techniques were all bound to have a positive impact on productivity. In turn, higher levels of productivity were presented as effective means of enlarging the economic pie, which could then be redistributed with all actors standing to benefit. Higher productivity, however, did not seem possible without the collaboration of at least a part of Western European labor. This implied a redefinition of industrial relations in Western Europe and a toning down of class conflicts. With this last objective in mind, American Marshall planners identified the findings of the Human Relations school as being particularly useful. All in all, mass production, higher levels of productivity, and the creation of a competitive environment at the European level were the main dimensions of the program for Western Europe as defined by the ECA.

Methods and Strategies

In his famous speech of June 5, 1947, Secretary of State George Marshall explained that 'it would be neither fitting nor efficacious for (the American) government to undertake to draw up unilaterally a program designed to place Europe on its feet economically'. 'The initiative', he went on, '[had to] come from Europe' and Europeans themselves should in part shape the program of assistance.[72] Each country participating in the Marshall scheme had first of all to assess its own needs and to sort out its own priorities. Then, within the framework of the CEEC—and after 1948 of the OEEC—European countries should discuss national plans as a group before making a common and global proposition for aid allocation.

Although real, European initiative nevertheless remained subject to American scrutiny and approval. According to the American lawyer, George Ball, the first version of the allocation plan drawn up by Europeans within the CEEC did not fit what was expected in Washington. The European proposal was perceived as being a much too expensive and mostly uncoordinated shopping list, not a global plan for European recovery. The Europeans were sent back to work.[73] Throughout the years, the ECA would favor this type of strategy. Advocating collaboration with local actors, the American agency still always retained powerful means of control and secured the possibility of last resort intervention.

The decentralized structure of the ECA favored direct contact with national actors. Each country receiving Marshall funds had had to create, under American pressure, an agency responsible for monitoring relationships with the ECA. In France, the official belt transmitter was the SGCI (Secrétariat Général du Comité Interministériel pour les Questions de Coopération Economique Européenne) headed by Pierre-Paul Schweitzer.[74] In the western territories of Germany, a committee was created in March 1948 to handle relationships between Bizonal institutions and the administration of the ECA.[75] After the creation of the Federal Republic of Germany in September 1949, this role was taken over by the Bundesministerium für den Marshallplan, under the responsibility of Franz Blücher.

For each project they undertook, ECA national Missions naturally worked through these official contacts. They also attempted to identify other local actors who might be likely to support or to help implement each particular project. When they could not find local institutional support, members of the ECA did not hesitate to prompt the creation of new institutions. When at the end of 1948, for example, the ECA launched the technical assistance program, it demanded that each participating country create specific institutions responsible for monitoring the productivity effort. Those institutions, it was hoped, would give national momentum to a program which had clear American origins. When the ECA decided in 1949 that the agricultural sector in France should be made more dynamic and more productive, the chief of the Paris Mission, Barry Bingham, suggested that the best strategy might indeed be to 'find or create through persuasion influential groups in the French government who want to see instituted the type of dynamic agricultural program we have in mind and of working with them towards its accomplishment'.[76] Through those national institutions created for that very purpose, American Marshall planners could thus have a direct influence on any national decision relating to the Marshall plan. Those were official channels through which they could orient and control the use of counterpart funds, help prepare demands for appropriations which had to be presented to Congress every year, and push for the participation of European countries in OEEC work.

Official channels, however, were not always the most efficient. American Marshall planners sometimes preferred to work through other national actors or institutions they particularly trusted and knew to be highly sympathetic to their projects. The French planning board, Jean Monnet's Commissariat Général du Plan, was one such institution. As already documented, the French planning board and the ECA had common structural features and they drew from the same ideological tradition. There was a particularly good fit between both institutions and Jean Monnet was a close personal friend of most high ranking Marshall planners, whom he had met during his years in Washington.

Members of the ECA administration therefore found it much easier to communicate and collaborate with members of the planning board than with French politicians or for that matter French businessmen.[77] From the very beginning, the ECA gave considerable support to the French planning board and its investment program. This support found concrete expression in the direct allocation of a large share of Marshall assistance to the French plan. A direct flow of this nature shielded the French investment program not only from disturbances such as inflation or increasing budget deficits but also from political instability on the national scene. In addition, the existence in France of a planning board they trusted and of an investment plan they supported allowed members of the ECA to relax, to a certain extent, their control over the use of Marshall funds in that country as they themselves acknowledged:

You might indicate to the French that in several other participating countries, ECA's interest in investment projects has gone to extent of approving releases of funds only on basis of detailed examination of specific projects involved. Existence of Monnet plan in France makes such procedure less necessary, but ECA will continue to elicit cooperation of French in specific cases where it feels some change in investment plans is desirable.[78]

The French were fortunate that their own decisions and choices were perfectly compatible with American projects, at least most of the time. The ECA administration therefore rarely had to resort to strategies of coercion. In fact, French planners and modernizing civil servants sometimes used this situation of dependence to put pressure on French politicians. Acting in collusion with members of the ECA, they argued that certain policies might put an end to American assistance and they warned of the dangerous consequences for the French polity and economy of an American disengagement.[79]

In the Federal Republic of Germany, on the other hand, Americans were not merely friendly providers of funds. The USA had won a war that had led to German collapse and they were a powerful occupying power. The American impact on institutions and economic policy making could therefore be even more direct in Germany than in France. Starting in 1948, however, the Americans attempted to grant more responsibilities to the Germans, trying to work with them rather than systematically coerce them into reform. The ECA administration in Germany, merged with the High Commission, thus set out to collaborate with selected German actors and institutions. While the Federal Ministry for the Marshall Plan was their official German interlocutor, members of the ECA in fact preferred to work directly with the Federal Minister of Economic Affairs, Ludwig Erhard, and members of his team, with whom they had privileged relationships.

Through the launching of the Marshall plan and the creation of an apparatus for managing it, a progressive American élite thus institutionalized, in the late 1940s, its collaboration with a number of Western European actors on economic and industrial issues. The common ambitious objective of this cross-national network was to foster the emergence, in Western Europe, of conditions perceived to have been at the origin of American industrial success and wealth. The American side of the network pertained to a tradition of pragmatic Keynesianism that had roots in the New Deal and war periods. This American group was genuinely convinced that the American system of industrial production, in its corporate version, was a most efficient and superior model. It saw its mission as spreading around the 'free' world the seeds of the American experience, the 'miracle of mass production'. Convinced that reforms and transformations would not survive a period of direct dependence if they were forced onto European countries, they fostered collaboration with a small number of carefully selected actors and institutions in each of those countries. American Marshall planners also chose co-optation as a strategy in part to avoid too direct and visible an involvement in the internal affairs of foreign countries.

ITALY: THE WEAK POINT OF THE CROSS-NATIONAL NETWORK

In Italy, the cross-national modernizing network broke down. Members of the ECA failed to identify and co-opt, on the Italian national scene, actors with whom they could collaborate to bring about a radical transformation of economic and industrial structures. Moreover, Italy never represented for the USA, in its confrontation with the USSR, as significant a stake as France or West Germany. A systematic and large-scale involvement in Italian affairs therefore appeared less crucial to the American administration. From the end of the Second World War and particularly after March 1947, the main objective of the USA in Italy was essentially to weaken the Italian communist movement. The threat of a communist takeover and of political destabilization was the prime motive behind American bouts of financial generosity towards Italy (Hughes, 1965; De Cecco, 1972; Miller, 1986; Harper, 1986). By the spring of 1947, unsystematic and fragmented American efforts had brought little relief to a battered and depressed Italian economy. At the same time, it appeared increasingly obvious that the American Congress was unlikely to give financial assistance to those countries where communist parties remained involved in governmental coalitions. Under strong American pressure, the Italian Prime Minister, Alcide de Gasperi, thus formed a new government at the end of May, leaving out communists and left-wing socialists. The American Ambassador to Italy, James Dunn, also urged de Gasperi to take appropriate measures for a stabilization of the economic and financial situation. Self-help, he indicated, would be a key condition for obtaining American aid (Harper, 1986: 132–4).

The new Italian government put together by Alcide de Gasperi at the end of May 1947 was dominated by members of the Christian Democratic party

(Democrazia Cristiana). By 1947, the US government had come to support the Christian Democratic party as the only alternative it could identify in Italy to communism or fascism. This party was heir to the prewar Popolari, the people's party led by Don Sturzo. By the end of the war, the Christian Democratic party brought together all those Italians wary of extremism and fearful, in particular, of communism. It thus emerged as a patchwork of many different political trends, united essentially around a preference for the West in the geopolitical confrontation that was dividing the world. The middle classes were dominant in the electorate of the Christian Democratic party, with a prominent group of craftsmen, shopkeepers, and small business entrepreneurs.

The new Italian government also counted, in addition to members of the Christian Democratic party, a few apolitical experts and technicians. Alcide de Gasperi was an astute politician, but he was not an expert on economic issues. After driving the communists and left-wing socialists out of the governmental coalition, as he had understood was the wish in Washington, he brought in a group of economists and experts to deal with the second American requirement. Prominent Italian economists and experts—'liberal' in the European sense of *laissez faire* advocates—were given the responsibility of improving the economic and financial situation of the country so that it would be ready to receive American assistance. Luigi Einaudi was appointed Vice-Prime Minister and Minister of the Budget; Menichella became Governor of the Bank of Italy; Gustavo del Vecchio and Giuseppe Pella shared the Ministry of Finance and the Treasury while Cesare Merzagora became Minister of Trade.[80]

Until 1943, Italian economic policy making had been characterized by mercantilism, protectionism, and significant state intervention. The creation of a united Italian Kingdom in 1861 had brought to power men with high ambitions for the new country. Even before fascism, a modernization of the Italian economy had been attempted from the top down, through authoritarian and coercive means. This period of state intervention and mercantilism had led, in reaction, to the emergence of a small group of Italian economists preaching a pure and orthodox version of the *laissez faire* doctrine.[81] Although marginal on the Italian national scene, both before and during the war, their reputation was firmly established in academic circles worldwide. For the first time, in 1947, this group gained institutional power after de Gasperi and the Christian Democratic party had identified them as experts who could handle American demands for economic and financial stabilization in Italy.

The similarities between Italy and Germany are undeniable with respect both to the emergence of a small group of liberal critics and to their somewhat surprising arrival in positions of power. The Italian liberal school, though, was much more orthodox and systematic in its defense of *laissez faire* than the Freiburg school and Italian experts proposed a drastic stabilization program. In the beginning, Washington gave its full support to a series of harsh measures with the triple objective of curbing inflation, creating a sound currency, and balancing the budget. Those measures, however, rapidly took their toll on production levels and brought a worsening economic depression and increasing unemployment. A clash between the Italian government and members of the ECA became unavoidable. Italian liberal experts wanted to continue with the stabilization program while members of the American administration were starting to advocate reflationary measures. It soon became obvious that members of the ECA did not give priority to financial and economic stabilization. They had supported the Italian program as being necessary to some extent but this program, they believed, should only be a temporary first step, creating the right conditions for future economic growth and ultimately for the 'politics of productivity'. Italian liberal economists, on the other hand, apparently considered their economic and financial stabilization program as an end in itself. They lacked a vision for Italy and often repeated that 'the age when Italy [had been] a Great Power was over' (Vigezzi, 1986).

From 1948, the ECA country Mission in Italy was headed by James Zellerbach. Zellerbach had been board chairman of the Crown Zellerbach Corporation and a prominent member, during the war, of the Committee for Economic Development (CED). He had a project for Italy that was similar to ECA projects for the rest of Western Europe. The transformation of Italy towards a mass-producing, mass-consuming society would, according to him, quell political conflicts and rule out the possibility of communist takeover. This transformation, however, would require the creation of large firms in most industrial sectors and necessitate a significant increase in productivity levels.[82] The ECA Mission in Italy was ready to elaborate and to help implement programs that would increase production capacities and bring about the modernization and restructuring of Italian industry. Members of the ECA Mission in Italy, in fact, pointed to what was being done in France. Marshall aid should be used to invest in a few key industries that would have, in turn, a multiplier effect on the rest of the economy. But Keynesian productivists in the ECA did not find any collaborators sympathetic to their project on the Italian political and technocratic scene.[83] Members of the ECA Mission in Rome and those men in positions of institutional power in Italy seemed to be separated by an abyss. Communication was impossible most of the time and both groups generally worked at counter purposes.

After the national elections of 1948 and the adoption of a new constitution, de Gasperi reshuffled his government. The coalition led by the Christian Democratic party had won a clear victory and Luigi Einaudi became the first President of the new Republic. On the whole, Italian economic policy did not change. The conflict between Keynesian productivists from the ECA and orthodox champions of a *laissez faire* economic policy in the Italian administration only became more acute. At that point, the main source of disagreement was the use that should be made of Lira counterpart funds. Italians never took full advantage of this original device and when they did, it was essentially to decrease budget deficits and rarely to finance productive investments. The ECA, on the other hand, wanted all European countries to use those funds for large-scale capital investment and industrial restructuring, on the model of what was being done in France.[84]

The cross-national modernizing network thus broke down in Italy. The Italian group co-opted by the USA after the war—selected as the only alternative to communism and fascism—did not live up to expectations. State holdings, such as the IRI or ENI (Ente Nazionale Idrocarburi), inherited from the fascist years, could have been used as powerful tools in a state-led strategy of economic and industrial modernization. There was, moreover, a tradition of modernizing Italian technocrats dating back to the period of national unification. After the end of the Second World War, a few Italian modernizers could still be found but mostly amongst those businessmen and managers running the few large industrial units. Sometimes extremely powerful, their impact on the Italian economy as a whole was nevertheless limited. Enrico Mattei at the head of ENI or Oscar Sinigaglia, who was leading IRI's Finsider (the steel sector of the state holding) were relatively sympathetic to the Keynesian and productivist values characteristic of the ECA and they often developed direct contacts with members of the Italian Mission or with American business leaders. They never gained control, however, of those key state institutions that could have allowed them to have an impact on the Italian economy and industry as a whole. In the Italian case, the Americans had clearly failed in their strategy of co-optation.

By the late 1940s, a cross-national modernizing network was thus clearly in place both in France and in West Germany, while it had failed to emerge in Italy. A complex web of institutional and individual relationships had been spun between Keynesian productivists in the American administration and French or West German modernizers in key positions of power in their own countries. In Italy, on the other hand, the national administrative or governmental élite and representatives from the Marshall plan administration often worked at counter purposes. In France and West Germany, the emergence of such a cross-national modernizing network significantly increased the likelihood that a large-scale, cross-national transfer process would be launched and successfully implemented. In Italy, the absence of such a network further reduced the chance that such a process would even be considered. At the same time, however, significant differences between France and West Germany, particularly with respect to the degree of geopolitical dependence or to the nature of cross-national institutional channels, would account for the predominance in each of those two countries of different types of transfer mechanisms and patterns of implementation.

Notes

1. Commencement address at Washington University, Missouri, June 7, 1949. Hoffman had been appointed administrator of the ECA in 1948.

2. A detailed account of the origins of the French plan can be found in Djelic (1996). On Monnet, see his memoirs and two recent biographies, Duchêne (1994) and Roussel (1996).

3. A direct heir to prewar Keynesian boards, the War Production Board was responsible for the coordination and optimization, through planning, of American war production. For more on the Combined Production and Resources Board, see Monnet Foundation, AME (ii. 14/7) and interview with Robert Nathan (1981).

4. The list of Monnet's professional acquaintances and personal friends in the USA reads like a Who's Who. It includes many of the men, who, at the articulation of business and government, held after the war key positions in the American administration and in particular within the Marshall plan apparatus: Paul Hoffman, Milton Katz, Averell Harriman, and also Dean Acheson and John McCloy.

5. See Kaspi (1971), Roussel (1996), and Monnet Foundation, AME (iii). Monnet was sent to Algiers in 1943 by the Americans, officially to coordinate the supply effort for troops in North Africa. In reality, the key part of his mission, kept secret at the time, was to rally French forces, divided by the leadership fight between Giraud and de Gaulle.

6. George Ball (1981), interview for the Monnet Foundation. David Silberman and Sid Lerner were other American experts employed by the CFA.

7. 'Eugen Rostow in Yale to Monnet in Washington, July 30, 1945.' Monnet Foundation, AME (iv. 56/2/27).

8. Robert Nathan, interview for the Monnet Foundation (1981). In April 1946, Monnet introduced Nathan to members of the planning board in the following way: 'Nathan can give you the benefit of his experience with the War Production Board, when at the beginning of 1942, the US faced the same problems as we do in connection with the carrying out of the Victory program.' Monnet Foundation, AME (iv. 65/7/38).

9. AN-80AJ/1 for Monnet's December memorandum and de Gaulle's January directives.

10. More traditional understandings of French postwar planning have tended either to replace it within a well-entrenched French tradition (Saint Jean, 1947; Mioche, 1981, 1987) or to see it as pragmatic and *ad hoc* tinkering (Beigel, 1947; Margairaz, 1982; Bloch-Lainé and Bouvier, 1986; Bossuat, 1992).

11. For more on the American interpretation of Keynesian thought, see Sweezy (1972), Jones (1972), Skocpol and Weir (1985), Salant (1989).

12. Monnet Foundation, AME (ii. 14/5/4) and AME (ii. 16/12/17).

13. Monnet (1976: 336). Monnet had been ready to resign if this was not granted. An outsider to the French administration, he did not trust it as an agent of change: 'I respect French administration but it appeared obvious that it could never elaborate a plan to deeply transform the country.'

14. Apparently, Robert Nathan discovered Pierre Uri at the ISEA in 1946 and brought him over to the planning board (Roussel, 1996: 448).

15. See Fourquet (1980), Rosanvallon (1989). Keynesian ideas came to France through practitioners and technocrats before being adopted by professional economists. The ISEA and François Perroux worked in close collaboration with Simon Kutznets and the National Bureau for Economic Research to set up a French version of national accounting.

16. Commissariat Général du Plan (1946). In this report on the French plan, the

American economy is clearly identified as the model for the modernization of French structures.

17. 'The French Investment Program: a Defense of the Monnet Plan, November 1951', AN-80AJ/7. Lubell went on: 'When planning the programs for investments in the non-nationalized sectors of French industry, modernization commissions had clearly in mind that one of the express purposes of the Monnet plan was to foster concentration and thereby rationalization of French industry.'

18. 'Gouvernement Provisoire de la République—Instructions à Monsieur le Commissaire Général du Plan, 10 janvier 1946', AN-80AJ/1. The concept of productivity was unknown in France before 1945 and there was no French word for it. The concept was imported and the word *productivité* coined by the planning board as a direct transcription of the American word.

19. See in particular 'Eugen Rostow, Letter to Monnet, July 30, 1945.' Monnet Foundation, AME (iv. 56/2/27).

20. Those institutions were necessary tools for a Keynesian state and the planning board had been instrumental in creating them. INSEE stood for Institut National de la Statistique et des Etudes Economiques and SEEF for Service des Etudes Economiques et Financières.

21. See Fourquet (1980: 88–9). For more on relationships between the French Treasury and the planning board, see also Bloch-Lainé (1976), Bloch-Lainé and Bouvier (1986).

22. Taking over a number of key institutional advanced posts in order to gain ground within French administration was a conscious strategy, as a debate thirty years later between those early modernizers showed quite clearly (Fourquet, 1980).

23. See Journal Officiel (June 22–23, 1945). In particular, the speech by Jules Jeanneney, minister in the provisional government in charge of the project for the creation of a civil service school and the speech by André Philip, socialist representative.

24. This was a major achievement of Bloch-Lainé and his team (Fourquet 1980: 192). Taking over the ENA allowed them to train and shape to their own will the next generation of civil servants, without having to deal directly with the old administrative élite. This takeover would facilitate the diffusion of a modernizing spirit and of the technical tools required by the modernization project.

25. Kesler (1964, 1985). Throughout the postwar period, the impact of ENA was not limited to the administration. After the nationalizations of 1945, ENA students came to hold positions of power within the state sector. They were also and still are to be found in a number of large private firms. In 1973, 43 per cent of the chairmen of the 100 largest French firms had been civil servants at some point (Bauer, 1985).

26. Simon Nora, then economist in the national balance-sheet commission (SEEF), would claim thirty years later: 'To a large extent, we bred and trained the next generation of private leaders and managers'. Fourquet (1980: 181).

27. For the difference between 'infrastructural' and 'despotic' power of the state, see Mann (1986). On the nationalization program, see Michel and Mirkine-Guetzevitch (1954).

28. For more on Mendès-France, see Lacouture (1981), Bédarida and Rioux (1985).

29. Georges Boris had published a book on the New Deal, *La Révolution Roosevelt*, in 1933. The economic program proposed by Mendès-France was in the end very cautious, amounting to some price controls, a mild increase in government spending, and a tax rise.

30. Around thirty members of the French national assembly boarded the *Massilia* on June 21, 1940, determined to carry on the fight from North Africa. The Vichy government seized the opportunity to taint the reputation of those politicians—many of whom were on the left of the political scene, some of whom were Jewish—accusing them of treason and desertion (Paxton, 1973: 19; Azema, 1979: 67–9).
31. On the financial reform and on this disagreement, see Rioux (1980: 100), Lacouture (1981: 168), Bloch-Lainé and Bouvier (1986: 69).
32. 'Délégation à l'Equipement National—Plan d'Equipement National, Rapport Général, Tranche de Démarrage, novembre 1944', AN-80AJ/276.
33. Bloch-Lainé and Bouvier (1986: 120) and Fourquet (1980: 226).
34. On Walter Lippmann, see Steel (1980). Jean-Jacques Servan-Schreiber certainly pictured himself as the French Lippmann, unofficial consultant and *éminence grise*, making and unmaking politicians at will.
35. See *L'Express* (1953–1955), Siritzky and Roth (1979). According to Boltanski (1982: 182), '*L'Express* called for concentration of firms, rationalization of production, productivity, the advent of a consumer society, and changes in the system of education . . . . It also did its part in the creation of a group of competent managers, in the training of those managers and more generally in the vulgarization of economic concepts and knowledge.'
36. 'JCS1779, July 11, 1947, § 21' in Office of the Historian (1986: 124).
37. 'Internal memorandum, Decartelization Branch, 15 July 1947', OMGUS Rds, Bd42, #17/224-2/12.
38. 'While in the United States, the antitrust division's work is largely legal, the situation is different here. It seems to me that in our program here we are dealing with an economic problem perhaps more than with a legal problem.' 'Charles Dilley, Assistant Chief for Deconcentration, Internal memorandum, Decartelization and Deconcentration Branch, 22 September 1947', OMGUS Rds, Bd18, #11/11-3/7.
39. 'OMGUS, USA Zone and Land Bremen Law #56: Prohibition of Excessive Concentration of German Economic Power, 12 February 1947.' The constructive paragraph of this preamble was the only concession made to German reviewers of the American proposal (Damm, 1958: 138–9).
40. Industrial firms over 10,000 employees were 'excessive concentrations of economic power'. Under 10,000, occupation authorities had some leeway to define excessive concentration of economic power.
41. 'Memorandum, Economics Division: Reaction of Industry Branch to Decartelization Plan, August 24, 1946', OMGUS Rds, Bd42, #17/263-2/10-11. A number of American businessmen also filed complaints with OMGUS on the decartelization and deconcentration program (Taylor, 1979: 36–7; Martin, 1950).
42. Speech of Lawrence Wilkinson, Chief of the Industry Branch, Economics Division, October 1946, quoted in 'Report of the Ferguson Committee, April 1949', OMGUS Rds, Bd41, #3/142-1/9.
43. 'Revised Functional Program: Decartelization, July–December 1947', OMGUS Rds, Bd17, #3/214-7/3.
44. 'Charles Dilley, Assistant Chief of Branch for Deconcentration, Memorandum to Phillips Hawkins: Explaining Decartelization to the Germans, September 10, 1947', OMGUS Rds, Bd18, #11/11-3/7.
45. 'Objectives of the Decartelization Program, November 15, 1947', OMGUS Rds, Bd18, #11/11-3/7.

46. 'Explaining Decartelization to the Germans, September 10, 1947', OMGUS Rds, Bd18, #11/11-3/7.
47. 'Memorandum from General Clay to General Draper, October 1946', OMGUS Rds, Bd41, #3/142-1/9.
48. The debate on the meaning of 'technical efficiency' that took place within the Branch during 1947 illustrated perfectly the arbitrary use made of this concept. Nobody within the 'new team' managed to provide a convincing answer to members of the 'old team' who were asking for a clear definition, for tools to measure it, and for the demonstration that a correlation existed between efficiency and the size of the firm. 'Explaining Decartelization to the Germans, September 10, 1947' and a series of other memoranda dated September 1947, OMGUS Rds, Bd18, #11/11-3/7.
49. OMGUS Rds, Bd42, #17/247-1/5. See also 'Lawrence Wilkinson, Economics Adviser, Brief for the Military Governor', OMGUS Rds, Bd41, #3/141-3/6.
50. 'Richardson Bronson, Chief of the American Decartelization Element to John McCloy, July 30, 1949', OMGUS Rds, Bd18, #11/10-2/15.
51. They were sometimes called 'neo-liberals' or 'ordo-liberals', 'liberal' being understood in a European sense, more or less synonymous with 'free-market' advocate.
52. This article was entitled 'Our Task' (Peacock and Willgerodt 1989: ch. 2).
53. To the extent that they were calling for government intervention, German 'neo-liberals' differed from traditional European *laissez faire* and free market advocates. See the interesting argument in Allen (1989) that the Freiburg school was, in Germany, a functional equivalent to a Keynesian school. This could explain in part why Keynesian ideas did not seem to have a lot of influence in that country.
54. Alfred Müller-Armack was the only member of the Freiburg school who joined the Nazi party (Peacock and Willgerodt 1989).
55. 'Speech in front of the German Federal Parliament: Aims of the Law against Restrictions of Competition, March 24, 1955' (Erhard, 1963).
56. I agree with Berghahn (1984) who claimed that being aware of those differences was essential if one was to understand the postwar evolution of West German capitalism. I also agree that with respect to competition and economic concentration, American influences had more impact on Erhard's thought and policy than the program of the Freiburg school.
57. In Erhard's program, according to Müller-Armack, 'competition is viewed primarily as a way of accomplishing technological and economic progress with the least possible hindrance. Hence its justification is a constant increase in productivity.' In Peacock and Willgerodt (1989: 85).
58. 'I regard the material rise of the German worker and other sectors of our people as an absolute political, social and economic gain. . . . I have consciously worked towards this end and am happy with its success.' Erhard (1958: 169–71). See also Berghahn (1984: 185).
59. Erhard (1958: 120). German critics of Ludwig Erhard, particularly within the business community, accused him of being a mere puppet of American occupation authorities. In order to build his own legitimacy, he systematically tried to keep his distance from American models, at least officially. Americans in fact understood and encouraged such a strategy.
60. For more on the career of Ludwig Erhard before and during the war, see Berghahn (1984). It is important to mention that Erhard stayed away from the Nazi regime,

which pushed him further up on the American list of 'worthy' Germans with whom it was possible to cooperate.

61. 'Arthur Vandenberg, letter to George Marshall' in Vandenberg (1952: 393). Arthur Vandenberg was the chairman of the Senate Foreign Relations Committee. The fact that he had called for a bipartisan support of the Marshall plan represented a significant achievement for the Truman administration.
62. The expression 'politics of productivity' is taken from Maier (1978).
63. Van der Pijl (1984) and Carew (1987) have argued that the predominant role of business within tripartite boards dated back to the war period and the Second New Deal.
64. A few ECA administrators had belonged to another organ of business/government collaboration, the Business Advisory Council (BAC) by the Department of Commerce.
65. Harriman had been a member of the BAC, which he drew on to staff his Paris office.
66. Hogan (1985: 56 ff.) gives a still longer list of American businessmen who joined the ECA. Most had been prominent members of the CED. See also Carew (1987: 42).
67. The watering down and virtual uselessness of the Employment Act enacted in 1946 symbolized the loss of influence, after the war, of progressive businessmen on the American national scene. The original version of the bill had been sponsored by the CED and provided that government would guarantee full employment through of a vast array of Keynesian tools. The watered down version, on the other hand, had been redrafted under the influence of the US Chamber of Commerce.
68. See in particular Hoffman (1951), Maier (1978), Milward (1984), Van der Pijl (1984), Hogan (1985, 1987), and Carew (1987).
69. 'Paul Hoffman to Averell Harriman, ECA file, box 46, February 14–March 10, 1949.' Quoted in Hogan (1985: 63).
70. 'John Foster Dulles: Europe must Federate or Perish, America must Offer Inspiration and Guidance. Speech, February 1, 1947.' Quoted in Hogan (1984).
71. 'Paul Hoffman, Washington, September 15, 1949', FRUS (1949, iv).
72. 'Remarks by the Honorable George Marshall, Secretary of State, at Harvard University on June 5, 1947', FRUS (1947: iii).
73. Ball (1982: 77–8). George Ball, a close friend of Jean Monnet, was in the summer of 1947 working with him on the French part of the European allocation proposal.
74. Interministerial committee for questions of European economic cooperation. See AN-F60ter, for archives of this committee.
75. Berater für den Marshallplan beim Vorsitzer des Verwaltungsrates des Vereigniten Wirtschaftsgebiet (Committee for the Marshall plan by the presidency of the Bizonal economic council). Bundesarchiv Koblenz, Bestand Z14.
76. 'Barry Bingham to ECA in Washington, September 8, 1949', FRUS (1949: iv). An editorial note at that point in the FRUS volume goes further: 'This had been the secret of the Mission's success in influencing the French in such matters as credit control, non-inflationary financing or trade liberalization.'
77. A series of interviews with French civil servants and politicians convinced Cohen (1969) that many 'viewed Monnet's office as the principal link with the Marshall plan and with Washington. [Civil servants and politicians] pointed out that in their own dealings with the Marshall plan administration, they often worked through Monnet's office.'

78. 'Deputy Administrator to ECA Washington, William Foster, to ECA Mission in France, April 21, 1950', FRUS (1950: iii).
79. Interview with Pierre Uri, Wall (1991: 186). See also Girault (1986: 63).
80. For more on Italian liberal experts, most of whom were followers of the Italian *laissez faire* school dominated by Pantaleoni, Walras, and Pareto, see De Cecco (1972, 1989), Esposito (1994).
81. It is interesting to point out here the difference with the French case. In the interwar period, before Marshal Pétain took over under exceptional circumstances, the French state had very much adopted a hands-off policy with respect to the economy. In direct reaction to this period of relative *laissez faire*, a small group of planners became increasingly vocal before and throughout the war, state intervention becoming the new French orthodoxy after the war. The comparison between France and Italy highlights the impact dominant institutions and ideologies can have on opposition groups, to some extent shaping and defining them.
82. 'Report of the State–War–Navy Coordinating Committee's Ad Hoc Committee on Italy, April 4, 1947.' Quoted in Miller (1986: 226–7). See also Harper (1986: ch. 9).
83. Italians clearly lacked at the time a generation of modernizing technocrats similar to the French group, who would have talked a language that Americans in the ECA could understand and agree with (Zamagni, 1986).
84. De Cecco (1989), D'Attore (1981), Miller (1986). On counterpart funds, see later, Chapter 7.

PART III:

CROSS-NATIONAL TRANSFER: MECHANISMS

After the Second World War, a national crisis combined with geopolitical dependence in both France and West Germany to increase the likelihood that the American system of industrial production would become a model for national reconstruction and modernization. A small cross-national network had taken over and held on to key positions of institutional power, both in the USA and in these two Western European countries. Spinning dense webs of personal and institutional relationships across the Atlantic, French, West German, and American members of the cross-national network shared similar objectives and worked together in close synergy. The large-scale transfer to these two Western European countries of structural arrangements—peculiar until then to American industry and understood to be at the source of its success—was, in particular, a key common project.

Substantial differences, however, set apart the French and West German situations. First, the nature of the geopolitical link between the USA and each of these two countries was not the same. The degree of dependence remained higher in the West German case, even after the end of military occupation and well into the mid-1950s. In addition, cross-national channels were quite different. The German element in the cross-national network owed its institutional position of power on the national scene to direct co-optation by American actors. Relationships between these two sides of the network were thus highly asymmetrical. In France the modernizing group had secured national power on its own, using American support only to strengthen its position. Furthermore, amongst French and American members of the network, some were linked through close personal friendship, making for a more symmetrical relationship.

As a consequence of these differences, whether in the degree of geopolitical dependence or in the nature of the cross-national channels, transfer mechanisms were not the same in each case. In the French context, both sides of the cross-national network tended to rely on voluntary imitation as the main mechanism. The French modernizing group spontaneously took upon itself the task of transferring the American structural model to the national economic and industrial scene. The predominance of spontaneous and voluntary imitation in the French case, however, did not prevent the American side of the network from occasionally resorting to more coercive types of transfer mechanisms. Coercive mechanisms could speed up the transfer process.

They could also provide support to and help, in an indirect manner, French modernizing actors facing powerful resistance on the national scene. In the West German context, the American military government had started by using only coercive mechanisms, imposing on the western territories of Germany a large-scale structural transfer. However, having identified and co-opted a small group of nationals on which they could rely, the Americans increasingly left more space for spontaneous West German undertakings. Towards the end of the 1940s, voluntary imitation thus became an operative transfer mechanism in West Germany.

In time, normative types of transfer mechanisms also came to play a role in these two Western European countries. Members of the cross-national network all understood that, in order to last and to be successful in the longer term, a structural transfer of the sort they were advocating and sponsoring should become deeply embedded and appropriated at the receiving end. Ideally, the transferred system of industrial production should come to be perceived as their own by French and West German civil societies. This would naturally imply a radical shift in mentality, values, and economic and industrial ideology in both countries, which would in turn foster and further embed the structural transformations already in process. Antitrust legislation, management and business education, or a common market on a Western European level, once successfully institutionalized, had the potential to turn into normative transfer mechanisms. Throughout the 1950s, members of the cross-national network were working towards the implementation of such normative mechanisms of transfer in Western Europe but it would take some time before their impact could be felt.

In postwar Italy, the lack of a national sense of crisis had combined with the failure of a cross-national network to emerge, thus decreasing the likelihood that a large-scale, cross-national transfer of structural arrangements would be undertaken or even considered. The Italian group that came to power after the war did not systematically question pre-existing social and economic arrangements. Italian power holders did not advocate a radical transformation of industry structures nor the large-scale transfer to their country of the American system of industrial production. In the meantime, American modernizers within the Marshall plan administration, attempted to institutionalize in Italy the same coercive or normative transfer mechanisms that were proving to be quite effective in France and West Germany. Most of the time, these attempts failed. The lack of sympathetic Italian interlocutors and institutional relays frustrated and curtailed the efforts of American modernizers in that country. In the longer term, the creation of a Western European economic community and of a large common market, of which Italy became a member, would have some impact on the national economy and industry. As documented in the Introduction, however, the scale and scope of transformations in the Italian system of industrial production during the two decades following the Second World War does not compare with what was taking place in France and West Germany at the very same time.

It could be argued, therefore, that the launching and successful implementation of a large-scale cross-national transfer process requires that a number of transfer mechanisms be not only institutionalized but also operated. Empirical cases in this book brought out three main types of transfer mechanisms. Following DiMaggio and Powell's (1983) terminology, they were labeled respectively 'mimetic', 'coercive', and 'normative'. Those three sorts of mechanisms are naturally ideal types, in the Weberian sense (Weber, 1978). In real life situations, these mechanisms tend to operate jointly and identifying their respective impact can sometimes be difficult. However, the predominance of one given type of transfer mechanism over another has undeniable consequences for the transfer process and its potential success. The speed of the process, the extent of adaptation and reinterpretation of the original model that takes place, or the degree of resistance and opposition within civil society all depend, in part, on the particular mix of transfer mechanisms and on the type, within this mix, which plays the most significant role throughout the process. It appears useful, therefore, to define theoretical tools that will facilitate the identification of each type.

A transfer mechanism is labeled mimetic when it is the expression of a logic of imitation and reflects a spontaneous decision, locally, to replicate and appropriate foreign models. A process of voluntary imitation will generally be motivated by the perception, amongst groups of local actors, of problems and inadequacies at a national level and by the conviction that foreign models are superior. When an acute sense of national crisis and a search for solutions combine with dependence on the geopolitical scene and in particular asymmetrical dependence, such a conviction will be bound to emerge. Indeed, a relationship of geopolitical dependence has a tendency to increase the density of contact between two countries. Asymmetrical dependence, furthermore, creates a subjective ranking between both countries, a feeling of inferiority being even more likely to emerge within the dependent country. There will be voluntary imitation, in those circumstances, only if the dependent country has, at the same time, a sense of its own worth that is being painfully contradicted by its position in the geopolitical relationship. Indeed, voluntary imitation can be seen as a means, ultimately, of severing the relationship of dependence that appears unfit to the status of the country.

A second type of transfer mechanism, labeled coercive, is at work whenever the process of large-scale transfer is being imposed rather than eagerly pursued. A coercive mechanism in a cross-national transfer process implies the direct intervention of foreign actors, groups, and institutions, generally from the model country. The capacity to coerce another country into radically transforming or redefining some of its key features follows naturally from a strong power position in a geopolitical relationship characterized by asymmetrical dependence. Conversely, the more dependent a given country and the less bargaining power it enjoys, the more it can be subjected to coercive transfer mechanisms. Still, the fact remains that nationals from the dominant country have to have strong motives to justify pressing radical change on a foreign country. Indeed, the costs for the dominant country of such a process may be very high. Those motives may be essentially economic, nationals from the dominant country expecting increased synergies between both countries and ultimately economic benefits. Motives can be political and geopolitical, nationals from the dominant country hoping to increase their capacity to understand, control, and manipulate the dependent foreign entity. Nationals from the dominant country may also simply be driven by a missionary spirit. Deeply convinced of the superiority of the model their own country embodies, they may desire to shape at least parts of the world following that model.

A third type of transfer mechanism, finally, labeled normative, may come to operate in an indirect manner, for example through the globalization and homogenization of norms, rules, legislation, or values. A normative transfer mechanism is neither voluntarily chosen, nor forced upon a given country in any direct way. It is generally the unavoidable consequence of former commitments or undertakings and follows, in particular, membership within cross-national organizations. The role and the impact of normative types of transfer mechanisms have undeniably increased throughout the second half of the twentieth century, precisely due to a multiplication of international bodies. Ever since the end of the Second World War, those organizations—the United Nations, the International Monetary Fund (IMF), the General Agreement on Tariffs and Trade (now World Trade Organization), or the European Economic Community (now European Union) for example—have been defining, diffusing, institutionalizing, and embedding within member countries common normative rules. The worldwide development, at the same time, of professional associations with their own sets of norms has led, in most countries, to increased pressure stemming from normative types of transfer mechanisms.

There is a direct relationship between the nature of geopolitical dependence and the type of transfer mechanisms that is bound to be dominant in any particular case. In a situation of clear asymmetrical dependence with little bargaining power, transfer mechanisms of the coercive type can operate relatively easily and are bound to have a significant and rapid impact. The original model, moreover, is likely in those circumstances to be transferred with little transformation or adaptation. But the impact of coercive transfer mechanisms may be relatively short-lived and might not survive, in particular, the end of the period of dependence. A transfer through imitation, on the other hand, will certainly lead to more stable transformations, as foreign patterns are voluntarily adopted. The original model, in this case, might come to be interpreted or translated somewhat in order to fit local conditions. Normative transfer mechanisms, finally, appear essential to the embedding and long-term appropriation of foreign models within a national community. Such mechanisms might not have an immediate impact, however, and they may lead to a

Table 9. Mechanisms of cross-national transfer—key characteristics

	Coercive	Mimetic	Normative
Conditions	Asymmetrical dependence	Dependence or asymmetrical dependence	Dependence or interdependence
Agents	Model country	Local	Foreign or local
Process	Imposing	Imitating	Embedding
Speed	Rapid	Medium	Slow
Impact	Short-lived and fragile	Stable and long lasting	Fairly permanent
Result	Similar to model	Partial adaptation	Partial adaptation
Reactions	Rejection, opposition	Resistance or support	Indifference or support

significant reinterpretation and adaptation of the original model. The type of transfer mechanism dominating in a given large-scale, cross-national transfer process will also, to some extent, determine the nature of local reactions to that process. Coercive transfer mechanisms are likely to prompt the most violent rejection, even though local opposition may be successfully brought under control during a period of acute dependence. Mimetic transfer mechanisms may lead to a wide range of reactions within local civil society, from resistance and organized opposition to strong support. As to normative transfer mechanisms, they will tend to arouse less passion once institutionalized and local reactions may vary in this case from indifference to support. Table 9 brings together, in a summary and somewhat schematic form, the key characteristics of these three types of transfer mechanisms.

5
Voluntary Imitation
Adopting the Corporate Model in France

How could the French business class finally come round to the American model, visiting the United States without always speaking the language? How could French business leaders take pride in and benefit from technological innovations the French state had had to urge on them and still appear, in the end, as the champions of free entrepreneurship against the administration?
François Bloch-Lainé (1976: 124)

After the Second World War, a small French modernizing élite proved to be instrumental in launching and fostering the large-scale transfer of American structural models to France and more generally to Western Europe. Working from key positions of institutional power on the French national scene, this small modernizing group elaborated and operated, on its own initiative, a set of mechanisms that were to bring about radical transformations within the French economy and industry. This small group, however, was not only an agent of the cross-national transfer. It was also an intervening variable, responsible for the adaptation and interpretation of the foreign model. The French modernizing group partly redefined the American system of industrial production before diffusing it onto the national scene through the planning and productivity institutions it had created.

This same French group was also a driving force behind the emergence of a Western European economic space. Defining new rules of competition and market regulation, the Western European space was to have an impact, in turn, on national systems of industrial production. Implementing and operating transfer mechanisms of a mimetic or of a normative type, the French modernizing group benefited all along from the strong support of the American side of the cross-national network. Taking advantage of their position of power on the geopolitical scene, the Americans intervened sometimes in a coercive manner. Their objective was then generally to back up their French partners by helping to counter or defuse resistance and opposition to the cross-national transfer process, widespread at the time within French or West European civil societies.

OPERATING THE FRENCH PLANNING INSTITUTIONS

During its early years, the French planning board or Commissariat Général du Plan was the main interface between the French and American worlds, the key

point of articulation in France of the cross-national network. The elaboration
of a national plan and the creation of a planning board had not merely been
devices to obtain American support and financial aid, as it was sometimes
argued (Margairaz, 1982; Bossuat, 1992). They pertained of a general strategy
of economic and industrial modernization as defined by national actors. It is
undeniable, however, that Jean Monnet and his team had factored in American
financial assistance as an essential condition for the successful implementation
of the French plan.[1] Mostly thanks to Jean Monnet, the French planning board
turned out to be, until about the mid-1950s, at the heart of a Franco-American
collaboration and the unavoidable meeting point of a transatlantic network.
American consultants significantly influenced the overall framework of the
first and second French plans, which unmistakably came to reflect the American model and experience. The American system of industrial production was
always implicitly and often explicitly used as a reference by French planners in
their attempt to foster the redefinition of French structures of industrial
production.

The First French Plan and its Objectives

General guidelines for the first French plan were defined in official directives
sent by General de Gaulle to the planning board in January 1946. This national
undertaking had two main dimensions. The first French plan, otherwise labeled
plan de modernisation et d'équipement, was naturally going to be a scarcity
managing tool. It was to be an instrument through which rare resources could
be channeled in the most efficient manner to an economy in dire straits.
Reconstruction was for France an imperative and it was argued that the central
allocation of resources and flexible planning could speed up the process,
limiting waste and redundancies at the same time. The first French plan had
also a longer-term objective, which seemed even more important to the planning team. The *plan de modernisation et d'équipement* should prepare and
foster the modernization of structural arrangements within the French economy and industry, essentially through a systematic and large-scale investment
program. For members of the planning board, who believed that modernization
was not only a 'state of things' but also a 'state of mind', this second objective
required a significant transformation of mentalities within French economic
and industrial communities (Commissariat Général du Plan, 1946). Modernization was thus a difficult and long-term undertaking and the strategies of the
French planning board would naturally have to fit the scope of the project.

The first French plan identified six sectors within the national economy—
coal, steel, electricity, cement, agricultural machinery, and transportation—to
be given priority. A centrally-led and coordinated investment effort in those
sectors, spread over four years, should lead to higher levels of production and
to the removal of many bottlenecks.[2] The French planning team believed that
higher levels of production in those particular sectors were bound to provide

the necessary steam to both drive and pull the rest of the economy. On the other hand, higher levels of production were deemed to be not quite enough and capital investment in those sectors should be reinforced by systematic efforts to 'modernize archaic structures' and to 'improve productivity'. Members of the planning board pointed in particular to the small size of French production units and firms as an obstacle to the adoption of mass-production techniques and technologies.[3]

While focusing primarily on the six priority sectors, the French planning board hoped to have an impact on French economy and industry as a whole. Eighteen modernization commissions were created, each bringing together labor, business, and government representatives for a given sector of the French economy and industry. Modernization commissions were responsible for the elaboration of detailed plans for each sector. Work within these commissions lasted in fact almost a year and the first French plan, in its final and detailed form, was enacted in January 1947 by government decree. Its clearly stated goal was 'to bring all Frenchmen and women the benefits of material well-being accruing to citizens of more advanced countries'. The reference was 'American high standards of living' which were essentially due, it was argued, 'to a production of goods and services by worked hours always on the increase' (Commissariat Général du Plan, 1946: 12). In its detailed version, the French plan gave a clear definition of what was understood by 'modernization'. Modernization meant concentration within each sector of industry, larger production units and firms, the adoption of machines and technologies that would make mass production possible, and a rationalization of management and production methods. Machines and technologies would be imported from the USA as would structures and management methods.[4] As early as October 1946, members of the French planning board were also proposing the creation of a productivity committee, the role of which would be to foster, monitor, and coordinate, across French industry as a whole, an increase in productivity levels.

Strategies of the Planning Board and Workings of the Plan

Within public and newly nationalized sectors of French industry, the plan was compulsory and had the force of law.[5] The impact of the planning board in those sectors could thus be direct and significant. In all other sectors, the plan was in theory merely indicative. In reality, members of the planning board had at their disposal a fair number of tools and incentives through which they could bring most sectors of the industry to comply with the provisions of the plan. Making use of the tools or not was left in each case to the discretion of members of the planning board. Their decision, in this respect, tended to reflect the priorities they set themselves. Incentives were generally used in those sectors the planning team considered 'key' while this was not so systematically the case in those sectors that were viewed as being of less strategic importance:

In the industrial sectors which are not nationalized but . . . the importance of which is
key to the achievement of our general objectives, the execution of the plan will imply
special agreements between public authorities and the interested sectors, where the
latter will commit themselves to the execution of the plan, and the public authorities
will promise to supply them with the necessary means or to help them secure those
means.[6]

Members of the planning board had soon realized, though, that without a
budget for financing—at least in part—the planned investments, the national
plan was unlikely to be implemented, particularly in its modernization dimension. On that front, Jean Monnet won a significant battle in 1948, when he got
the ECA and the French government to agree that Marshall plan counterpart
funds be allocated to the financing of the French plan. However, he did not
manage to achieve, for the planning board, direct control of those funds. The
Fonds de Modernisation et d'Equipement or FME was created in 1948, as a
division of the French Treasury, to handle counterpart funds and, in effect, to
become the bank of the planning board. Under the leadership of François
Bloch-Lainé, the FME did collaborate quite closely with the planning board.
Marshall plan counterpart funds were thus used to ensure the execution and
proper implementation of the plan as well as to foster efforts at modernization
and restructuring.

   A conditional granting of funds rapidly became the preferred strategy of the
planning board. Modernization investments, restructuring, mergers, or concentration became necessary conditions for the allocation of FME controlled
funds. Conditional strategies were also used with other sources of capital.
By the end of 1945, French public authorities had the power to control most
credit allocation in France. A new public agency, the Crédit National, had
become responsible for overseeing the entire French credit system, a significant share of which was nationalized in 1945. The planning board managed to
impose, in 1948, that the Crédit National should request its approval for all
credit allocation to the private sector over a given threshold (Brochier, 1965;
Fourquet, 1980). In fact, conditional strategies could be particularly efficient
at the time due to an increased dependence of French industrial firms on
external financing and to the significant expansion of state power and involvement in the economic sphere after 1945.[7] Members of the planning board
soon identified other types of possible strategies. They understood, for
example, that a properly designed tax system could help to implement the
national plan. In 1946, the French tax system was much more of an obstacle
than an incentive, as it heavily penalized mergers and concentration.[8] The
team around Jean Monnet therefore started to work on this issue. By 1948,
they had significantly amended the relevant legislation and tax exemption
became a tool to foster mergers and restructuring. Legislative amendements
'facilitated and rendered less expensive mergers and acquisitions, earlier
precluded by heavy fiscality'.[9]

   In the short to medium term, these strategies of an essentially coercive nature had a direct and significant impact. Large-scale restructuring in steel or electronics for example, both identified as priority sectors during the 1950s or 1960s, can be traced back to the industrial policy of the French planning board. Figure 7 sketches out the rapid transformation of the French steel industry into a duopoly. All listed mergers were negotiated under pressure from the planning board, as conditions for credit allocation, tax exemption, or direct subsidies that generally helped buy machinery and equipment in the USA.[10]

The planning board was thus largely responsible for bringing about both a radical restructuring of the steel industry and a modernization of its plant. Those far-reaching transformations took place despite the reluctance and

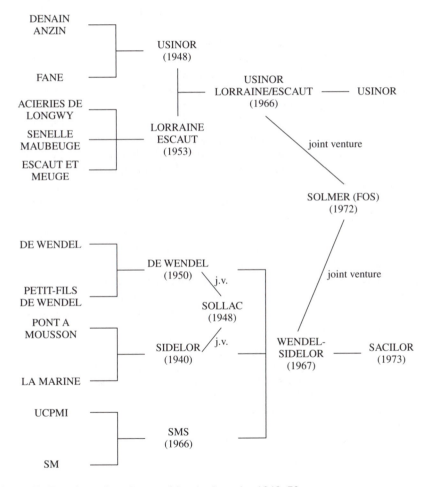

Figure 7. French steel or the transition to duopoly, 1948–73
Source: Hayward (1986: 36).

misgivings of traditional French iron masters. Apparently, the Wendel family, owning large steel works in the Lorraine region, was particularly opposed to change (Monnet, 1976; Bloch-Lainé and Bouvier, 1986). The Wendels would finally adopt mass-production technologies and techniques but only because their direct competitors—Denain-Anzin and Fane—had themselves accepted a deal with the planning board. The latter were to merge into a new entity, Usinor, and received, in return, public funds to finance imports of American technology and machines.[11] A relatively similar evolution characterized the electronics industry in the post-Second World War period with mergers generally being prompted by the planning board. By 1967, the planning board had managed to turn the French electronics industry from a sector dominated by many small, traditional, and family-owned firms into what was essentially a duopoly.[12]

The impact of coercive strategies was thus in the majority of cases direct and significant. However, members of the planning board were aware that in spite of their short-term efficiency, those strategies should not be systematically relied upon. Modernization, they understood, was also a 'state of mind', a particular mentality. Structural tranformations would not be long lasting, nor would they bring the expected results of increased production and productivity, if they remained imposed upon national actors and if they did not come to reflect changes in attitude within French economic and industrial communities. As it turned out, the planning board played a significant role in this attempt to 'modernize the minds' of French business and labor communities, through modernization commissions in particular, although precisely measuring such a role would naturally prove quite difficult. Jean Monnet's idea was to bring together, within modernization commissions, the few progressive leaders of a given industry with more conservative members, thus fostering interactions between them. The planning board undeniably contributed, in this manner, to the re-education and renovation of French economic élites. Those national efforts were furthered, starting in 1949, by the American-sponsored 'productivity drive'. Etienne Hirsch, who replaced Jean Monnet as Commissaire Général in 1952, would later acknowledge that a synergy indeed existed between the objectives of the planning board and the goals of the American 'productivity drive':

One cannot really grasp how revolutionary the idea of modernization was when compared to the prewar period. . . . Investment had [then] been considered a dangerous luxury. We had to transform that mentality. This took time. Productivity missions to the USA have been very helpful, showing [French] businessmen how backward we were. The plan also, as an educational tool, has been important. . . . It is only in 1951–52 that mentalities have started to change.[13]

Assessment of the First Plan and Elaboration of a Second

The first French plan or *plan de modernisation et d'équipement* had initially been designed to last four years, from 1947 to 1950. When Marshall dollars started to flow in, in 1948, the plan was extended until 1952, so that it would end with American assistance. The short-term objective of the first plan had been to overcome shortages and to remove bottlenecks strangling the French postwar economy. The target, more precisely, had been a 25 per cent increase in general production levels over the 1929 figure, with some variation across sectors. By 1950, there was still some way to go and targets had to be re-evaluated downwards for most sectors. The extension of the first plan, how-ever, meant that by its end in 1952, results on average were fairly good, even if somewhat short of the target in steel and agricultural machinery.[14] Another key objective of the French planners had been to keep the level of capital invest-ment at around a quarter of the total national income, a significantly bigger share than during the pre-Second World War period.[15] Under pressure from a French government concerned about rampant inflation, the investment pro-gram for 1948 had to be cut somewhat, although the general upward trend was not threatened. Total investments in 1952 were more than four times what they had been in 1947 (Bossuat, 1992). A large share of those investments was financed through public funds, within the public and nationalized sectors as well as in the private sector. In the prewar period, 80 per cent of total investments had been self-financed, bank credits having covered most of the rest (Caron, 1981). The state had not even been a player. During the period of the first plan, on the other hand, the French state was the main national investor, as documented in Table 10.[16]

While the first plan was fairly successful in helping the French economy to overcome scarcities and bottlenecks, the planning team was much less satisfied with its results with respect to modernization. According to members of the planning board, the process of modernization was in fact just starting in 1952 after a period where reconstruction had had the priority. A lot still remained to be done and there was apparently room for a second plan with a clear focus on modernization. By the end of the first plan, the necessity appeared to be 'much less an investment policy than systematic tracking of numerous structural, technical, legal, or psychological barriers to production and productivity increases'.[17] The planning board had been created in 1946 as a temporary

Table 10. Modernization investments in France and share of the State, 1948–51 (1952 FF billions)

	Investments (A)	Public Financing (B)	B as per cent of A
1948	546	316	58
1949	725	451	62
1950	715	462	64
1951	756	331	44

Note: Only modernization (and not reconstruction) investments are included.
Source: 'Note de Jean Monnet à Antoine Pinay, 8 mars 1952', AN-F30/2860.

institution that should normally not outlast the task it had been created for—launching and implementing a national plan. The planning team, as a consequence, had to plead in 1951 for a renewal of the planning experience and for its long-term institutionalization. This was granted by decree in December and the elaboration of a second national plan started right away.

The second French plan set a target for the economy as a whole. Production was to increase by 20 per cent between 1954 and 1957. The emphasis, however, was not so much on quantity as on quality, with productivity levels and the modernization of structures being identified as particularly important. Priority this time was not given to a few industrial sectors but to 'basic actions' that were to apply horizontally, across all sectors of the French economy. Those basic actions included the 'diffusion of modern methods of management', 'industrial restructuring through mergers in order to promote production on a large scale', a 'modernization of the distribution system', or 'long term programs to lower costs in capital goods industries'.[18] The objective was clear. The French system of industrial production had to be reshaped. There were too many small or medium-sized firms, with 'archaic' legal and organizational structures, old machines, and 'inefficient' production methods. For members of the planning board, mergers and concentration seemed necessary, so that 'modern' legal and organizational structures could emerge and so that 'advanced' technologies and 'efficient' production methods could be imported. What French planners understood by modernity was clearly, once more, mergers, large size, and mass-production techniques. However, while they equated size with efficiency, none of them ever attempted to test the validity of this assumption.[19]

Many of the strategies adopted to implement those 'basic actions' had already been tried and tested during the period of the first plan. Cheap and conditional credit allocation, subsidies, conditional access to public markets, tax exemptions, or American technical assistance were all used as incentives to bring about mergers, internal restructuring, or a rationalization of modes of production. One particular strategy, however, was more original and specific to the second plan. During the process of elaboration of the second plan, members of the planning board started to advocate the enactment of antitrust legislation, which could lead, they argued, to the disappearance of 'inefficient', 'morally and materially backward' companies by outlawing cartels and other anti-competitive organizations. The position of French planners, however, with respect to antitrust legislation was far from radical. They distinguished between *ententes* or cartels destructive of competition and those that appeared to foster cooperation or specialization, making a point to welcome the latter.[20] On August 9, 1953, the French government issued a decree, labeled by some 'the Sherman Act of the IVth Republic'. The decree was in reality fairly weak and essentially an abuse legislation. Cartels and *ententes* that could be shown to 'improve the market or to insure the development of economic progress through rationalization and specialization' did not fall within the purview of the law.[21] Moreover, the administrative agency in charge of implementing the decree only had advisory powers.

In fact, this decree would rarely be used, and the issue of non-competitive behavior more or less disappeared after 1953 from the second French plan.[22] However, the apparent contradiction between the enactment of a regulation against 'cartels, *ententes*, or other forms of cooperation in restraint of trade' and the general objective, characteristic of the planning board, of bringing together production units disturbed business actors. By the beginning of the third plan, members of the modernization commissions were asking public authorities to make it clear to business leaders that 'their efforts to accomplish in common the rationalization of production, far from falling under the sanctions of the law will benefit from real encouragements from public authorities' (Cohen, 1969: 75). The planning team was reassuring and, throughout the end of the Fourth Republic and well into the Fifth, planners and civil servants would sometimes tolerate, or even encourage, the emergence of cartels or *ententes*, as second best to mergers and only for as long as they seemed to create the conditions for cooperation or specialization.

LAUNCHING AND INSTITUTIONALIZING THE PRODUCTIVITY EFFORT

Well before the American federal administration had considered elaborating a systematic program to improve the productivity of European industries, productivity levels had been a concern of the French planning board. Ever since the drafting of the first plan, productivity issues had been at the center of a debate that was largely framed by the American experience. To begin with, the concept of productivity and the word itself were American imports. Furthermore, American levels of productivity represented a benchmark against which French figures were being systematically contrasted, in official reports as well as in internal memos. Once again, but this time with respect to productivity, the objective of the planning board was to try and catch up with the American model.[23]

In 1946, in order to document the need for a large-scale productivity effort in France, members of the planning board made extensive use of two sets of industrial data produced during and immediately after the Second World War. On the one hand, the Vichy administration during the war had systematically started to compile data on French industry. On the other hand, a bureau of industrial monographs (Service des Monographies et d'Analyse Industrielle) had been created in the USA at the end of the war and integrated into French diplomatic services. The stated mission of the bureau was to produce detailed studies on the American industry. By 1946, the planning board had extended its influence and secured its control over this bureau that became, from then on, one of its main institutional outposts in the USA and a key provider of American data.[24] A systematic comparison of both sets of data, although often questionable with respect to methodology, was the basis of the planning board's work on productivity. Starting in October 1946, well in advance of the productivity drive of the 1950s, members of the planning board were already advocating the multiplication of direct contacts with American economic and industrial actors. Working with the bureau of industrial monographs in Washington, they were putting together a project whereby members of French business and labor communities, handpicked by modernization commissions, would go to the USA on study tours to learn about the American system of industrial production.[25]

Early Attempts at Institutionalization

Building on their experience with the national investment plan, members of the planning board were convinced of the need to institutionalize and thus embed the productivity debate. In the summer of 1948, a working group in charge of productivity was created within the planning board as a first step towards institution building. Jean Monnet and his team hoped to be able to co-opt and bring together, through this working group, a few key actors relatively sympathetic to their general objective of increasing productivity levels. Chaired by Jean Fourastié, a collaborator of Jean Monnet within the planning board, the working group was responsible for spreading the productivity debate throughout France. The few permanent members of the working group had generally had experience in the USA and were thus relatively familiar with the American model. Armangaud and Donn had previously been in charge of the bureau of industrial monographs in Washington, while Ménard had worked for a private company in Washington during the war. Pons, a French consultant in organization, had spent a lot of time training and working in the USA. The structure of the working group was flexible enough to allow non-members to be invited to contribute on particular issues. The external consultants tended, however, to favor French references. Noël Pouderoux, for example, chairman of a private research institute—Centre d'Etudes Générales d'Organisation Scientifique or CEGOS—who contributed from time to time, pertained to a French technocratic and *saint simonian* tradition.[26]

The working group was created in the summer of 1948 and it was asked to prepare by the fall an action plan to increase productivity levels in France. While external consultants deplored the impact of foreign models on the French productivity debate, most members of the working group still believed that the idea of productivity was essentially new in France.[27] Since the American economy appeared to be the reference, many within the working group argued that the objective should be to 'take full advantage of the American experience'. In 1948, the working group in charge of productivity was thus clearly calling for the large-scale transfer of managerial knowledge and methods from the USA to France:

In order to transfer and diffuse [to the French industry] the new methods of production and organization, it is only necessary to train seriously a significant number of carefully selected individuals. The new knowledge will then spread through competition and by its own appeal. . . . Those specialists should be French, and since there are none right now, they should be trained, theoretically and practically, in the United States.[28]

The working group was also calling for the adoption in France of a number of structural features, believed to be important factors of productivity in the USA. Ever since the beginning of the twentieth century, members of the working group emphasized, American industry had been characterized by the predominance of large, mass-producing units, by a specialization and standardization of the productive process, and by a rationalization of organizational structures. Those particular features, they argued, accounted to a significant extent for high levels of productivity in the USA. The failure of those features to emerge in France explained, on the other hand, low levels of productivity in that country. As a consequence, members of the working group were adamant that one should not only foster the transfer of methods and managerial knowledge, but that one should also 'pay particular attention to the problem of structural rationalization [concentration, specialization, market organization], as the only way in which productivity levels [might] be brought to improve radically'.[29] While the influence of American models and references on the working group was unmistakable, it remains true that such an understanding of economic and industrial modernization was not widespread in France at the time. Nevertheless, the power of French modernizers and the impact of their vision were much more significant than sheer numbers could lead one to expect. Their web-like control over key institutions explained that. Financial and logistic support coming from the USA would furthermore soon increase this power and influence.

Prior to systematic American involvement in French productivity issues through the technical assistance program, a peculiar French tradition had had some impact on the modernization and productivity discourse. In line with the interwar rationalization movement led by a small group of *saint simonian* engineers and with the corporatist policies of the Vichy regime, consultants to the working group had proposed solutions to the French productivity problem.[30] Most were members of research organizations—or with stretching the label somewhat, consulting agencies—inherited from the prewar period such as the CNOF, the CEGOS, or the BTE.[31] In the prewar period, those organizations had mostly specialized in the implementation of time and motion studies within industrial production units. After 1945, they offered a two-pronged solution to the French productivity problem. Together with the systematic implementation of a scientific division of labor within industrial production units, they advocated an extensive and formal organization of markets. Such a combination, they believed, would create the appropriate conditions for industrial productivity levels to increase in France.

The influence of both traditions, the American on the one hand and the French or continental European on the other, could unmistakably be felt in a report by the working group in charge of productivity that was written in July 1948. Unsystematic management methods, the absence of formal organizational structures and of a formal administrative division of labor, the lack of specialization, standardization, and rationalization of the productive process, or the small size of production units were all identified as sources of low productivity levels within French industries. In line with a French or continental European heritage, however, and in radical contradiction with the dominant and official discourse in the USA, the 'lack of a systematic organization of markets and the absence of cooperation between companies within a single industry' also had a prominent position on the French list of obstacles to increasing industrial productivity.[32]

Empowering French Institutions for the Productivity Effort

By the end of 1948, the working group in charge of productivity proposed an action plan, more or less meeting its fall deadline. This 'program for the improvement of French productivity' called for training, a transfer of knowledge, and structural transformations on a large scale.[33] Those were expensive undertakings and in all likelihood the productivity effort would have stalled due to lack of funds had it not been for the American technical assistance program. After he became chairman of the OEEC subcommittee for productivity studies, Jean Fourastié acknowledged that 'United States dollars and the visits by teams to the United States [had] made it possible to accelerate the movement in France and Great Britain and to start it in other countries in a way that would otherwise have been inconceivable' (Fourastié, 1953: 346). From 1949, increased American influence over French productivity matters led to the setting up of more stable and powerful institutions, through which a transfer of knowledge, expertise, or structures could take place on a wider scale.

The creation in the UK, in September 1948, of an Anglo-American Council on Productivity was the first sign of American interest in European productivity issues. The main task of this bi-national council was to launch joint productivity actions and indeed American experts came to Britain and British teams were sent to the USA on study tours. Funding for this productivity program had become available after the enactment of the 'US Information and Educational Exchange Act' in the spring of 1948. In fact, the Anglo-American Council on Productivity turned out to be the first stage in a significant American undertaking at a Western European level. James Silbermann, who was in charge of productivity issues within the American Department of Labor and an advisor to the ECA, contacted French representatives in Washington at the end of September 1948. He let them know that the USA, through the ECA, was ready to extend its productivity program to France. He added, however, that for clear political reasons Paul Hoffman, chairman of the ECA, did not want to be seen to put any pressure on the French government. The ECA therefore asked the French to officially take the initiative. The scenario proposed by Silberman was that the French government would express 'spontaneous' interest and officially request to be included in the American-sponsored productivity program.[34] In the end, this scenario prevailed. At the formal request of the French government, James Silbermann came to France late in 1948. He spent more than a month assessing the productivity situation and elaborating a program in collaboration with the French authorities. Not surprisingly, American intervention received wholehearted support from members of the working group in charge of productivity: this intervention was likely to solve the key problem of financing. Once again, therefore, the synergy proved unmistakable between the projects of French technocrats and the objectives and financial resources of the American foreign aid administration.

President Harry Truman's speech to Congress on the State of the Nation, in January 1949, gave a major impetus to the American technical assistance effort. Point IV of Truman's proposed 'program for peace and freedom' turned technical assistance into official American policy and in March 1949, a special division was set up within the ECA. While the USA had spent US$6 million on technical assistance projects in 1948–9, the figure for 1949–50 went up to US$17 million.[35] Arguing from the strength of the Communist party on the national scene, French authorities refused an official Franco-American colla-boration through a joint council on productivity on the British model. In the French case, therefore, Americans had to fall back on the strategy of indirect cooperation that had characterized their intervention in France until that time. In matters of productivity as in matters of productive investment, they would have to deal with a French-led and French-controlled institution, the objectives of which were relatively similar to their own.

In May 1949, a temporary committee in charge of productivity took over from the working group. It was in charge of organizing the first French study trips to the USA. This temporary committee was a technocratic institution, just like the working group, made up of civil servants and experts. The American administration, however, was insistently asking for the creation of a tripartite productivity council that would bring together not only civil servants and experts, but also labor and business representatives. There was an unmistak-able reluctance, within traditional political and administrative circles in France, to the creation of a committee of this type and to the allocation of budgetary resources to productivity projects.[36] In the end, though, the Amer-icans won their case. After a forceful intervention by Jean Monnet, a tripartite Comité National de la Productivité or CNP was created in the spring of 1950. It included civil servants and members of the planning board as well as members of business and labor communities even though the communist trade union, the CGT, was not represented.[37]

The CNP and the planning board had many common features and they were

soon working in close collaboration. Jean Fourastié was the official representative of the planning board to the productivity committee. The role of this
committee was to elaborate a general productivity program and to propose and
launch productivity projects. Its members were responsible for overseeing the
diffusion of knowledge or information and for coordinating all institutions and
organizations involved in the productivity effort. The productivity committee,
just like the the working group a few months before, could use thę expertise of
outside consultants, expertise often acquired in the USA. The structure of the
CNP was similar, in many ways, to the structure of the French planning board.
Several commissions shared the work, each within a particular domain or on a
particular project. One commission was in charge of training and education,
another of propaganda and information. There was a commission focusing on
fiscal policy and another on full employment. The productivity committee was
thus essentially a planning and coordinating agency. The concrete setting-up
and monitoring of study trips to the USA or of propaganda and information
projects were delegated to another organization, the Association Française
pour l'Accroissement de la Productivité or AFAP, also created in March
1950. The publication and diffusion of productivity documents, books, or
reports on study trips were entrusted to a publishing company created for
that purpose, the Société Auxiliaire de Diffusion des Editions de Productivité
or SADEP.[38]

Bringing the French Productivity Discourse into Line

The institutionalization of the French productivity effort thus coincided with
increasing American intervention. The USA came to finance a large proportion
of the productivity effort through the technical assistance program and American productivity experts were soon touring French factories, companies,
farms, and administrations. Study trips or 'productivity missions' to the
USA undeniably created the conditions for the American system of industrial
production to become known first hand by a fair number of French economic
actors. An increased familiarity with the American model combined with the
dependence of French productivity institutions on American funds to bring the
French productivity discourse fully into line with the American tradition. This
was particularly striking with respect to issues of cartelization and market
organization.

   While the working group in charge of productivity had identified cartelization as a condition of high productivity levels, the temporary committee was
already questioning, in 1949, the existence of a positive correlation between
cartelization and productivity.[39] In March 1950, the ECA Mission in Paris sent
the French planning board and French productivity institutions the results of a
study it had conducted. The report made it clear that the ECA saw French
problems as essentially structural and accounted for low levels of productivity
essentially in three ways. This report pointed, first of all, to the small size of

firms and production units. Then, it highlighted the lack of dynamism and the risk averse attitude of the French entrepreneur whose main objective remained the preservation of the *status quo* and of his personal or family interests. Finally, it deplored the lack of competition or its systematic restriction through *ententes* and cartels.[40] By the end of 1950, this third element was at long last integrated in the official discourse of the planning board and of French productivity institutions. At least in principle, French institutions would from then on denounce cartels and *ententes*, making clear their disastrous impact on productivity levels.[41] Over a period of a few months, the official French discourse on cartelization had changed radically. From initially creating the conditions for high productivity levels, cartels and *ententes* had turned into key obstacles to the productivity effort.

When the Mutual Security Agency (MSA) took over from the ECA in 1952 to run and monitor American economic and technical assistance, it defined the fight against restrictive practices as one of its top priorities.[42] Increasing pressure was thus brought to bear, at the time, on the French authorities to act on the double problem of restrictive practices and limitation of competition. This had a direct impact, as already discussed, on the process of elaboration of the second French plan. Nevertheless, the small team of French modernizers would find it very hard to import and integrate competition into the French industrial discourse and landscape. For the most part, members of the French industrial community strongly resented and were forcefully opposed to all measures tending to limit cooperation, market organization, and restrictive practices. In the medium to long term one could argue that in the fight between the new French modernizing technocracy on one side and the traditional business community on the other, the former ultimately came to have the upper hand (Bloch-Lainé and Bouvier, 1986). In the late 1940s, however and up until the 1950s, the French planning board and productivity institutions had to accept their share of compromise. When cartels and agreements could be shown to have a positive impact on rationalization or on specialization of the productive process, they were often tolerated as a second best alternative to outright mergers. By 1952 therefore, although a convergence between French and American discourses on productivity was unmistakable, particularly on the issue of competition, the dedication of the French authorities to an active fight against restrictive practices still remained short of American expectations.

While ready to compromise to a certain extent on the issues of competition and restrictive practices, French planning and productivity institutions were, in the 1950s, particularly dogmatic in their equation of large size and mass production with productivity. In March 1953, the French productivity committee was confronted with a report on what were, undeniably, Italian achievements. An Italian engineer, Patrignani, had developed a set of working methods and techniques allowing small production units to be 'at least as productive and efficient as American companies producing on a large scale

could be'. The key assumption behind these methods was in direct contradiction of Taylor's understanding of a scientific division of labor. The idea was
that 'the entire production of a single object or piece could be made by
successive and simple manipulations on a single work station (and that) the
total needed time could be fairly comparable to that achieved with an assembly
line that would have as many machines and work stations as there were
manipulations'.[43] By systematically reducing the time needed to adapt and
prepare the machines for new objects, production in a short series could be
made at least as productive and profitable as mass production. Implementation
appeared simple and cheap. A number of firms had already successfully
adopted those methods in Italy, including in the auto and aircraft industries
or in electrical and mechanical construction. A representative of the French
peak business association (CNPF), M. Vallée, presented the results of this
Italian experience to members of the CNP. From the minutes of the meeting,
however, it appears that members of the productivity committee considered the
Italian achievements as being essentially marginal, a mere curiosity. The
report did not trigger a debate or any collective questioning of the dominant
equation between large size and productivity characteristic of the French
modernization project. Large production units, standardization, and mass production would remain the foundations of French industrial policy and for many
years to come this choice was never questioned.[44]

TOWARDS AN INTEGRATED EUROPEAN MARKET: THE SCHUMAN PLAN

On May 9, 1950, Robert Schuman, then French Minister of Foreign Affairs,
put forward a project to pool European coal and steel industries. The 'Schuman
plan' had in fact been elaborated by the planning board, under the leadership of
Jean Monnet, but its appropriation by Robert Schuman gave it political legitimacy.[45] For some time now, France had had to deal with the consequences of a
redefined American policy in Germany. In the context of the Cold War, West
Germany was becoming a stronghold of the Western alliance. As a consequence, restrictions and controls weighing down on the German economy
since the early occupation period were being lifted one after the other. In
particular, by 1950, the USA was making it increasingly clear that France
would not be able to retain for much longer the control it had held since the
end of the war over the Saar region (Bossuat, 1992: 664–6). Considering the
relative weakness of France on the geopolitical scene at the time, the Schuman
plan was a master stroke, offering an original solution to the Franco-German
problem. The pooling of coal and steel industries on a European level led to an
implicit recognition of German sovereignty while still allowing France to
maintain a degree of control over the core of German industrial power.

In reality, the Schuman plan was also much more than a short-term answer
to a specific economic and geopolitical problem. It turned out to be the first

stage in the process of construction of a large, integrated, Western European market. It seemed to answer, to that extent, pressing demands from the USA and more particularly from the ECA for the creation of such a Western European framework. In the end, the Schuman plan was a European initiative, monitored all along by the French planning board. The process of elaboration of the Schuman plan bore witness, once again, to the close and efficient collaboration that existed between French and American elements of the cross-national modernizing network.

The Spirit of the Early Proposal

The proposal drafted by Jean Monnet and his team called for the pooling of French and German coal and steel production, with the possible participation of other European countries.[46] A joint high authority would be responsible for bringing about a convergence of productive processes, a rationalization of coal and steel industries at the European level, and for gradually lifting trade barriers. The stated long-term project—to prepare the construction of a common market—was ambitious. The Schuman proposal embodied a vision, that of a united and possibly federated Europe. The creation of a common market, starting with coal and steel products, was defined as a means to an end, a strategy to institutionalize cross-national interdependence at the European level and create common interests between former enemies. The ultimate aims were political and geopolitical, to reconcile a divided continent and 'to create the first concrete foundations for a European federation which [appeared] so essential for the preservation of peace'.[47]

The vision of a peaceful and united, mass-producing and mass-consuming European continent as entertained by Jean Monnet and his team had been shaped, to a large extent, by their familiarity with and admiration for the American economic space. As early as 1945, Jean Monnet had been talking with his American friends about the possible features of a united Europe.[48] After May 9, 1950, a number of Americans were still closely involved, as experts and consultants, in the concrete process of turning the coal and steel project into a treaty and a community. George Ball played a key role even though a mostly unofficial one, both throughout the elaboration of the project and throughout the negotiation proceedings of the European Coal and Steel Community or ECSC treaty.[49] Raymond Vernon, in the State Department, apparently studied the treaty very closely and commented on all successive drafts, while William Tomlinson, top Treasury official with the ECA Mission in Paris, was the contact between Vernon and Monnet (Duchêne, 1994). In the fall of 1950, Robert Bowie started working on the antitrust provisions of the project. A Harvard Law School antitrust specialist, Robert Bowie was also General Counsel to the American High Commissioner in Germany, John McCloy, one of Monnet's closest friends.

Compatibility between the proposal of the French planning board on the one hand and, on the other, the general objectives of the American administration was striking once more. The vision of a single European economic space lay behind the French proposal. A common European market, creating the conditions for lasting peace and cooperation on the continent, was also a key objective of the American administration in charge of foreign aid and in particular of the ECA (Hoffman, 1951; Maier, 1978; Hogan, 1984, 1985). The belief was widespread in Washington and in ECA Missions throughout Europe that the integration of European markets was a necessary precondition to mass production. On the basis of American experience, it was further argued that mass production meant lower costs, higher productivity, increasing living standards for all, and, as a consequence, greater social and political stability.

In the late 1940s and early 1950s, some of the most zealous advocates of a European economic union could thus be found within the American foreign aid administration. Americans were ready to use the position of power they enjoyed as providers of financial and economic assistance or of military protection to push for closer economic and potentially political union in Western Europe. Once again, however, they undeniably preferred to work towards the construction of the 'United States of Europe' in collaboration with Europeans—even if only a small group—rather than against them. By the end of the 1940s, the UK was distancing itself from the affairs of the continent and the Federal Republic of Germany remained politically powerless and dependent. The 'key to progress towards integration' therefore clearly lay, in the words of the American Secretary of State Dean Acheson, 'in French hands'.[50]

After some hesitation, the Americans welcomed the Schuman proposal as a step in the right direction and as essentially compatible with their own objectives for Europe. The initial hesitation was mostly due to American wariness with regard to the potential of the project to turn into a European-wide cartel. On May 10, 1950, in an immediate reaction to the French proposal, Dean Acheson, while praising the initiative, held back his full support on those very grounds. The lukewarm American reaction immediately led to a heightened level of activity within the French planning board. On May 12, the French team sent a memorandum to the American State Department, documenting differences between the French proposal and an international cartel.[51] The memorandum emphasized that the main objective of the proposed organization was to increase production and productivity 'by an improvement of methods, the broadening of markets, and a rationalization of production' and not to 'maintain stable profits and acquired positions'. The goal was to create a competitive environment for coal and steel industries within Western Europe. This, the French argued, required that governments be involved. Only a political and technocratic initiative could break the resistance to competition characteristic of European coal and steel industries and business communities. In the end, those arguments proved convincing.

What really made a difference, however, and got the better of American hesitation, was the fact that Jean Monnet was behind the project. Members of the American administration knew that Monnet believed in the model of expanded production and markets. They were also aware of the close collaboration existing between the planning board and a number of American lawyers and consultants. Members of the American administration were thus convinced that they would get systematic feedback and that they could have an indirect impact, whenever necessary, through the web-like network spun around Jean Monnet. Knowing that they had in this way a fair degree of control, the Americans were ready, by June 1950, to step back from negotiation proceedings in order to minimize their apparent involvement in European affairs.[52]

Negotiation Proceedings

Towards the end of June 1950, negotiation talks started between the six countries that had accepted the Schuman proposal—France, West Germany, Italy, Belgium, the Netherlands, and Luxemburg. The UK had excluded itself, rejecting the supranational nature of the project and the partial loss of sovereignty it seemed to imply. The object of these talks was to define the features and workings of the future community and to prepare the implementation stage. Negotiation proceedings were long and difficult and the European Coal and Steel Community (ECSC) only started to operate in 1953. For the small team around Jean Monnet, the battle during negotiation proceedings had to be waged on several fronts. French modernizers had, first of all, to prevent the project from drifting towards an international cartel. Next, the supranational nature of future community institutions had to be explained to and imposed on national representatives. Finally, support for the project had to be secured in the USA and created in participating countries.

The main obstacle, throughout the talks, was the systematic opposition of business and labor communities, particularly in West Germany and in France. Some problems also emerged from the parallel reorganization of coal and steel industries that was carried out by Allied occupation forces in West Germany. The strategy of Jean Monnet and his team had been to pre-empt conflicts with industry representatives by altogether excluding them. The planning board had not even consulted members of the coal and steel industries before drafting the early proposal. Jean Monnet had then strongly insisted that official country delegates to the negotiation proceedings should not be members of national industries who would only consider their own interests, but 'independent personalities who [had], besides technical capacity, a concern for general interest'.[53] Excluding members of the industries from negotiation proceedings was naturally difficult, but it appeared to the team around Jean Monnet to be essential if the final treaty was to reflect the objectives and spirit set forth in the 1950 proposal. Involvement or input on the part of members of the coal and steel industries could only increase the likelihood of a drift towards cartelization.

The cartel issue, together with the supranational nature of future institutions and the reorganization of German coal and steel industries would remain key bones of contention throughout the negotiation proceedings. Despite their early wish not to get involved, the Americans soon acknowledged the strength of the opposition to the project and realized that they would have to intervene in order to help Jean Monnet and his team. During the early weeks of negotiation, national pressures were strongly felt. The Dutch were challenging the supranational character of the future community and the Italians were asking for special conditions. French, Belgian, and German industrial communities were violently denouncing the project and its anticartel orientation in particular. Their impact on country delegates to the talks, albeit indirect, was nevertheless real. As a consequence, early drafts of the ECSC treaty reflected and, to some extent, incorporated those pressures. This soon aroused concern within the American administration and prompted intervention. In the fall, the American administration imposed a redrafting to bring the future treaty into line with the initial objectives of the Schuman proposal. The revised project had, in particular, to address the cartel issue in a satisfying manner. Both French and German delegations were being asked to work in that direction. The Germans, however, only accepted with reluctance as the following account by the head of the West German delegation, Walter Hallstein, clearly shows:

Monnet's ideas are probably also influenced by the American desire that all cartel-like institutions be rejected—a desire that gains special weight due to the fact that it is supported by the funds that Americans are to provide at a later stage. The French side will examine the cartel question once more from this perspective. The [German] Federal Ministry of Economic Affairs is likewise asked to submit an appropriate proposal and has agreed to do so.[54]

At the end of October, the French came back with a draft that essentially rekindled the spirit of the Schuman proposal. The supranational character of the future community was embodied in a High Authority, patterned on American federal regulatory agencies and sheltered from direct national and political influences. Articles 60 and 61, written in large part by Robert Bowie, dealt explicitly with the cartel issue. Article 60 prohibited cartels and agreements although it made a partial exception for periods of crisis, when the High Authority could accept certain types of agreements. Article 61 dealt with abuses of market power due to excessive concentration, without prohibiting concentration *per se*. Mergers which could be shown to create conditions for increased efficiency and productivity without representing a threat to competition might be allowed by the High Authority. Were the French draft adopted, the 'rule of reason', that had come to frame the American antitrust debate, would thus undeniably be transferred to the new community through those two articles.[55] The draft proposed by the German delegation was, on the other hand, much less restrictive on the cartel issue. All national delegations except the French backed this second draft which was also more acceptable to industry members. The French draft, on the other hand, was closer to American objectives for Europe and it therefore received full American support. Such support would be crucial throughout the remaining months of negotiations and would tip the scales in favor of the French proposal.

Breaking German Resistance: The American Joker

The cartel issue was at the origin of disagreements and conflicts between French and German delegations during the negotiation proceedings. The problem was further compounded by the restructuring of West German coal and steel industries that was being imposed, concomitantly, by Allied occupation authorities. A common and competitive market for European coal and steel products required that the German Ruhr industry be decartelized and deconcentrated. Vertical links in particular between coal producers and iron makers needed to be destroyed or at least weakened. The Deutscher Kohlen-Verkauf (DKV), a centralized sales agency for the coal produced in the Ruhr region, would also have to disappear. Acting *de facto* as a cartel, the DKV was absolutely incompatible both with Allied anticartel legislation in Germany and with the spirit of the Schuman plan. The French draft of October 1950 demanded that those issues be settled and that the Germans agree on a large-scale restructuring of their coal and steel industries. Under strong pressure from members of the Ruhr business community, the German delegation resisted for more than three months. ECSC negotiations were stalled, but intensive and unofficial, behind-the-scene, diplomatic activity was still taking place. Jean Monnet started talking directly with the German Minister of Economic Affairs, Ludwig Erhard, and with the West German Chancellor, Konrad Adenauer.

The most efficient unofficial scheme, however, proved to be an indirect Franco-German discussion through an American mediator, John McCloy, High Commissioner to Germany. On the one hand, John McCloy and Jean Monnet were close friends who happened to share similar views and objectives as far as the European common market for coal and steel was concerned. At the same time, John McCloy as official representative of the American government in Germany had significant authority over German affairs, particularly in a domain like decartelization, a 'reserved field' under the Occupation Statute. He could exert strong pressure on the Germans or legitimately threaten to do so.[56] The role of McCloy (and more generally of the American administration) in bringing the Germans back to the negotiating table cannot be overestimated.[57]

The German delegation finally agreed to the restructuring of the German coal and steel industries and accepted a version of the ECSC treaty fairly close to that which had been proposed in October 1950 by the French delegation and had received full American support at the time. This rallying of the German delegation to the French draft would certainly not have taken place without repeated American pressure. On April 9, 1951, Ludwig Erhard reminded Konrad Adenauer that the final German decision had been 'influenced by the American negotiating partners in a fashion which amounted almost to an ultimatum'.[58] Nine days later, the six participating countries had officially signed the ECSC treaty.

As it turned out, the coal and steel community prepared the way for the creation of a wider common market, that was made official by the signing of the Treaty of Rome in 1957. The European Economic Community (EEC) integrated the coal and steel pool and appropriated its institutions. In fact, the Treaty of Rome extended to most sectors of Western European economies those principles initially defined for coal and steel by the ECSC treaty. In particular, articles 60 and 61 of the ECSC treaty were directly transferred to the Treaty of Rome where they became articles 85 and 86. In the words of Jean Monnet, those articles, 'drafted with great care by Robert Bowie, represented a fundamental innovation in Europe'. According to him, 'the essential *antitrust* [*sic*] legislation reigning over the common market today ha[d] its origins in those few sentences for which [he did] not regret to have fought during four months'.[59] And indeed, articles 60 and 61 of the ECSC treaty laid the foundations of antitrust legislation for the common European market. Such antitrust legislation was clearly foreign to European industrial traditions and had direct and unmistakable American origins.

The significance of those two articles was due to the fact that, together with the supranational character of institutions, they embodied the original spirit of the early Schuman proposal. They were essential to the creation of a unified, competitive and productive, mass-producing and mass-consuming European economic space on the American model. The fight over these two articles, marking the end of 1950 and the beginning of 1951, was in fact symbolic of the conflict between the two systems of industrial production. This explains why this fight reached such proportions and engendered so much passion. Throughout the early 1950s, representatives of a prewar European economic and industrial order were trying hard to resist the transfer of foreign—in this case American—models that a small cross-national group of modernizing technocrats was attempting to impose. By the end of the 1950s, anticartel provisions were directly incorporated within the Treaty of Rome. This incorporation did not generate particular resistance, at least nothing that could compare with the episode of the ECSC negotiations. It is too early to argue that the fight had been won by modernizing technocrats. It can still be claimed that, by the end of the 1950s, the original spirit of the Schuman proposal had been, to some extent at least, integrated and institutionalized within the Western European economic space.

Ultimately, the initiative both for the large-scale reshaping of the French system of industrial production and for the creation of a Western European economic space lay with a small group of French modernizers. The infrastructural power of the French state after the Second World War made it possible for this small group to have a significant impact over the national economy and industry. Holding strategic positions of power at the articulation of state and society, French modernizers had the necessary means and tools to launch and implement their ambitious project. The challenge they had set themselves was to transform the French economic and industrial landscape, following their own understanding of the American corporate model. With this objective in mind and building on their institutional power, French modernizers elaborated mechanisms—such as the national investment plan or productivity institutions—through which a large-scale cross-national transfer could take place. Having secured the support and the concrete material assistance of their American partners in the cross-national network, they were soon operating this set of mechanisms. Members of the small French team were aware of the radical implications of their project. They knew, in particular, that a restructuring of the national economy on such a scale would require, at some point, a redefinition of the Western European economic space. They initiated, as a consequence, the first stage of this radical redefinition, dragging along a few other Western European countries but also most of their fellow countrymen. This particular French undertaking would certainly not have succeeded without American intervention and support. It remains a fact, however, that the initiative lay with the French modernizers and that voluntary imitation was a key mechanism of the cross-national transfer process in the French case, from the very beginning. This was not the case in the West German context.

Notes

1. As early as October 1946, members of the planning board seemed convinced that a large part of proposed investments would be financed 'through the counterpart in Francs of foreign credits' (Commissariat Général du Plan, 1946: 99).
2. Originally, the first plan was to last four years, from 1947 to 1950. It was extended, in the end, until 1952 and made to coincide with the Marshall plan.
3. 'Gouvernement Provisoire de la République: Instructions à Monsieur le Commissaire Général du Plan, 10 janvier 1946', AN-80AJ/1. Increased productivity, the official directive provided, could come from a 'concentration of production units and firms, from the adoption of new methods, tools and machines, or from internal reorganization'
4. Commissariat Général du Plan (1946), detailed plans by sector, *passim.*
5. Through its program of nationalizations in 1945 and 1946, the French state gained direct control over key sources of energy (gas, electricity, coal), air transport (Air France), a sizable part of auto manufacturing (Renault), insurance and credit companies (in particular, the Banque de France and four commercial banks—Crédit Lyonnais, Société Générale, Comptoir National d'Escompte, and BNCI).
6. Commissariat Général du Plan (1946: 103).

7. Cohen (1969: 21) argued that 'as long as business was dependent on the state for upwards of 2/3 of the financing of its investments and approval of a proposed investment project by the planning board was an important determinant of the allocation of public investment credits, business would be compelled to cooperate with the plan'.

8. Commissariat Général du Plan (1946: 107). In 1946, a report from the modernization commission for the oil industry denounced the tax burden imposed on mergers 'demanded by the state' (AN-130AQ/22).

9. 'Commission sur la Production Industrielle, Assemblée Nationale, Avis sur le Deuxième Plan Français, 6 mars 1956', AN-80AJ/21. The planning board used a number of other strategies such as the conditional allocation of public contracts or direct subsidies to encourage mergers, restructuring, and programs to increase productivity. Commissariat Général du Plan (1946: 104).

10. See Commissariat Général du Plan (1946) and 'Premier Rapport de la Commission de Modernisation de la Sidérurgie, novembre 1946', AN-80AJ/11. See also Venturini (1971), Hayward (1986), and Hall (1986).

11. The account by Etienne Hirsch, then a member of the planning board, of this forced modernization can be found in Fourquet (1980: 238).

12. Both 'national champions' in the electronics industry—Thomson Houston and CSF—were in 1967 and would remain for years, aggregates of loosely coordinated smaller entities. The policy of prompting rapid mergers was not followed by systematic internal restructuring. Internal reorganization would only take place after the nationalization of the merged giant, Thomson-CSF, in 1982. Zysman (1983) and Hall (1986).

13. Etienne Hirsch, in Fourquet (1980: 237).

14. See Imprimerie Nationale (1961), *passim*. A 25 per cent increase over the 1929 figure was equivalent to a 66 per cent increase over the 1938 figure.

15. For 1938, the equivalent was around 16 per cent. Peterson (1953) as quoted in Kuisel (1981), p. 261, n. 62.

16. In fact, the role of the French state as an investor was greater than Table 10 indicates, since it also controlled, through nationalized institutions, a fair share of bank credits.

17. 'Note sur la nécessité d'un deuxième plan, juin 1951', AN-80AJ/17. See also 'Note sur les procédures d'établissement du deuxième plan', no date.

18. The list of basic actions presented here can be found in AN-80AJ/17.

19. AN-80AJ/17. This unverified assumption remained dominant throughout the Fourth Republic and well into the Fifth. See Lauber (1981: 231): 'The Gaullists favored a policy of industrial concentration out of a conviction that only a concentrated economy was efficient and capable of surviving international competition. Yet, no effort was made to verify the relation between size and efficiency and many observers have remained skeptical.'

20. 'Ententes can be as useful in promoting specialization as they are harmful when they restrict competition.' In 'Directives proposées en vue de l'établissement du 2ème plan, février 1953', AN-80AJ/17.

21. *Le Monde*, 20 août 1953 and Sélinsky (1979: 7).

22. See AN-80AJ/19. There is already no mention, in the version of the second plan submitted to the national assembly, in June 1954, of a regulation of non-competitive behavior and of the use that could be made of antitrust provisions.

23. See for example Commissariat Général du Plan (1946), *passim*, and AN-80AJ/77. The objective would remain the same throughout the 1950s and Jean Fourastié, chairman of the French working group in charge of productivity and later of the OEEC subcommittee on productivity studies, understood that it would take time: 'The action undertaken is essentially long term and often very long term. It will require more than a few months or even a few years to raise a nation in the present situation of Greece, Portugal or France to the level of the USA' Fourastié (1953: 344).

24. For more on the history and organization of the bureau of industrial monographs, see 'Histoire et Organisation du Service des Monographies et d'Analyse Industrielle, 19 juin 1947', AN-80AJ/77.

25. AN-81AJ/176 and AN-80AJ/77.

26. AN-81AJ/176 and AN-80AJ/178.

27. According to Noël Pouderoux, 'it [was] highly unfortunate that the [productivity] issue ha[d] been brought to the attention of our political and administrative leaders through foreign influences'. 'Noël Pouderoux, presentation to the working group, November 18, 1948', AN-81AJ/178.

28. 'Formation aux méthodes modernes d'organisation, 8 septembre 1948' and 'Comment tirer parti de l'expérience Américaine? 29 septembre 1948', AN-81AJ/176.

29. 'Note sur la Productivité, juillet 1948', AN-81AJ/176. See also AN-80AJ/77.

30. For more on the prewar rationalization movement in France, see Devinat (1927), Maier (1970), Kogut and Parkinson (1994). For more on the technocratic and corporatist heritage of the Vichy regime, see Paxton (1973), Azéma and Bédarida (1992).

31. Comité National de l'Organisation Française (CNOF), Centre d'Etudes Générales d'Organisation Scientifique (CEGOS), Bureau des Temps Elémentaires (BTE).

32. 'Note sur la Productivité, juillet 1948', AN-81AJ/176. As discussed in Chapter 1, the very idea of cartelization and market organization had come to be associated, in the American tradition—and this ever since the beginning of the twentieth century—with limits to competition, inefficiencies, high prices, and thus low productivity levels. The idea that organized markets could have a positive impact on productivity levels was thus undeniably in radical contradiction with the American tradition and experience.

33. According to Jean Monnet, this program took up 'concrete solutions already successfully implemented in the USA'. 'Lettre de Monnet au Président du Conseil, 8 janvier 1949', AN-80AJ/80.

34. 'Télégramme à l'arrivée de Bérard, Washington, 25 septembre 1948, pour le Ministère des Affaires Etrangères', AN-80AJ/80.

35. AN-F60bis/517, AN-F60ter/392, AN-80AJ/277, and Documentation Française (1953). For more on the American technical assistance program or 'productivity drive', see Chapter 7.

36. In December 1949, Monnet was deploring the insufficient scope of French efforts in productivity matters in particular when compared to American generosity. He argued that when the ECA was thinking of granting US$5 million to the French productivity program, an increase in the French contribution from FF180 to 275 million was certainly not asking for too much. 'Lettre de Monnet au Ministre de l'Economie et des Finances, 12 décembre 1949', AN-81AJ/206.

37. AN-81AJ/178 and AN-81AJ/179.

38. Productivity reports on study trips to the USA were presented in summary form in a bi-monthly publication—*Cahiers de la Productivité*. Starting in 1952, the SADEP also published a monthly magazine, *Productivité Française*.
39. 'Esquisse d'une Politique de Productivité, 18 novembre 1949', AN-81AJ/178.
40. 'Note sur la Productivité du Travail en France, Mission ECA Paris, mars 1950', AN-81AJ/207.
41. 'Discours de Buron, président du CNP, 10 octobre 1950', AN-81AJ/179.
42. 'MSA, Critères Relatifs aux Projets d'Assistance Technique, 29 janvier 1952, A toutes les Missions MSA et Washington', AN-81AJ/179.
43. 'P.v du 23 mars 1953 et annexe. Communiqué de M. Vallée (CNPF)', AN-81AJ/180.
44. One should naturally not dismiss the path dependencies and lock-in situations that political and economic choices can engender. Once productivity had been equated with large size and mass production, legislation, institutions, and industrial policy tools had been rapidly redefined and adapted to fit such an equation. By the mid-1950s, it would already have been fairly difficult and costly to go back on those early choices. However and in any event, the problem was not even discussed when clearly it could have been.
45. Monnet Foundation, AMG.
46. 'Proposal of May 9, 1950.' For the French version of the Schuman speech, see Gerbet (1956). For the English translation, see FRUS (1950: iii).
47. Commenting on this excerpt from the 'Proposal of May 9, 1950', Jean Monnet added in his memoirs: 'The last word was the key word—peace' (Monnet, 1976: 353).
48. With Robert Nathan, Eugen Rostow, and George Ball naturally. But also with Henry Luce and John Davenport of *Fortune Magazine*, John McCloy, or the former Morgan partner Dwight Morrow. See Monnet Foundation, AME (iv) and Monnet (1976).
49. In George Ball's words: 'I came back to work on the Schuman plan starting on June 18, 1950. . . . It was very funny because I had this little office under the stairs. . . . The European delegation was also there. He [Monnet] didn't want them to know he had an American working for him, so I was being smuggled up to his office and smuggled out the back door . . . Bruce [American Ambassador to France] and Tomlinson [American Treasury representative] were very happy that I was there. We were all working for the same side' (George Ball (1981), interview for the Monnet Foundation).
50. 'Acheson to Paris Mission, 19 October 1949', FRUS (1949: iv., 470–2).
51. This memorandum is reprinted in 'Telegram from Acheson to Dulles [Acting Secretary of State], London, May 12, 1950', FRUS (1950: iii).
52. 'The US government therefore should have no official association or even observers with the working committees engaged in the elaboration of this plan at this stage. The full knowledge of such negotiations can be obtained by us . . . and we believe that the French will be anxious to keep us currently informed.' 'Telegram from Bruce to Acheson, Paris, May 23, 1950', FRUS (1950: iii).
53. Memo of the French planning board, reprinted in 'Telegram from Acheson to Dulles, London, May 12, 1950', FRUS (1950: iii). The West German Chancellor, Konrad Adenauer, after a conversation with Jean Monnet, finally agreed not to

appoint as chief negotiator an industrialist who had been his first choice. He proposed Walter Hallstein instead, a German law professor (Schwartz, 1991*a*: 107).

54. 'Walter Hallstein to German government, October 19, 1950.' Quoted in Berghahn (1986: 140).

55. According to Eberhard Günther, cartel expert with the German Ministry of Economic Affairs, Monnet's proposal 'followed American antitrust legislation and went even beyond the anticartel legislation imposed on Germany by occupying powers'. Quoted in Berghahn (1986: 141).

56. FRUS (1951: iv) and Monnet Foundation, AMG (12/3/6). Towards the end of February 1951, McCloy was calling Monnet on the 'phone to tell him that the latest German demands were unacceptable. Monnet urged him to give the Germans an ultimatum—accept the French proposal or else the High Commission would impose a solution.

57. Jean Monnet was the first to acknowledge the help he had received from the American administration, and in particular from John McCloy, stating that the treaty 'would never have been signed but for McCloy's support' (Monnet, quoted in Schwartz, 1991*a*: 198).

58. Quoted in Berghahn (1986: 153).

59. Monnet (1976: 413). Jean Monnet deliberately used, in the French text of his memoirs, the unmistakably American term: 'antitrust'.

6

From Coercion to Imitation
Transplanting the Corporate Model to West Germany

We all recognize that one of the most important aspects of the occupation is in its educating the Germans in economic and political democracy. This can best be done, as I am sure you recognize, by example and not mere precept, and the decartelization program furnishes a most valuable and important area for such action.

Dean Acheson[1]

In the period just following the war, occupation authorities held all decision making powers in the western territories of Germany and the American element was particularly dominant. Consequently, at this early stage, the initiative for economic and industrial reforms could only come from the foreign administration and in effect from the American administration. After months of confusion, disagreements, and overt conflicts around what the economic policy for German territories should be, a clear project had finally been settled upon by the end of 1947. From that point on, the American administration did advocate the rebuilding of a healthy West German economy. It appeared essential, to that end, to foster a radical redefinition of West German economic structures and of the West German system of industrial production. The objective was to bring about an evolution of the economic and industrial landscape towards the model then dominant in the USA. Members of the American administration thus initiated a large-scale, cross-national structural transfer, mostly using coercive means at the beginning.

Americans, however, were perfectly aware of the shortcomings of coercive transfer mechanisms. Reforms that were merely being imposed had little chance of being long lasting. For transformations to outlast the period of acute geopolitical dependence, they would have to be actively appropriated by at least a small group of West German nationals. The American administration was therefore soon looking for local partners it could co-opt and place in strategic positions of institutional power within the new West German entity. It settled on the small and somewhat marginal group around Ludwig Erhard essentially because of the unmistakable similarities existing between the economic program of this group and the American project for West Germany. Once this group had been co-opted and its institutional position on the national scene had been secured, voluntary imitation could start to operate in West Germany as a mechanism for the large-scale, cross-national transfer process.

IMPOSING A REGULATIVE FRAMEWORK TO FOSTER COMPETITION

In the context of deteriorating relationships between East and West, in 1947, the USA had redefined their official policy towards Germany. Once the western territories of Germany became a front line against communism, the systematic destruction or weakening of German industry appeared to be counterproductive. By the end of 1947, the USA, and in particular members of the American military government in Germany (OMGUS), were therefore unambiguously working towards the rebuilding of a democratic, peaceful, and economically powerful West Germany. This followed a period, however, of heated debate and open conflict within the American administration, both in Washington and in Germany. The confrontation around a policy for the West German economy in fact paralleled the turn of the century antitrust debate in the USA. Two very different and incompatible economic world views at that time had indirectly confronted each other around the meaning and interpretation of antitrust policy. Champions of the emerging model of corporate capitalism had finally gained the upper hand, in this turn of the century confrontation, against advocates of small-scale, family capitalism.

Similarly, the post-Second World War American debate on the economic future of West Germany resulted in the victory of those who argued for the rebuilding of a strong West German industry, along the lines of the American corporate model. Emerging through the conflict around decartelization and deconcentration policies, the issue of competition once again appeared to be of key importance. By 1948, decartelization and deconcentration policies had unmistakably evolved towards antitrust legislation in the American sense of the term, where cartels were prohibited *per se* while mergers and tight combinations seemed to escape legal scrutiny, as long as they remained 'reasonable'. This evolution of the decartelization and deconcentration program after 1947 fitted perfectly the new agenda of the American administration in West Germany. Members of OMGUS were indeed arguing by then that 'the decartelization program [was] essentially constructive' and that 'it should raise the standards of living of the people of Germany'. This program, they went on, was 'interested in the eventual development of a society of free private enterprise in Germany . . . [because] freedom is good *per se* . . . [and because] lasting political democracy is impossible unless accompanied by economic freedom'.[2]

Breaking up German Aggregates of Industrial Power

Soon after Germany had surrendered and even before the beginning of the Potsdam Conference, Allied occupation authorities took over a number of

German industrial concerns. Allied powers agreed, by the end of the war, that those industrial leaders who had provided material resources for the German war effort shared responsibility with German political and military authorities and should therefore be tried and punished. Consequently in July 1945, the American military government in Germany seized the assets of the German chemical giant, IGFarben, located in the American zone of occupation. An IGFarben Control Office was immediately set up within OMGUS. With 140 American personnel in September 1945, this office was temporarily entrusted with the control and management of those assets. It severed most technical and commercial relationships between the 52 units of the IGFarben combine, forcing them to operate as independent entities (Clay, 1950; Stokes, 1988). The size and power of IGFarben had singled it out, making it a likely first target. It had been, both before and during the war, at the center of a dense network of international cartels. According to the Economic Warfare Unit in the Antitrust Division of the American Department of Justice, these international cartels had been responsible for reducing the American production capacity of a number of strategic materials. IGFarben had significantly contributed, according to this same source, to the German program of economic warfare.

IGFarben was not the only German firm, however, on the short list of the American occupation authorities. The heavy machinery (Henschel und Sohn, Bosch, Flick) and the banking sectors, for example, also fell under the systematic scrutiny of the American decartelization and deconcentration branch.[3] Large coal and steel combines were other targets of the Americans, but with the entire Ruhr region being located within the British zone of occupation, coal and steel were placed under the temporary trusteeship of the British military government. For all these industrial sectors, investigation and data gathering proved necessary before any deconcentration program could be put forward. During this preparatory work, investigating teams in the Decartelization and Deconcentration Branch or in the IGFarben Control Office naturally encountered significant resistance on the part of German business communities. They also came across resistance, as was documented earlier, from within other divisions of American military government.

In spite of these obstacles, most combines on the early short list of Allied occupation authorities did eventually undergo partial deconcentration or outright break-up. The restructuring that took place in the end, however, was in keeping with the redefined American policy for Germany. The American military government imposed a deconcentration of IGFarben assets but only to the point where the German chemical industry would become a competitive oligopoly. It appeared that General Clay and General Draper had 'agreed to a compromise solution for the sale of IGFarben assets: each separate economic unit would be made sufficiently large so that a corporation with a large stock issue could be set up as the successor owner'.[4] By 1951, the break-up of IGFarben was completed. There were three major successor companies—

Hoechst, Bayer, and BASF—and a number of smaller ones. This reorganization of the German chemical industry would prove long lasting and naturally meant a redefinition of the competitive environment in that industry (Dyas and Thanheiser, 1976; Berghahn, 1986). The break-up of IGFarben also had consequences for ownership structures within the German chemical industry since OMGUS had insisted on creating joint stock corporations with large stock issues and on placing a limit to the amount of shares that could be bought by a single individual.[5]

With respect to the banking sector, the restructuring followed a similar pattern. The German *Grossbanken*, that had collaborated with the Nazi regime, were liquidated and broken down into thirty-three small and local banking units. The banking operations of one particular unit were limited to the territory of a single German *Land* or state. Each *Land* could set up its own central bank, confirming the tendency towards a decentralization of the German banking system.[6] The institutionalization of the Bizone and an anticipated merger with the French zone led to the setting up of a Bank Deutscher Länder in March 1948. This bank became the central bank of the West German Federal Republic after 1949. In 1952, the Allied High Commission agreed to a second restructuring of the German banking sector, perfectly in line with its economic policies for West Germany. Through mergers, the thirty-three small and local banking units turned into nine larger ones, each having operations in several different *Länder*. Concentration and centralization went one step further in 1957 when three main banks came to dominate the German commercial banking sector. Far from being a sign of the failure of American policy in Germany, this reconcentration made perfect sense in the light of the redefinition of this policy after 1947.[7]

The coal and steel industries also fell under the close scrutiny of Allied occupation authorities. Located for the most part within the Ruhr region, under British control, the entire coal and steel sector came under trusteeship of the British Military Government in 1946. A controller was appointed—the North German Iron and Steel Control—to oversee and manage coal and steel firms in the short term.[8] The coal and steel industries had played a key role in building up German economic and military might during the 1930s and early 1940s. Restructuring in those industries, however, proved particularly complex due to the dense networks of cooperation linking coal producers on the one hand, iron and steel makers on the other and due also to the existence of powerful sales agencies in the coal sector.[9] A disagreement between British and American governments on the policy to be followed in these two sectors also contributed to delaying the restructuring process. The British Labour government was arguing that only the nationalization or socialization of the German coal and steel industries could prevent such staggering forms of economic and industrial power returning to private hands. The Americans had a position on the restructuring of coal and steel industries that was consistent with their overall program for West German industry as it had developed by that time. A few particularly huge individual concerns and combines should be broken-up and deconcentrated.[10] Ownership should remain private but corporate forms of ownership were favored over personal forms. Formal and less formal relationships between the coal and steel industries had to be destroyed while sales syndicates in the coal sector should be liquidated. In this Anglo-American dispute, the Americans ended up gaining the upper hand, mostly as a consequence of their dominant role in the Bizone. American occupation authorities made it clear to their British counterparts that there would be no further talk of socialization or nationalization of coal and steel industries in Germany, as long as a freely elected and sovereign German national assembly was not ready to initiate it. In the meantime, American occupation authorities were urging a rapid reorganization and restructuring of the coal and steel industries, essentially through the break-up of coal and steel combines and their sale to private actors. They were attempting, in fact, to create a *de facto* situation where the ownership issue would be settled before a debate on nationalization could even start.[11]

The particular weight of coal and steel industries in Germany, their peculiarly complex patterns of organization, and the symbolic dimension attached to their role before and during the Second World War called for specific legislation in that sector. A long period of investigation and difficult negotiations between the American and British occupation authorities held up the promulgation of such legislation for quite some time. Law #75, on the 'reorganization of German coal and iron and steel industries' in the British and American zones, was finally enacted in November 1948.[12] Article I provided that the ten largest concerns, producing around 90 per cent of German steel output and 50 per cent of German coal during the war, had to be broken-up. Articles II and III laid out the conditions and procedures for a systematic reorganization of the coal and steel industries. German trustees, selected and appointed by occupation authorities, were to impose and foster reorganization, in accordance with instructions issued by the military government.[13] The American proposal for a systematic reorganization of coal and steel industries in Germany amounted in fact to an attempt at rationalizing those industries, with the objective of bringing about lower costs, increased efficiency, and higher levels of production (Owen Smith, 1983; Berghahn, 1986). Law #75 made such rationalization possible by allowing the creation of new companies through 'mergers or amalgamations of seized assets, including assets outside the field of the iron and steel industry'.

The reorganization process took time. The resistance and sometimes outright opposition of members of the coal and steel communities slowed it down considerably. In the end—and this has already been told—the reorganization of the West German coal and steel industries was hammered out in 1951 during the Schuman plan negotiations, under strong pressure from the French delegation on one side and of the American High Commission and Marshall plan administration on the other. Out of the initial ten combines to be broken-up, twenty-six new companies emerged. The Vereignite Stahlwerke AG alone was divided into thirteen independent operating entities. Relationships between coal and steel industries were also significantly redefined. A mere 11 per cent of coal production would thereafter be controlled by steel firms, when the equivalent figure had been 55 per cent at the end of the Second World War. Finally, the agreement reached in 1951 also provided for a dissolution of sales syndicates in the coal industry (Owen Smith, 1983; Berghahn, 1986).

The largest of German combines were thus broken up throughout the late 1940s and early 1950s. A significant deconcentration and reorganization was forced upon German industry by the American occupation authorities. By 1947 however, the objective was no longer to destroy German industrial sectors but to bring about their transformation into competitive oligopolies, following a model pioneered in the USA. This objective implied rationalization—and thus possibly mergers and concentration—in those same industries where prewar combines had been systematically broken up. The contradiction was only apparent and the concentration process that started in a number of German industries in the early 1950s should not be interpreted as the failure of American economic reforms in Germany. On the contrary, it followed perfectly logically from the redefined American program for the West German economy and industry. Concentration or reconcentration did take place in German industry throughout the 1950s and the 1960s, but in a manner that differed radically from that which had characterized Germany before and during the Second World War (Dyas and Thanheiser, 1976; Berghahn, 1986; Cassis, 1997).

Prohibiting Cartels and Re-Educating German Actors

While the American deconcentration program for West German industry had undeniably been redefined by 1947, cartels and restrictive trade practices had remained a priority target of the American administration in Germany ever since the beginning of the occupation period. Law #56 and ordinance #78, promulgated in February 1947, prohibited 'excessive concentrations of German economic power, whether within or without Germany and whatever their form or character'.[14] Cartels, combines, syndicates, and trusts were declared in paragraph 2 of the first article of the law to be, *per se*, excessive concentrations of economic power. The prosecution and dissolution of cartels, combines, and syndicates, was entrusted to an Anglo-American decartelization commission or BIDEC (Bipartite Decartelization Commission).[15] Ultimate power and responsibility for decision making lay with this Bizonal commission. The occupation authorities, however, and in particular the American element, were convinced that implementing economic reforms through coercive means only would only lead to fragile results. Structural transformations, if they were to outlast the period of foreign occupation in Germany, had to be appropriated by West German actors. The decartelization program, or more exactly the project to transfer American antitrust legislation and tradition to West Germany, was thus designed so that it could be taken over, at some point, by West Germans. This implied, naturally, the systematic re-education and training of those West German actors who ultimately were to be in charge.

As a first step towards re-education, members of the emerging West German administration were involved in the implementation of law #56 and ordinance #78, under the strict supervision and control of the Bizonal commission or BIDEC. The British and American military governments created, in April 1947, German agencies that became responsible for the decartelization program.[16] A central German Decartelization Commission (GEDEC) was located in Minden, while each *Land* had its own Decartelization Agency (GEDAG). The duties of these German agencies were clearly defined. They were to serve as mediators between the Bizonal commission and German firms or combines. They collected and processed reports for BIDEC that had to be prepared by those German companies falling under law #56 and they passed along to German firms the instructions they received from BIDEC. They could help German firms and combines prepare decartelization, deconcentration, or reorganization proposals and they were also in charge of supervising the implementation of final plans, once those had been approved by BIDEC.[17]

The work of German decartelization agencies was regularly double-checked by members of the Bizonal decartelization commission. The ultimate objective in this case was not so much to control as to educate. Close collaboration between the bizonal decartelization element and German agencies represented an opportunity for Americans to 'educate and indoctrinate German personnel engaged in enforcing German decartelization laws'.[18] Members of West German agencies had to be trained in the peculiar role of enforcing a decartelization legislation that was foreign to German legal and economic traditions. American occupation authorities were very much aware that 'such a procedure [did] not serve to expedite enforcement'. They also knew, however, that a 'painstaking educational process to teach the Germans the meaning of the [decartelization] law [was] essential to obtain results'.[19]

This painstaking process of re-education was supposed to create, in the end, conditions for the successful transfer or transplantation to West Germany of the American antitrust tradition. Ultimately, German agencies should come to uphold on their own and voluntarily fight for rules of competitive behavior satisfactory to the American occupation authorities and compatible with their project of a redefined West German economy. The next step in the transfer of responsibilities to West German actors came with the creation of the Federal Republic of Germany. The Allied High Commission demanded that the new German government prepare a fair trade or anticartel law explicitly prohibiting all restrictive business practices. Responsibility for the drafting officially lay with German agencies but American occupation authorities closely monitored the work of those agencies until 1957 when the 'Law against Restrictions to Competition' was finally adopted by the Bundestag. In the meantime, from

1947 to 1957, law #56 remained the basis of competition regulation in West Germany.[20]

To comply with this American demand, Ludwig Erhard brought together in 1950 a task force that was to work on the drafting of West German anticartel legislation. The team counted a number of economists from the Freiburg school, and in particular Franz Böhm. The drafting process turned out to be long and painstaking. Numerous versions were rejected either because they did not conform to American directives or because they were violently denounced by German business leaders. In 1957, the West German Bundestag finally ratified the German anticartel act, albeit with some reluctance. Once again, unrelenting American pressure had clearly been instrumental in bringing the drafting process to an end. Throughout the ten-year long process, the Americans used different types of strategies. They favored, undeniably, a scenario where the Germans would voluntarily adopt the American antitrust tradition on its own merits. They were not ready to accept, however, for the sake of voluntary and spontaneous adoption, too radical a departure from their original demands as far as the contents of the law were concerned. The Americans thus seized every opportunity to 're-educate' or 'indoctrinate'—in their own words—members of the West German task force.

In the early 1950s, the American High Commission took advantage of the American-sponsored technical assistance program to put together a productivity mission, the aim of which was to provide 'a group of German lawyers with the technical knowledge required for the preparation of pending German antitrust legislation'.[21] Franz Böhm and Eberhard Günther, amongst others, met with representatives of the Federal Trade Commission, of the Antitrust Division, and of the Securities Exchange Commission. Eberhard Günther later became, in 1958, the first director of the German cartel office or Bundeskartelamt. At the same time, the office of Robert Bowie—general counsel to the American High Commission—made itself available to help the Germans with the drafting. Finally, whenever progress seemed too slow or a draft unacceptable, the Americans did not hesitate to adopt a tougher strategy, threatening to impose, in particular, their own version of anticartel legislation.[22]

Most members of the first West German government had initially been co-opted and placed in positions of institutional power by American occupation authorities. After September 1949, however, and with the creation of a democratic West German State, they also became accountable to their own citizens. The West German Ministry of Economic Affairs thus found itself throughout the drafting period in a very uncomfortable position. Under the occupation statute, West Germany was still not sovereign in a number of reserved fields, including deconcentration and decartelization. The West German Ministry of Economic Affairs could thus receive orders and directives from the High Commission and, at the same time, it increasingly had to take into account the German national scene and particularly the violent opposition of the German business class to anticartel legislation. Ludwig Erhard himself and the team around him shared the American negative view of cartels, on the grounds that they destroyed competition:

I am convinced and this is the nucleus of my attitude to cartels that only as a result of free competition shall we liberate those forces which will guarantee that economic progress and improvements in working conditions will not be absorbed in greater profits, private incomes and other benefits but that they will be passed on to the consumer. . . . Whoever wants to exclude the function of free prices—and it does not matter whether it is done by government or cartels—kills competition and allows the economy to stagnate.[23]

Without American support and active involvement throughout the 1950s, however, Ludwig Erhard and his team would certainly not have been able to push for a restrictive anticartel act. By providing material and intellectual support to a small group of West Germans ready to fight cartels, by helping to ground their institutional power, the Americans had in the end a significant impact on the West German anticartel debate. Still, after ten years of negotiations, drafting and redrafting, violent attacks from the business communities followed by American threats and promises, the result was bound to be a compromise.

The West German law against restrictions to competition or 'Gesetz gegen Wettbewerbsbeschrankungen', ratified by the Bundestag and the federal President at the end of July 1957, clearly reflected this lengthy and complex drafting process (Damm, 1958). The final version was a prohibition law in the American tradition and, in accordance with American directives, cartels and restrictive practices were outlawed *per se*.[24] Ludwig Erhard had stood firm against German business representatives and Bundestag members, who had actively lobbied for a legislation targeting only abuse. He had had to accept, however, a partial watering down of the prohibition clause. A number of exceptions could be granted in favor of agreements that were shown to increase efficiency, productivity, or competitivity on export markets and in a few sectors, traditionally within the public sphere in Europe.[25] A cartel office or Bundeskartelamt was created in 1958 to enforce and administer the new law. In 1966 and 1973, the powers of this cartel office were enlarged and the law amended to provide for control of mergers which had until then lain outside the domain of the German legislation.[26]

In any case, the enactment of the German act in 1957 marked a significant American victory. In 1954, when the final version was still being discussed in the West German Bundestag, the American magazine *Fortune* claimed that if the bill was to be ratified 'even in a modified form, [this] would mean a major victory, perhaps the greatest victory ever won in Europe for the principles of dynamic American-style capitalism'.[27] The final version of the German legislation proved powerful enough to lead most of German industry away from cartels and restrictive trade practices. While in the 1930s, the number of cartels and other agreements had been estimated at more than 3,000, the German cartel office in 1968 counted a mere 200 (Dyas and Thanheiser, 1976: 54). Concentration and reconcentration of German industry undeniably took place in the 1950s and 1960s, but along lines that were closer to an American corporate and oligopolistic model than to a German tradition of organized capitalism (Dyas and Thanheiser, 1976; Berghahn, 1986; Cassis, 1997).

As was also the case during negotiations for the Schuman plan, the violent nature of the struggle around German anticartel legislation revealed that high stakes were involved. The fight in fact opposed two systems of industrial production, two very different models of economic organization. German anticartel legislation was not only bound to redefine the rules of competitive behavior and to outlaw traditional patterns of cooperation between firms. If the American experience was taken as a reference, it was also likely to have an indirect impact on the size of firms and production units as well as on ownership structures. Ever since 1947, the ultimate American objective in West Germany had been to transform local industrial sectors into as many competitive oligopolies. The American decartelization program had even been reinterpreted to this end. The German anticartel legislation of 1957 represented, in effect, an institutionalization of this redefined decartelization program. It seemed to confirm and officialize the adoption and appropriation of this program by West German authorities. With the ratification of the act in 1957, the Americans had apparently succeeded in planting the seeds, deep within German institutions, of their own peculiar model of market organization, of their own specific system of industrial production. And this in spite of a violent and well organized opposition, that had essentially emerged from within West German business communities. Naturally, the process had been slow and time was needed before the impact of the new legislation could be felt or measured. As Eberhard Günther, director of the new German cartel office, acknowledged in 1960:

[Germans] had to fight for every piece of [their] political and economic freedom; the Americans enjoyed different starting conditions. And yet it took almost twenty years for the Sherman Act to establish itself in [American] legal consciousness. It was not to be expected that an incomparably more difficult process would assert itself with [Germans] in two years.[28]

Time, indeed, was of the essence but the evolution was unmistakable. The Americans had clearly had the initiative but a small group of West German actors did take over at some point, pushing further towards the transformation of the national economy.

IMPLEMENTING THE SOCIAL MARKET ECONOMY

The creation of the Federal Republic of Germany, in September 1949, led to a large-scale transfer of responsibilities—barring a few reserved fields—from occupying powers to the new German institutions and authorities. In September 1949, the task which lay ahead may have seemed daunting to the new West German government, particularly with respect to economic issues. It was clear that economic policy choices would affect the degree of support granted by national actors to the coalition in power and could thus weigh on future national elections. Those choices also appeared to be key to a progressive reclaiming of respectability—and thus ultimately of sovereignty—on the world scene. Allied powers, and more particularly the Americans, had been clear. West Germany had to deserve political sovereignty and it had to gain geopolitical recognition. This could be done step by step, through good conduct in economic affairs. The economy would provide a testing ground for Germany's rejection of Nazism and for the readiness of West German citizens to democracy and full-scale sovereignty. A stunningly clear presentation of this American position appeared in an issue of the German newspaper, *Der Volkswirt*, in the form of a letter from a prominent New York lawyer to a West German industrial manufacturer:

When I read the articles you sent me, I realized how little your authors know about the American industry and how much they desire that Germany should return to the old ways, because they are old, not because they are right. Supposing the German government would only prohibit cartels, would that not eliminate public criticism in America of the German industry? Would that not give Germany the characteristic features of a freedom loving democratic country? Would this step not be considered as a final rejection of nazism?[29]

The stakes were indeed high, and those institutions within the German administration in charge of economic issues had responsibilities that went well beyond those that generally characterize such institutions. The German Ministry of Economic Affairs and the German Ministry for the Marshall Plan were also, and *de facto*, in charge of relationships with foreign powers, a role that more traditionally falls to ministries of foreign affairs. Since foreign affairs were a reserved field under the occupation statute, such a ministry could not be created in West Germany before 1951. The German Ministry of Economic Affairs and the German Ministry for the Marshall Plan therefore took up the empty space. To a large extent, sovereignty and geopolitical recognition depended on them.

The message repeatedly sent by American occupation authorities was clear. German political sovereignty and a full integration of the Federal Republic of Germany into the community of Western nations were dependent upon the diligence of the German government in bringing about a radical redefinition of the German economy and industry. Americans were clearly running the show although, after 1949, they increasingly tried to do so discreetly and indirectly. A redefinition of the German economic landscape had to be satisfactory to American occupation authorities and to fit the general objectives of the Marshall plan. As already argued, this clearly meant drawing the German economy closer to the American model of corporate capitalism, as defined by competitive, mass-producing, highly productive oligopolies, and consumer-driven markets. A project of that sort was foreign and clearly distasteful to many Germans and in particular to members of industrial and business communities. It was close enough, on the other hand, to the program of the new West German government and administration. Ludwig Erhard's 'social market economy' was 'social' to the extent that 'it allow[ed] the consumer to benefit from economic progress, from the results of increased efforts and increased productivity'. The key to such a social market economy was 'to retain freedom of competition' as the guarantee that economic benefits would be turned into social benefits (Erhard, 1958). For Ludwig Erhard and his team, however, competition and a market economy were not going to emerge nor persist naturally. The new West German government was acutely aware that, in a country like Germany, competition had to be imposed and a free market economy had to be protected from many dangers. In order to counter a distaste of competition that was deeply rooted within German industrial traditions, the West German state had to intervene. It should take upon itself the responsibility for building and preserving the foundations of a market economy, for setting up a competitive framework, and for ensuring its long-term institutionalization. West German political and administrative actors defined it as their task to create the necessary conditions for a smooth working of 'free market' mechanisms in their country.

Laying the Foundations of a Competitive Economy

Ludwig Erhard and the small team of German economists working with him were convinced that monetary instability and financial crisis represented major obstacles to the setting-up of a competitive economy. Distorted signals in monetary and financial spheres could reflect negatively on production and investment levels, on the availability of goods, and on patterns of consumption. Once in charge, they immediately contemplated, as a consequence, launching a monetary reform of significant scope. American occupation authorities had themselves been concerned about the financial and monetary situation in West Germany. The June 1948 monetary reform was thus once more a collaborative undertaking between American occupation authorities and the West German administration in charge of economic policy. The Deutschmark was introduced and variable rates for the currency exchange made possible a sharp cut in an overflowing money supply while limiting the social costs of the reform.[30]

Monetary reform, however, could only succeed if the remaining money supply found outlets, particularly in terms of consumption. For Ludwig Erhard, currency exchange had to come with the lifting of price controls and of other restrictions. To the dismay of the American occupation authorities who agreed that liberalization was necessary but believed in a more gradual process,

Erhard abolished all price controls shortly after announcing the monetary reform. Positive developments followed quickly that can be more or less directly traced to that particular decision. Goods suddenly became available, production levels increased, and prices came to better reflect the existing balance between supply and demand.[31] By 1949, one key condition of a healthy and smoothly running supply and demand economy had thus been successfully set up (Bark and Gress, 1992). Indeed, a stable currency could be a powerful regulating tool, allocating resources and maximizing the benefits of competition provided, naturally, that nothing else got in the way of the free play of competitive forces. According to Ludwig Erhard and the team around him, the lifting of price controls and monetary reform could create conditions for a demand-driven economy where the consumer reaped the benefits of growth, but only if they combined with the setting-up of a regulative framework prohibiting restrictions to competition. This was necessary to ensure that Germany's brand of capitalism would come to be 'social', meaning in Erhard's terms a source of prosperity for all.[32]

The fight against cartels and the struggle to impose anticartel legislation or a regulative framework prohibiting restrictions to competition were thus naturally key dimensions of the institution building program of Ludwig Erhard and his team. Since competition, according to them, drove growth, value-creation, and a fair distribution of wealth, it should be nurtured and protected at all costs. In West Germany, the danger seemed to lie particularly with various forms of private agreements and Erhard 'declare[d] war against all forms of cartels and against those aiming at a limitation of competition' (Erhard, 1958: 117). It is fair to argue, as has already been done, that Ludwig Erhard managed to transplant and institutionalize the American antitrust tradition to the postwar West German economic and industrial landscape, and this in spite of opposition essentially stemming from within German civil society. The legislation that was imposed by American occupation authorities in 1947 structured for around ten years the West German competitive environment in a manner that represented a sharp break with the German industrial past and traditions. The West German anticartel legislation, that was finally adopted in 1957, and for which Ludwig Erhard had fought all along and with all his energy, confirmed and institutionalized further such a radical break. The creation of a German cartel office or Bundeskartelamt, responsible for implementing the legislation, was a symbolic institutionalization in Germany of an American definition of competition. Countering accusations that he was 'acting on American orders', Ludwig Erhard insisted repeatedly on the natural fit that existed between the 'social market economy' and a fight against cartels (Erhard, 1963: 135). He still knew how to use, though, throughout this period, the support the Americans were ready to provide. He did not hesitate, in particular, to point to the threat of American pressure and intervention to further his own agenda even though the latter was in fact, most of the time, quite compatible with American objectives.

On the Road to Prosperity: Preparing for a Mass Economy

Together with monetary reform and the institutionalization of anticartel legislation, the new West German government also took it upon itself to stimulate production. It appeared obvious, indeed, that a necessary prerequisite to the emergence of a mass-consuming society in West Germany was to increase production capacities. This, in turn, meant boosting investments. Since private actors did not seem willing nor able, at the time, to launch investment programs on a sufficient scale, West German political authorities saw it as their duty to take the lead. In fact, boosting investment in capital goods was perfectly in line with the objectives of American occupation authorities and with the mission of the Marshall plan administration. Combined with competition, an increase in production capacities was expected to lead to a sharp fall in prices, to mass consumption, and higher standards of living for all. The new West German government agreed with members of the American administration that a mass-producing and mass-consuming economy meant prosperity and freedom for all and that it would ultimately build the foundations of a free democratic society.[33]

While Ludwig Erhard was convinced that he would have to lead the process, at least in the beginning, he clearly disliked the idea of systematic and large-scale state intervention in the national economy. He hoped in fact that private initiative would rapidly take over and he generally preferred, in any case, to act in indirect and unofficial ways. The key mechanism allowing the West German government to have a discrete and nevertheless significant impact with respect to productive investments owed a lot, once more, to the Americans. The German economic council, led by Ludwig Erhard, had created in October 1948 a reconstruction loan corporation or Kreditanstalt für Wiederaufbau. The mission of this corporation was to provide the German economy with medium- and long-term credits to be granted either directly or through various credit institutions. In fact, the idea of the Kreditanstalt had originated within the American administration that had then passed it along to the Germans.[34] When the Marshall plan was launched, this institution became responsible for managing and controlling Deutschmark counterpart funds of Marshall dollars. The Kreditanstalt thus became the functional equivalent in West Germany of the French Fonds de Modernisation et d'Equipement (FME).

Naturally, the use of German counterpart funds was subject to the scrutiny of members of the Marshall plan administration. Herman J. Abs, chairman of the Kreditanstalt, thus had to work in constant and close collaboration with Americans from the ECA. At the same time, relationships between the Kreditanstalt and the West German Ministry of Economic Affairs were close, although unofficial and systematically downplayed. In fact, Ludwig Erhard used the Kreditanstalt as a mechanism of last resort allowing him to set a general direction and to stimulate investment in capital goods without officially appearing to be involved (Abelshauser, 1993). From 1948 to 1952, more than 11 per cent of West German investment in capital goods was financed through counterpart funds of American dollars and, as a consequence, indirectly controlled by the West German Ministry of Economic Affairs.[35] If anything, though, this figure underestimates the impact of this ministry on the national economy. Indeed, investments controlled through the counterpart mechanism and the Kreditanstalt turned out to be key investments, of the kind having a significant multiplier effect on the economy as a whole. Those sectors given priority then in West Germany were pretty much the same as in France—transportation and electricity, coal and steel industries. Counterpart funds were essential to German postwar investments in yet another way. They often sparked off a process, launching a project which then received further funding from other sources, whether private or public. Through its indirect control of counterpart funds, the West German Ministry of Economic Affairs was thus able to set the general orientation for West German capital investment and to encourage initiatives in a few key industries (Wallich, 1955; Abelshauser, 1993; Hardach, 1993).

Combining Competition and Cooperation: Trade Liberalization

The liberalization of trade was another objective of the new West German government and it was identified as such in its program for a social market economy. The idea, once again, was to create the conditions most favorable to the free play of competitive forces. Such an ambition, naturally, received full support from the American administration. Well into the 1950s, Ludwig Erhard had to defend himself against accusations, once more and this time with respect to the issue of trade, that he was acting under American or foreign orders.[36] Throughout the 1950s, negotiations for trade liberalization increasingly took place on a multilateral level, within the GATT, OEEC, EPU (European Payments Union), ECSC, or EEC frameworks. The Americans always played a key role, including in those negotiations that officially brought together only Europeans. During such negotiations, members of the American administration paid particular attention to West German involvement and contributions. In fact, in a number of circumstances, the Americans had significant influence on the negotiation proceedings, supporting, coaxing, or threatening the West German delegation. The Americans tended to treat West Germany as a 'cockpit'—Ludwig Erhard being the pilot—for their pet project of worldwide free trade.

When the need arose, at the same time, the West German Ministry of Economic Affairs was able to work in close but discrete collaboration with members of the American administration. Ludwig Erhard used American support but also American threats to counter opposition in his own country and to further his agenda on trade liberalization. Both sides, clearly, had something to gain from such collaboration and Ludwig Erhard felt perfectly comfortable with the role the Americans expected him to play. As he privately told members of his team, he laid great hopes in the special relationship that was emerging between West Germany and the USA. He

argued that in the future, the Americans would rely on the Federal Republic as a sort of stronghold of the American economic concept in Europe. To ensure this support, Germany would have to continue to adapt itself to the American mentality, especially with regards to liberalizing its trade policy and abolishing cartels.[37]

The Americans exerted real and significant economic and political power in Germany through the institutions of the American High Commission for Germany or HICOG. This was particularly true in a number of reserved fields as defined by the occupation statute. This power, furthermore, gained some legitimacy thanks to the launching of the Marshall plan and its extension to the western territories of Germany. The Americans were thus able to exert a strong influence over West German delegations during multilateral negotiations.

Relying primarily on the goodwill of the West German government with respect to trade liberalization, the Americans still never shrank from threatening or bullying the West Germans when the need arose. The fragile position of the West German government on the national scene and the asymmetrical nature of its relationship with the USA meant that collaboration could not be overt. Even though it might boast about the good student image of German economic policy in an American-dominated Western world, the West German government also had to claim, high and loud, its autonomy and independence. The unfolding of negotiation proceedings around the Western European coal and steel community, presented in greater detail earlier, was a good illustration of the complex patterns of collaboration and confrontation existing between American and West German actors.

On the issue of foreign trade, the USA clearly came to favor multilateral negotiations after 1945. In fact, the American administration initiated many negotiations of that type.[38] This did not prevent, however, a number of bilateral agreements from emerging and being implemented. Those agreements had a double advantage. They were generally easier to negotiate and their impact could be felt much more rapidly. A number of mechanisms were thus set up in the early 1950s to liberalize trade between West Germany and the USA and to increase exchanges between both countries. Trade liberalization on a bilateral level, however, was threatening to many West German actors due to the striking asymmetry that characterized relationships between their country and the USA. The creation, in June 1950, of a society for the development of German–American trade (Gesellschaft zur Förderung des deutsch-amerikanischen Handels) thus proved to be a tricky undertaking requiring a step by step and cautious strategy.

Despite its unmistakable American origins, the Gesellschaft had to be presented as a German initiative. The ECA therefore sponsored a communication campaign praising a project to be 'launched by West German businessmen' and this well before the Gesellschaft was even set up.[39] In reality, West

German businessmen had little to do with this undertaking that had followed a pattern fairly usual in West Germany at the time. The proposal to create a trade agency, with the objective of closing the dollar gap, had been made originally by members of the ECA. This proposal came after Paul Hoffman's European tour in September 1949 and his pressing call for organized efforts to stimulate European exports.[40] ECA officials in West Germany had then passed the idea of the trade agency along to the German Ministry of Economic Affairs. The latter, finally, had attempted to minimize and conceal its own role by packaging the initiative as a private undertaking.[41] In reality, the idea of a German-American trade agency had initially found close to no support within the West German industrial community as the ECA administration would acknowledge when making a first assessment a little later, in 1951:

The proved success of the Gesellschaft zur Förderung des deutsch-amerikanischen Handels is especially gratifying for ECA trade development officials who first conceived the idea of a super trade promotion organization, because their suggestion was looked at askance initially by German industrialists whose cooperation was a necessarily integral part of such a plan. . . . Actually we had only three German industrialists with us when we began and they were not completely optimistic.[42]

The Gesellschaft was thus in fact one more American initiative, endorsed by the German Ministry of Economic Affairs, and packaged as a private German undertaking. Notwithstanding the official discourse, the trade agency was far from private and independent. It was financed for the most part through Marshall aid counterpart funds with additional subsidies coming from the West German Ministry of Economic Affairs.[43] The financing by West German private actors of such an agency, the objective of which was to increase commercial exchanges and to stimulate trade between the USA and West Germany, was simply unthinkable in 1950. Members of the West German and American administrations agreed that the West German industrial and business community was not yet ready for that:

I consider it an impossibility that the Trade Promotion Society be financed exclusively through the establishment of a company, whose shares are subscribed by the German industry. Even if in this case tax advantages could be given, I believe that in view of the present attitude of German industry towards exports to the United States and in view of the present lack of capital, not enough financial means could be accumulated to make possible even the most humble of beginnings of the dollar drive. . . . Financing the whole project from public funds cannot be circumvented.[44]

The West German effort towards a liberalization of foreign trade was thus one more example of an initiative stemming from the public sphere and reflecting complex patterns of cooperation between West German and American administrative agencies. In this case as in others, mimetic and coercive transfer mechanisms undeniably combined.

Coordinating the Productivity Effort: The Marshall Plan Ministry

In the spring of 1948, the American administration had demanded the creation of a German office to be particularly responsible for handling Marshall plan issues in collaboration with ECA representatives. A councillor on Marshall plan affairs was appointed, reporting directly to the German economic council. The office of the councillor was to coordinate German agencies with respect to Marshall plan issues. It also had to handle day-to-day relationships between ECA representatives and the West German administration.[45] In the fall of 1949, following the creation of the Federal Republic of Germany, a Ministry for the Marshall Plan (Bundesministerium für den Marshall Plan) took over from the office of the councillor. Relationships with the OEEC were added to its functions. On October 4, 1949, Franz Blücher became the first West German Minister for the Marshall Plan. In France, the functional equivalent to this West German ministry was the SGCI (Secrétariat Général du Comité Interministériel pour les Questions de Coopération Economique Européenne), a relatively powerless administrative agency. That Marshall plan issues and relationships with the ECA administration were handled in West Germany at ministry level was not surprising. The Marshall plan, indeed, took on particular significance in that country. A treatment of the West German economy within the Marshall scheme on a par with other European economies seemed to herald its full reintegration into the Western economic space. The Marshall plan, in fact, was an opportunity for West Germany to take a step forward in the direction of sovereignty and geopolitical recognition. Much more was at stake than mere economic interests and the importance of the Marshall plan was symbolically expressed by giving ministerial status to the German administration that was to be officially in charge:

One should not disregard the fact that the Marshall plan is a construction with both political and economic dimensions. . . . Without the Marshall plan, Germans would not be fed. Without the Marshall plan, the reconstruction of the West German economy would not be possible. Without the Marshall plan, West Germany would not (or at least not so fast) be brought back into the economic and political community of European nations.[46]

In reality, however, and on the ground, the influence of the West German Ministry for the Marshall Plan was somewhat undermined by that of the Ministry of Economic Affairs. The personality of Ludwig Erhard and his undeniable clout within American circles were clear obstacles to the full assumption by the Minister for the Marshall Plan of his potential powers and prerogatives. The direct and personal relationships Ludwig Erhard had nurtured with a number of American officials within military government or in the civil High Commission also made him a privileged interlocutor for ECA representatives.[47] The implementation of Ludwig Erhard's social market economy required systematic and coordinated state intervention, even if ideally this was to be not too visible. The German Minister of Economic Affairs thus attempted to retain maximum control in those areas of policy making that were key to the successful implementation of his overall economic program. Investments qualified as such a key issue and it was argued earlier that Ludwig Erhard and his Ministry had secured an indirect hold over the handling of those investments to be financed through Marshall aid counterpart funds. As a consequence, the core of the Marshall plan, financial assistance and the handling of counterpart funds, was in effect outside the reach of the German Ministry for the Marshall Plan. As far as Marshall plan affairs were concerned, Franz Blücher and later Karl Albrecht, who replaced him, were mostly left with the handling of technical assistance and of the German productivity effort. Despite their significance and impact in the medium to long term, these programs were low budget, as Table 11 shows, and tended to be perceived by West German actors as relatively marginal in the overall context of Marshall assistance.

The German Ministry for the Marshall Plan thus ended up being mostly responsible for technical assistance projects and in particular productivity missions or visits of foreign experts to West Germany. The Ministry worked in close collaboration with the ECA Special Mission to Germany and with two German agencies. In the summer of 1949, a German ERP delegation had been set up in Washington to serve as *liaison* office between the West German administration and the central office of the ECA. This delegation was to look after West German interests and it was also responsible for handling, on the German side, the concrete implementation of the productivity missions program in the USA.[48] Starting in 1950, a productivity center—Rationalisierungs-Kuratorium der Wirtschaft or RKW—assisted the Ministry with the practical side of productivity projects in West Germany. This institution was essentially responsible for dealing with the members of productivity missions before, during, and after their trips.[49]

Applications for technical assistance projects could originate from anywhere within German civil society. However, applications had first to be approved and reformated by the German Ministry for the Marshall Plan before they could be sent to the ECA Special Mission to Germany. In collaboration with

Table 11. Total Marshall aid in Europe and West Germany (US$ millions)

	Total Europe	West Germany
Financial aid	13,300	1,400
Counterparts withdrawn	8,400	1,000
Technical assistance	43	1.4

Note: Counterpart funds withdrawn are the amounts that were both released, that is agreed to by the Americans, and used indeed in each country.
Source: Mayer (1969: 94–9).

competent services in the American High Commission, the German Ministry for the Marshall Plan was also responsible for screening applicants on the basis of their political past. The decisions of denazification courts were particularly crucial to this selection process.[50] The uncompromising attitude of Americans on the issue sometimes placed the German Ministry for the Marshall Plan in a predicament. As the interface with respect to technical assistance issues between German social and economic actors on the one hand and the American administration on the other, the Ministry was often faced with contradicting pressures. German companies sending employees to the USA within the framework of productivity missions had to pay in Deutschmarks the equivalent amount of what was spent in US dollars by the ECA for the trips. Thus, for individual German companies technical assistance was not a gift and, as a consequence, they generally had trouble accepting the political demands that went with the program. The Ministry for the Marshall Plan, a natural outlet for their dissatisfaction, passed on their complaints and grievances to the American administration. The following letter sent by Franz Blücher to John McCloy, on November 23, 1949 provides a clear illustration of the nature of those complaints:

In view of the fact that the ECA provides only the necessary dollar sums and that the participants have to raise the total expenses in DM, each plant endeavors to send only the best experts. . . . If however these experts would have to be replaced by second class substitutes for the mere reason of their being formally incriminated because of their membership in the NSDAP mostly acquired under pressure, German industry and agriculture cannot participate in technical assistance to the desired extent.[51]

The setting-up and day-to-day management of technical assistance projects were only the first stages in a longer term process. The German Ministry for the Marshall Plan shared responsibility with the ECA Special Mission to Germany for the advertising and exploitation of technical assistance projects upon the return of productivity missions. The Ministry therefore had to develop strategies for the dissemination of teaching and knowledge acquired through those productivity missions and to prepare implementation programs adapted to the West German economic and industrial context. With the assistance of the RKW, in the 1950s the Ministry for the Marshall Plan published close to one hundred reports on every aspect of the American system of industrial production—mass production, standardization, specialization, rationalization, antitrust, human relations, trade unions. The Ministry also helped members of productivity missions, upon their return, to write implementation reports as demanded by the ECA administration. Indeed, six months after the end of each productivity mission, its members had to assess the extent to which the knowledge gained during the trip had been used and concretely implemented in their respective organizations or companies. Building on those early experiences and reports, the Ministry then set up a number of projects with the objective of stimulating wider and more systematic implementation.[52]

Beyond the general handling of productivity projects, whether study trips to the USA or visits from American experts to West Germany, the Ministry for the Marshall Plan was also instrumental in bringing about cooperation and collaboration within the West German industrial community. The national productivity effort provided an opportunity, in particular, to experiment with a collaboration scheme which brought together labor and business representatives. A number of formal committees were created around productivity issues where members of trade unions and business associations worked together under the guidance of representatives of the Ministry for the Marshall Plan.[53] While the initiative appeared to lie with the West German Ministry, the ECA administration had naturally had to apply a degree of pressure for such collaboration to become institutionalized. This particular experiment paved the way to some extent, in West Germany, for agreements of co-determination that developed between labor and employers. Later on, co-determination would be identified as a factor of high productivity and as an essential dimension of the German economic miracle.

The progressive reclamation by West Germany of its economic and political sovereignty, in the late 1940s and early 1950s, did not lead to a sharp redefinition of German economic and industrial policy. Starting in 1947, the American occupation authorities had defined and started to implement in the western territories of Germany, a program for economic recovery that implied, in particular, the structural reshaping of West German industry following the model of American corporate capitalism. Consequently, they were soon launching and imposing what amounted to a large-scale, cross-national, structural transfer using mostly coercive types of transfer mechanisms. The effectiveness of coercive transfer mechanisms, though, in the West German case was closely related to the situation of acute geopolitical dependence that characterized Germany at the time. Members of the American administration had quickly realized that transformations would have to be appropriated by at least a small group of West German nationals if they were to outlast the period of dependence. Americans were therefore searching in the late 1940s for West German partners they could sufficiently trust to progressively hand over responsibilities.

In their search, the Americans stumbled upon the small and marginal group around Ludwig Erhard, who was putting forward an economic program sufficiently similar to their own project for the western territories of Germany. By securing institutional power for this small group on the West German national scene, members of the American administration ensured a degree of continuity with respect to economic and industrial policy beyond the period of military occupation. In the West German case, voluntary imitation became an operative transfer mechanism from the early 1950s onwards. Americans remained in West Germany and the capacity of the American administration to intervene in that country was still significant throughout the 1950s. During that period, however, American involvement in West German economic and industrial affairs increasingly tended to take place in the context of a more general involvement of the USA in Western European affairs. We will now turn to this American involvement at a European level and show that the American administration, in this case, strove for a balance between using coercive transfer mechanisms and pushing for the implementation of normative mechanisms.

Notes

1. 'Draft of letter from Dean Acheson, American Secretary of State to Ernest Bevin, British Foreign Secretary, May 17, 1950', OMGUS Rds, Bd42, #17/247-1/5.
2. 'Charles Dilley, Objectives of the Decartelization Program, November 1947', OMGUS Rds, Bd18, #11/11-3/7.
3. OMGUS Rds, Bd18, #11/17-1/9.
4. 'Philips Hawkins [Chief Decartelization Branch] to General Lucius Clay, 18 July 1947', OMGUS Rds, Bd42, #17/224-3/1.
5. OMGUS Rds, Bd42, #17/224-3/1.
6. State central banks took over the assets of the former Reichsbank, each in their respective *Land*. During the early years of occupation, those local central banks could not issue currency. For more on American-led reforms of the German banking system, see Zink (1957) and Owen Smith (1983).
7. I agree, here, with Berghahn (1986). The structure of each individual bank and the nature of its links to German industry changed enough in the postwar period, that it seems fair to claim that the German banking sector was then fairly different from what it had been before the Second World War. See Dyas and Thanheiser (1976: ch. 5).
8. 'General Order #7 to Law #52, British Military Government, August 20, 1946.' OMGUS Rds, Bd17, #3/262/6.
9. There were two main sales agencies in that sector: the Deutscher Kohlenverkauf (DKV) in the British zone and the Kohlenkontor in the American zone. The peculiar German system of vertical agreements combining with horizontal cooperation or *Verbundwirtschaft* had led in both coal and steel industries to systematically organized markets. OMGUS Rds, Bd42, #17/224-1/3.
10. The Vereignite Stahlwerke, producing in 1938 around 39 per cent of Germany's steel, was naturally to be deconcentrated. Friedrich Krupp AG, Hoesch AG, GHH und Mannesmann Röhrenwerke AG were other targets of American occupation authorities.
11. OMGUS Rds, Bd42, #17/250-2/17.
12. 'Military Government, Law #75, Reorganization of German Coal and Iron and Steel Industries', OMGUS Rds, Bd 18, #11/12-1/22. Law #75 was replaced in May 1950 by law #27, covering the entire West German territory including the French zone.
13. OMGUS Rds, Bd 18, #11/12-1/22 and Bd 42, #17/250-2/17.
14. OMGUS Rds, Bd18, #11/23-2/1.
15. Regulation number one, issued by the American military government, defined the procedure for prosecution and gave a set of directives for the implementation of law #56. OMGUS Rds, Bd18, #11/23-2/1.

16. 'OMGUS: Office of the Chief of Staff. Letter to the directors of military government for Bavaria, Württemberg-Baden, Hesse and Bremen, April 21, 1947', OMGUS Rds, Bd18, #11/23-2/1.

17. 'Procedural Memorandum: Administrative Procedures of German Decartelization Agencies and German Decartelization Departments, no date', OMGUS Rds, Bd42, #17/229-2/4.

18. To this aim, the Department of Justice in Washington was of significant help. The Assistant Attorney General, Herbert Bergson, sent BIDEC material and documents to 'aid in the objective of implementing the decartelization laws and giving the German people a clearer understanding of the operation of a free economy'. 'Letter from Bergson to BIDEC, December 27, 1948', OMGUS Rds, Bd42, #17/247-1/6.

19. 'Report on Progress of the Decartelization Branch since February 12, 1947. June 1947', OMGUS Rds, Bd18, #11/23-2/1.

20. Throughout that period, the enforcement of law #56 rested on the use of American antitrust cases, which implied the familiarity of German officials and lawyers with that particular tradition. According to Damm (1958), a majority of German lawyers 'agreed that for an equitable interpretation of the Allied Law, it would be necessary to use American antitrust cases as a precedent because only these cases could fill the vague definitions of common law terminology with substantive meaning'.

21. 'Internal Memo, Antitrust Project L501, September 20, 1950', OMGUS Rds, Bd42, #17/246-1/6.

22. Damm (1958: 212ff). A threat of that sort could apparently have an impact not only on German administration but also on the business community. According to the *Industriekurier* (January 24, 1950), the relative softening of the position of the Bundesverband der Deutschen Industrie (BDI—peak German business association) could be explained by 'the need to show a regard for certain foreign policy interests, the question of foreign credits playing certainly a role in this connection'. Quoted in Berghahn (1986: 165).

23. Erhard (1958: 124–5).

24. 'Agreements made by enterprises or associations of enterprises are null and void if they are suited to influence, through restraints of competition, production or market conditions with regard to the trade in goods or commercial services.' Article 1 of the 'Gesetz gegen Wettbewerbsbeschrankungen', translated by Damm (1958: 258). This article compares fairly closely with Sections I and II of the Sherman Act.

25. Damm (1958: ch. IX).

26. By drawing a sharp distinction between deconcentration and decartelization and keeping control over the first program while asking the Germans to enact a law against restraints of trade, Americans had in fact placed mergers outside the reach of German legislation.

27. Gilbert Bruck, 'The German Business Mind' in *Fortune* (May 1954), quoted in Berghahn (1986: 175).

28. Eberhard Günther, *Der Spiegel* (February 27, 1960). Figures presented in the introduction tend to show that the impact of the legislation could already be measured in the late 1960s and early 1970s.

29. *Der Volkswirt* (May 12, 1950). Introducing the letter was a comment from the editors: 'We could not find any statement that would explain more clearly, out of which spirit the American attitude against cartels has arisen'. The shortcut from

cartels to Nazism is striking but consistent with an American view of the world as being essentially shaped by economic factors (Sutton *et al.*, 1956).

30. From 1935 to 1945, the total money supply in Germany had increased tenfold and the German currency was thus close to worthless. With the 1948 monetary reform, 60 Reichsmark could be exchanged at parity with the new Deutschmark. Beyond that amount, monetary assets were to be exchanged at the rate of 1 DM for 10 RM and even less in the case of particularly huge holdings.

31. Hardach (1993), Pohl (1993). The monetary reform of June 1948 was also one more step towards the division of Germany. Soviet occupation authorities ordered a blockade of the western parts of Berlin to prevent an influx of worthless Reichsmarks to their zone. The deterioration of relationships between Western Powers and the USSR that followed swelled the numbers of refugees from the East and thus unemployment figures in the West—from 450,000 in June 1948 to 1.3 millions one year later.

32. Erhard's fellow countrymen accused him in that period of leading West Germany towards a soulless materialistic society. His answer was that he strongly believed in the virtues of a mass-consuming society and that he was indeed trying to bring about such a society in Germany: 'What could be more human than to consume and to enjoy? . . . Ever-increasing numbers of people are able to afford a higher standard of living, that is they are able to buy more goods in a variety of ways which has hitherto been out of their reach. I have consciously worked towards this end, and I am happy with this success' (Erhard, 1958: 171).

33. See Erhard (1958). See also 'Proposal for a German Economic Administration', OMGUS Rds, Bd17, #3/261-3.

34. This is clearly shown in 'Principles for the Establishment of the Reconstruction Loan Corporation, 28 May 1948', OMGUS Rds, Bd18, #11/12-1/8. See in particular the comments from Hawkins, then Acting Economic Adviser in OMGUS: 'It is assumed that, if and when the paper is passed from the bipartite board to the German economic council, it will be in terms that the latter is authorized to establish a reconstruction loan corporation in accordance with the principles set forth in this paper'.

35. Hardach (1993: 483). 8 per cent of total financing came from German counterpart funds of Marshall dollars, while another 3 per cent was the Deutschmark counterpart of the early American GARIOA aid program (Government Account for Relief in Occupied Areas).

36. See for example 'Erhard, Speech at the Bundestag, 153rd meeting, June 26, 1956.' Quoted in Erhard (1958: 98). According to Wallich (1955: 372), the idea of trade liberalization 'fitted in so well with the ideas of Economics Minister Erhard and was so energetically taken over by the German government that its Allied origin has somewhat become obscured. There can be no doubt, however, that the original impulse towards liberalization of European trade came from the ECA, and that the American authorities in Washington and Paris had decided to make Germany into a test or showcase of liberalization.'

37. 'HICOG, Intelligence Report, January 13, 1950.' Quoted in Schwartz (1991*b*: 192).

38. This was naturally true of the GATT and OEEC negotiations. The initiative also belonged to the American administration in the case of negotiations for the European Payments Union (EPU). Jean Monnet deserves credit for the ECSC but, in

this case also, as has already been shown, American support was key to the project and to its success.

39. '*Stars and Stripes* (official publication of the ECA), December 28, 1949.' Bundesarchiv Koblenz, Bestand B140-#1.

40. 'Visit of Paul Hoffman to Europe, September 1949.' Bundesarchiv Koblenz, Bestand Z14-#6.

41. In the end, most members of the executive committee of the Gesellschaft were German businessmen. Official announcements pointed to the support and encouragement of the Ministry of Economic Affairs while insisting on the independent and private nature of the organization.

42. 'Promoting German Trade: Review of Progress Achieved during the First Year of the German-American Trade Promotion Society', *Monthly Information Bulletin of the Office of the US HICOG*, July 1951. Bundesarchiv Koblenz, Bestand B140-#49.

43. Before December 1950, DM2.3 million were allocated to the Gesellschaft from counterpart funds. An additional DM800,000 was provided by the German Ministry of Economic Affairs and private funds amounted to only DM120,000. Bundesarchiv Koblenz, Bestand B140-#1 and Bestand B140-#130.

44. 'German report, November 1949.' Bundesarchiv Koblenz, Bestand B140-#1.

45. The office of the councillor or Berater für den Marshall Plan beim Vorsitzer des Verwaltungsrates des Vereiniten Wirtschaftsgebietes was located in Frankfurt. Bundesarchiv Koblenz, Bestand Z14.

46. 'Arguments for the creation of a Ministry for the Marshall Plan, September 1949.' Bundesarchiv Koblenz, Bestand Z14-#98.

47. This was naturally reinforced by the fact that, in West Germany, the High Commission and the ECA administration merged under the single chairmanship of John McCloy (Schwartz, 1991*a*).

48. Bundesarchiv Koblenz, Bestand B146-#51 and Bestand Z14-#92.

49. Bundesarchiv Koblenz, Bestand B146-#304 and Bestand B146-#416.

50. Bundesarchiv Koblenz, Bestand B146-#416.

51. Bundesarchiv Koblenz, Bestand Z14-#159.

52. Bundesarchiv Koblenz, Bestand B146-#416.

53. A few examples were the committee for increased production in coal mining or Ausschuss für Produktionssteigerung im Kohlebergbau and the German productivity council or Deutsche Produktivitätsrat. Link (1991: 300–5).

7

From Control to Conversion
Embedding the Corporate Model in Western Europe

As the largest producer, the largest source of capital, we must set the pace and assume the responsibility of the major stockholder in this corporation known as the world. . . . Nor is this for a given term of office. This is a permanent obligation.

Leo D. Welch.[1]

The launching of the Marshall plan in 1948 represented an opportunity for the USA to extend their hold over Western European economic affairs. The American agency in charge of foreign assistance, the Economic Cooperation Administration or ECA, was indeed a powerful instrument, through which the USA could play the role and take on the responsibilities 'of the major stockholder in the corporation known as the [Western] world'. The small group of businessmen, trade union members, experts, and government officials running the Marshall plan administration was well organized and institutionally powerful but it was not quite representative of American civil society. In the first place, a Keynesian understanding of the role of the state in the economy, dominant within the ECA, was denounced as heresy by a majority of American business leaders. Members of this progressive minority were also connected, in one way or another, to large American public corporations and were generally convinced of the superiority of the American model of corporate capitalism. This was far from being the case of all American business leaders and the US Chambers of Commerce or the National Association of Manufacturers (NAM) were in fact dominated by representatives of a smaller-scale, family type of capitalism. Finally, the small group running the ECA was characterized at this time by its interventionism and a desire to institutionalize American involvement in foreign countries quite peculiar within the USA.

Through management of the American program of foreign assistance, this small group came to control a set of powerful institutional tools. Its members used this institutional framework to further their ambitious objectives. Indeed, they saw it as their mission to bring about a structural reshaping and redefinition of the Western economic and industrial world along the lines of the American model of corporate capitalism. The very nature of this model implied that they would have to intervene both on a national and on a European level. The construction of a common market crossing over national borders seemed to be a necessary step to ensure the success of their project. As already discussed, the American project for Western Europe received support from a few local actors in a number of Western European countries. It also encountered significant resistance and opposition on the old continent and this will be documented in greater detail in the following chapters. Consequently, while favoring conversion strategies to bring about the structural redefinition of Western European industries, members of the American administration still had to resort occasionally to coercive or control mechanisms. Coercion and control were necessary to impose rapid changes in the face of strong national resistance or opposition. They were also vital if members of the American administration wanted to limit the extent of adaptation and reinterpretation of the original model that was bound to take place in each case. On the other hand, it was clear that structural changes would outlast the period of direct American involvement only if appropriation and a systematic embedding took place at the national level. American missionaries therefore also relied on normative types of transfer mechanisms.

COUNTERPART FUNDS: A POWERFUL CONTROL DEVICE

It could be argued that the impact and success of the Marshall plan was due to its being much more than a mere program of financial assistance. The European Recovery Program had been accepted and adopted by the American Congress on the condition that it would not be one more program of foreign aid, loosely coordinated and controlled and lacking in effective results. To ensure efficient management, Congress had demanded that the ERP be run in a 'business-like way' and had insisted upon significant involvement of the American business community (Arkes, 1972). The small group of businessmen, who came to exercise control over Marshall plan institutions after the war, was a peculiar team. They were bearers of a new business creed (Sutton *et al.*, 1956). They believed in the efficiency and superiority of an economic space where 'competition' combined with large-scale mass production, where corporate ownership structures implied a professionalization of management and ensured relative economic democracy through a fragmentation of property rights.[2] Regardless of their ultimate motives, Marshall plan administrators undeniably shared a vision. Beyond a politically and economically fragmented territory, they pictured the 'United States of Europe', a continent where the workings of the economy would be patterned after the model of American corporate capitalism.

They believed American financial assistance was necessary to help further an integration of markets on a European level and to foster an increase in productive and consumption capacities. Marshall assistance, they agreed, should be used to stimulate productive investments. It should also be used as an instrument to bring about collaboration on a European level and to foster the emergence of European-wide markets. Indeed, Marshall planners identified economic integration as a *sine qua non* condition of the transformation of Western European systems of industrial production. They knew 'that there [was] no possibility of Europe becoming the kind of economy that [would] make it a great factor of strength in the Atlantic community' if existing barriers between political subdivisions were not broken down 'so that you [could] have a single market, or something close to it in which you (could) have large-scale manufacturing because you [had] a large market in which to sell'.[3] Marshall plan administrators had the means, both institutional and financial, to carry through their project for Western Europe. The mechanics of the Marshall plan were designed and devised to facilitate the implementation of such an ambitious project and to increase the likelihood of its success.

The Mechanics of Marshall Assistance

The Act actually launching the Marshall plan and creating the Economic Cooperation Administration (ECA), was adopted by the American Congress on April 3rd, 1948. On April 16, the Organization for European Economic Cooperation (OEEC) became the forum for European collaboration around Marshall plan issues. Altogether, the USA transferred more than US$13 billion to Western Europe, within the framework of the Marshall plan, between 1948 and 1952. This tranfer was, for the most part, in the form of donations which were not to be repaid.[4] Figure 8 shows that flows were mostly of goods and to the benefit of national governments, not individual economic actors.

The ECA procured for national governments raw materials, consumption goods, and industrial equipment, according to the pre-approved allocation scheme collectively agreed upon by Western European countries within the OEEC framework. Local economic actors had to buy the goods they needed from their national governments. They deposited in special accounts the equivalent amount in local currency of the dollar value of those goods. These special accounts came to be known as counterpart funds. Five per cent of the counterpart funds were allocated back to the ECA to help finance its running costs. The rest could be re-injected by national governments into the local economy provided the ECA had given its approval to the projected use of those funds.

The counterpart device was a smart mechanism. It maximized the potential impact of Marshall assistance while at the same time institutionalizing American control over the national use that was made of Marshall goods and funds. It significantly increased, in fact, the multiplier effect that the flow of American aid could have on Western European economies. At the first stage, goods came in directly and free of charge for the country as a whole, fueling and stimulating national economies. Table 12 lists the types of goods that were shipped to Western Europe thanks to Marshall assistance. The chances are that dollar-starved European economies would not have been able to

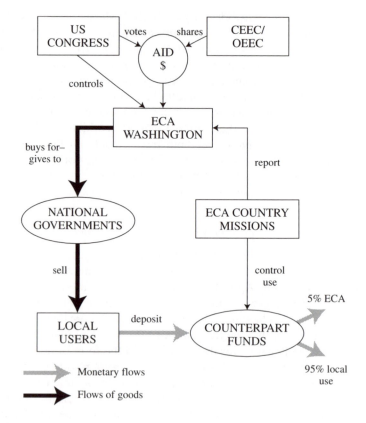

Figure 8. Mechanics of Marshall assistance
Source: Adapted from Bossuat (1984: 36).

afford these goods without Marshall assistance. Imports of machinery, in particular, or of raw materials would certainly have been much less significant.[5] At the second stage, the counterpart mechanism made it possible to re-inject into the local economy up to 95 per cent of the value of those 'free'

Table 12. ERP shipments to Western Europe, April 1948–December 1951 (%)

Food, Feed, Fertilizer	32.1
Fuel	15.5
Cotton	14.0
Raw materials, Semi-finished products	18.8
Tobacco	4.4
Machinery and Vehicles	14.3
Other	0.9

Note: The total value of shipments in US dollars over the period was 10 billion.
Source: Milward (1984: 101).

goods, provided the ECA had granted its approval to the projected use of these funds. The counterpart mechanism in fact amounted to a process of forced savings at the level of the country and it could have a particularly significant multiplier effect when counterpart funds were being re-injected to finance capital investment in the national economy and industry.

The Power of the ECA and its Strategies of Control

The mechanics of the Marshall plan undeniably provided the ECA with a powerful means to exert direct or indirect control. The allocation and distribution of goods, within the framework of the Marshall plan had been made conditional on European-wide collaboration. Marshall assistance in its very definition thus gave members of the ECA significant leverage to push for closer European integration. The division and allocation of Marshall aid was a yearly task, dependent upon the calendar of the American Congress. It was to emerge, on the other hand, from negotiations between the sixteen European members of the OEEC. Work within the OEEC was a systematic attempt at collaboration on a European level with no historical precedent. Despite its shortcomings, the OEEC was undeniably a success in this respect. Merely three years after the end of a bloody and traumatic war, cooperation on such a scale would certainly not have been possible without the stimulus of American assistance and the pressure brought to bear by the ECA on Western European countries.

Fairly unexpectedly, another source of leverage and control for the ECA was its relationship with the American Congress. Members of the ECA had originally hoped that funds for the ERP would be voted once for the entire four year period. They did not win on this point, however, and Congress would monitor closely the ERP. Appropriations had to be negotiated each year and they could be re-evaluated. Congress set regular deadlines and, during the yearly budgetary discussions, projects and realizations were systematically scrutinized. Members of the ECA, whether in Washington or in national Missions, generally treated these compulsory hearings as tedious duties. They realized, however, that those hearings could be used to put pressure on Western European governments. Western European countries being highly dependent in the short term on Marshall deliveries, the threat of re-evaluated appropriations was highly effective. Members of the ECA therefore used Congressional hearings as a scarecrow in all kinds of situations. They pointed to an upcoming deadline when trying to stimulate cooperation or to foster productive investments, when imposing austerity measures, or even when attempting to negotiate with national actors the launching of 'propaganda' or information drives around Marshall plan achievements.

In the end, however, the main source of leverage, the essential means of control for the ECA, lay in the counterpart device itself. In each participating country, national users deposited in special accounts the dollar value in local currency of Marshall goods. Counterpart funds were not American funds. They belonged to those countries participating in the Marshall scheme. Nevertheless, their use was subject to approval by members of the ECA.[6] A small percentage of these funds, no more than 5 per cent, was earmarked for the running costs and administrative expenses of the ECA, including the financing of propaganda and information drives in each country. The remaining 95 per cent could be used for investment in capital goods or debt retirement, as long as this use was regularly validated, through the appropriate agencies, by the ECA. Marshall plan administrators naturally advocated the re-injection of the largest possible share of counterpart funds into national economies. Those funds could have, according to them, a significant multiplier effect on distressed national economies. Counterpart funds were also a key mechanism through which the American administration could control European economic policies.

With respect to the use that was to be made of counterpart funds, Marshall plan administrators had clear preferences. They generally favored investment in capital goods over debt retirement.[7] They believed, indeed, that a key objective of the ECA should be to stimulate production and productivity in Europe. This they saw as the cure to all European evils from which everything else would follow—freer trade, increased competition, and higher living standards.[8] Priority was to be given, in particular, to investments, and thus to production and productivity growth, in a few key sectors that could have a significant multiplier effect within national economies. In this respect, coal, energy, and the steel industry were singled out by members of the ECA, as exemplified in the following comment made by Paul Hoffman:

We take a ton of steel and put it in an automobile and you know very few people can afford to buy an automobile in Europe. So, if you start this process, raising wages and lowering prices, you get that great expanding market in Europe and that will take care of this increased production. Henry Ford introduced us to that new principle and when he did he started a revolution that we are still benefiting by.[9]

Counterpart funds, in fact, were powerful tools which members of the ECA used to launch and monitor a productivist and consumerist 'revolution' in Europe.

On a day-to-day basis, the handling of counterpart funds by Marshall plan administrators also took into account the situation on the ground and in particular the priorities of the coalitions in power within each country. The decentralized character of the ECA machinery made such pragmatism possible and allowed, moreover, close monitoring of the use that was ultimately made of counterpart funds. Within the framework of the Marshall plan, ECA country Missions had to approve all projects to be financed, in part or entirely, through counterpart funds. Country Missions were located on the ground close to those national offices that were responsible in each country for the handling of counterpart funds. This allowed systematic scrutiny of the economic affairs of European countries and a tight control, down to the smallest amounts, of counterpart funds. At the same time, differences in national contexts required the partial adaptation and redefinition of strategies locally. The degree of control exercised by members of the ECA over the use of counterpart funds was inversely proportional to the trust they had in local authorities. The priorities of local authorities themselves as well as their capacity to implement measures and policies in the national economy were two important variables conditioning this American trust.

Shaping Policy in France: Stabilization, Propaganda, and Housing

In France, the very existence of the planning board tended to spare the ECA an overly systematic and detailed monitoring of counterpart funds and of their use. Thanks to the intervention of Jean Monnet, the French planning board had secured the allocation of counterpart funds to the French investment plan, albeit only indirectly through the FME. As already shown, trust and synergy characterized relationships between members of the French planning board and members of the ECA. Production and productivity growth were key common priorities. Other projects such as a European-wide integration of markets were also important, but Jean Monnet believed that 'cooperation [would] come later, basing itself on the national efforts that [were to] precede and prepare it'.[10] The French plan and the Marshall plan were highly complementary. They strongly reinforced each other and the key point of articulation was the counterpart fund mechanism.

In 1946 and 1947, the French planning board had prepared a national investment plan which then received the full support of American Marshall planners. The implementation of this plan required investment in machinery and equipment goods. And indeed, throughout the period of implementation, the French planning board demanded or recommended investments, particularly in those industrial sectors it considered to be key. At the time, machinery and equipment could only be imported from the USA. French funds, whether public or private, were not available in significantly large amounts to finance the importation of this type of goods. Counterpart funds were a welcome device, in such circumstances, allowing French planners to grant individual companies or industrial sectors subsidies and loans to buy in the USA the equipment necessary for their planned investments. The fit between the French plan and the Marshall plan was so good, in fact, that members of the ECA could relax their guard somewhat, relying on a solid partnership with French modernizers. Amongst those countries participating in the Marshall scheme, France was undeniably the one to make the fullest use of the counterpart device. Table 13 shows that all of French counterpart funds were re-injected into the national economy which was not the case in all Western European countries.

From Control to Conversion

Table 13. Marshall aid and counterpart funds, 1948–52 (US$ millions)

	Europe	France	FRG	Italy	UK
Marshall aid	13,300	2,700	1,400	1,500	3,200
Counterpart released	8,400	2,700	1,000	1,000	1,800

Sources: Mayer (1969: 84–5) and Margairaz (1993: 162–3).

In fact, the first French plan, otherwise known as the *plan de modernisation et d'équipement*, was financed for half its total amount through counterpart funds.[11] This showed the significant dependence of French investments on American funds. It also testified to the good working relationships existing between the French planning board and the ECA. Those two institutions had common objectives and priorities for the French economy. The very existence of a French plan was a guarantee for members of the ECA that, generally, the counterpart mechanism was used in France in accordance with their own preferences and that it was bound to have a significant impact in that country. Indeed, as Table 14 illustrates, approximately three-quarters of the total of French counterpart funds were used to finance investments in capital goods. The case of the UK has been added to Table 14 to present an entirely different strategy with respect to the use of counterpart funds.

Despite this overall synergy between the French planning board and the ECA, however, there still were some tensions, power plays, or even confrontations between French and American modernizers. In 1948 and 1949, a number of disagreements emerged over French choices with respect to macroeconomic policy. The French Fourth Republic was at the time a highly unstable regime. Political coalitions and governments were weak, being made and unmade in rapid succession. Governmental musical chairs in France were all the more worrying to Americans in that the French communists remained powerful and well organized. Furthermore, this high level of political instability led in turn to irresponsible policy making with respect to macroeconomic issues. Decisions tended to be made with the next election in mind, to soothe coalition

Table 14. Counterpart funds in France and the UK, 1948–52 (%)

	France	UK
Debt retirement	6.3	96.8
Development of production	74.1	0.1
Arms production	7.6	2.7
Construction/Housing	11.7	—
Other	0.3	0.4
Total	100.0	100.0

Note: Total counterpart funds released in France: US$2.7 billion and in the UK: US$1.8 billion.
Source: Adapted from Margairaz (1993: 162–3).

partners, or in response to strikes or labor action. The priority for members of the ECA was undeniably to stimulate production and productivity in Western Europe. They were nevertheless not ready to accept that production and productivity growth take place in an unstable or unhealthy macroeconomic environment. There was little justification, Americans argued, for the spending of American taxpayers' dollars, if the French themselves did not make any effort, if they squandered their resources around, or badly managed the national budget.

In the summer of 1948, the ECA therefore demanded that French authorities elaborate a convincing program of macroeconomic stabilization. Inflation, in particular, should be kept within bounds which implied control over both wages and prices. Solutions should be found, as well, to the chronic deficit of the French budget, through a restructuring of the tax system for example or through cuts in government spending. Throughout 1948 and 1949, the ECA used counterpart funds as an instrument to impose on successive French governments the adoption and implementation of a macroeconomic stabilization program. Counterpart funds releases were approved on a monthly basis and this gave the ECA significant leverage to closely monitor French macroeconomic policy.[12] By the early months of 1950, the French macroeconomic situation had improved sufficiently for the ECA to relax somewhat its control. From then on, the release of counterpart funds would not be negotiated monthly anymore but annually, on the basis of French proposals officially drawn up by the SGCI—but in reality by the planning board. Table 15 shows that, despite the stabilization effort imposed by the ECA, the French investment program was not curtailed nor significantly slowed down in 1948 or 1949. In addition, there was no disagreement during that period on the use that was to be made of counterpart funds once they had been released.

The situation changed in 1950, when disagreements emerged between the French and American administrations precisely on the use that should be made of counterpart funds. The French investment program was not challenged nor called into question. Nevertheless, members of the ECA believed that the time had come to reorient somewhat their priorities in France. This closely followed the publication in the fall of 1949 of a report on ERP implementation, that came to the conclusion that efforts to publicize Marshall plan undertakings and achievements in Western Europe were not sufficient.

Table 15. French public finances, 1947–49 (FF billions)

	Budget deficit	Public investment	Counterpart funds
1947	184	151	—
1948	338	445	140
1949	151	605	263

Source: Esposito (1994: 88).

The Watchdog Committee, which produced this report, was an American parliamentary committee precisely created to monitor the European Recovery Program. The conclusions of the report were buttressed by opinion polls and the results in the French case were particularly disturbing. Amongst those individuals polled in France, 13 per cent had never heard about the Marshall plan. A mere 38 per cent of those who had heard of it were in favor of Marshall aid and only 4 per cent believed that it had made a difference in France to the economic recovery.[13]

Both the American Congress and the ECA were unhappy with these results and therefore called for a systematic and large-scale French information drive. Members of the ECA put pressure on the French authorities by threatening that such a negative report could bring Congress to reassess its appropriations for France. A propaganda drive seemed all the more necessary in France because anti-American feelings were particularly strong and often violently conveyed by communist groups. The French, it was argued in American circles, should be told clearly and repeatedly what the USA was doing for them. They should also be given a chance to experience the benefits of Marshall assistance. This naturally required systematic and large-scale information and propaganda campaigns. A more significant implication, however, was that investments should be partially reoriented towards projects with a concrete and direct impact on the everyday life of French citizens (Bossuat, 1993; Margairaz, 1993; Esposito, 1994). In 1950, the ECA therefore demanded that a proportion of French counterpart funds be allocated to the construction of schools, hospitals, and social housing. French authorities were highly reluctant to adopt this reorientation. They believed that a large-scale propaganda effort would be in reality counterproductive, fueling anti-American feelings. They were convinced that underplaying the role of the USA in the French economic recovery was in fact much more reasonable. The planning board, on the other hand, did not like the idea of making cuts in its investment program to finance what it considered to be non-priority sectors.

Overall, however, the balance of power was clearly in favor of the ECA and the latter retained full control over the release of counterpart funds. Therefore, in 1950, the French *liaison* office in charge of relationships with the ECA, the SGCI, had to launch and oversee a large-scale information and propaganda drive. It organized, in particular, official unveiling ceremonies for a number of realizations financed through the Marshall plan, to which both American and French journalists were invited.[14] Jean Monnet himself also had to accept a partial reorientation of his investment program. While the planning board had initially not budgeted an amount for construction and housing in 1950, the balance sheet showed that, in the end, 7 per cent of all counterpart funds released that year were directed towards the low-cost housing program put forward by the ECA. In 1951, construction and housing appeared at the top of the list elaborated by the planning board with one third of counterpart funds releases for that year (Bossuat, 1993: 188–91).

Shaping Policy in West Germany and Italy: Capital Investment

In West German territories, the handling of counterpart funds proved to be quite a different process. For obvious political reasons, those territories were not full blown partners in the Marshall scheme, especially during the first two years.[15] In the case of West German territories, Marshall assistance initially took the form of loans, to be repaid in dollars. Both the procurement of commodities and the handling of counterpart funds were then the entire responsibility of the American administration. Partnership and collaboration between the Americans and the West Germans only started on those issues in 1949, after the decision to create a West German state had been taken. Still, paradoxically, the ECA appeared ineffective during the first year of the Marshall plan in a country where, in fact, Americans could be all powerful. This turned out to be the consequence of a conflict between members of the American military government (OMGUS) and Marshall plan administrators. Competition for power and influence within the American administration accounted to a significant extent for the slow start of the ERP in West German territories. By the end of 1948, ERP deliveries only amounted to a US$100 million, 90 per cent of which was either food or cotton.[16] On the other hand, the release of counterpart funds had not even started by then. In this early period, the Marshall plan did not play in West German territories the key role for which it had been designed. It was still a long way from stimulating economic recovery and industrial restructuring.

However, this situation started to change in 1949 when the period of military government ended and when the Federal Republic of Germany was put under the supervision of a civilian Allied High Commission. The merging of the American High Commission for Germany with the ECA Mission in Germany under the single chairmanship of John McCloy was symbolic of this change. John McCloy was personally close to many members of the ECA and he shared their vision and their sense of mission. Although it remained difficult, until the end of the Marshall plan, to justify large-scale imports of machinery or strategic raw materials to West Germany, the attitude towards counterpart funds evolved in a radical way after 1949.[17] The American civilian administration in Germany set out to use counterpart funds to stimulate investments in capital goods. Following a pattern that was proving reasonably successful in France, members of the ECA in Germany called for a national investment plan. Such a plan would help them monitor the use that was being made of released counterpart funds and it would give them a more direct control over West German industry.[18] A West German investment program was finally put together, although the West German Ministry of Economic Affairs greatly disliked national planning. While on a much more modest scale, this German program shared with the Monnet plan the idea of defining priority sectors with potential multiplier effects. Electricity, coal-mining, transport, and housing were singled out and consequently they received a large proportion of German

Table 16. Counterpart funds in West Germany, 1948–52 (%)

Debt retirement	—
Development of production	75
(including coal, energy, and transport)	(33)
Arms production	—
Housing	10
Other/non-specified	15

Note: The total of counterpart funds released in West Germany over the period was US$1 billion.
Source: Margairaz (1993: 162).

counterpart funds, as documented in Table 16.[19] By the end of the Marshall plan period, three-quarters of German counterpart funds had been re-injected to finance productive investments, in a pattern that closely fit the objectives of members of the ECA.

Once the difficulties of the first year had been successfully overcome, the monitoring of counterpart funds proved particularly effective in West Germany, due to the power position of the American administration. The ECA had the means and the right to monitor and control the release and the use of German counterpart funds, project by project and month by month, as a letter from the ECA to the German Ministry for the Marshall Plan made quite clear:

The industry division is interested to receive through your Ministry detailed English reports, covering all industrial applicants. . . . The first report is due here on April 1st, 1950, and should cover all releases of counterpart funds cumulative to March 1st, 1950. Thereafter, monthly reports on firms approved for credit over DM2 million and quarterly reports on firms with credits in smaller amounts will be adequate.[20]

Thus in West Germany, the ECA used the counterpart funds mechanism as a tool to shape and stimulate national investment. While the Americans had the same objectives in Italy, the results proved much less satisfactory there. In 1948, the political and economic situation in Italy was similar in many ways to the situation in France. Large budget deficits and rampant inflation were factors of destabilization in a political context which was already quite volatile. The existence of a large communist opposition represented a threat that the American authorities could not dismiss lightly and it undeniably had a significant impact on their action in that country. Italy, on the other hand, lacked its Jean Monnet. In contrast to what had happened in France, a national modernizing élite had not taken over key positions of institutional power after the Second World War (Zamagni, 1986). Postwar Italian governments were dominated by members of the Christian Democratic party. Around Alcide de Gasperi, these successive governments favored a conservative economic policy, essentially advocating a program of macroeconomic stabilization. This particular political and governmental configuration was to a significant extent responsible for the slow start of the ERP in Italy. In France, FF140 billion had already been released by the end of 1948 through the counterpart funds mechanism. This represented 18 per cent of the total amount of counterpart funds that were ultimately released in France. In the meantime, in Italy, the counterpart mechanism remained virtually blocked until the spring of 1949 (Margairaz, 1993; Esposito, 1994).

Members of the ECA believed that Italy needed both a serious stabilization effort and an ambitious national investment program. The Italian government was undeniably willing to work on macroeconomic stabilization. It did not have, however, a national investment plan nor did it apparently intend to elaborate and implement one. In those conditions, the counterpart device appeared relatively useless. As long as there was no plan on the Italian side to make use of counterpart funds or Fondo Lire, the counterpart device could clearly not increase the leverage of American Marshall planners on Italian economic policy. The first year of the European Recovery Program in Italy was therefore characterized by intense negotiations, numerous confrontations, and frustration on both sides. The Italians feared that the inflationary effects of counterpart funds might endanger their stabilization effort and consequently refused to use them. Members of the ECA, on the other hand, were highly critical of the Italian government for failing to seize the ERP opportunity. They deplored the unwillingness to use American assistance to fuel recovery and to rebuild the national economy.

By 1949, the ECA and in particular the Rome Mission around James Zeller-bach was putting systematic pressure on the Italian government so that it finally would elaborate a national investment program.[21] Members of the ECA were adamant that in Italy as everywhere else in Europe, 'one should concentrate upon locating those investments which permit the breaking of important bottle-necks and will thereby lead to increases of output and improvements of per-formance out of proportion to the investment itself'.[22] In Italy, the ECA was undeniably using France as a model. Members of the Rome Mission called for the creation of an Italian planning board that would be responsible for elabor-ating and implementing a national investment plan. In 1948, however, and well into 1949, the only Italian response to American demands was in the form of vague and uncoordinated plans for a small number of industrial sectors.[23] Under these conditions, the ECA questioned the capacity of the Italians to use counter-part funds in a satisfactory way. Members of the Rome Mission therefore decided to retain a controlling process allowing them to screen every single project. The complexity of such a process and the overall dissatisfaction of members of the ECA with unclear and uncoordinated Italian projects explained the chaotic and limited release of counterpart funds in that country.

By the fall of 1949, members of the ECA had become convinced that they would have to take the Italian situation in their own hands. According to them, a large-scale and coordinated investment program was becoming increasingly urgent in Italy and unused counterpart funds were not acceptable. The first step was to create a joint committee bringing together the Italians and the

Americans. This committee was put in charge of elaborating a national investment plan. Members of the ECA had deplored the small share of capital goods
in Italian imports financed through the ERP between 1948 and 1949. A second
step was therefore for the ECA to threaten a cut in appropriations for Italy if no
effort was made to increase the share of capital goods in ERP shipments for
1950. In return, the Rome Mission agreed to relax somewhat the screening and
control process for Italian projects financed through counterpart funds. The
distribution of ERP imports was indeed modified along the lines set by the
ECA. While machines and vehicles had represented 6.9 per cent of Italian ERP
shipments in 1949, this rose to 30 per cent in 1950 (Milward, 1984: 103–4). In
addition, the use of counterpart funds was significantly stepped up. While the
counterpart mechanism had remained virtually blocked well into 1949, US$1
billion in counterpart funds had been released by June 1952. This represented
around 70 per cent of total ERP assistance to Italy. Table 17 shows that a large
proportion of those counterpart funds did help to finance the 'development of
Italian production', in apparent conformity with the demands stemming from
the ECA.

In spite of American pressure, however, the Italian government never proposed a systematic and coordinated national investment plan. In keeping with
their *laissez faire* convictions, Italian decision makers refused to contemplate a
national Italian state with central planning functions. Starting in 1950, they
nevertheless had to accept—even if only reluctantly—the idea of public
investment. They reconciled themselves to the use of counterpart funds to
stimulate investments but only in those sectors where private initiative was
unlikely to emerge. During the last two years of the Marshall plan, Italian
counterpart funds were thus mostly used in the transportation sector (32 per
cent of released counterpart funds), for housing (17 per cent), or in the Italian
South to finance agrarian reforms and programs (13 per cent) (Margairaz,
1993: 162–3).

Altogether, American involvement in Italian economic affairs had mixed
results. On paper, the ECA had managed to stimulate imports of capital goods
to Italy. It also had apparently succeeded in ensuring that a significant share of
counterpart funds be re-injected into the development of Italian production.
The lack of a coherent national plan, however, and the priority granted to

Table 17. Counterpart funds in Italy, 1948–52 (%)

Debt retirement	—
Development of production	79
Arms production	—
Housing	17
Other/non-specified	4

Note: The total of counterpart funds released in Italy over the period was US$1 billion.
Source: Margairaz (1993: 162–3).

infrastructural over truly productive investments left members of the ECA frustrated. Throughout the fall of 1950, Leon Dayton—who had taken over from James Zellerbach as head of the Rome Mission—was publicly and bluntly criticizing both the Italian government and the Italian business community for their apathy and resistance to change. Italian business and industrial leaders were giving 'lip-service to the need for raising the standard of living and to the basic principles of low cost and high production. But of all the firms in Italy, he deplored, you could count those which practice these precepts on the fingers of your two hands.'[24] By the early 1950s, members of the ECA generally shared the feeling that the Italians had refused to seize the opportunity provided by the ERP to undertake a deep transformation and redefinition of Italian economic and industrial structures. In the Italian case, the Americans had to acknowledge the relative failure of their strategy of co-optation. They had been unable to select a small group of Italians with whom they could have worked towards a redefinition of the Italian system of industrial production. They had not managed to identify and co-opt in Italy those individuals who would have embraced and championed the American model of large-scale, mass-producing, corporate, and competitive oligopolies.

'POLITICS OF PRODUCTIVITY': TOWARDS CONVERSION STRATEGIES

The Marshall plan was originally defined as an American program of financial and material assistance. It provided for a large-scale transfer of machinery and equipment from the USA to Western European nations. The counterpart mechanism associated with this program of assistance could be a powerful control device for the American administration in charge. It could allow members of the ECA to have an indirect impact upon Western European economic and industrial policies. The Americans used it in fact to stimulate productive investments and industrial restructuring. The ambitions of Marshall planners, however, went beyond putting together a large-scale investment program for Western Europe. Their common objective was the radical transformation and redefinition of the European economic and industrial landscape along the lines of the American model of corporate capitalism.

Considering this ultimate objective, the large-scale transfer of machinery and a fostering of investments were clearly not sufficient. Members of the ECA had realized from the outset that knowledge, know how, and the will to make the most of new machines and equipment were also quite important. The 'productivity' or 'expansion spirit' as this came to be labeled, was essential to the success of their ambitious undertaking. In order to be long lasting, structural and technical transformations had to be grounded in appropriate institutional and cultural environments. Institutions, practices, and mentalities should therefore also be evolved in Western Europe. To that end, mechanisms of control and coercion could only play a limited part. More complex strategies of conversion, indoctrination, and re-education were necessary if the process of change was to achieve a momentum of its own and to survive beyond the period of strong geopolitical dependence. American Marshall planners were not only controllers managing a large-scale program of assistance. They were also 'missionaries' trying to convert Western Europeans to the new American 'business creed'.

The Technical Assistance Program or Productivity Drive

As already argued, the very idea of productivity had American origins. The word itself had not existed in most European languages and it was coined in the early post-Second World War period as a direct transcription of the American word. According to both American and European specialists in productivity issues, the 'science of productivity' had originally emerged in the USA at the turn of the twentieth century. In postwar Western Europe, the term 'productivity' was generally used in its straightforward sense of 'production per man hour'. High levels of productivity in the USA and in particular within American industry were generally explained by a mixture of mass production, competition, scientific management, and 'human relations' in the work place.[25] Systematic productivity measures and the quest for higher productivity levels had been institutionalized in the American industrial context during the New Deal period with the creation of the Works Progress Administration. Members of that administration had soon established a close working relationship with economists from the National Bureau for Economic Research (NBER) and with representatives of professional associations such as the American Management Association (AMA) or the Society for the Advancement of Management (SAM).[26] The emergence of such a network contributed to the institutionalization of the productivity movement in the USA. In 1938, the Works Progress Administration was dismantled. American interest in productivity issues, however, was reasserted and the responsibilities of that administration were simply transferred to the Federal Bureau of Labor.

From 1945 and until the end of 1948, the issue of productivity emerged on the Western European scene but not in any kind of systematic way. In 1946, the French planning board claimed that differences in productivity levels between France and the USA revealed much more than technological or even structural differences. A modernization of the French economy and industry, it was argued, required a radical redefinition of methods, practices, and mentalities. There was a systematic attempt, in that early period, to document and measure gaps in productivity levels between American and Western European industries. However, measurement problems were quite significant and, in particular, figures giving production per man hour were rarely available in Western European countries. Therefore, comparisons pointing to a significant European backwardness were, in general, based on rough and questionable estimates.[27]

In the summer of 1948, an Anglo-American Council on Productivity was created on the joint initiative of the ECA and of James Silbermann, chief of the productivity division in the American Bureau of Labor. A key objective of this binational council was to fight the lack of interest in scientific production methods and technical efficiencies characteristic of British labor and management. This council also hoped to transform the 'complacent attitude' towards restrictive practices and limits to competition dominant in those same communities (Hogan, 1985: 62). In the fall of 1948, the ECA was indicating to the French government that it was ready to extend its program in favor of productivity to France. The productivity drive, however, was only launched on a large scale in 1949. President Harry Truman's speech to Congress in January 1949 gave this productivity drive legitimacy and indicated that it had official support on the national American scene.

Point IV of Truman's 'program for peace and freedom' called for the elaboration and implementation of bold plans and programs that would allow 'backward' parts of the world to benefit from American 'industrial and scientific progress'.[28] A special technical assistance division was created within the ECA in March 1949. In July, the American Congress passed the International Technical Cooperation Act defined as 'a bill to promote the foreign policy of the United States and to authorize participation in a cooperative endeavor for assisting in the development of economically underdeveloped areas of the world'.[29] On the American side, the 'politics of productivity' were the result of a collaboration between the ECA, the Federal Bureau of Labor, and traditional partners of the latter. Those traditional partners were private professional associations or research agencies such as the National Management Council, the SAM, the AMA, or the NBER. The very nature of the productivity drive reflected such a collaboration. The concept of productivity came to include all those features characteristic of the corporate and managerial version of American capitalism. To the ECA's initial emphasis on mechanization, size of production units or firms, structures, and competition were added the characteristic focus of the Bureau of Labor on scientific management, standardization, output per man hour, and 'human relations' in the work place. Productivity could be measured as 'production per man hour'. By the late 1940s, however, it had come to mean much more than that for a number of American and Western European modernizers:

Increases in productivity levels are necessary for the success of the ERP . . . . Beyond the obvious need in machinery, equipment, and modern methods of production, fundamental institutional transformations will be necessary. Attitudes and mentalities should be radically altered. Competition should become a normal element of economic life leading to the elimination of inefficient companies as its normal role should be.[30]

Notwithstanding a relatively limited overall budget, the American technical assistance program thus had significant ambitions.[31] Its objectives were long term. It was to further and reinforce the program of large-scale investment and structural reshaping at the core of the Marshall plan. Assessing the American program of technical assistance is however, quite difficult. Evaluating the extent to which institutions and mentalities were transformed is indeed a much more complex exercise than measuring the size of firms and production units or the value of imports.

At the core of the technical assistance program was a large-scale transfer of knowledge, know-how, managerial practices, and values from the USA to Europe. The proposed mechanism for the conversion of European economic and industrial actors to the American 'business creed' was a two-step process of trickle-down transfer or diffusion. In the first stage of the technical assistance program, a selection of European economic and industrial actors were offered a direct and intensive American experience. In the second stage, a systematic plan was elaborated to ensure the implementation of the methods, know-hows, and practices with which those actors had become familiar. A dissemination and communication plan also had to be defined during this second stage to maximize the impact within each national country of the initial American experience.[32]

Type A productivity missions, from Europe to the USA, were at the core of this two-step process of cross-national transfer but all other forms of technical assistance projects pertained to the same logic. Amongst these other projects were the sending of American experts to Europe, the training of future European trainers in management, the reorganization of European business education, the diffusion of American technical and business literature, the pilot factories projects, and the questions and answers service.[33] The main objective behind all technical assistance projects was always as wide a diffusion as possible with the learning process taking place in a trickle-down fashion. Within the framework of the American technical assistance program, interactions between Western European and American actors always had to be as direct as possible. National administrations and governments had a role to play in setting the process in motion. They were nevertheless to wither away after a while. The technical assistance program purported to be a cross-national program of cooperation between actors at the grass-roots level. Indeed, members of the American administration were convinced that conversion in Western Europe would be neither large-scale nor long lasting if it were not grounded at the level of individual actors, firms, business leaders, managers, and workers:

The success of such a vast undertaking as technical assistance to European countries is highly dependent, according to the Americans, on the cooperation of business leaders. . . . The ECA is adamant that the role of administrative and political agencies should fade—at least in appearance—behind the role of business leaders and managers themselves, who would be supposed to be moved by the spontaneous desire of improving and transforming their own methods.[34]

Thus in the beginning the technical assistance program was essentially imposed on grass-roots Western European actors through political and administrative *fiat*. The American administration played a particularly significant role in this respect, pushing for the involvement of business and labor representatives at all levels of the technical assistance program. National agencies, created under pressure from the ECA administration to handle the technical assistance program, were generally tripartite and included labor, business, and government representatives. European teams leaving for the USA in search of the 'sources of productivity' also had to include members of both labor and business communities, with the partial exception of a few teams of experts.

The technical assistance program outlasted the Marshall plan. In 1953, the Blair-Moody amendment gave the productivity drive a new life, setting aside a special US$100 million fund for purposes of technical assistance.[35] Starting in 1953, productivity missions became more specialized and technical, 'general missions being [by then] less necessary'.[36] On the other hand, the largest share of Blair-Moody funds was to be directly allocated at the firm or industry level for projects that were likely to 'stimulate an economy of free enterprise through increased productivity and the fair sharing of its benefits between consumers, labor and capital'.[37] By the end of the 1950s, American funds were still available to finance a few productivity projects in Western European countries.

Go West Young Men! The Productivity Rush

Productivity missions were undeniably the most striking and original feature of the American technical assistance program. During the first period of this program, from 1949 to 1952, type A missions—Western European teams sent to the USA and marginally to other Western European countries—were the main type of productivity projects to be financed through technical assistance funds. Starting in 1953, the Blair-Moody amendment led to a partial reorientation of the productivity drive. Direct loans to private companies were given priority, the objective being to finance structural or technological transformations with a positive impact on productivity. Considering the ultimate objectives of the technical assistance program, the reorientation of 1953 made perfect sense. In the end, private initiative was supposed to prevail and the large-scale financing of productivity missions through public funds was legitimate only on a temporary basis. With respect to the 'productivity crusade', both the ECA and the Mutual Security Agency taking over in 1952 hoped, in time, to be able to hand over responsibilities to the Western European private sector.[38] It was assumed that Western European economic actors and industrial communities would come to appropriate the productivity drive. By the late 1950s, this seemed indeed to be the case in some Western European countries. And the French government justified its partial disengagement from the productivity drive in this way:

If state intervention appeared at some point necessary to revive the modernization spirit of business leaders, this intervention was to decrease once private initiative had regained sufficient vitality. The work which has been done through those years allows us today to have greater confidence in the spontaneous initiative of private companies.[39]

The 1950s undeniably witnessed in Western Europe the institutionalization of a 'productivity spirit'. This process of institutionalization was undeniably given its first and main impetus by the productivity missions program. By the end of June 1953, France had organized 291 type A missions, West Germany 266, and Italy 173. Most productivity teams had been sent to the USA, although the ECA administration and later on the MSA (Mutual Security Agency) also encouraged productivity missions from one OEEC country to another.[40] Throughout the 1950s, more than 4,000 Frenchmen (and only very few women) were sent to the USA through type A missions (Boltanski, 1981; Kuisel, 1988). In two years, from 1950 to 1951, 5,000 Germans went to the USA, whether through type A missions or through an exchange program sponsored by the American High Commission in Germany (HICOG).[41] Type A missions were national and in some rare cases cross-national teams of Europeans. They lasted on average six weeks and each team had between ten and thirty members. Those teams were to learn, through immersion and direct contact, about American productivity achievements. The objective was that Western European economic actors find direct 'inspiration in the model which the American economy represent[ed]'.[42] European team members were to bring back methods, practices, know-how, and knowledge that should help to increase levels of productivity within an individual company, a particular industrial sector, or even the national economy as a whole. Productivity teams shared responsibility with national productivity agencies for implementation and for the diffusion of knowledge acquired during the trips.

Officially, projects for type A missions had to originate from within European civil societies. After a first screening, carried out by national productivity agencies, those projects were then sent for approval to the ECA administration.[43] In reality, however, the initiative often lay with national administrations and governments or even with the American administration. All projects for type A missions on general issues such as antitrust legislation, fiscality, trade unions, or business education were for example proposed and put together by the ECA administration. 'Suggestions' or 'proposals' made by the ECA or other American administrations generally amounted to unofficial orders and American-initiated projects were therefore often given priority. Those projects had to be packaged as national projects emerging from local actors so as to conceal their American origins as much as possible. National productivity agencies thus reformulated the proposals, sending them back to ECA country Missions through formal channels. Figure 9 presents in summary form the official and unofficial workings of the productivity missions program. In the end, the final decision on type A projects was the prerogative of the American administration in Washington. Once projects were approved, the ECA worked with other American public and private actors or with European

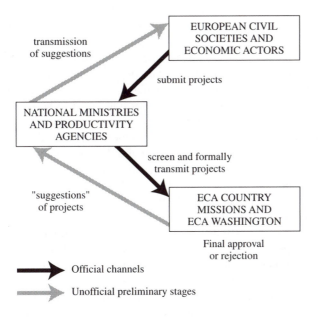

Figure 9. Type A missions program: official and unofficial workings

productivity agencies to concretely set up each productivity mission, closely controlling the selection of team members and the organization of trips.

The ECA had set up formal rules with respect to the structure and membership of productivity teams, rules that varied in part with the nature of the proposed mission. Teams of experts were sometimes necessary when the productivity mission required specialized knowledge and specific skills. Membership could then be fairly homogeneous and participants tended to be experts in their field. A special case was the 'young experts' team where participants were promising young men sent to American universities or schools of business administration for periods of up to one year. Generally, however, the ECA favored productivity missions that brought together business and labor representatives and required that several firms work together. The Americans had been very clear about their preference for this particular type of team structure and membership but national productivity agencies had sometimes to be reminded of this fact.

In France, the ECA regularly had to fight a tendency to favor teams of experts and the inclusion of too many civil servants. The representation of labor within French teams was another contentious issue. ECA labor advisers criticized in particular the control exercised by business owners and top level managers over the choice of labor representatives. The ECA finally deplored the fact that French business decision makers refused to work together with competitors within the framework of a single productivity team. The ECA thus repeatedly had to put pressure on French national productivity agencies to ensure that 'more workers take part in productivity missions, [that] trade unions have a say in the selection of labor representatives for productivity missions, and [that] several different firms be represented in the same mission'.[44] French productivity agencies undeniably tried to take those American criticisms and demands into account but labor continued to be slightly under-represented in French productivity teams.

In West Germany, the political past of team members proved to be the main bone of contention. The ECA administration and the American High Commission in Germany insisted that West Germans sent to the USA through the productivity missions program should have a clean political record, validated by an Allied denazification court decision. German productivity agencies pointed to the complexity of the selection process in those conditions, claiming that the existence of strict political criteria for team members considerably slowed down the productivity program in West Germany. They relayed numerous complaints on such a conditional selection process stemming from German economic and industrial actors.

Altogether, it could be argued that the selection process of team members was conflict-ridden by its very construction. Within the technical assistance framework, business owners and decision makers had to pay the transatlantic travel expenses of members of their company. They naturally expected, as a consequence, in France, in West Germany, or in other Western European countries, to have a significant say in the selection process of team members. Conflicts between national actors and the American administration on the structure and membership of productivity teams could sometimes considerably delay a productivity mission. The relatively slow start of the productivity missions program, both in France and in West Germany, can partially be explained in this way.

Once agreement had finally been reached on a particular productivity mission and its members arrived on the shores of the New World, the American administration could assert full control. In the USA, all dollar expenses were covered by the ECA and the day-to-day preparation and organization of missions was the joint responsibility of the ECA administration and of the Federal Bureau of Labor. The elaboration of a busy schedule, the choice of factories, companies, institutions to visit, and of individuals to meet were prerogatives of American administrative agencies.[45] European team members were supposed to learn from the American model they discovered during their trip to the USA. The systematic control exercised by the ECA and the Federal Bureau of Labor over the schedule of European productivity missions allowed those institutions to shape, in fact, the American model to be 'discovered'. Ultimately, European teams were essentially given a tour of mass-producing, corporate, and managerial American industry. The factories they visited were 'model' factories to the extent that they were characterized by large size, modern technology, the use of scientific management techniques, up-to-date management methods, and a progressive attitude, quite often, with regard to 'human relations'.[46] Through their politics of productivity, members of the ECA were therefore setting up American corporate capitalism as a superior and universal model. They were also encouraging conversion of parts of the world to this particular model.

The work of productivity team members did not end upon their return to Europe. Both the implementation of conclusions and the diffusion of knowledge were also crucial responsibilities of productivity teams:

Conclusions arrived at by productivity missions have an exemplary value, and they should be given as wide a diffusion as possible. While we should increase the number of missions, we should also multiply the means thanks to which economic actors who stay in France could be informed and could understand the benefits of such conclusions for their own activity.[47]

The ECA believed that a two-step process of cross-national transfer could be particularly effective. It therefore attached great significance to the diffusion and dissemination of knowledge acquired during the trips and of conclusions reached by productivity teams. Within the framework of the technical assistance program, the ECA demanded that national productivity agencies set up systematic mechanisms ensuring that productivity missions would have an impact well beyond the small group of participants.[48]

Upon returning to their home country, European productivity teams had to write a report. National productivity agencies were then responsible for publishing those reports and for diffusing their results. Under pressure from the ECA, those agencies came to devise a number of other strategies to enlarge the scope of the dissemination effort. They launched monthly or bi-monthly specialized magazines on productivity, where summaries or excerpts of reports were reprinted.[49] They multiplied contacts and developed working relationships with the press, passing along information on productivity missions. Special radio broadcasts were created to give regular accounts of the productivity missions program to a wide audience.[50] Seminars and conferences were organized, where members of productivity missions told of their experience in a direct way. Roving ambassadors sent by productivity teams spread the word across the national territory using, in some cases, movies made in the USA during the productivity mission.[51] In addition, in West Germany, each productivity team was responsible for the elaboration of an implementation report four to six months after the end of the mission. This report had to lay out 'the extent to which plans have been made and work carried out using the information gained as well as the results already achieved'.[52] As a result of these implementation reports, the ECA could control the use that was being made of productivity mission conclusions in West Germany. Members of the ECA could also intervene rapidly in order to stimulate or reorient efforts at dissemination and implementation.

The lack of systematic mechanisms made it much more difficult to have any control over implementation in France. This clearly bothered members of the ECA and in 1951 they asked French productivity agencies to organize, for French and ECA officials, a tour of those French companies that had been involved in the productivity missions program. The objective was to assess the extent to which productivity mission conclusions had been implemented and at the same time to stimulate further implementation and diffusion.[53] In a few industrial sectors—particularly in the smelting, shoe, and clothing industries—ECA members intervened even more directly. They took the initiative to stimulate themselves the implementation of conclusions reached by productivity missions in those sectors. The pilot-factory program, as this initiative was generally called, heralded the reorientation, starting in 1953, of American 'politics of productivity'.

There was a double objective behind the pilot-factory program. A number of 'model' factories or companies were to be created first of all. This program would also show how conclusions reached by productivity missions could be implemented. Building on the reports made by productivity teams in those sectors, the ECA—and starting in 1952 the MSA—worked with a limited number of companies which were ready to cooperate. American experts were sent to the factories for significant periods of time. Specialization of production by company or factory was encouraged, as a way of working around small size. For each production unit, machinery was brought in from the USA. In each case, American experts launched and oversaw time and motion studies in order to simplify and rationalize the production process. Those companies participating in a pilot-factory scheme had to work together to standardize accounting practices, develop marketing tools, and to create the bases for good relationships between labor and management.[54] Short of legal merger, the pilot-factory scheme thus led to a significant modernization of participating companies along the lines of the corporate model of American capitalism.

In Italy, the fate of the productivity missions program was relatively similar to the fate of the counterpart funds program. The Italian government was clearly not enthusiastic about the productivity drive and it did not like the idea of getting further involved in the national economy. Italian political decision makers were anxious, furthermore, to keep the American influence within bounds and were not attracted to the model of low-cost mass production that champions of the technical assistance program hoped to transfer to Europe.[55] The productivity missions program was therefore slow to start in Italy. In 1950 and 1951, the Italian government had spent a mere 15 per cent of available funds and the Italian national productivity committee was created only in the fall of 1951. The ECA tried to compensate for the slow start of the productivity missions program in Italy by sending American experts to Italy (type B missions) and by extending the French pilot-factory program to that country. In the end, however, members of the ECA and later of the MSA shared the feeling that the Italians had failed once again to take full advantage of available opportunities. The Italian case illustrated once more the limited degree of control exercised by the American administration in those Western European countries where its policies and undertakings did not have the support of local actors with a powerful institutional base.

Creating Institutions for Social Reproduction: Business Education

Throughout its involvement in Western European affairs, the ECA was perfectly aware of the fragile nature of its achievements in that region. The procurement of Marshall goods, the counterpart fund device, and the productivity missions program were all efficient mechanisms through which a fair number of Western Europeans could become familiar with the American system of industrial production and come to view it as a model. For members of the ECA, however, complete success would require that Western Europeans appropriate this model and see it as theirs. The transformation of structural arrangements, changes in methods and practices, the redefinition of business knowledge and values would have to outlast the period of direct American involvement. Younger generations of Europeans should one day come to claim those redefined structures, methods, knowledge, and values as their own.

In order for those reforms initially imposed or prompted by the ECA to survive, they had to be rooted deeply in Western European countries. The presence in positions of institutional power, both in France and in West Germany, of actors sympathetic to the project of the ECA represented a partial guarantee of continuity in policy. Ideally, however, the transformations themselves would have to be embedded in Western European social systems, both through institutions of control—the legislation—and through institutions of social reproduction—the education system. Members of the ECA had understood the importance of both types of institutions for the success of their project. Not surprisingly, they became closely involved in the development of systems of business and management education in Western European countries. In the short term, business education programs were mostly used to increase the impact of the productivity missions program and to enlarge its reach. European actors already in the labor force were given the opportunity to become familiar—this time in their own country and using their own language—with structures, practices, management methods, and knowledge identified as being at the foundations of American economic and industrial success. In the medium to long term, an institutionalization of business education in Western European countries was designed to create a new generation of economic actors and business decision makers who would take those particular structures, methods, practices, and knowledge for granted.

Before the end of the Second World War, business education in the American sense of the term, had not existed in Europe (Locke, 1989). This was partly explained by the fact that European national economies had not undergone, during the first part of the twentieth century, transformations that could compare with the American corporate and managerial revolution. In Western European industries where family firms were still dominant, management was rarely defined as a profession or a science. Leadership was generally understood to be a gift, an hereditary quality transmitted from father to son together with the family business. In so far as professionalization existed in Western Europe for a small minority of industrial leaders, it mostly occurred within engineering schools and only marginally within a few schools for advanced commercial studies.[56] In any case, before the Second World War, professionalization was far from necessary and it was certainly not the main source of legitimacy for Western European industrial leaders. This situation changed only after the end of the war and the initiative, once again, lay with the ECA. Other American institutions also took some interest in the transfer to Western Europe of business education. Professional associations, in particular, such as the American Management Association (AMA) and the Society for the Advancement of Management (SAM) were closely involved in this cross-national transfer process:

The SAM has consistently adhered to the purpose of helping executives approach all phases of the management problem—production, distribution, finance, administration, industrial relations—in an engineering manner. This means discarding prejudgment, thumb rule, guessing, haphazard methods and adopting instead the scientific method in the solution of all management problems. . . . The SAM, as a member of the National Management Council, is promoting sound, scientific management practices and doctrines on a world-wide basis.[57]

The role of the Ford Foundation should also be mentioned here. Until the early 1970s, it generously sponsored a number of initiatives, financing in particular the training in American universities of future European professors of business administration.

Within the framework of the technical assistance program, those American actors thus encouraged the development in Western Europe of training programs and seminars around management related issues. As a follow-up to productivity missions, the ECA sponsored for example a series of training sessions where a lecture by an American expert was combined with an open debate. Themes ranged from 'structural and organizational problems of the firm' to 'leadership', 'human relations in the firm', 'planning and control', 'market studies and marketing', or 'professional management associations'.[58] American experts for these sessions were selected through the National Management Council, an organization federating a number of American professional associations. National participants were European business leaders, managers, engineers, or technicians. In certain circumstances, a two-step training process was considered in order to enlarge the audience. American experts trained national trainers who then worked with business owners and local managers.[59]

Within European countries, national productivity agencies also took the initiative to hold training seminars and to institutionalize continuing education programs in business management. Some of those training seminars, on time and motion studies, accounting, or marketing techniques for example, could be highly specialized and technical. Overall, however, national productivity agencies tended to favor programs giving a large number of business leaders and managers a general overview of modern methods of management.[60] Private or semi-private research and consulting organizations were called upon to help set up the training sessions and seminars. European research and consulting organizations had been well represented in early productivity teams. Some of their members had benefited from the 'young experts' program and had thus attended, for periods of up to one year, a 'complete indoctrination session in principles of industrial and business administration' in an American graduate school of business administration.[61] By the early 1950s, members of those organizations were thus characterized by their first-hand knowledge of the American system of industrial production, which they generally admired. They were therefore ready to become its champions in their own country.

In France, the Comité National de l'Organisation Française (CNOF) and the Centre d'Etudes Générales d'Organisation Scientifique (CEGOS), private organizations created during the interwar period, deserve special mention for their role in the development of continuing education programs. As early as 1950, 20,000 engineers and middle managers had attended evening classes organized by the CNOF on scientific management.[62] A small minority of French business leaders soon jumped on the bandwagon, thus amplifying the process. A dynamic group within the CNPF, the French peak business association, set up in 1954 a Centre de Recherche et d'Etudes des Chefs d'Entreprise (CRC), the mission of which was to organize training and information sessions of up to three weeks on 'modern methods of management'.[63] In Western Europe as a whole, private undertakings emerged in the 1950s and multiplied in the 1960s. In fact, many of the initiators of these private programs had taken part earlier in one of the numerous productivity projects sponsored by the ECA (or the MSA) or by national productivity agencies.[64]

Continuing education and the development of short-term training programs in business administration were necessary to reinforce the impact of the productivity missions program. The short-term training effort was specifically aimed at European actors already in the labor force. Another stage, however, had to be the training of a new generation of European business decision makers. A radical reshaping of the Western European education system was therefore in order. The creation, in particular, of tracks or programs in management and business administration seemed essential. The ECA (and from 1952 the MSA) once again gave the impulse to such an in-depth reform. A number of productivity teams were sent to the USA to study the American business education system. When the European Productivity Agency (EPA) was created in 1953 under American pressure, it singled out the development of business

education as one of its most pressing responsibilities.[65] Working with the
MSA, the Ford Foundation, and the National Management Council, the EPA
did stimulate national efforts and help with the development of business
education in all Western European countries. The EPA set up programs for
the training of future European professors in management and business administration. By 1958, it had sent around 225 future professors to American
universities for periods of up to one year. Short-term summer sessions were
also organized for those academics already working as professor. Thanks to
Ford Foundation funds, American professors were brought to European institutions or universities for full teaching cycles.[66] The EPA also regularly
organized conferences and meetings where national delegations could share
their experiences, learn from each other with regard to business education, and
compare methods or curricula. A climax in the work of the EPA was the
creation in 1959 of a European business school, INSEAD, in a small town near
Paris. This project had been in the making ever since the early 1950s and the
main objective was 'to create an institute for the formation of top European
managers, similar to the Harvard Business School but covering the program in
a shorter period of time'. The new institution would benefit, naturally, 'from
substantial American assistance, both financially and with respect to
teaching'.[67]

While, from 1953, the EPA showed significant initiative, a great deal was
also being done at the national level. Under pressure from national productivity agencies, public institutions and universities were restructured in order to
accommodate management curricula and to offer diplomas in business administration. At the same time, a significant number of new private schools were
created in Western Europe throughout the 1950s and 1960s, specializing in
business education. In the case of France, the Ministry of National Education
defined in July 1955 a new university curriculum in management and business
administration. New establishments, labeled Instituts d'Administration des
Entreprises (IAE), were thereafter created in rapid succession in the largest
French universities. The prewar private French schools for commercial studies,
on the other hand, and in particular HEC or ESSEC, were reorganized following the American business school model. Faculties were professionalized and a
permanent body of professors was constituted in these schools. Many members
of the new faculties obtained an American diploma or at least gained some
experience in America through training opportunities offered by the technical
assistance program.[68] In conformity with the American model, research in
management and business administration was systematically fostered in these
schools, thus leading to the institutionalization of management as a 'science'
and to an increasing legitimacy of business education on the national scene.[69]
The structure, organization, and curricula of the schools were entirely revamped
following the model provided by the most famous of American graduate
schools of business administration. Active pedagogy in particular, based on
case studies, slowly made its way into French 'business schools', in radical

contrast to teaching methods then dominant in French universities.[70] A number of less prestigious business schools were created in the 1950s and 1960s in France. They also tended to be patterned, with more or less success, after American graduate schools of business administration. By the end of the 1960s, there were eighteen semi-public schools of management in France (Ecole Supérieure de Commerce or Ecole Supérieure de Commerce et d'Administration des Entreprises), all of which had been created since the early 1950s. There was around thirty private schools of business administration, nine of which had been created in the 1950s and sixteen in the 1960s.[71]

By the mid-1950s, the implementation of a large-scale, cross-national, structural transfer process from the USA to Western Europe was thus well under way. A small but institutionally powerful and well coordinated cross-national network had set up, for both France and West Germany, transfer mechanisms of the 'mimetic', 'coercive', or 'normative' types. A number of these transfer mechanisms were operating at the national level but Americans within the cross-national network tended to encourage a coordination of the transfer process on a European level. A few transfer mechanisms had also been set up in Italy, either at the national level or through European institutions. In that country, however, the break-up of the cross-national network made transfer mechanisms relatively ineffective.

While a large-scale transfer was attempted in both France and West Germany, the actual mix of transfer mechanisms was quite different in each of those two countries. In France, voluntary imitation had launched the transfer process while mechanisms of the coercive type had been initially predominant in the western territories of Germany. From 1948, the American administration had the means to use coercive pressure in France as well, if only to give the French modernizing group some support against resistance and opposition on the national scene. At the same time, American occupation authorities in the western territories of Germany were progressively giving up some of their responsibilities and prerogatives, mostly to the benefit of the few West Germans they had co-opted and placed in institutional positions of power. Mimetic transfer mechanisms, as a consequence, were becoming operative on the West German national scene. The early 1950s were also characterized in both countries by a systematic attempt to put in place normative types of transfer mechanisms. The objective was to embed the transfer process in national and European institutional contexts, to integrate and ground structural transformations locally. Operating those various types of transfer mechanisms was not always an easy task, as we will now attempt to show. Resistance or opposition on the part of more or less powerful and organized groups set serious obstacles to the large-scale transfer of the American structural model. Interestingly, the main source of resistance in fact lay in civil societies and more precisely within business and labor communities.

Notes

1. Leo D. Welch, Treasurer, Standard Oil. Speech in 1946. Quoted in Carew (1987: 40).
2. An essay putting forth this new American business creed was published in the early 1950s and had significant impact in the USA under the title *USA, the Permanent Revolution*. This essay claimed that 'more goods at lower cost and price is the basic principle of American industry. . . . Workable competition (which has been defined as the pragmatic concept which has succeeded the Darwinian notion of all-out competition) provides a good check on how a company is doing and the soundest way to ensure survival. . . . The success of the Sherman Act is among the chief reasons why American business today is so vastly different from European business.' Quoted in Sutton *et al.* (1956: 177).
3. 'Paul Hoffman. Speech to the Senate Foreign Relations Committee.' Quoted in Van der Pijl (1984: 159).
4. More than 90 per cent of Marshall assistance was in the form of donations and did not have to be repaid (Milward, 1984: 94). At the time, the American gross national product hovered somewhere around US$200 billion.
5. Figures can be found that partly validate this counterfactual argument. ERP-financed imports amounted in 1950 to 15 per cent of all French imports and in Germany ERP and GARIOA financed a third of all imports. Imports financed through the ERP, on the other hand, included a significant share of capital goods. While in 1950, machinery and vehicles represented a mere 10 per cent of total French imports, they represented 40 per cent of ERP shipments. Equivalent figures for Italy were respectively 3 per cent and 30 per cent, for Germany 2 per cent and 4 per cent. Milward (1984: 103–4).
6. Initially, Germany had represented a partial exception. Counterpart funds did not belong to the Bizone and were understood to be savings accounts for the later repayment of Marshall assistance. Fairly rapidly, however, after the creation of the Federal Republic, the special and unfavorable treatment of that country was no longer justified and the idea of a German repayment of Marshall aid was given up.
7. The preference of the ECA administration for investments in capital goods was unmistakable. This did not prevent members of this administration, however, from conditioning in some circumstances the release of counterpart funds on a limited number of austerity measures.
8. In reality, a debate opposed within the ECA administration the 'producers'—those for whom increased production was the priority—and the 'traders' who acknowledged the importance of increased production but nevertheless emphasized that the key to higher levels of production was an expansion of trade, through integration of European economies. This debate did not lead to a confrontation. There was general agreement, overall, on what Europe needed and the difference lay merely in the ordering of priorities. Price (1955) and Hogan (1984).
9. Quoted in Van der Pijl (1984: 149).
10. 'Letter, July 13, 1948.' Quoted in Frank (1986: 277).
11. Margairaz (1993: 155). The proportion of counterpart funds financing the French plan corresponded to what Monnet expected it to be in 1948. He had, at the time, budgeted investments of FF 1,500 billion, out of which FF 800 billion were to be financed through counterpart funds (Bossuat, 1993: 177).

12. Bossuat (1993), Margairaz (1993), Spagnolo (1993), and Esposito (1994). Esposito has described in great detail this monthly arm-wrestling and has argued that in a number of cases, releases were still accepted by the ECA despite insufficient progress on macroeconomic issues, mostly for political reasons, to prevent the fall of weak and nevertheless relatively well-meaning French governments.

13. As a comparison, 82 per cent of individuals polled in the Netherlands and 67 per cent of those in Norway believed the Marshall plan had made a difference. See AN-F60ter/381, particularly the telegrams from Henri Bonnet, French Ambassador to the USA, on October 16 and December 13, 1949. Information and propaganda had clearly been stipulated as a condition of Marshall assistance in all bilateral agreements signed in 1948 between the ECA and beneficiary countries.

14. AN-F60ter/393 and AN-F60ter/394 give a general overview of propaganda undertakings and projects in 1949 and 1950, going from a list of official unveiling ceremonies to detailed transcripts of radio programmes. In one American project for a radio program, the famous French singer, Edith Piaf, was to dedicate songs to the workers of a number of French factories having benefited from ERP financing, after praising the Marshall plan and its significant achievements. The French managed to resist the wildest of these American projects.

15. While the Americans, starting in 1948, wanted to bring about economic recovery in West Germany, they could naturally not treat those territories exactly on a par with their Allies and fellow occupying powers, the UK and France. West Germany only got 10 per cent of total Marshall assistance over the period 1948–52, while France received 21 per cent and the UK 25 per cent. On the other hand, West Germany benefited from other American programs such as GARIOA.

16. Abelshauser (1993: 430). This represented only 27 per cent of the amount initially planned for 1948 (US$367 million) and 7 per cent of the total ERP amount that would effectively be received by West Germany.

17. Until 1952, capital goods were a very small share of total ERP shipments to West Germany, 4 per cent in 1950 (Milward, 1984: 102–4).

18. 'HICOG, Memorandum: Counterpart Committee Meeting on February 6, 1950', OMGUS Rds, Bd26, #FIN/13/3-5.

19. OMGUS Rds, Bd26, #FIN/13/3-5, Milward (1984: 110) and Abelshauser (1993). Iron and steel industries were not on the list of German basic sectors for clear political reasons. Housing, as we have seen, was becoming a central concern of the ECA administration by 1949. It appeared on the German list even before it was imposed in France.

20. 'ECA, Office of the Special Mission to Germany. Letter to the German Ministry for the Marshall Plan, Karl Albrecht, March 10, 1950', OMGUS Rds, Bd26, #FIN/13/5.

21. Zamagni (1986) and Esposito (1994). Esposito has argued that there was a debate in 1948, within the ECA administration, on the Italian case. Zellerbach and the Rome Mission were adamant that an investment plan should be elaborated and that counterpart funds should be used to rebuild and transform the Italian economy. ECA Washington and the Office of the Special Representative (OSR) in Paris, on the other hand, believed that stabilization was a necessary precondition in Italy to a successful national investment effort. The latter had therefore been ready, in 1948, to grant the Italian government more time for the implementation of the stabilization program. By 1949, however, the ECA came to speak with a single voice. In January, Paul Hoffman wrote to James Zellerbach agreeing that the Italians 'were not taking

full advantage of the opportunity afforded by our assistance' and indicating that he was concerned 'by the possible future consequences of this slow start.' Quoted in Esposito (1994: 139).

22. Hirschman in 1948, quoted in Esposito (1994: 141).
23. A key obstacle to the efficient management of the Marshall plan on the Italian side was the lack of an institution or of a group of individuals with clear and legitimate responsibility on ERP matters. There was in fact competition within the Italian government for the handling of ERP issues, between ministries and the CIR-ERP (Comitato Interministeriale per la Ricostruzione). This latter institution was the counterpart to the French SGCI. For more on the Italian 'bureaucratic nightmare', see Esposito (1994: ch. 6).
24. 'Leon Dayton, Speech before the American Chamber of Commerce for Italy in Genoa, October 1950.' Quoted in Esposito (1994: 190).
25. See AN-81AJ/176 and in particular various reports on James Silbermann's visit to France. Silbermann was the chief of the productivity division in the American Bureau of Labor and in his discussions with the French working group in charge of productivity, he defended the idea that productivity was a 'science'.
26. The Society for the Advancement of Management (SAM) was founded in 1936 through the merging of the Taylor Society with the Society of Industrial Engineers. The Taylor Society had itself been created in 1912 to diffuse the ideas of Frederick Taylor and his associates. AN-80AJ/77 and AN-81AJ/176.
27. The January 1949 report of the French working group in charge of productivity provided striking examples of bold conclusions resting on questionable figures. Members of the French working group underscored in this report French backwardness with respect to productivity, quantitatively measuring the gap between France and the USA, industry by industry (the average being a 1–3 ratio). Three pages later, however, they were deploring the lack of 'studies comparing French and American productivity levels or comparing productivity levels across firms within the same industry'. They clearly and straightforwardly defined, at some point, productivity as 'production per man hour' a measurable reality while they argued somewhere else that 'productivity was before anything else a mentality, the mentality of progress, ever increasing progress' (Documentation Française, 1950).
28. 'Excerpts of Truman's 1949 Speech', AN-80AJ/277.
29. 'Report on the Bill of July 12, 1949, 81st Congress', AN-F60bis/517.
30. 'Report on French Productivity, elaborated by the ECA Mission, March 1950', AN-80AJ/207. This more complex definition of productivity was also used by European productivity experts: 'The notion of productivity should become a trend in public opinion, a general desire for technical progress as well as economic and social progress'. 'Note by Jean Fourastié, February 20, 1950', AN-80AJ/207.
31. While the core program of the Marshall plan—the transfer of material goods—represented US$13 billion altogether, the budget of the technical assistance program amounted to a mere $43 million for all Western European countries over the same period. Mayer (1969: 94–9).
32. AN-81AJ/207 and AN-81AJ/176. 'The objective is to give members of those teams information, to familiarize them with American methods to increase productivity, and to turn them into propagandists of the idea of productivity.' 'Note on productivity teams to the US, March 23, 1949', AN-F60bis/517.
33. The forms of technical assistance listed here are taken from the ECA expanded

program elaborated early in 1950. See 'Memorandum from Bingham, chief of the ECA Mission in France, to the SGCI, January 31, 1950', AN-81AJ/208: 'I am glad to inform you that this Mission is now authorized to invite the French government to participate in a greatly expanded program of technical assistance. . . . The expanded TA program is viewed by us as only one part of a broad and systematic plan to raise productivity and distribute its benefits to all parts of the population. Included in this broad plan of course are maintenance of financial stability, removal of trade barriers, elimination of restrictive practices, promotion of competition, and other basic measures.' The revised technical assistance program then followed.

34. 'Letter from Donn, chairman of the Service d'Analyse Industrielle [earlier Service des Monographies et d'Analyse Industrielle] in Washington to French Ministry of Commerce and Industry, November 11, 1949', AN-81AJ/208.

35. This was more than double the total amount spent on technical assistance during the entire Marshall plan period (US$43 millions).

36. 'Note sur les Missions pour 1953, 15 novembre, 1952', AN-81AJ/180.

37. Blair-Moody amendment as presented in Documentation Française (1953). See also AN-81AJ/180 and AN-81AJ/215.

38. The term 'productivity crusade' was used by Georges Villiers, chairman of the French peak business association, the CNPF. Villiers was himself calling in 1949 for an organized and systematic effort within the French business community towards increased levels of productivity, independently of public pressure and undertakings. *Bulletin du CNPF* #30 (15 March, 1949).

39. 'Décret #59-254 du 4 février 1959 portant fusion du Commissariat Général du Plan et du Commissariat Général à la Productivité', AN-81AJ/215.

40. 'OEEC Report on Technical Assistance, July 10, 1953.' Bundesarchiv Koblenz, B146/303 and B146/304.

41. Bundesarchiv Koblenz, Z14/159 and Link (1991).

42. 'Secrétariat d'Etat aux Affaires Economiques. Esquisse d'une Politique de Productivité, no date', AN-81AJ/179.

43. 'Procédure d'Envoi de Missions aux Etats-Unis, 28 Mars, 1950', AN-81AJ/178. 'Memorandum from HICOG, Office of Economic Affairs, January 1950', Bundesarchiv Koblenz, B146/416.

44. 'Letter from Bingham (Chief ECA Paris Mission) to SGCI, July 26, 1949', AN-81AJ/179. See also AN-81AJ/207 and AN-81AJ/208. The problem of labor participation led to an open conflict between ECA labor advisers in Paris and the French administration, the latter denouncing an 'inopportune interference from certain American officials in matters that must be considered as exclusively French'. 'Letter from CNP to Taff, chief technical assistance, ECA Paris Mission, July 24, 1951', AN-F60ter/522.

45. 'Letter from Donn to Fourastié, June 24, 1949' and 'Letter from Donn to SGCI, February 14, 1950', AN-81AJ/208: 'Contacts with those [American] firms accepting to receive our missions are still made by the ECA, which retains, in this respect, total exclusivity.'

46. The Crown Zellerbach Corporation of San Francisco, a 'model of peaceful labor relations' in the USA, was one of those American companies that was visited by a number of European productivity missions. Hogan (1985: 63) and Esposito (1994: 129). See Kuisel (1988), AFAP (1952), AFAP (1953), and Comité National de la Productivité (1953) for a general overview of productivity missions.

47. 'Secrétariat d'Etat aux Affaires Economiques, Esquisse d'une Politique de Productivité, no date', AN-81AJ/179. See also 'CNP Meeting, October 10, 1950', AN-81AJ/179.

48. It took time to set up such mechanisms in France. This was one more source of dissatisfaction for members of the ECA. 'Letter from Bingham, chief ECA Mission in Paris, to SGCI, December 2, 1949', AN-81AJ/207. In West Germany, the ECA Mission officially shared responsibility with the Bundesministerium für den Marshall Plan for the diffusion of conclusions, which allowed the ECA closer control. Bundesarchiv Koblenz, B146/416.

49. *Cahiers de la Productivité* and *Productivité Française* in France, *ERP-Informationen* in West Germany, or *Produttivita* in Italy.

50. In France, radio broadcasts on productivity issues started early in 1949 with the weekly 'Ronde des Nations'. 'Chronique de l'Efficience' or 'Production et Productivité Française' were other specialized broadcasts dealing with productivity issues. AN-F60ter/393, AN-81AJ/206, and AN-81AJ/181.

51. 'Memorandum from Taff, chief technical assistance, ECA Mission in Paris, to CNP, January 4, 1950', AN-81AJ/208. 'Letter from HICOG and MSA, February 2, 1952', Bundesarchiv Koblenz, B146/416. See also Gonod (1962: 241).

52. 'Memorandum from HICOG, Office of Economic Affairs, January 1950', Bundesarchiv Koblenz, B146/416.

53. 'CNP meeting, February 13, 1951' and 'Memo on technical assistance and on French politics of productivity, July 6, 1951', AN-81AJ/179.

54. In the shoe industry, for example, four companies were involved in the pilot-factory experiment. Each had a single factory with an average of 200 employees. Those four companies had previously taken part in a productivity mission. 'CNP meeting, May 12, 1952', AN-81AJ/179.

55. D'Attore (1981) and Carew (1987). It seems that Italian productivity teams were mostly interested in those personnel management techniques brought together under the label 'human relations'. The Italian institutional and cultural context proved conducive, in fact, to a 'human relations' drive.

56. In France, the most famous of those schools were HEC (Ecole des Hautes Etudes Commerciales) and ESSEC (Ecole Supérieure des Sciences Economiques et Commerciales). Both would come to play a significant role, after the Second World War, on the new French 'business education' scene (Locke, 1989).

57. OMGUS Manpower Division (1949: 2–4), 'What It Is—What It Does, descriptive booklet on the SAM'.

58. OMGUS Manpower Division (1949) and 'Projets d'action soumis à la commission "Formation du Personnel d'Encadrement", CNP, par Rolf Nordling, 30 janvier, 1952', AN-81AJ/198. See also Commissariat Général à la Productivité (1956).

59. 'We could have [for each theme] two American experts, one of whom should speak both languages and know both countries. Those American experts could train 10 national trainers. . . . The objective would then be to reach 2,000 business owners and around 5,000 managers.' In 'Projets d'action soumis à la commission "Formation du Personnel d'Encadrement", CNP, par Rolf Nordling, 30 janvier, 1952', AN-81AJ/198. A note was added: '2,000 is the number of French firms having 50 employees or more'. This project was implemented on a somewhat smaller scale towards the end of 1952 (AN-81AJ/181).

60. Commissariat Général à la Productivité (1956: 58).

61. This sentence is taken from a memorandum sent by Taff, chief technical assistance, ECA Mission in Paris to the French CNP in March 1950 and setting forth the conditions for sending a 'young experts' team to the USA (AN-81AJ/208).
62. The CNOF also helped with the preparation of a series of lectures sponsored by the ECA (AN-81AJ/181). For activities of the CEGOS, see Boltanski (1981, 1982).
63. A total of 2,500 business leaders took part in those training sessions between 1955 and 1963 (Boltanski, 1981: 31; Commissariat Général à la Productivité, 1956: 61).
64. 'A recent survey has shown that 40 per cent of all business leaders who have started up training programs in the past few years, were initially prompted to do so by the teachings of productivity missions.' Commissariat Général à la Productivité (1956: 59). See also Harbison and Burgess (1954: 22), D'Attore (1981: 95), and Carew (1987: ch. 11).
65. Documentation Française (1959: 4).
66. Documentation Française (1959: 8).
67. 'CNP meeting, April 25, 1952', AN-81AJ/179.
68. Before the Second World War, professors were teaching in those schools only on a part-time basis. They were often university professors, civil servants, or politicians and the curriculum thus did not differ radically from what could be found in French universities (Locke, 1989: 104).
69. The transformation of those schools undeniably had significant consequences. Less than 5 per cent of French business leaders had gone to HEC in 1952, more than 20 per cent by 1972 (Boltanski, 1982: 192).
70. To this day, the influence of the American model is unmistakable in French business schools. An unusually high percentage of faculty members hold American diplomas (in ESSEC for example, half of the faculty in 1994 had an American diploma). French business schools have adopted a tenure system, which also makes them quite unusual in the French education system. Cases, textbooks, and teaching materials often still come from American graduate schools of business administration.
71. Boltanski (1982: 32). For more on business education in France and also in West Germany, and on the radical transformation of the post-Second World War period, see Locke (1989: ch. 5).

PART IV

CROSS-NATIONAL TRANSFER: NATIONAL LIMITS

After the Second World War, several types of transfer mechanisms rapidly became operative in Western Europe, and particularly in France and in West Germany. A network of individuals in positions of institutional power and working in close synergy across national borders was responsible for setting up and operating those mechanisms. This took place, for France and for West Germany, in the context of national geopolitical dependence. It was made possible by the significant infrastructural power of state institutions in both countries over the national economy and industry. The large-scale structural transfer process, however, launched and monitored by the small cross-national modernizing network, was not a laboratory experiment. It took place within preexisting institutional environments and necessarily disturbed the social balance in each country. This process was bound to challenge vested interests and to run into more or less significant resistance and organized opposition in each national context. As it turned out, resistance stemmed mostly from within civil societies and more precisely from those very communities directly concerned by changes to come: the business and labor communities. Business leaders had trouble accepting the radical questioning of their traditional ways of organizing and doing business which the modernization project implied. Those parts of Western European labor communities under communist influence reacted violently against the projected transfer and mostly on political grounds. Non-communist labor groups, finally, feared that voluntary cooperation and participation on their part might in return be used to manipulate and exploit them.

While resistance and opposition stemming from those communities could undeniably create obstacles to the cross-national transfer process, the capacity of these various groups to mobilize and organize on the ground differed for each country and through time. This capacity naturally depended on whether or not these groups had an institutional reality but also on the fit that existed between the resources they were able to muster and their concrete goals and strategies. The capacity to rally and mobilize was also contingent upon the homogeneity of those groups and upon a relative identity of views and interests between their members. Those three elements defining the capacity of opposition groups to mobilize and organize resistance on the ground are brought together in summary form in Table 18.

The organization of resistance can be difficult in situations where opposition

Table 18. Capacity of opposition groups to mobilize and organize

Institutional Representation	Relevance of resources	Community of interests

groups do not have any institutional or structured representation—whether official or non-official. Indeed, institutional or structured representation helps bring about group consciousness. It also establishes patterns of resource mobilization and communication and significantly increases the likelihood of collective action. In addition, representative organizations will be effective only if there is a degree of 'fit' between their structures, strategies, and resources and the social, political, and institutional framework of the particular context in which they are trying to have an impact (Skocpol, 1992). Finally, diverging views and interests between members of a group tend to limit its capacity to mobilize and act, irrespective of other conditions.

In the period that followed immediately the end of the Second World War, business communities did not have the means to mobilize effectively against the structural transfer process, in both the western territories of Germany and also France. They were neither allowed nor able, for reasons to be specified later, to have institutional and structured representation. This directly translated into a lack of resources and significantly impaired their capacity to organize systematic resistance. After a while, however, those communities would come to regain power and influence. Once they were allowed to organize and have institutional representation, they managed to reassert control, collectively, over a number of resources. The fees of participating members in newly restored business associations were naturally essential. The control of press outlets with wide readership or privileged relationships with political actors, possibly nurtured through donations for campaign funds, were also important. Making use of these resources, French and West German business communities did initiate and monitor, as early as they could, organized and systematic resistance against those features of the transferred model they were reluctant to accept. In West Germany, business communities were particularly opposed to the break-up of cartels, to a redefinition of the competitive environment, and to the transfer to the West German industrial scene of American antitrust tradition. In France, business communities reacted first and foremost on issues of size and ownership structures. In both countries, the strategies of business communities were essentially a combination of large-scale and violent communication or propaganda campaigns with political lobbying.

With respect to labor communities, on the other hand, the situation was quite different in each of the two countries. In France, communist influence was significant in the working class through the dominant trade union, the Confédération Générale du Travail (CGT). A strong presence at the grass-roots level combined with rigid centralization to explain how the French communist trade union could very rapidly mobilize a large share of the working class. The CGT could also count on those resources controlled by the Communist Party: funds, press outlets, or other propaganda tools. Making use of these institutional strengths and resources, French communist labor did monitor violent movements bordering on the insurrection to resist, starting in 1947, the projected large-scale transfer. Together with the Communist Party, it also launched and fueled violent propaganda campaigns.

At the same time in West Germany, labor communities mostly belonged to a christian and social democratic tradition and communist influence was all but non-existent. In the postwar period, West German labor hesitated between an alliance with national business communities against the projected transfer of antitrust tradition and voluntary cooperation, under certain conditions, to the politics of productivity and to the more technical and technological side of the modernization project.

In Italy, business and labor communities shared many common features with their French and West German counterparts. However, the resistance, and opposition stemming from those communities was a lot less significant. In reality, there was not much for members of the business and labor communities to oppose in Italy. The modernization project of the American foreign aid administration had not been relayed in that country within the national administrative and political élite. Under such conditions, systematic resistance and opposition was neither justified nor necessary. Under Soviet pressure, the Italian Communist Party and communist trade union did prompt and monitor a series of violent strikes to denounce Italian participation in the Marshall scheme. Labor protest, however, rapidly died down. As it turned out, the labor and business communities would frequently be objective allies of the Italian administrative and political élite in its resistance to the American sponsored transfer project.

These three empirical cases in effect clearly reveal that the characteristic features of opposition groups can define in part the nature of the obstacles that might emerge to the cross-national transfer process in a particular national context. At the same time, however, it seems that the impact of a group might be relatively limited despite a capacity to mobilize and to organize resistance. Both in France and in West Germany, for example, powerful opposition groups were not able to call the cross-national transfer process to halt, although this clearly was their ultimate objective. They managed at best to impose a partial adaptation and redefinition of the original model. Such limited impact can be explained in the following way. First of all, the national élite supporting the modernization project was small but institutionally powerful both in France and in West Germany. Throughout the postwar years, the modernizing groups in both countries were relatively shielded from civil society pressure. Their partial autonomy was strongly reinforced, furthermore, by the control they exercised over a set of powerful institutional tools allowing them to have influence on national economies and industries. Building on these two empirical

Table 19. Conditions for an impact of opposition groups

Groups with capacity to mobilize and organize	Porosity of state institutions	Limited infrastructural power of state

cases, we can therefore identify those conditions which seem necessary for an opposition group to have any real and significant impact in a particular social context, beyond its capacity to mobilize. These conditions are presented in summary form in Table 19.

The very nature of an institutional and political system can make it more or less subject to the influence of various civil society actors. The values and objectives of politicians and state administrators might come to reflect, to a greater or lesser extent, the values and objectives of particular interest groups, depending precisely on the nature of the system. The 'porosity' of state institutions will make it possible for certain interest groups to increase their power significantly while drastically reducing the autonomy of political and administrative actors. On the contrary, insulated state institutions will create a sphere of autonomy for political or administrative actors thanks to which they might be able to get things done in spite of strong opposition from civil society. This capacity to get things done will naturally increase with the infrastructural power of state institutions (Mann, 1986). Leverage in the national economy may be gained through a control of credit sources or even through the direct involvement of the state on the economic and industrial scene as investor, buyer, supplier, or producer. On the other hand, those state institutions with limited infrastructural power may clearly find it difficult to impose their policies on the ground in the face of a strong and organized opposition movement.

8

The Resistance of European Business
Organized Opposition to Structural Transformations

German industrialists have waged a violent, elaborate and expensive cam-
paign against deconcentration and decartelization and the Schuman plan.
They have won the support in other countries of those vested interests, private
collectivities, who are so habituated to restrictive practices and monopolistic
purposes, that they have set in motion a wave of reaction against the kind of
progressive and competitive economy which the Schuman plan envisages.
                    New York Herald Tribune (March 5, 1951)

Throughout the late 1940s and the early 1950s, a network of cross-national dimension had been woven and successfully institutionalized, drawing together the USA and a number of Western European countries. Originally, this institutional framework lay within the public sphere. It was constituted, on both sides of the Atlantic, by governmental agencies and administrative units. In the USA, these agencies were in charge of foreign assistance. They were controlled by business leaders who had been pioneers with respect to colla-boration between government and business. Those American business leaders were convinced that the state should intervene in economic affairs. They also felt vested with a mission, that of transforming European economies following the model of American corporate capitalism in order to build the foundations of a wealthier and more democratic Western European space. In each Western European country participating in the Marshall scheme, the Americans had been more or less successful in identifying and co-opting local partners sympathetic to their ambitious objectives. Initially, those partners were for the most part civil servants, experts, or government officials. Local business and labor communities would become involved in the large-scale transforma-tion of Western European economies and industries but progressively and mostly under American pressure, rarely on their own initiative.

In fact, well into the 1950s, members of those communities tended to resist and oppose the large-scale transformation project. The violence of the reaction amongst Western European business leaders was particularly striking and surprising. Throughout the late 1940s and well into the 1950s, most members of the European business communities were clearly not ready to accept a radical questioning of their traditional ways of organizing and doing business. They resented the transfer on a large-scale of a foreign model they believed was not adapted to European conditions and potentially dangerous for their own interests. In West Germany, the issue of competition and the transfer of an antitrust tradition prompted particularly violent reactions. In France—and to a lesser extent in Italy since the transfer process never reached a significant level in that country—demonstrations of opposition were mostly directed towards the planned redefinition of physical and ownership structures within the national industry.

Patterns of resistance and opposition were therefore specific to each Western European country. They created obstacles and set limits to the transfer of the peculiar American system of industrial production. The success of such a transfer required that the transferred model be embedded within Western European civil societies and thus, ultimately, that a new generation of business leaders emerge. Large-scale actions of 'indoctrination' and 're-education' had rapidly been launched but their impact could only be long term. In the short term, early patterns of resistance and opposition came to shape the transfer process itself. Consequently, the model was partially adapted and reinterpreted. In each national context, some of its features combined with specific institutional and organizational legacies, leading in each case to unique systems of industrial production. A number of Western European systems of industrial production therefore became increasingly similar to the American corporate model while retaining significant specificities that clearly set them apart.

GERMAN BUSINESS AND THE ISSUE OF COMPETITION

In the post-Second World War period, members of the cross-national modernizing network identified competition as being a key feature of the American system of industrial production and an essential dimension of its success and efficiency. Furthermore, the lack of competition in Europe was largely blamed for significant differences between Western European and American systems of industrial production and in particular for gaps in levels of productivity and efficiency. As a consequence, European business was openly criticized by American and local modernizing élites for resorting to restrictive practices and for systematically favoring cartels and collective agreements. The German business community was singled out in this respect and received particularly harsh criticism.

Muted Opposition in the Early Postwar Years

In conformity with American antitrust tradition, members of the modernizing network described cartels and collective agreements as being essentially collusion schemes set up to control competition, preserve stability, and ensure high profits. Collective agreements were blamed for high price levels, restricted output, and consequently for limited levels of consumption in Europe. In the case of France, the modernizing network identified cartels and collective agreements as key mechanisms of a *malthusianism* that had been characteristic of the prewar economy and had significantly slowed down the industrialization of the country (Monnet, 1976; Bloch-Lainé and Bouvier, 1986). In the case of West Germany, cartels and collective agreements were systematically denounced as being power tools to the detriment, overall, of the consumer. Furthermore, their role during the Nazi period and their basically anti-democratic character were repeatedly emphasized (Erhard, 1958; 1963). In striking contrast, members of the modernizing network put forward an American tradition of competition and claimed that the American system of industrial production was in essence democratic. The argument was that, by outlawing cartels and collective agreements, the Sherman Antitrust Act had in effect preserved a competitive economic environment in the USA. This argument, however, had to be reconciled with the reality of American industry—the large size of firms and oligopolistic markets. This was achieved by introducing the concept of efficiency. In a given industrial sector, a few large companies benefited from significant economies of scale and scope, their size allowing them to mass produce and to reduce costs. Savings on the production line were eventually passed on to the consumer, since antitrust legislation guaranteed healthy competition between these few companies.

Systematic attacks against cartels and organized capitalism filled with dismay many members of European business communities. In the early postwar period, however, reactions could be little more than muted and resistance was by necessity unorganized. The period following the war was indeed difficult for business communities. The role and choices of a number of business leaders during the war, not only in Germany but also in France, had brought into disrepute the business communities as a whole and had inflicted on them a severe loss of legitimacy. In fact, in Germany, the business community was initially one of the main targets of the denazification campaign launched by Allied powers, whereby all former members of the Nazi party 'who had been more than nominal participants in its activities' should be 'removed from positions of responsibility'.[1] A significant number of German business leaders were in fact suspected of having played an active role in building up Nazi industrial and military might. It was soon obvious, however, for many industrial and business positions, that no replacement could be found with an equivalent level of skills. The counter-élite was much too small. As a consequence, the denazification of the German business class turned out to be relatively short-lived and it never reached the extent initially anticipated. By the end of the 1940s, Western occupying powers—and in particular the USA— came to the pragmatic conclusion that they had to work, at least for the time being, with the German business élite which was already in place.[2] The make-up of the West German business community was therefore characterized in the end by stability and continuity, even though the early period of

Allied occupation tended to breed feelings of insecurity amongst members of this community.

By the early months of 1950, the Allied prohibition on the formation of trade associations was finally allowed to lapse and a federation of business associations, the Bundesverband der Deutschen Industrie (BDI) was created in West Germany. The West German business community regained the right to be institutionally and officially represented. This was not only highly symbolic, it also made it possible for members of the West German business community to organize themselves and to act or react collectively.[3] The steel processing industry had been instrumental in setting up the BDI and heavy industries therefore had significant weight within the leading West German trade association from the very beginning.[4] Most members of the BDI had belonged, before and during the war, to the former German federation, the Reichsverband der Deutschen Industrie (RDI). A number had been involved in the corporatist organizations of the Third *Reich*.[5] Altogether, the BDI was therefore quite conservative. Fritz Berg, who became the first chairman of the BDI, had joined the Nazi party in 1937 and had been a prominent citizen of Nazi Germany. Appointed *Bürgermeister* or city mayor of a small German town in 1945, he had then been rapidly dismissed by Allied occupation authorities because of his political past. A local denazification court had in fact advised in 1946 against employing Fritz Berg in any position. Otto Friedrich, a leading rubber manufacturer, was another BDI board member with a problematic past. A powerful figure in Nazi Germany, he had been denied a position as adviser to the German economic council 'due to [American] Intelligence objection to his confessed belief in Nazi doctrine'.[6] It was clear, by the end of the 1940s, that this older generation of German business leaders had managed to survive the transition period. They held on to positions of power on the West German economic and industrial scene and their influence was indeed still significant.[7] In 1950, members of the BDI were for the most part quite anxious to preserve the old German way of doing business. They were particularly inflexible on the issue of cartels and they were ready to try and defend their own style of organized capitalism against both German and American champions of competition.

Launching Systematic and Organized Resistance

In defense of cartels and collective agreements, members of the West German business community initially used fairly traditional arguments carried through from the prewar period. Free competition, they claimed, led to dangerous price wars, the consequence of which in turn was generally a series of failures, particularly amongst smaller and medium-sized concerns. They insisted that competition was highly disruptive of the economic and also of the social environment in a given country. They presented, on the other hand, cartels and collective agreements as being essentially sound mechanisms to 'avoid ruinous competition and to prevent the waste of material and labor capacities'.[8] Cartels and collective agreements, German business leaders argued, were a superior form of economic regulation much more efficient than free markets. By smoothing out the ups and downs of business cycles and by protecting smaller concerns, they had historically preserved the economic and social balance of a country like Germany where the small firm was also a way of life.[9]

Rapidly, however, the West German business community became much more aggressive in its rhetoric. Feeling increasingly secure and powerful after the creation of the BDI, West German business leaders launched a systematic and violent propaganda campaign against competition and its champions in the West German political and administrative élite. Ludwig Erhard and the West German Ministry of Economic Affairs were clearly the main targets of these attacks. Throughout the 1950s, the West German business community repeatedly accused the Ministry of Economic Affairs of being the instrument of American occupation authorities and of implementing an American policy that had originally been designed to weaken the German economy. Ludwig Erhard was badly hurt by those accusations as he himself acknowledged and he spent a lot of time and energy trying to defend himself:

I sometimes feel a certain bitterness when attacks on the cartel law force me by their very nature to the conclusion that I am obviously suspected of being prepared to gamble lightheartedly with the German economy and with the future of smaller concerns, to say nothing of the even more sordid suspicion that I am acting on American orders.[10]

In their fight against the Ministry of Economic Affairs, West German business leaders knew how to exploit, smartly and to their own advantage, the confusion that had temporarily characterized the American debate around decartelization and deconcentration. Pointing to a relative continuity between the early deconcentration and decartelization program on the one hand and anticartel or antitrust policy on the other, they claimed that the logic was in both cases punitive and that the common objective was to weaken if not to destroy West German industry (Braunthal, 1965: 239). Acting as an official representative of the West German business community, the BDI was thus, in the early 1950s, violently criticizing and rejecting a transformation which it claimed was being imposed upon the community by a foreign power with the complicity of the German Ministry of Economic Affairs. Members of the BDI, indeed, found it 'hard to understand why the Federal Minister of Economic Affairs wishe[d] to lead and force industry into economic freedom against its own will'.[11]

The technical assistance program and the early West German productivity teams supplied members of the BDI, in a surprising and unexpected manner, with other powerful arguments that were used in defense of cartels and organized capitalism. Productivity missions made it possible for a number of West German business leaders to confront directly the dominant image of an efficient and competitive American economy with American business and industrial reality. They came back to the Federal Republic of Germany comforted in their belief that cartels and collective agreements had a significant role to play for the development of a healthy economy and industry in their country. American industry was far from competitive, they argued, and this in spite of antitrust legislation and of a general prohibition of cartels and collective agreements. The large size of American business units and the patterns of price leadership that emerged naturally as a direct consequence of the oligopolistic structure of American industries more than made up, according to West German business leaders, for the cartelization of West German industry:

> By any means, 'complete' competition and 'perfect' markets do not exist in the United States in the meaning of the classical market theory. On the one hand, the individual trust organizations have restricted to a considerable extent complete competition by their mere size. On the other hand, as is clearly shown by the example of price leadership, there exist other methods of restraint of competition beyond capital concentration.[12]

At about the same time, a similar argument was being put forward by members of the French business community. Pierre Ricard, vice-president of the French peak business association, the Conseil National du Patronat Français or CNPF, was a champion of cartels and of a systematic organization of industry. Invited, in January 1952, to an international congress sponsored by the American National Association of Manufacturers (NAM) in New York, he reacted violently to American criticisms of European industry on the issue of cartels. He emphasized what appeared to him were blatant contradictions between American business ideology on the one hand and American industrial reality on the other, arguing that US Steel, for example, produced much more than a hundred European steel firms put together ever would.[13]

European business leaders therefore questioned the very validity of the claim, then dominant within the modernization network, that American capitalism was competitive. They proposed at the same time a reinterpretation of the cartel tradition characteristic of their national industries. Cartels and collective agreements, they argued, were in fact functional equivalents in Europe to the large American corporate entities. Western European business leaders claimed that such looser forms of collaboration could be used very efficiently to foster rationalization, standardization, or specialization in European industries. They could help to create the conditions for the adoption of mass-production techniques and technologies and thus for an increase in productivity levels. European business leaders argued further that cartels and collective agreements were better suited than the large corporate entity to Western European conditions. They did not require the large-scale disruption of economic and social arrangements which was bound to take place if the American model of corporate capitalism was indeed adopted and transferred. This argument was then quite widespread but it was particularly well articulated in the following comment of a German manufacturer in the weekly *Der Volkswirt*:

Nobody doubts that the enormous progress of the American economy would not have been reached without the big, efficient, mass-producing concerns, which were created by merging formerly competing and independently managed firms. I think, however, that it is more adequate to the structure and character of the European economy to carry through the technical cooperation on the basis of an agreement between independent enterprises.[14]

European business leaders were very much aware that the prohibition of cartels and collective agreements in the USA—or competition the American way— had led to numerous mergers of significant scope in that country and thus to a series of failures at the turn of the twentieth century. They understood that, beyond potential productivity gains in the short term, a transfer of the American definition of competition would also have a significant impact on the basic features of national systems of industrial production in Europe and ultimately on the very nature of European societies. Such a transfer, as a consequence, was not appealing to them.

Towards Violent Confrontation, in West Germany and in Europe

In time, the issue of competition became much more than a matter for debate in West Germany. It turned out to be the source of a violent confrontation between the small group of technocrats and civil servants around Ludwig Erhard on the one hand, and on the other a large share of the West German business community, increasingly able to assert itself and to organize its resistance. The central stake of this confrontation was the elaboration of German anticartel legislation. Throughout the 1950s, the drafting and enactment of such legislation were key objectives of the West German Federal Ministry of Economic Affairs. The personal commitment of Ludwig Erhard to the fight against cartels combined with the American demand for a German anticartel act to explain that the West German Ministry kept to those objectives against overwhelming odds. The enactment of anticartel legislation, on the other hand, would undeniably mark for West Germany a significant departure from deeply rooted industrial traditions. The fight against such legislation was therefore highly symbolic for the national business community. With such determination on both sides, the struggle was bound to be long and rough. Indeed it lasted for close to eight years.[15]

Before the West German legislative elections of 1953, the strategies of the BDI were essentially those of a pressure group more or less excluded from the policy making process. The federation of German business launched first of all a systematic and large-scale information and propaganda campaign, using all the arguments presented above. The main publication controlled by the West German business community was the economic weekly, *Der Volkswirt*. It became a key instrument of the fight against anticartel legislation and an efficient propaganda tool. The BDI also used more direct means of pressure, through its political contacts within the Christian Democratic party (CDU). Bypassing the Minister of Economic Affairs, Ludwig Erhard, members of the BDI even tried to appeal directly to Konrad Adenauer, German Chancellor and leader of the CDU. Complaining about Ludwig Erhard's rigid attitude with respect to anticartel legislation, they threatened to reduce their campaign contributions to the CDU for the 1953 elections if the bill was not modified (Braunthal, 1965). In conformity with American antitrust tradition, the first version of the bill drafted by the West German government had indeed been based on the prohibition principle. This first version was put before the German parliament in 1952. Essentially due to pressure and delaying tactics by members of the BDI, a discussion of the bill was still pending by the time of the legislative elections of 1953.

During this early period, the power of Ludwig Erhard and his ability to withstand pressure and to stand up to bitter attacks from the German business community could largely be traced to the strong support of the American administration. The West German Ministry of Economic Affairs also tried to implement a Trojan horse strategy. Identifying a minority group within the business community with more to lose than to gain from a cartelized environment, Ludwig Erhard attempted to work through them. The Arbeitsgemeinschaft selbstständiger Unternehmer (AsU), an association of small independent businessmen, became his main institutional relay within the business community. Erhard often used the support of this group to bypass and counter the systematic opposition of the BDI and of German heavy industries (Braunthal, 1965; Berghahn, 1986). The open conflict, in this first period, between the Federal Ministry of Economic Affairs and a large share of the West German business community still virtually brought the legislative process to a halt. In the meantime, the American administration in Germany was still pressing for an anticartel act to be enacted. The strategies of actors on both sides obviously had to change.

In October 1953, following elections, Ludwig Erhard created an *ad hoc* commission to work on anticartel legislation. This commission brought together officials from the Ministry of Economic Affairs as well as a few members of the BDI acting as representatives of the West German business community. Ludwig Erhard had radically redefined his strategy, deciding to involve business leaders earlier on in the process. He thus hoped to prevent the systematic use of obstructive tactics by members of the Bundestag at the very end of the process. Against the relative assurance that an anticartel legislation would finally be enacted, Ludwig Erhard seemed ready to accept that business leaders propose, under his close supervision, a number of modifications to the bill. The bipartite commission managed to agree on a revised version by 1955. Ludwig Erhard had held tight to the prohibition principle, which the American administration also considered essential. The revised version of the bill thus outlawed, *de facto*, cartels and collective agreements. The West German Ministry of Economic Affairs had accepted, on the other hand, a number of exceptions to the prohibition clause which had been proposed by business representatives. The process, however, was not yet over and the bill was put before the Bundestag in 1955. Hostilities were immediately reopened and the confrontation lasted until 1957, when the anticartel law was finally passed.

Despite its collaboration with the government through the bipartite commission, in 1955 the BDI launched a major new offensive. The objective was to try to weaken the bill further so as to make it essentially harmless by pushing for all sorts of legislative amendments. Ludwig Erhard, however, could still count on American support. He also managed to enlarge his pool of allies within the West German business community to representatives of the consumer goods industries.[16] In July 1957, after eight years of protracted and difficult negotiations, including sometimes violent confrontations, the Bundestag finally voted for a West German anticartel law. The West German legislation, in the end, was a prohibition act but it included a number of exceptions. It appears undeniable, on the whole, that the West German Ministry of Economic Affairs had won, with the support of the American administration, the anticartel fight. Despite the systematic resistance and organized opposition of a mobilized business community controlling significant resources, Ludwig Erhard and the small team around him had managed to impose, in less than ten years, a legislation that was likely to alter in a fundamental way the rules of the German economic game. Cartels and collective agreements were, *de facto*, outlawed and competition was redefined in West Germany following an American tradition. A federal cartel agency was created to implement the anticartel act. Eberhard Günther, who until that time had run the cartel section in the West German Ministry of Economic Affairs, was appointed director. His appointment was in fact a symbolic confirmation that the West German government had won the fight. Indeed, Ludwig Erhard managed to impose Günther even though members of the BDI, who saw him as an enemy of cartels and feared a strict implementation of the legislation, were violently opposed to his appointment.

During the early 1950s, while confrontation on the national scene was still in full swing, the West German business community became involved in a parallel fight on a European level. The emerging coal and steel community (ECSC) was a source of significant concern for West German heavy industries, particularly with respect to the cartel issue. Although the confrontation was taking place in a different context, the pattern was fairly similar. On one side, a few European—and even more precisely French—technocrats and civil servants were working with members of the American administration to institutionalize a competitive logic in the emerging European market for coal and steel. On the other side, national representatives of the heavy industries were apparently intent on fighting this project.

The common enemies of all Western European coal and steel communities were undeniably Jean Monnet and the small team around him. There was no institutional framework, however, that could formally bring together all Western European coal and steel industries. Their common objectives and interests, furthermore, were often offset by national rivalries. There was thus little likelihood of an organized, transnational resistance movement. And indeed opposition to the coal and steel community remained essentially national. The strategy of Jean Monnet and his team had been, from the very beginning, to exclude entirely all national representatives of European heavy industries. However, they could not prevent—except in the French case—the weaving of informal links between industry members and members of national delegations. Private interests and corporatist claims were thus bound to influence, even if only partially and indirectly, negotiation proceedings. This was clearly illustrated when, under strong pressure from heavy industries' representatives, the West German delegation denounced the anticartel provisions of the ECSC treaty. Negotiations were consequently stalled for several months and if it had not been for American intervention they may never have started again. Indeed, the American administration and John McCloy in particular, then American High Commissioner in Germany, were instrumental in dragging the German delegation back to the negotiation table and in bringing Germans finally to accept and ratify the anticartel provisions of the ECSC treaty.

On the French side, Jean Monnet had managed to exclude entirely industry members from ECSC negotiations. He also kept to a strict minimum informal relationships between the French delegation and representatives of the French coal and steel industries. Needless to say, the latter resented this exclusion and they systematically tried to bypass Jean Monnet and his small team of technocrats. They used lobbying tactics with members of the national assembly. They also complained directly to the Prime Minister, René Pleven. Jules Aubrun, president of the French steel industry business association, sent him a letter 'to bring to [his] attention the unbearable position in which the French steel industry has been placed since the beginning of the ECSC negotiations'. 'Our future', he added, 'is being decided without any input on our part.' He explained further that the steel industry could not 'agree with the ECSC scheme, since as it [stood then] it [went] against the vital interests' of the community.[17] In the end, however, Jean Monnet and his team were entirely in control, on the French side, of ECSC matters. Such letters of complaint therefore ultimately found their way back to Jean Monnet's desk.[18] His replies generally left little space for compromise. As head of the French delegation to ECSC negotiations, throughout the talks he held tight to his vision of the community as a competitive space where cartels and collective agreements were banned and he loudly denounced the conservative position of members of the French coal and steel industries:

Public opinion will not understand that, after all that has been done [by the French planning board] to endow the French steel industry with the most modern machines and techniques, it still shies away from entering the vast and open market which it is being offered . . . . You were demanding that the French steel industry keep the advantage it enjoyed thanks to the low price it paid certain supplies such as ore while, on the other hand, the price of more expensive supplies like coal should go down. Notwithstanding all this, you also asked to keep the benefit of all kinds of protection against competition. You will understand, I am sure, that the head of the French delegation could not be the spokesman for such an indefensible position.[19]

FRENCH BUSINESS AND THE ISSUES OF SIZE AND OWNERSHIP STRUCTURE

Throughout the 1950s, in fact, a large share of the French business community feared competition and championed, just like its West German counterpart, an organized type of capitalism where cartels and collective agreements secured a stable environment for individual firms. On the French national scene, however, the issue of competition was not the main source of conflict between business leaders and the French team of modernizers. Problems tended to emerge more often about the size of firms or with respect to ownership structures. A small group of French technocrats had set out to bring about, after the Second World War, a modernization of the national economy and industry following its own reading of the American model. The French team had identified, in particular, the large size of production units as being a key feature of the American system of industrial production and as accounting for American economic success, at least to some extent. In the project of French technocrats, a modernization of the national economy and industry would thus require large-scale restructuring, the disappearance on the one hand of many small firms and a multiplication, on the other, of larger production units. At the same time, they proposed that personal and family management should increasingly give way to administration by professional managers. Pointing once again to the American model, they argued that a private technocracy would better serve the interests of French firms and of the national economy as a whole than traditional business owners whose main objectives were to secure their own position and to preserve the social status of their families.

The first and second French plans were in part designed to implement such a modernization project. They rested upon a systematic comparison of American and French economies and industries, where French weaknesses were generally attributed to 'the very structure of French industry, the large number and small size of individual firms as well as their low degree of specialization'.[20] In the second French plan, restructuring through mergers in order to promote large-scale, specialized production was clearly singled out as a priority, and was one of the five key basic actions that were to apply across all sectors of the French economy.[21] To increase the chances of success for their ambitious project, French modernizing technocrats rapidly adopted a strategy of progressive co-optation and contagion. They systematically involved dynamic members of the French business community in the restructuring process, hoping that the latter would then slowly influence the rest of the French business community.

A Divided Federation: The Conseil National du Patronat Français

In the late 1940s and early 1950s the restructuring of the French economy and the modernization of the French business community were still in their early stages. Most French firms were still owned and run by a generation of business leaders who had already been in place during the war or before. Many of those traditional business leaders were without doubt strongly opposed to a large-scale restructuring and to a systematic transformation of the French industry and economy. They understood that such a transformation was bound to bring about failures and bankruptcies, particularly for those economic and industrial entities that did not conform to the modernization paradigm. Within this paradigm, small-scale or family ownership and management were 'archaic' by definition and thus likely to be the first targets.[22]

In postwar France, the most prominent federation of business associations was the Conseil National du Patronat Français or CNPF. Created in December 1945, it was heir in many ways to the prewar federation, the Confédération Générale de la Production Française or CGPF. Just like its predecessor, the CNPF was largely controlled by 'big business' or in other words by the largest of French companies. Ironmasters, in particular, and private owners of a few large concerns were active members. So were a small number of professional managers, who were running firms in the newly nationalized sector and were keen to implement modernization objectives. Due to such diverse membership, it was difficult to mobilize the CNPF as a whole against the modernization project. In fact, a few prominent members of the federation were convinced that French industry needed to be restructured and that many French firms were far too small. This minority could in certain circumstances champion the modernization project as illustrated in this speech by Robert Norguet, a key figure of the CNPF, to students of a top engineering school:

The parceling out of industry in France is considerable . . . . This is due both to the small size of firms and to their lack of specialization . . . . I understand, naturally, that the more firms there are, the more owners—that is independent men (or at least who believe to be so) . . . . Let's be careful, though. In a modern world where concentration and specialization are the rule, we should not foolishly go against the stream. We would not be winners in this game . . . The solution is painful but unavoidable: those firms too small to be modernized will have to disappear.[23]

Although a few of the most prominent figures in the CNPF would certainly have agreed, this nevertheless remained a minority position in the federation well into the 1950s. Pierre Ricard, vice-president of the CNPF, warned the French planning board in the late 1940s that his federation was not all of the same mind. Many members, he indicated, were highly suspicious of the modernization project and reluctant to collaborate with the planning board.[24]

Small-Scale Capitalism in France and its Fight for Survival

Divided as it was on the issue of restructuring, the CNPF turned out to be quite a poor instrument of collective action. Another French trade federation, the Confédération Générale des Petites et Moyennes Entreprises or CGPME, in fact proved better able to mobilize its members who, on the issue of modernization, had a clear and common position. If modernization implied the failure and disappearance of smaller or 'marginal' firms, then members of the CGPME were ready to fight it through all possible means. They denounced, furthermore, those members of the CNPF partial to the modernization project as traitors to the French business community. The CGPME had been created in 1944. It brought together small and medium-sized firms whose owners also generally ran the business. By the late 1940s, the federation claimed to represent 50 per cent of French industry as well as 95 per cent of the distribution sector and to employ 48 per cent of French labor (Lavau, 1955). Léon Gingembre, president and spokesman, defined the small or medium-sized French firm or PME as 'any enterprise, whatever its legal identity, that is being financed by the personal capital of the owner and his family, where risks are assumed entirely by the owner, and in which the employer has direct contact with his personnel'.[25] The modernization project of the French technocratic élite appeared to threaten directly not only the economic interests and the social status of most members of the CGPME but also their very existence as a group constitutive of the French social order. The CGPME could thus easily mobilize its members against the modernization project and the fairly homogeneous membership of this federation made it a particularly effective and active pressure group. It was able to sustain throughout the 1950s a systematic and organized war against the modernization project. It truly entered a crusade, dedicating a significant share of its resources to defend small-scale, family capitalism against repeated attacks coming from the modernizing network.

In the immediate postwar period, the CGPME remained discrete. Its members were clearly waiting to see how things evolved, hoping in particular that the social and political environment would become less hostile. In a situation of relative powerlessness they could only observe changes, paying particular attention to new institutional actors such as the planning board, the objectives of which they initially had trouble reading. In November 1946, when the first plan was about to be launched, Léon Gingembre was thus merely warning the planning board against 'a tendency to simplify and a will to centralize, that have always led the [French] administration to prefer large-size production units over smaller or medium-sized ones'.[26] At that time, members of the CGPME still understood the postwar planning effort to be more or less a continuation of those corporatist policies that had characterized the Vichy regime. Their only fear, as a consequence, was that the largest of French firms would come to dominate the process, enjoying full control within each industrial branch as this had already been the case during the war.[27]

Rapidly, however, members of the CGPME came to understand that the modernization project, as defined by the planning board, was in reality much more threatening than that to their own interests. They came to realize that the objective of modernizing technocrats was a systematic restructuring of French industry on a scale unheard of before. The postwar modernization project clearly implied and required the disappearance of many small family firms, generally labeled 'marginal' or 'archaic' by French technocrats. The modernization project also seemed to question the traditional definition of ownership dominant until then in France and associated with the right and power to manage or decide. It was becoming increasingly clear that the technocratic group was planning to bring about in France a type of capitalism that differed radically from traditional family capitalism. The small team of French modernizers seemed to favor those companies (whether nationalized entities or joint stock companies—*sociétés anonymes*) where management was a profession and not a birthright.[28] Once this had become clear, the CGPME naturally radicalized its position and adopted much more aggressive strategies. Not surprisingly, the anger of its members and their organized resistance crystallized around Jean Monnet and the planning board.

In the early 1950s, the CGPME launched a violent propaganda campaign— today we would call it a communication campaign—attacking and trying to discredit Jean Monnet and the planning board. The CGPME more or less directly controlled a number of professional and local newspapers or magazines—*La Volonté du Commerce et de l'Industrie, Le Journal des Finances, Informations Confédérales, AGEFI*, or *Cahiers Financiers* for example. These publications would prove to be powerful tools for the diffusion of systematic attacks against the planning board and its modernization project. Denouncing one day 'the socialist and bureaucratic Monnet plan', the CGPME could shortly thereafter regret the lack of social orientation of a plan that did not seem to take into account the dramatic consequences for workers of multiple failures and bankruptcies amongst small and medium-sized firms.[29] The fiercest attacks, however, were directed at Jean Monnet and at the planning board, questioning in particular their legitimacy. A widespread opinion amongst members of the CGPME was that Jean Monnet had created the planning board and elaborated the first plan on the mere 'strength of his own personal convictions'. He had been able to impose those convictions, bypassing French 'institutions and regular powers'. Members of the CGPME clearly asked the question: 'Who supports Jean Monnet?'[30] They then proposed their own answer: since Jean Monnet and the planning board had, according to them, no national legitimacy or power base, support certainly came from outside and more exactly from a foreign power. This opinion was quite widespread and diffused repeatedly through the publications controlled by the CGPME. Jean Monnet, the rumor went, was a foreign agent. Many West German business leaders believed that Ludwig Erhard's stubborn fight against cartels was part of an organized Allied program to weaken Germany and the West German economy. To many members of the CGPME, the large-scale restructuring imposed by Jean Monnet and the destruction of a number of small and medium-sized firms was in fact a systematic plan 'to lead the French economy to its doom'.[31] The fascination for the American model that characterized members of the planning board as well as their close relationships with the American administration had convinced many members of the CGPME that Jean Monnet was an American agent. A few particularly conservative members, on the other hand, charged him with communist sympathies, pointing to Jean Monnet's insistence on involving trade union representatives at each step of the modernization project and to the initial enthusiastic reaction of the communist trade unions to the French plan.[32]

In addition to their propaganda campaign, members of the CGPME also developed political strategies, building on the traditional relationships linking French business to conservative elements of the political class. Taking advantage of a fragmented national assembly and of fragile coalition governments, the CGPME turned out to be a powerful, homogeneous, and well organized pressure group. The clear objective of the CGPME was to bring to power a man who would defend the cause of family capitalism. It finally succeeded in 1952, when Antoine Pinay became Prime Minister—Président du Conseil— and formed a new government.[33] Antoine Pinay was himself a small businessman, owning and running a family firm. He came to power as the symbol of an 'eternal' France, the France of farmers, family firms, and craftsmen, already extolled during the war by Marshal Pétain who had officially vowed to be its champion.[34] In the short term, members of the CGPME obtained a number of direct payoffs for helping Antoine Pinay come to power and in particular a general amnesty for tax evasion.[35]

The ultimate objective, however, was longer term. Members of the CGPME undeniably hoped that, as Prime Minister, Antoine Pinay would be able to offset somewhat the power and influence of French modernizing technocrats. The general expectation was that the new Prime Minister would bring to a halt the threatening modernization project or at least slow it down considerably. Therefore, when the outline of the second French plan started to circulate in the fall of 1952, members of the CGPME were flabbergasted. The general orientation in favor of large-scale units and towards systematic restructuring was indeed clearly reasserted. The CGPME reacted immediately. In a letter to Antoine Pinay, its members demanded the outright dismantling of the planning board on several grounds. First they argued that 'the administrative and political roles of the planning board had never been properly defined'. They added that the existence of the planning board 'outside the established ministries had led to a duplication of work'. They emphasized, finally, that 'the planning board had always maneuvered to escape control of the national assembly and to present the latter with a *fait accompli*.[36] In the meantime, the CGPME was also lobbying the national assembly, counting on sympathetic reactions from the centre and conservative parties and on a general feeling of exasperation amongst members of the national assembly at being systematically bypassed by members of the planning board.

The National Assembly and its Role in the Confrontation

Throughout the transformation process, French modernizers were wary of the national assembly which they found to be a particularly conservative and unreliable institution. The great dependence of deputies on their constituencies was highly conducive, throughout the Fourth Republic, to patronage. Well organized lobbies could undeniably have a great deal of influence on the decisions of the French national assembly. The strategy of members of the planning board had therefore been to avoid dealing with that particular institution and to resort, as often as was possible, to statutory orders. As it turned out, in a number of circumstances when members of the planning board had not been able to bypass the national assembly, the results had been such as to justify their deep mistrust of that institution. In June 1949, for example, a bill prepared by the planning board and the working group in charge of productivity was put before the assembly. It proposed rewarding those companies working towards increased levels of productivity by granting them significant tax incentives. The bill was rejected by a majority of deputies, on the grounds that such a measure 'would in fact grant further advantages to large companies that [we]re already being favored to the detriment of smaller ones and agricultural concerns'.[37] It appeared that in this particular case, the CNPF had actually joined forces with the CGPME against the bill, thus increasing the pressure on members of the national assembly. Even the productivity commission of the CNPF, chaired by Robert Norguet, had clearly expressed its opposition 'to the principle of discriminating tax cuts dependent on productivity gains, which could only alter the normal conditions of competition'.[38] The immediate reaction of members of the planning board was to prepare a number of statutory orders that took up the contents of the bill. One of those statutory orders expanded the scope of a June 1948 law that had rewarded mergers with tax incentives. Another granted significant tax cuts to corporations (joint stock companies or *sociétés anonymes* but also private limited liability companies or SARL) that were reinvesting benefits into machinery and tools.[39]

Overall, the strategy of the planning board had thus been to avoid as much as possible the involvement of political and legislative actors. In postwar France, the involvement of these actors could considerably slow down the modernization project if not altogether bring it to a standstill. The first plan was not even put before the national assembly. It was enacted through a statutory order in the exact version emerging from the work of the planning board. Policy making through statutory orders, however, was possible only as long as the government remained sympathetic enough or relatively neutral towards the modernization project and the planning board. The leverage and power of the planning board on the national scene were also explained in part by the significant support and assistance it received from the USA.

In 1952, however, by the end of the first plan, both the national and the international contexts were clearly becoming less favorable for the planning board. Marshall assistance was coming to an end, thus depriving the planning team of the key financial instrument of its autonomy and of a powerful source of leverage on the national scene. The second plan had to be financed on French funds only and decision making with respect to the national budget was the sole prerogative of legislative and political actors. On the other hand, the balance of power on the national scene was clearly in the process of changing. The French business community had by then regained its capacity to organize and to mobilize. Business leaders were making their comeback on the social and political scene. A large proportion of these businessmen being violently opposed to the modernization project, the planning board increasingly had to face powerful and organized resistance.

The coming to power of Antoine Pinay in March 1952 was a symbolic sign of this radical change in the national balance of power. At the end of 1951, statutory orders were guaranteeing a long-term institutionalization of the planning board and launching the process for the elaboration of a second plan. From 1952, however, the political situation in France was considerably slowing down work on the second plan. Things were particularly difficult between March and December, at which point the Pinay government finally fell. The second plan was thus elaborated in 1953 and started, belatedly, in 1954.[40] The planning board could not avoid putting the second plan before the national assembly. In order to limit the impact of the assembly, however, the second plan was only sent before it at the end of 1954, when it was already being implemented. The opposition of members of the national assembly was in this way neutralized in advance. This proved to be a smart strategy on the part of the planning board. As it turned out, the national assembly and in particular its more conservative members strongly denounced the second plan and its modernization project. Their reaction in fact reflected the discontent of the business community which had been conveyed through lobbying channels. Members of the national assembly particularly opposed the restructuring of French industry and the marginalization of family capitalism:

We want to react against a perspective which seems to be that of the second plan and which is a narrow and simplifying one, that of systematically privileging large companies. We have heard civil servants in charge [of the plan] declare, sometimes publicly, that they welcomed the failure and disappearance of those firms 'the size of which is incompatible with modern production techniques' . . . . Such a state of mind is unacceptable. I ask you, who will be the unfailing judge, deciding whether the size of this or that firm is compatible or incompatible with modern production techniques?[41]

In the meantime, mergers, reorganizations, and restructuring were already in progress and they only multiplied throughout the course of the second plan.[42] The national assembly finally passed the second plan in March 1956. No amendments had been made to the project as it had originally been proposed by the planning board. Adjustments would have been useless by then, in fact, since the second plan was scheduled to end in 1957.[43]

Throughout the 1950s, business communities were thus characterized in both West Germany and France by their strong mobilization against the large-scale structural transfer process championed by the cross-national, modernizing network. Following a short period of transition at the end of the war, during which they had been somewhat marginalized, those groups then rapidly reorganized, developing various strategies of resistance. Business leaders in both countries were violently opposed to the systematic questioning of their traditional ways of organizing and doing business. They strongly resisted the attempt to bring about a radical redefinition of national systems of industrial production, following a model they believed was 'foreign' and 'unsuited' to Western European conditions. In West Germany, business leaders privileged the fight against the transfer of an American antitrust tradition. In France, opposition came mostly from traditional business leaders wanting to preserve family capitalism. Business communities in both countries launched systematic information and propaganda campaigns against the modernization project and against members of the cross-national network. In both countries, but also on a European level, they tried to weaken or bypass the technocratic élite in charge of the modernization project by appealing to politicians and resorting to lobbying tactics. In the end, however, West German and French business communities could not prevent the large-scale structural transfer from taking place. The synergy between American and European members of the cross-national modernizing network certainly explains in part the fact that the modernization project was able to withstand repeated and violent attacks from the business communities.

However, patterns of resistance in both countries did have some impact on the transfer process itself. The very strength of opposition sometimes made compromise necessary and the transferred model was also partially adapted, reinterpreted, or 'translated'. A successful implementation of normative transfer mechanisms and the passing of the old generation of business leaders would have an impact in the longer term. Business communities in those two countries slowly came to reconcile themselves with the structural transformations undergone by their national industry. As early as the 1960s, a new generation of business leaders was claiming responsibility for and taking pride in some of those structural changes, stimulating and institutionalizing further a process originally fought against, sometimes quite violently, by their predecessors. In the end, still, patterns of resistance and compromise were institutionalized, together with features of the transferred model. The systems of industrial production dominating in each of those two countries by the late 1960s therefore reflected not only a common model but also different patterns of resistance that had brought about a number of adaptations in each case.

Notes

1. 'Allied Control Council, Directive #24, January 12, 1946.' Quoted in Edinger (1960: 59).
2. According to Edinger (1960: 71 ff.), close to 97 per cent of German business leaders in the early 1950s had held a similar position in Nazi Germany. 'There simply was no counter-élite source of qualified people to assume technical or economic tasks . . . . Intensive or extensive socio-economic dislocation or intensive or extensive military occupation (or both) was a price which the Western powers were unwilling or unable to pay to denazify all the German élites.'
3. 'Bundesverband der Deutschen Industrie, October 23, 1950', OMGUS Rds, Bd42, #17/249-1/8. In France, the peak business association, the Conseil National du Patronat Français or CNPF, was created in June 1946. The French situation was in fact quite similar to the West German one. The business community had lost legitimacy and influence due to its role and political choices made during the war. Until the end of the 1940s, its capacity to organize and to have an impact on the French scene would be singularly limited (Ehrmann, 1957).
4. Although German heavy industries (including the steel producing and coal sectors but also the chemicals industry) were not allowed initially to join the BDI, their interests were, from the very beginning, well represented in that organization. See 'BDI, October 23, 1950', OMGUS Rds, Bd42, #17/249-1/8.
5. See 'BDI, October 23, 1950', p. 15, for a list of those members of the BDI who had held prominent positions in Nazi Germany. OMGUS Rds, Bd42, #17/249-1/8.
6. 'BDI, Confidential Information on Members, August 3, 1950', OMGUS Rds, Bd42, #17/249-1/8.
7. The situation was relatively similar in France. Members of the French business community managed to escape for the most part the purge of the immediate postwar period which hit much more severely politicians, intellectuals, and journalists (Paxton, 1973; Fourquet, 1980; Rochebrune and Hazéra, 1995).
8. 'Antitrust and the European Cartel Problem, Reply of a German Manufacturer to a New York Lawyer.' Printed in *Der Volkswirt* #20 (May 19, 1950). OMGUS Rds, Bd42, #17/247-1/6.
9. Those arguments were all used by the BDI in its defense of organized capitalism. Fritz Berg exchanged numerous letters with Ludwig Erhard on the matter in the early 1950s (Braunthal, 1965: 238).
10. 'Ludwig Erhard, Ten Theses in Defence of the Anticartel Legislation, Open Letter to Fritz Berg, President of the BDI, July 10, 1952.' Reprinted in Erhard (1963: ch. 16). See also Erhard (1958: 120).
11. Telegram of protest sent by a large German industrial combine to Ludwig Erhard, reprinted in Erhard (1963: ch. 16). The reaction of Ludwig Erhard to the content of

this telegram was one of great exasperation and he exclaimed: 'The unanimity in industry with regard to its desire for cartelization goes much too far for my liking.'

12. Article translated from *Der Volkswirt* #35 (1950), OMGUS Rds, Bd42, #17/247-1/6. According to the editors of the weekly, the article was written by a member of the German committee in charge of anticartel legislation, which would indicate the extent of support for cartels at the time in West Germany.

13. *Nouvel Observateur* (January 24, 1952) and Villiers (1978: 175). See also the comment by François-Poncet, French High Commissioner in Germany, reprinted in 'Antitrust and the European Cartel Problem, Reply of a German Manufacturer to a New York Lawyer', *Der Volkswirt* #20 (May 19, 1950): 'The Americans are determined adversaries of all economic cooperation, of trusts and cartels. But at the same time, there are American corporations, each of which is more powerful than the eventually united German and French companies of the corresponding industrial branch would ever be.'

14. 'Antitrust and the European Cartel Problem, Reply of a German Manufacturer to a New York Lawyer', *Der Volkswirt* #20 (May 19, 1950), OMGUS Rds, Bd42, #17/247-1/6.

15. For more on this fight see, Part III, Chapter 6.

16. Starting in 1954, those representatives, members of the BDI, began to voice their opposition to the official position of the federation with respect to the cartel issue (Braunthal, 1965: 241).

17. 'Letter from Jules Aubrun, president of the steel industry business association—Chambre Syndicale de la Sidérurgie—to René Pleven, Président du Conseil, November 13, 1950.' Reprinted in Monnet and Schuman (1986).

18. One should add here that René Pleven had been a collaborator of Jean Monnet during the war and that they were close personal friends.

19. 'Reply from Jean Monnet to Jules Aubrun, November 17, 1950.' Reprinted in Monnet and Schuman (1986).

20. 'Documents Relatifs à la Première Session du Conseil du Plan, 1946', AN-80AJ/1.

21. The third, fourth, and fifth plans only confirmed this clear preference of French technocrats for large size and their hope to create a small number of large national champions in each industrial sector (Morvan, 1972).

22. The terms archaic (*archaïque*), antiquated (*vétuste*), backward (*en retard*) and malthusian (*malthusien*) were all used to describe those sectors within French industry characterized by small-scale, family ownership, and family management. See in particular 'Documents on the elaboration of a second French plan', AN-80AJ/17.

23. 'Discours de Norguet à l'Ecole Polytechnique, 15 novembre 1950', AN-81AJ/206.

24. This was not, he hastily added, his own position nor that of his friends on the board of the CNPF, but the position nevertheless of many members. '2ème Session du Conseil du Plan, 27 novembre 1946', AN-80AJ/1.

25. Léon Gingembre as quoted in Ehrmann (1957: 174). Firms were labeled 'small' under 50 employees and 'medium-sized' between 50 and 300.

26. '2ème Session du Conseil du Plan, 27 novembre 1946', AN-80AJ/1.

27. During the war, small business owners had denounced the overwhelming role played by the largest French firms and by a few powerful industrial families (Renault or Wendel for example) in the institutions of corporatism. They had directly appealed to Marshal Pétain to correct the discrepancy between, on the

one hand, the reality of a domination by the 'big' and, on the other, the project of the National Revolution that was to preserve a France of small family firms, farms, and craftsmen (Barbas, 1989 and AN-F12/9966).

28. Such preference was based on an assessment of family capitalism that was clearly not to its advantage. French technocrats agreed entirely in this respect with the analysis developed by members of the American administration and prominent members of the American business class. 'French family firms represent the foundation of the wealth as well as of the social status of the families who own them . . . . Instinctively, the private owner thus chooses security over risky and potentially lucrative ventures . . . . Since he got his position through heritage rather than through his own efforts and capacities, he defends as a vested interest, for himself and his family, the income of his firm.' 'Note sur la productivité du travail en France établie par la Mission ECA, March 1950', AN-81AJ/207.

29. Article in *AGEFI* (April 7, 1954) and article in *Cahiers Financiers* (December 7, 1954).

30. Article in *Cahiers Financiers* (December 7, 1954). See also *La Volonté du Commerce et de l'Industrie* (February 1952).

31. *La Volonté du Commerce et de l'Industrie* (February 1952).

32. That a few French conservative businessmen, blinded by radical anticommunist feelings and a fear of change, would come to attribute communist sympathies to Jean Monnet and the planning team might, after all, not be so surprising. That American labor advisers in the ECA Paris Mission—Harris and later Shishkin— 'linked the policy of the French planning board to the influence of the communist trade union, the CGT' and questioned Jean Monnet's foreign allegiance is, on the other hand, quite astonishing. 'Letters from Donn to Fourastié, April 6, April 27 and November 15, 1949', AN-81AJ/208.

33. The CGPME never denied that it had played an essential role in the accession to power of Antoine Pinay (Lavau, 1955: 375).

34. Under the Vichy regime, Antoine Pinay had been a member of the Conseil National, a small group of close advisers to Marshal Pétain (Paxton, 1973: 193–5; Rioux, 1983: ch. 1; Rémond, 1982: ch. 12).

35. Tax evasion was fairly widespread at the time amongst small and medium-sized firms. Indeed, under a certain level of turnover, French firms could opt for a lump sum tax. This system called BIC (Bénéfices Industriels et Commerciaux) was particularly conducive to tax evasion and was one more incentive to keep firms small. The planning board had denounced the unfortunate consequences of this tax regime and, in the early 1950s, the planning team was working on an in-depth reform of the French tax system. 'Meeting of the Fiscality and Productivity Commission, January 25, 1949', AN-80AJ/77. See also 'Memo from Fourastié to Monnet, July 23, 1950', AN-81AJ/207.

36. 'Excerpts of a letter from the CGPME to Antoine Pinay, October 1952', AN-80AJ/ 7.

37. 'Projet de Loi Relatif à Diverses Dispositions d'Ordre Economique et Financier— Discussion à l'Assemblée Nationale, 2 juin 1949', AN-81AJ/178.

38. *Bulletin du CNPF* (July 20, 1953).

39. 'Décrets portant réformes fiscales', AN-80AJ/77. 'Lois et décrets fiscaux pour augmenter la productivité', AN-81AJ/179. See also 'Rapport présenté par la commission ''Productivité et Fiscalité'' du Comité National pour la Productivité, avril

1952', AN-81AJ/198. The enactment of a French anticartel act followed a similar pattern. Bills submitted to the national assembly until 1952, under pressure from the planning board, were systematically rejected by a vast majority of deputies. An anticartel act would finally be enacted through statutory order, with great discretion, on August 9, 1953 (Sélinsky, 1979).

40. The government led by René Mayer enacted a number of statutory orders in May and July 1953, giving a new impetus to the planning process. See AN-80AJ/17.

41. 'Discussion à l'Assemblée Nationale, 10 mai 1955', Journal Officiel (May 11, 1955). See also 'Avis de la Commission de la Production Industrielle sur le Projet de Loi du Deuxième Plan', AN-80AJ/20.

42. It is somewhat ironic that members of the CGPME used precisely those transformations brought about by the first plan to attack the second plan: 'The second plan denounces the "rigidity of industrial structures" in France. This is a ready-made idea. Rigidity of industrial structures? France is right now the country with the highest number of bankruptcies. Every week brings its share of new mergers.' *Les Informations Industrielles et Commerciales* (November 23, 1953).

43. 'Law #56–342, March 27, 1956', AN-80AJ/19.

9

European Labor and Productivity
Between All-Out War and Active Participation

We refuse to hand over the working class of our country, tied hand and foot, to international capitalism and its strategies.

CGT-FO Congress (October 1952)

The speech of the American Secretary of State George Marshall at Harvard in June 1947 had helped to crystallize, we argued, a division of the world already in the making. This division scarred the European continent for more than forty years. The demarcation line between a communist and a 'free' Europe coincided with the border setting apart European countries participating in the Marshall scheme from those that did not. This geopolitical split also had a significant impact on the internal political balance of power within a number of 'free' European countries. In France and in Italy, Communist Party members were ousted from governing coalitions in 1947 in anticipation of the launching of the American assistance scheme. Communist parties settled in the opposition denouncing and resisting, sometimes quite violently, American involvement in Western Europe and the Marshall plan. In both countries, communist parties had close links with national labor movements. A significant share of labor therefore also came to systematically oppose transformations on the industrial scene having something to do with the Marshall plan or having clear American origins. Such systematic resistance was in the end highly political and little could be done to tone it down. Members of the cross-national modernizing network, in fact, generally chose to try and bypass communist actors rather than counter them. Both in France and in Italy, members of the American administration set out to identify and help—or even to create—labor groups with whom they could work and cooperate.

In West Germany, communist influence was much less of an issue on the national scene. The geopolitical division of the world had led to the creation of two German countries out of the former German *Reich*. In the western territories of Germany, soon to become the Federal Republic of Germany, the geopolitical division reduced communist influence and contributed to uniting the labor movement. In the geopolitical confrontation, West German labor clearly took sides against the communist bloc. This did not mean, however that labor organizations accepted and supported unreservedly American involvement in European and West German economic affairs. They joined forces in fact, in a number of circumstances, with members of the West German business community to oppose transformations they denounced as decidedly too foreign to German industrial traditions.

RESHAPING THE LABOR SCENE IN WESTERN EUROPE

The confrontation on the geopolitical scene between the USA and the USSR had led, in France and in Italy, to the break-up of postwar coalitions and had significantly toughened the national political debate in those two countries. This geopolitical confrontation also had an impact on labor movements and their overall make-up. One of its indirect consequences was a redefinition in both countries of the institutional and ideological framework within which labor action was taking place. Ever since the second half of the nineteenth century, labor organizations in France and in Italy had developed close links with the communist movement. The courageous involvement of Communist Party members in the national Resistance during the Second World War had legitimated the communist movement further in both countries, strengthening its hold over labor organizations. By the end of the war, the largest French trade union, the Confédération Générale du Travail or CGT, had become a communist federation. The main Italian trade union, the Confederazione Generale Italiana del Lavoro or CGIL, was created immediately after the fascist defeat in 1943. Bringing together Christian Democratic, socialist, and communist workers, the Italian trade union was soon in fact controlled by communists.

Communist influence over labor in France and in Italy disturbed and greatly worried members of the American administration but also union officials from the American Federation of Labor (AFL), who were staunch anticommunists.[1] Right after the end of the war, in the fall of 1945, the AFL sent one representative to Europe. The mission of Irving Brown was to help organize non-communist labor in Europe and to coordinate American financial and logistic support to 'free' European labor. Starting in 1947, the newly created Central Intelligence Agency (CIA) and the American State Department joined in this undertaking. In the end, this systematic American intervention had some part in the split affecting French and Italian labor movements in 1948 (Carew, 1987; Wall, 1991). A number of non-communist groups left the French CGT in April to create a 'free' trade union, the CGT-FO or Force Ouvrière. Throughout the early 1950s, Americans helped to finance and strengthen this new organization. The ECA significantly contributed, in particular, to the institutionalization of 'free' labor in France, intervening mostly via its labor advisers.

In a relatively similar pattern, the joint action of the AFL, of the American State Department, and of labor advisers in the ECA Rome Mission was clearly instrumental in bringing about a break-up of the powerful Italian communist union, the CGIL, in June 1948. The breakaway organization, the Libera

Confederazione Generale Italiana del Lavoro or LCGIL, had close links with the Christian Democratic party. In the following years, the Americans stayed closely involved in Italian labor affairs. They gave their full support to the building up in that country of a non-communist labor movement, fostering in particular mergers between the LCGIL and remaining non-communist minority groups from the CGIL (Carew, 1987: 102 ff.). Both in France and in Italy, those new trade organizations slowly came to impose themselves on the labor scene, becoming legitimate actors and shaking off, after a while and to a certain extent, their dependence on American support. In the meantime, communist trade unions were radicalizing their discourse and toughening their actions, retaining a large following in both countries. The geopolitical confrontation of the late 1940s therefore had a direct and significant impact on the labor movement in those two countries, bringing about conflicts, division, and radicalization.

In West Germany, on the other hand, the geopolitical situation contributed in fact to uniting labor against communism. In 1945, the weakness of the communist movement in Germany was easy to understand. The German communist party had been outlawed in Nazi Germany and its former members systematically persecuted.[2] In 1946, the small communist group within the Soviet zone of occupation merged with the local branch of the much more powerful Social Democratic party. The consequence was the creation, in that zone, of a mass party that would later lead the 'proletarian' takeover. In the western parts of Germany, on the other hand, the Social Democratic party (Sozialdemokratische Partei Deutschlands or SPD) refused to accept a merger of that sort. Kurt Schumacher, the leader of the SPD, naturally got significant support from Allied occupation authorities with regard to this decision.[3] In the emerging Federal Republic of Germany, the communist party (Kommunistische Partei Deutschlands or KPD) remained therefore a minor political actor.[4] The SPD of Kurt Schumacher was the only strong party on the left of the West German political scene and it would stay in opposition for many years to come.[5]

While relationships between the SPD and the CDU/CSU coalition were sometimes quite stormy, these parties had in effect common enemies—communism and the USSR. Political confrontation in West Germany was kept within the bounds of an anticommunist framework. Consequently, it turned out to be relatively benign, particularly when compared to what was happening at the same time in France or in Italy. In turn, the West German political situation had an impact on the labor movement and West German trade unions proved relatively immune to communist influence. Federated in October 1949 in the Deutscher Gewerkschaftsbund (DGB), those West German trade unions belonged either to a Social Democratic or to a Christian tradition. In Cold War language, West German labor was thus essentially 'free'.

Western European trade unions naturally reacted to transformations affecting national industries in the postwar period. Reactions differed, however, and those differences revealed the complexity of the Western European labor scene as it had come to be redefined by the late 1940s. Each labor organization had its own position on the issue of cartels and competition, on the problems of firm size and ownership structures, or on the projected coal and steel community. More important and significant, however, were the reactions of the organizations to the Marshall plan and its politics of productivity, which concerned labor in a direct way. Both in France and in Italy, trade unions had until 1947 been key actors in the national effort towards economic recovery. In both countries, communist ministers within coalition governments had called for a mobilization of labor to wage the 'battle of production'. Communist trade union leaders had accepted the challenge and the CGT in France or the CGIL in Italy had announced a social truce. In France, the CGT agreed to a longer working week—48 hours—during the period of reconstruction. It gave full and enthusiastic support, initially, to the planning board and to its ambitious objectives.[6] In Italy, the CGIL also collaborated, accepting the macroeconomic stabilization program of the Italian government, which by controlling inflation could prevent, it was argued, dramatic losses in the purchasing power of workers. In fact, in those two countries, the collaboration of the Communist Party and of communist trade union leaders sometimes went too far for the rank and file. A number of grass-roots movements broke out spontaneously during this period, essentially motivated by wage claims.[7]

By the fall of 1947, the situation had changed radically. Communist ministers had been dismissed from national governments in France and in Italy and the Marshall plan was being denounced by the USSR as an American scheme to take over and dominate Europe. After officially refusing to participate in the Marshall plan, Soviet leaders asked Western European communist parties, in the fall of 1947, to launch an all-out war against the Marshall plan and against those actors who seemed ready, in each country, to accept collaboration with the USA. Communist parties and trade unions complied, both in France and in Italy, and they were soon systematically opposing American intervention in Western European economic affairs. They also came to denounce the national economic policies to which they had given full support only a few months before. The social truce was over and the launching of the Marshall plan had undeniably contributed to a radicalization of Western European labor, particularly in France but also in Italy.

COMMUNIST LABOR IN FRANCE AND AMERICAN IMPERIALISM

The first reaction of the French communist trade union was, by the end of 1947, to boycott the French plan and all its institutions. The CGT withdrew from the various committees and commissions, on the grounds that the French plan was to be financed, starting in 1948, by Marshall funds. French communists often repeated that they did not so much oppose the French plan as its integration within and dependence upon the Marshall scheme. Leaders of the CGT made it clear that they 'still espouse[d] most of the early objectives of the Monnet plan. [They] refuse[d] and denounce[d], though, all foreign financing which impose[d] conditions dangerous to the independence of [the] nation.'[8] After the USSR had officially refused to participate in or let Eastern and Central European countries participate in the Marshall plan, the latter was presented by communist parties across Europe as essentially a tool of American imperialism and as a weapon in the Cold War. Since the Monnet plan was to be financed through Marshall funds, the French Communist Party and trade union could only become its resolute opponents. They therefore launched a war, not only against the Marshall plan, but also against the planning board and the French plan. The legitimacy and influence of the Communist Party and of the communist trade union within French labor made them quite formidable opponents. Through a dense and well organized network of committees, both deeply embedded at the grass-roots level and centrally coordinated, the CGT and the French Communist Party had the capacity to organize a movement of resistance on a scale that was not to be underestimated.

Stirring up Revolutionary Strikes

The opposition of labor to national economic policies and to the Marshall plan first of all—and quite naturally—took the form of strikes. The first wave started at the grass-roots level in the summer of 1947, spreading and intensifying in the fall. Claims had originally been about wages but the strikes were soon controlled and monitored by the communist trade union. Consequently, by September, the movement had reached quite a different scale and had become highly political. It proved extremely violent, verging on insurrection (Esposito, 1994: ch. 1). In return, the French government did not hesitate to send troops in to crush the movement. Throughout 1948, the political and social situation remained highly unstable in France. In the fall, CGT leaders launched another wave of strikes, which were once again quickly politicized. The ultimate objective was to bring the communists back to power and to question French participation in the Marshall plan.[9] On the ground, the struggle was fierce and the French government had once more to send in troops to reassert its control. There were casualties on both sides but the show of strength by the government brought workers back to work by the end of November. It turned out, in fact, that after this particular wave of strikes, the French communists had to give up any hope of coming back to power and of pulling France away from the Marshall scheme. The country was by then solidly anchored in the West. Becoming regular, the flow of Marshall funds was creating a situation of strong dependence. At the same time, the economic situation had undeniably improved. There were still some strikes in 1949 and 1950 but of a much less violent type. Labor claims and demands stayed within traditional, purely economic bounds.

'Yankees Go Home!'

The strikes monitored by the French Communist Party and trade union in 1947 and 1948 clearly showed that those organizations could mobilize rapidly and on a mass level. This was due in part to their very structure, a combination of rigid centralization with a dense network of grass-roots committees. It revealed also the power of the communist propaganda machine and the significant impact it had within French labor. To a large extent, the war against the USA and the Marshall plan was an ideological war, a struggle for the control of minds. As it turned out, a significant proportion of French labor was, in the immediate postwar period, relatively sympathetic to the Soviet vision of the world. French communist propaganda denounced American imperialism and the attempt, in particular through the Marshall plan, to 'colonize' France and 'enslave' Frenchmen. The American assistance scheme, French communists argued, was in reality a cover through which American products, investments, and culture were flooding in, threatening the independence of France and its very identity. Drawing a parallel with the period of German occupation during the war, French communists accused the Fourth Republic of being a collaboration regime. Resistance was therefore in order and American presence or intervention in France, whatever the shape it took, had to be fought. 'Yankees Go Home' or 'US Go Home' became rallying watchwords of French communists and appeared on the walls of many French cities.[10] The ratification of the NATO pact in 1949 was a confirmation for French communists of the aggressive aims of the USA, already implicit in the Marshall plan. It brought to light, they claimed, the American strategy of using France and other Western European countries as advanced posts in the war against the communist bloc.

Not surprisingly, French communists also opposed the politics of productivity and the technical assistance program. They denounced the false promises of the latter, pointing to the traps of the American dream. 'One could starve with a telephone' ran *L'Humanité*, the communist daily, in 1948.[11] Beyond the glossy image of a land of plenty and social harmony conveyed through the productivity missions program, communist propaganda documented the failures of an American society which was also defined by racism, segregation, violence, despair, and misery. French communists warned that, behind the promise of a fridge or a Ford, lay alienation and exploitation. The politics of productivity, they argued further, were a fool's deal for French workers through which the latter was bribed and bought so as to willingly participate in their own exploitation.[12] Starting in 1949, a publication controlled by the communist trade union, *Le Peuple*, repeatedly denounced the 'productivity crusade', the 'submission of French political and business leaders to the diktats of the Marshall plan', the illusory freedoms of a mass-consumption society, and the real exploitation of workers through a rationalization of production, systematic deskilling, and a forced pace of work.[13]

The American administration had excluded the CGT and its members from the productivity missions program in order to ensure that all members within French teams would participate in a constructive manner. When productivity missions returned to France, however, the communist trade union had the power and resources to hinder implementation. Through their capacity to mobilize and their control over powerful propaganda tools, members of the CGT could slow down and sometimes even bring to a halt the adoption of new methods or the redefinition of structures. They strongly resisted, in particular, the implementation of scientific management. A systematic rationalization was bound to lead, they argued, to higher rates of unemployment and, for those workers who kept their jobs, to deskilling and an unbearable work pace.

Throughout the early 1950s, labor resistance and opposition, stirred up and monitored to a large extent by communist organizations, could be neither ignored nor underestimated. Indeed, the communist trade union was largely dominant within French labor and the French Communist Party represented about a quarter of the total national vote. To handle labor resistance and opposition, whether real or potential, members of the cross-national network used various strategies. They first tried to bypass, as often as was possible, the communist trade union. Communist labor representatives were thus systematically left out of the various French committees and commissions bringing together government, business, and labor around economic policy making. The CGT was also excluded from all Marshall plan related institutions and projects. Starting in 1950, communist attacks and propaganda were also countered by a large-scale propaganda and information campaign, praising the merits of American assistance, pointing to the achievements of the Marshall plan, and disproving communist arguments. The investment program of the French government was, under American pressure, partially reoriented to cater more directly to the needs of French labor particularly in terms of housing. This social dimension was deliberately highlighted in Marshall plan propaganda. Members of the modernization network, finally, also attempted to bring about in the medium to long term an erosion of communist influence within French labor. This was essentially done by co-opting, helping, and building up 'free' trade unions.

FROM PARTICIPATION TO MANIPULATION: 'FREE' LABOR IN FRANCE

Starting in 1948 and with the launching of the Marshall plan, non-communist organizations became the only reliable partners within French labor for members of the cross-national modernizing network. The newly created and American sponsored CGT-FO or the Christian Federation of French labor (Confédération Générale des Travailleurs Chrétiens or CFTC) sent representatives to committees and commissions of the planning board when members of the CGT were leaving them. The success of the productivity program launched in 1949 was clearly dependent upon a constructive participation of labor. The American administration consequently relied on a collaboration with the CGT-FO and the CFTC as much as on the exclusion and boycott of the CGT. Non-communist French labor became a key partner in the productivity missions program which was at the core of the American politics of productivity. In 1951, non-communist trade unions created, together with the federation of managers (Confédération Générale des Cadres or CGC) a union center for research in productivity matters—Centre Intersyndical d'Etudes et de Recherches de Productivité or CIERP. This productivity center was designed as a forum for independent trade union work and discussions on productivity issues.

Conditional Participation in the Productivity Drive

In order to be successful, politics of productivity undeniably required an effective and constructive partnership between business and labor. This implied in turn the identification or definition of interests common to both groups. The French national productivity council (CNP) was created in 1950. It brought together representatives from non-communist trade unions, the CGT-FO and the CFTC, members of the federation of managers, the CGC, and of business associations, CNPF or CGPME. The attempt to build consensus and to create the conditions for a collaboration between these various groups followed a pattern that was proving successful in the USA at about the same time. The promise that increased productivity levels would mean a bigger cake to be shared by all was traded for the participation of 'free' labor in the productivity drive and for its commitment. Members of the productivity network argued that increased levels of productivity were ultimately bound to have a positive impact on the well-being of French labor thanks both to higher wages and to the availability of cheaper, mass-produced goods. The objective was to start building a consensus for the productivity drive on a narrow basis, amongst those business and labor actors directly involved in the program. The hope was then that a process of contagion would lead in time to collaboration and consensus on a much wider scale.

As it turned out, however, their participation in politics of productivity rapidly put 'free' trade unions in an uncomfortable position on the French labor scene. The Communist Party and the CGT loudly denounced the betrayal of the French working class by non-communist trade unions and their representatives. The CGT-FO and the CFTC were accused of 'collaborating' with French 'capitalists' against the interests of the working class. The fact that a segment of French business gave its support to the politics of productivity as a means of extracting more from labor was used to lend weight to those accusations. During the first meetings of the national productivity council, members of the CGT-FO and of the CFTC thus felt the need to reassert the conditional character of their collaboration to the politics of productivity. In order for the productivity drive to receive their wholehearted support, they indicated

clearly, it had to come with a social package, with the guarantee of full
employment, with higher wages, and with more buying power for labor.[14]

By 1951, the partial misgivings of 'free' labor organizations about the
French productivity program appeared increasingly justified. After three full
years of Marshall assistance and already two years into the productivity drive,
wages were still on average below prewar levels. Production and productivity
levels had increased but this had not led to better living standards or greater
purchasing power for the French working class. Those criticisms of French
politics of productivity were echoed by American labor representatives. Labor
advisers in the ECA Paris Mission sent the Washington office a series of
reports denouncing the disastrous handling in France of the productivity
program. Not only was labor under-represented in French productivity teams
but trade unions were also too rarely involved in the choice of participating
members, employers retaining full control. Worst of all, however, was the fact
that the ERP did not appear to have a direct impact on the living conditions of
the French working class. Wages were still low, prices high, and industrial
relations conflictual.[15] Those criticisms led the ECA to react and by the fall of
1951 it was publicly scolding the French business community for its 'feudal
mentality' and its failure to share with labor the benefits of increased levels of
productivity. Such clear American support, however was for non-communist
trade unions a double edged sword. It did give one more argument to those
who were accusing them of being the 'lackeys of American imperialism'.

A Bitter Feeling of Manipulation

By the end of 1951, members of the ECA were preparing and announcing a
reorientation of the technical assistance program or productivity drive. This
reorientation was officialized through the Blair-Moody amendment. The
American administration was planning to use pilot experiments at the industry
and factory level or productivity loans to impose the negotiation of agreements
on wages and profit sharing between workers and employers. Discussions at
that level, however, generally turned out to be stormy and agreement was
rarely reached. By the fall of 1952, non-communist trade union members felt
bitter and increasingly distrustful of French business leaders. They questioned
the possibility of a collaboration, and the very survival of productivity committees and commissions was therefore threatened. Members of the Christian
Federation (CFTC) were arguing that the productivity drive had only increased
profits with little or no benefits for workers and consumers.[16] They asked for
guarantees that labor claims would thereafter be taken into consideration and
that satisfactory agreements would be negotiated. This was the condition, they
warned, of their support for productivity projects in the future. Members of the
CGT-FO went one step further, threatening to withdraw from all productivity
committees and commissions. They refused to continue to back the pilot
experiment program on the grounds that, in the hands of French business

leaders, it was merely an instrument to exploit labor.[17] In the early spring of 1953, CGT-FO representatives to productivity committees and commissions had decided to 'refuse to take a stand on productivity projects and this attitude [was not to be] interpreted as tacit approval'. 'The reservations this revealed bore on the productivity program as a whole.'[18] Very soon after that, in fact, 'free' trade unions withdrew altogether from all productivity institutions.

Nevertheless, this did not mean the end of the productivity drive in France. The episode was merely a symbolic confirmation that labor was excluded from the French politics of productivity. Productivity committees and commissions continued to function but only as bipartite boards with government and business representatives.[19] The withdrawal of 'free' trade unions from French productivity institutions was an indirect confirmation that the French productivity drive had in fact favored the technical dimension over the human factor. Throughout the 1950s, the French productivity drive gave priority to rationalization and standardization, time and motion studies, the development of marketing techniques, the training of managers, or the restructuring of organizations and industries. At the level of the firm, labor proved to be more or less favorable to those technical and structural changes. The latter were implemented anyway, with labor or against it and by 1955 gains in productivity were unmistakable in French industry. From 1949 to 1956, the productivity of French labor had apparently risen by 5 per cent each year. As a basis of comparison, 5 per cent was the overall increase in productivity levels for the period between 1900 and 1939 (Kuisel, 1993: 352–3). At the same time, the human side of the politics of productivity had clearly been left by the wayside in France. Particularly striking, in this respect, was the failure to set up in France a framework for collective bargaining and for negotiating general agreements on wages, profit sharing, and working conditions.[20]

WEST GERMAN LABOR: CHOOSING CONSTRUCTIVE COLLABORATION

It was argued earlier that the labor situation had been quite different in the Federal Republic of Germany. Consensus was easier to reach in that country and collaboration could be negotiated. Indeed, the communist influence was weak and 'free' trade unions were clearly dominant in the West German working class. West German trade unions belonged either to a Social Democratic or to a Christian tradition, in direct continuity with the prewar period. Traditionally, they favored negotiations and a reformist approach over revolutionary outbreaks. In the post Second World War period, a majority of West German workers did not question the capitalist framework. The objective of West German trade unions was merely to increase, within this framework, the place of labor and to defend its interests. They were therefore likely to agree to a production and productivity drive provided labor could benefit from it.

Endorsing the Transfer of Scientific Management

Ever since the 1920s, German trade unions had been quite receptive to Taylor's scientific management and to the fordist mode of production, to the point of playing a part in the transfer of those techniques and methods to Germany (Guillén, 1994: ch. 3). Both Social Democratic and Christian trade unions had been ready to accept a rationalization of the production line on the condition that workers shared in the benefits, through higher wages or through an increase in living standards. As a condition of rationalization, German trade unions had also asked for closer involvement and participation of workers in the life of the firm. German trade unions had thus been playing with the idea of 'codetermination' ever since the early years of the Weimar Republic. The argument for 'codetermination' was that joint decision making at the level of the firm could help control and limit lay-offs, which may potentially follow from the process of rationalization. For employers, on the other hand, the participation of workers in decision making represented a guarantee of labor collaboration (Guillén, 1994: 112). Christian influences over German labor only rooted more deeply in the German tradition demands for formal collaboration and worker participation. The social doctrine of the Catholic Church, originally articulated in the 1891 encyclical 'Rerum Novarum', was reasserted in 1931 by Pope Pius XI. In the encyclical 'Quadragesimo Anno', Pius XI called for partnership contracts through which 'workers could become sharers in ownership or management or participate in some fashion in the profits received'. The social doctrine of the Church thus confirmed German workers in their claims for a 'codetermination' framework.

West German trade unions in the post Second World War period were undeniably heirs to this German labor tradition. In American eyes, the very nature of their claims and their preference for a gradual approach and for reformist strategies were clear assets. West German trade unions were therefore identified as potential partners for the American-sponsored technical assistance program. Although the politics of productivity were slow to start, most trade union members in West Germany seemed ready to cooperate in a program where the objective was to bring about rationalization, mechanization, and standardization in the national industry. As long as they were guaranteed a degree of control over the process, West German workers were apparently willing to contribute to an increase in production and productivity levels. In the post Second World War period, West German trade unions reasserted their support for scientific management and for a rationalization of production. They did not need, however, to endorse the human side of the American politics of productivity, as they had their own traditions from which to draw. Indeed, compared to German trade union demands for a 'codetermination' framework, the American Human Relations school clearly lacked ambition (Guillén, 1994: ch. 2). Participation and motivation techniques, meaningful integration in the group, fair working conditions, or material rewards were compatible with, but much less ambitious than demands for a share in management and for the institutionalization at the level of the firm of a framework for collaboration with employers. Instead of accepting what was offered by the American-sponsored politics of productivity, West German trade unions thus clung to their 'codetermination' project.

Building an Institutional Framework for Codetermination

Early in the spring of 1951, when the coal and steel business community was in a position of relative weakness and disturbed by ECSC negotiations, West German trade unions obtained the enactment of a law establishing codetermination in the coal and steel industries. Workers were represented both on supervisory boards, with five positions out of eleven, and on managing boards, with one labor director.[21] Owners and employers retained the right to decide and impose their views, as a last resort, if disagreements could not be overcome. Still, a framework had been institutionalized in two major West German industries allowing the participation of labor in management and decision making.[22] In the end, the West German business community did manage to prevent an extension of this codetermination legislation to other industrial sectors. West German trade unions only obtained the creation of work councils in all industrial firms with five or more employees and they had to fight for that against the organized opposition of business leaders.

Those work councils became the framework for discussions between labor and management at the level of the firm. Negotiations on wages, working conditions, welfare schemes, or even major organizational or technological transformations were thus grounded and institutionalized in West Germany at the level of the firm. Undeniably, work councils in West Germany had much more power and prerogatives than their French counterparts. Together with the codetermination framework in coal and steel industries, they institutionalized an industry-wide, decentralized scheme that made possible step by step, constructive, and local negotiations. In this way the conditions were created in West Germany for a dialogue between labor and management to take place at the firm level around issues of daily operation. This explains a relative consensus and social truce at the national level, both of which were important conditions for the success of the American-sponsored politics of productivity.

In this respect, West Germany represented an exception amongst those European countries benefiting from Marshall assistance. To some extent, West Germany was even more successful than the USA in building up and institutionalizing the social foundations of a mass-producing, corporate capitalism. The mobilization, in the USA, around 'Human Relations' was too limited and too short-lived to have a comparable impact. When West German workers were losing an average of 0.04 work days per year in industrial conflicts in the 1950s, the equivalent American average was still 0.55 (Guillén, 1994: 131).

The institutionalization, in West Germany, of a dialogue between labor and management at the level of the firm created favorable conditions for the negotiated adoption of new organizational structures or technological innovations. In contrast to what was taking place in other Western European countries, a redefinition of the work process, the rationalization of production, or the adoption of techniques to increase productivity were not systematically opposed by labor in West Germany. In the end, this institutional framework for codetermination—or more exactly for a collaboration between labor and management—significantly contributed to the postwar West German 'economic miracle', smoothing out the process of restructuring of West German industry.

COMMUNISM AND CHRISTIAN DEMOCRACY IN ITALY: UNLIKELY AFFINITIES

In the immediate post Second World War period, the Italian labor movement had features quite similar to its French counterpart. The main Italian federation of trade unions, the Confederazione Generale Italiana del Lavoro or CGIL, was by 1947 clearly dominated by communists. The American administration and American labor federations were instrumental in bringing about the break-up of this federation in 1948. A 'free' Italian trade union was thus created, the Libera Confederazione Generale Italiana del Lavoro or LCGIL.[23] Throughout the 1950s, the Americans helped to build up and strengthen non-communist labor in Italy. They provided the LCGIL with financial and logistic support. They also encouraged the merger in 1949 between the LCGIL and the remaining non-communist groups from the CGIL. The result was a new 'free' trade union, the Confederazione Italiana Sindicati Lavoratori or CISL.

Resisting the Marshall Plan: Communist Opposition in Italy

In Italy just as in France, the American foreign aid administration was planning to turn these newly created non-communist trade unions into local partners. Indeed, to implement their politics of productivity, the Americans needed the support of at least some groups within the local working class. The Americans hoped that, above anything else, 'free' trade unions could bring about a redefinition of industrial relations in Italy. Institutionalized bargaining and negotiation should increasingly replace class-based political confrontations. Such a redefinition of industrial relations was a necessary condition, according to members of the American administration, for the successful implementation of the politics of productivity.

Starting in 1947, however, the Americans in Italy had to face the fierce opposition and organized resistance of a majority of the working class. Following Soviet orders, the Italian Communist party and communist trade union managed to launch or take over several waves of strikes throughout 1947 and

1948. These strikes mobilized a large number of Italian workers around a platform which was more political than economic. Indeed, the ultimate objective of communist leaders was to denounce the Marshall plan and to protest against Italian participation in the American assistance scheme. The strikes reached insurrectionary proportions, in particular in July 1948, when Palmiro Togliatti, leader of the Italian Communist party, was shot and badly wounded in front of the Italian Parliament (Hughes, 1965). Just as in France, the Italian government did not hesitate to send in the police to break those strikes, thus asserting and consolidating its authority. By the end of 1948, the communist threat had subsided in Italy. The country had been lastingly anchored to the West partly as a result of the regular flow of Marshall assistance. However, similarities with the situation in France went no further. The institutional context was not the same in each of the two countries. Furthermore, the political and administrative élites had made quite dissimilar choices while the communist opposition in each case selected different strategies.

The Peculiar Origins of Italian Communism

By 1949, the communist movements in France and in Italy had to reconcile themselves with the fact that those two countries had been firmly tied to the American sphere of influence. A direct consequence of this geopolitical allegiance was to relegate the communist movement, in both countries, to the opposition. In the two cases, however, the communists settled down to their new role and position in quite different ways. Palmiro Togliatti, leader of the Italian Communist party, had been in Moscow throughout most of the fascist period. He nevertheless managed, after the beginning of the Cold War, to preserve a degree of independence from the Soviet line for his party. Furthermore, while the Italian communist party had been dismissed from the national government in 1947, it had retained control over a number of local strongholds particularly in the province of Emilia-Romagna, in the heart of the region that would later be called the Third Italy. Within those local strongholds, the Italian communists had a very pragmatic and constructive approach to economic issues, partly contradicting the violent opposition that defined their handling of those same issues at the national level. In fact, communist constituency in Italy was not limited to the working class, particularly within the Emilia-Romagna region. Locally, on occasion, there was even direct competition between Communist and Christian Democratic parties for the same voters (Weiss, 1984; 1988). In fact, the platform and agenda of those two parties was often quite similar, primarily with respect to small business. At the local government level, they both fought for the defense of small-scale capitalism, even though they did so on somewhat different grounds.

The Italian Communist party was heir to a prewar Socialist party, which nationally had been in the opposition but had also been closely involved in local government, at least before the fascist period. The creation of an Italian state in 1861 had not led to political centralization. The *comune*—a traditional territorial unit dating back to the Roman Empire—remained after 1861 a very important political and administrative entity and the source of cultural identity in Italy.[24] Bringing together a city and its surrounding countryside, *comunes* guaranteed over the years relative political, administrative, economic, and cultural stability in a quite turbulent national environment. They were also the natural framework, for most Italians, of participation in government and the scene of local democracy. Before the fascist period, socialists, who were excluded from political life at the national level, had thus turned to local government and in particular to running the affairs of the *comune*.

The Italian Christian party had also adopted such a strategy. The Christian party was opposed to a united Italian state and it favored political involvement at the level of traditional local communities (Romano, 1977). In fact, the tradition of utopian socialism from which the Italian socialists drew had a lot in common with the social doctrine of the Church, which was the ideological foundations of the Italian Catholic movement. Both socialists and Catholics fought for the 'defense of local society'. They denounced, with a single voice, large-scale capitalism and the exploitation of workers, proletarianization, and the alienation of man which were destructive, they argued, of local society. They championed, on the other hand, communities of independent craftsmen (*artigiani*) and small firms as the best possible form of economic and social organization. They did so concretely, within the *comunes* they controlled, by fostering the emergence of cooperatives and associations and by stimulating collaboration between small, independent entities. They helped to create local banks and financial networks in order to channel savings towards small industry and craft. They also created institutions which specialized in adult education with a technical and professional orientation that fitted the needs of smaller firms (Goodman and Bamford, 1989: 14–15).

Communists, Christian Democrats, and 'local society' after 1945

The post Second World War political scene in Italy reflected to some extent this peculiar pre-fascist heritage. The Communist party, direct heir to the pre-fascist socialist group, was still well established in a number of local communities. It strongly valued 'local society' and was ready to champion it and make it prosper. This clearly was a peculiar feature of the Italian Communist party, with origins in its own specific history and traditions and which had survived the influence of Soviet communism. On the other hand, while in charge at the national level, the new postwar Catholic party—Democrazia Cristiana (DC)— was also well established locally. In keeping with a tradition going back to the pre-fascist period, the Democrazia Cristiana praised 'local society' and favored small-scale, family capitalism partly because it came closest to a Christian ideal of economic and social organization:

The craft business helps to form a personal and direct commitment to production; it offers moral satisfaction from labor since it is not based on standardized labor which diminishes the capacity of the worker. It is therefore necessary that a party like the Democrazia Cristiana sees the problem of unemployment also under the profile of craft employment which is exquisitely and traditionally Christian.[25]

Italian Christian Democrats wanted to 'eliminate wage labor' and 'deproletarianize the worker'.[26] Italian communists intended to 'free labor' and to put an end to 'relations of exploitation'.[27] Beyond language differences, the objectives were in fact more or less the same. As far as was possible, individual workers should be helped to shake off their dependence and alienation. They should be encouraged to become independent entrepreneurs, owning the means of production. The strategies adopted by both parties, within the communities under their control, to achieve those objectives also proved to be quite similar. Within the regions under communist or Christian Democratic control—the center and the northeast of Italy, better known today as the Third Italy—those strategies clearly favored small firms and the development of the craft sector. Under a given size, industrial or craft units benefited from generous tax incentives, cheap credit opportunities, access to structures providing training or management support, and various types of local subsidies.[28]

At the national level, the Italian Communist party was a party of opposition, hostile to the Christian Democratic government. At the local level, on the other hand, a relative convergence in objectives and strategies between Communist and Christian Democratic parties could sometimes bring them to cooperate. The consequence was a surprising alliance—including at the national level—of members from both parties around legislative or policy proposals that seemed to favor small-scale industry and the craft sector. A number of legislative tools and institutions were set up in the 1950s at the national level, reinforcing local initiatives. They undeniably helped to preserve small-scale capitalism in Italy and certainly contributed to its dynamism throughout the post Second World War period. The Artisan Statute, for example, enacted in 1956, gave production units with less than twenty employees numerous benefits—cheap loans, lower taxes, exemption from keeping accounts, and more flexibility with respect to the management of labor. Created in 1947, the Artigiancassa launched a large-scale loan scheme in 1952, offering ten-year loans at very low interest rates for the creation or the modernization of small workshops. The Third Italy was by far the prime beneficiary of this scheme. Altogether, it received more than 57 per cent of those funds between 1953 and 1971 with only 41 per cent of Italian workshops.[29] A dense network of 'special credit institutes' was also set up at the national level, with the objective of catering to the financial needs of small and medium-sized firms intent on modernizing their equipments. Once again, with 45 per cent of all Italian small and medium-sized firms, the Third Italy received 50 per cent of total loans and funds allocated by those credit institutes.[30]

Communist 'opposition' was therefore quite peculiar in Italy and a collaboration with the party in power, the Democrazia Cristiana, was not inconceivable at times. This, naturally, had some impact on the positions and strategies of Italian labor. In regions under communist control, the communist trade union or CGIL tended to support local efforts and projects which favored small industry. A relative social truce existed in those regions and the local situation was in the end quite surprising, particularly in the Emilia-Romagna district where

a communist local authority presided over an industrial district which exemplifies in extremely efficient form all the characteristics of a capitalist system described by the classical economists: some thousands of small textile firms for example (many of them employing fewer than ten people) competing with each other, producing high-quality goods, achieving remarkable success in export markets and bringing great prosperity to the district.[31]

In regions under communist control, the CGIL was particularly strong but its members were often ready to cooperate. The relative goodwill of communist labor in those parts of Italy guaranteed that conflicts generally found a nonviolent and negotiated resolution. The strength and power of this trade union ensured, on the other hand, that once they had been negotiated, agreements could be readily and rapidly accepted by workers.[32] The partial convergence of economic and industrial agendas between Communist and Christian Democratic parties throughout the 1950s also led to a moderation of trade union claims in regions under Christian Democratic control. This was further reinforced by the peculiar status of labor and trade unions in those regions. The small size of firms indeed limited trade union pressure while in the craft sector the legislation left owners more discretion with respect to labor issues.[33]

In a partly unexpected manner, conditions for social truce had thus emerged this way in the post Second World War period in those regions better known as the Third Italy. Communist labor and small Italian business owners had agreed to collaborate, at least to some extent, on an economic and social project that was common in its broad outlines to both Communist and Christian Democratic parties. This project was radically different from the one championed at about the same time by a small technocratic élite in France and violently opposed by French communist labor. Despite the American presence in Italy, despite large-scale American assistance, and the systematic pressure of ECA members, the corporate system of industrial production had not found institutional champions there. Instead, a relative social compromise had been reached, particularly within the Third Italy, around a traditional system of industrial production where small, independent, family-owned and run units were predominant.

Reactions in Italy to the American technical assistance program were shaped, not surprisingly, by this quite specific national context. The Italians finally set up a national productivity council in 1952 and only then under significant American pressure. This council was made responsible to the office of the Italian Prime Minister and lacked real power. In fact, the American politics of productivity were no more appealing to the Italian government than the counterpart fund program. Italian officials were mostly anxious to limit American involvement in Italian national affairs and to prevent further encroachment by members of the ECA on the industrial policy of their country (Carew, 1987). The American productivity drive did have a lot to offer, from scientific management techniques, methods and tools of mass production, machines and modern technologies, to rational structures of organization, or 'human relations' techniques of personnel management. While the Italians tended to refuse scientific management, large-scale mass production, or the corporate and managerial revolution, they accepted mechanization and technological innovations, but only to a certain extent. A modernization of the means of production could be contemplated but only as long as it did not threaten the small-scale, family structure of the firm.

Italian industry was also quite interested, as it turned out, in the findings of the 'human relations' school. The Italian politics of productivity would in fact focus mainly on the human side of the politics of productivity, in striking contrast to what was taking place in a country like France. The American 'human relations' school, with its particular emphasis on the meaning of work, on the participation of workers, or on the building of consensus between labor and business, fit particularly well the social doctrine of the Church and the ideological tradition characteristic of the Italian Christian Democratic party. It was also perfectly compatible with the agenda of the Italian Communist party in those local strongholds that were under its control. As a consequence, government, labor, business actors, and the Catholic Church, all seized upon the 'human relations' school as one rare element of the American technical assistance program that could be imported and integrated in Italy.[34]

Altogether, it appears that the patterns of resistance and opposition within the working classes had a significant impact on the process of cross-national structural transfer. A strong communist influence over labor, both in France and in Italy, meant that resistance and opposition to the Marshall plan took, within the working classes of those two countries, a political dimension. A systematic and violent reaction on the part of labor was all the more disturbing to members of the American foreign aid administration in that the success of their large-scale modernization project hinged upon at least partial support from and collaboration of the working class. Joining forces with American trade union representatives, they therefore set out to foster the creation and development of non-communist trade unions in France and Italy. The hope was that such 'free' trade unions could become privileged partners in the implementation of the modernization project.

Similarities between France and Italy with respect to this issue of labor did not go much further, however. Differences in the structure of political and economic institutions and a much greater decentralization of power in the Italian case undeniably had an impact on the nature of communist opposition. In Italy, the communists had significant power at local government level in a number of strongholds in the center and northeast of the country. Furthermore, in contrast to the situation in France, Italy did not have an institutionally powerful national élite working in close synergy with American Marshall planners. The strategies of opposition groups were, consequently, quite different in each of these two countries. In an Italian context where the group in power was itself not favorable to the American modernization project, systematic resistance and violent opposition often proved unnecessary. In fact, the peculiar features and intellectual heritage of Italian communism could even lead, on a number of issues, to a collaboration between communist organizations and the Christian Democratic majority in power. In France, the violence of labor resistance meant that the French working class remained all along a minor partner, when it was involved at all, in the modernization project. The human side of the American politics of productivity was all but forgotten in France and the modernization project took place essentially against and in spite of labor.

At the same time, partly for historical reasons, communism had little impact on the West German labor movement. West German trade unions belonged either to a Christian or to a Social Democratic tradition. They were ready to contemplate collaboration with the cross-national modernizing network but only to a limited extent and under certain conditions. They asked for, and obtained, the creation of an institutional framework allowing negotiations at the level of the firm and workers' participation. As it turned out in the years that followed, those institutions for 'codetermination' created the conditions of a lasting and widespread social truce in West Germany. They proved highly compatible with the human side of the American politics of productivity. They were key, ultimately, to the peculiar collaboration between business and labor characteristic of West Germany. They undeniably contributed, in the end, to the successful restructuring of West German industry and to the West German 'economic miracle' in the post Second World War period.

Notes

1. On the American labor movement and its opposition to communism, see Rupert (1995).
2. The German Communist party was outlawed in 1933. The Reichstag fire in 1934, shown since to have been set up by the Nazi government, was blamed on communists and used to justify their systematic persecution (Shirer, 1959: ch. 7).
3. This was in fact quite unusual. Relationships between Kurt Schumacher and occupation authorities were in general far from smooth. The leader of the SPD indeed became famous for his violent attacks against the American occupation policies or against the 'Chancellor of the Allies' as he once called Konrad Adenauer (Adenauer, 1966: 212 ff.; Bark and Gress, 1992: 251).

4. After the elections of August 1949, the KPD had only obtained fifteen seats in the Bundestag out of a total of 402. Between 1956 and 1968, the KPD was banned by the High Court of the Federal Republic of Germany.

5. Within the German economic council, the SPD had been attributed twenty seats, on the basis of its strength within local governments. This was as much as the Christian Democratic Union, CDU, and the Social Christian Union, CSU, altogether. The 1949 elections brought to the Bundestag 131 members from the SPD against 141 CDU/CSU out of a total of 402 representatives. Despite these good results, the SPD was not involved in government at the federal level (Adenauer, 1966; Bark and Gress, 1992: 182).

6. AN-80AJ/1 and Monnet (1976). See also Carew (1987: ch. 2).

7. For example the Renault strikes in 1947, used to justify the dismissal of communist ministers from the French government, had begun in this way. After trying without success to break this wildcat strike, the CGT and the Communist party, belatedly took it over, claiming leadership (Carew, 1987: ch. 2).

8. *Le Peuple* (June 23–30, 1949), AN-81AJ/206.

9. Back in power, the French communists would certainly have tried to pull the country away from the Marshall plan. It seems also quite clear that Americans would in this case have been loath to keep on helping France (Carew, 1987: ch. 7; Esposito, 1994: ch. 2).

10. For a literary account of the confrontation, within a small French community, between those two incompatible value systems, see the novel by Pascal Quignard (1994), *L'Occupation Américaine*. Quignard tells quite vividly of communist attempts to demystify the 'American dream' and to take apart 'American propaganda'. See also Kuisel (1993: ch. 3) on communist propaganda.

11. Quoted in Kuisel (1993: 40).

12. For example, 'Parliamentary Debates, June 2, 1949, Intervention of Alfred Costes, Member of the Communist Group', AN-81AJ/178.

13. Articles from *Le Peuple* (1949), AN-81AJ/206.

14. 'Conseil National de la Productivité, Réunion du 10 octobre 1950', AN-81AJ/179.

15. 'Letter from ECA Paris to SGCI, July 26, 1949', AN-81AJ/179. See also AN-81AJ/208. Kuisel (1993: 345 ff.) quotes reports sent by American labor advisers and trade union members to the Washington office of the ECA.

16. 'Higher living standards, that had originally motivated free labor to participate in the productivity drive never materialized: productivity increases in a number of industrial sectors have been diverted from social ends.' 'CFTC representative, May 1953', AN-81AJ/181.

17. 'CGT-FO Congress, October 1952', AN-81AJ/180. Members of the CGT naturally applauded. ECA labor advisers upheld the demand of French labor for guarantees. They did their best, though, to prevent a drift of 'free' trade unions away from the politics of productivity. AN-81AJ/180 and Kuisel (1993: 48 ff.).

18. 'Comité National de la Productivité, Réunion du 16 mars 1953, Représentant CGT-FO', AN-81AJ/180.

19. A productivity board—Commissariat Général à la Productivité or CGP—was created late in 1953 to take over from the productivity committee (CNP). Labor was not represented on the new board, made up of civil servants, management representatives, and members of business associations (AN-81AJ/181).

20. The fate of French work councils (*comités d'entreprise*) illustrates such a failure.

From 1946, the creation of a work council was compulsory in firms with fifty employees or more. The real power and role, however, of those councils was rapidly limited to the handling of social and leisure activities. Decision making remained the prerogative of management and work councils did not even become a forum for collective bargaining (Rioux, 1980: 113 ff.).

21. All West German firms employing more than 500 persons, whether joint stock companies (*Aktiengesellschaft*—AG) or private limited liability companies (*Gesellschaft mit beschränker Haftung*—GmbH) have a two-tier board system. The supervisory board (*Aufsichrat*) has functions similar to those of a board of directors in an American joint stock company. The management board (*Vorstand* for the AG and *Geschäftsführung* for the GmbH) is responsible for day-to-day executive decision making.

22. Bark and Gress (1992, iii., ch. 4).

23. Carew (1987). See also Miller (1986: 255 ff.): 'In May 1948, the [American] Department of State instructed the embassy in Rome that the US was to exert all possible efforts to strengthen non-communist labor. The success of the ERP depended on the ability of non-communists to capture and hold control of the major labor federations. In the event that non-communists could not control CGIL, the US would covertly support an effort to split it. . . . American unions followed suit.'

24. After the elections in 1920, the Italian socialists controlled more than 2,000 *comunes* out of a total of 8,059 (Romano, 1977: 177; Goodman and Bamford, 1989).

25. 'Report to the Seventh National Congress of the Democrazia Cristiana, 1959.' Quoted in Weiss (1988: 89). The 1891 'Rerum Novarum' encyclical had proposed a Christian 'third way' between liberalism and socialism, pleading for small-scale, private property, and family business: 'when men know they are working on what belongs to them, they work with far greater eagerness and diligence. . . . The law therefore should favor ownership, and its policy should be to induce as many people as possible to become owners.'

26. In its 1946 proposal for an Italian constitution, the Democrazia Cristiana defined its ultimate aim as being 'the elimination of wage labor and of the consequent servitude of the proletariat, by favoring access of labor to ownership.' The credo of the DC was 'non tutti proletariani ma tutti proprietari'. Weiss (1988: 108 ff.).

27. Weiss (1988: 51), Goodman and Bamford (1989: introduction).

28. This was undeniably quite different from what the French administration was doing at about the same time.

29. Weiss (1988: 60). By 1976, more than 35 per cent of workshops in Italy—not including the south of the country—had benefited from one or more loans from the Artigiancassa.

30. Weiss (1988: 69) shows that 75 per cent of small manufacturing firms created between 1960 and 1970 had been financed through this network of credit institutes specializing in small and medium-sized production units.

31. Goodman and Bamford (1989: 15). See also, for a detailed and systematic description of the 'Emilian model', Brusco (1982).

32. Brusco (1982: 173 ff.): 'Even though the union exercises a real control over working conditions in the plant, the employer enjoys a secure climate which makes possible a greater degree of planning of the volume of production and investment.'

33. This proved in fact to be one more argument used by members of the Italian Christian Democratic party to justify their defense of small-scale industry: 'in craft

enterprises as in small industries, conflicts can be more easily dealt with and are more or less stifled by the modest dimensions of the firm and above all by the particular figure of the entrepreneur, personally present as the craftsman or small industrialist.' 'Statement made before parliament by a Christian Democratic leader in 1954.' Quoted in Weiss (1988: 89).

34. Attempts were made during the 1950s to adapt 'human relations' techniques in Italian companies. Under the leadership of a Catholic priest, Father Gemelli, the Italian Catholic University became a training and research center on 'human relations' techniques. Numerous articles, studies, and essays were written in Italy throughout the 1950s on 'human relations' techniques and their impact on industrial productivity (D'Attore, 1981; Carew, 1987).

Concluding Remarks

Insofar as Europe has a common culture, it is primarily American.
Anthony Sampson[1]

Although its blunt character may appear as somewhat of a provocation, Sampson's claim does ring quite true in light of the interpretation that has been proposed here of a key period in Western European economic history. It was argued indeed, in previous pages, that the postwar transformation of national systems of industrial production was the consequence of an organized and large-scale attempt to 'Americanize' the Western European industrial landscape. Twenty years after the end of the Second World War, many of the features common to Western European systems of industrial production could be traced back to a peculiar American model that had itself emerged in unique institutional and historical circumstances. Although partial, convergence was an unmistakable trend in postwar Western Europe and, to this day, this trend has not subsided. At the same time, however, while convergence in postwar Western Europe had essentially meant 'Americanization', significant differences in the structure of national industries could still be identified by the end of the period under study. In fact, a number of local peculiarities have remained to this day, so that national systems of industrial production can even now be contrasted and set apart from each other.

Unpacking historical contexts and institutional conditions has allowed us to propose an explanation for this puzzling and apparently contradictory combination of convergence with persistent differentiation. As it turns out, the fate of the peculiar American system of industrial production was closely linked, throughout the twentieth century, to the fate of the USA as a country. When the USA took on the leadership of the Western world in the immediate post Second World War period, parallels were quickly drawn between American geopolitical and economic power on the one hand and the unique American system of industrial production on the other. In the context of national crises and radical questioning that characterized a number of Western European countries, the American system of industrial production not surprisingly became the model to be transferred and adopted. And indeed, a large-scale structural transfer process was launched and fostered by a small cross-national network which controlled key resources and positions. This process was institutionalized through the systematic setting-up and operation of various cross-national transfer mechanisms, whether of mimetic, coercive, or normative types. Such a transfer process was bound to disrupt preexisting economic and social arrangements. It did encounter obstacles and sometimes even triggered organized resistance and opposition within national units. As a direct consequence, the transfer was not equally successful in all Western European countries. The original model was more or less significantly adapted or 'translated' and this largely accounted for the persistence, in the long term, of significant differences not only across Western European national industries but also between European and American industries.

The story that has been told in this book is thus the story of an attempt to radically redefine systems of industrial production in Western Europe. This attempt was deliberate, systematically monitored, and institutionalized by a few actors who together made up a cross-national network. Models, at the time, were American, and the transformation of Western European industries—or their 'modernization'—seemed to call for the transfer, on a large scale, of features until then quite peculiar to American corporate capitalism. This transfer, I have shown, was attempted and it did have an impact on Western European systems of industrial production. However, it took place in each case within unique institutional contexts and, not surprisingly, ran into obstacles and encoutered resistance that proved, at times, quite significant. The attempted transfer, as a consequence, was not equally successful in the three countries under study. The transferred model, furthermore, was never simply adopted. It was always adapted and 'translated', quite often in order to fit local institutional conditions and national legacies.

It seems difficult not to try and assess, at this point, how successful overall the attempted transfer process has been. The answer proposed here has two sides to it. To the extent that the attempted transfer has led to a redefinition of key rules of the game in Western European industries, it has undeniably been a success. In the long run, the Western European economic space was indeed redrawn, definitions of the firm and of competition were evolved, and the professionalization of the managerial function was imposed. The attempted transfer, however, appears much less successful if success is measured by the degree to which Western European systems of industrial production have converged with the American model. I have shown indeed that obstacles and resistance on the one hand, and significant adaptation and translation of the original model on the other, have prevented full convergence. Western European systems of industrial production have been and still are embedded in particular institutional contexts and some of their most peculiar features can to this day be traced to unique national legacies. The peculiar role of the state in France, patterns of collaboration between labor and business in Germany, or the network organization of industry in certain regions of Italy, for example, only make sense in light of national institutional histories.

> *Setting the Stage for the 'American challenge'* [2]

The focus, throughout this book, has been on historical developments and institutional contexts as key explanatory variables. This does not mean that economic change and technological evolution were considered altogether unimportant. The assumption has been, however, that economic and techno- logical conditions are not givens. They are themselves problematic, institu- tionally and historically situated, and consequently they also have to be accounted for. Economic and technological conditions are shaped, sifted, and interpreted by surrounding institutional frameworks and legacies while this does not prevent them, in turn, from having an impact on the structural features of national industries, on national institutions, or even on national cultural schemes. Emphasizing timing and contextualization, the approach developed here has brought out the embeddedness of economic and technolo- gical factors and of their evolution, the partly contingent character of that evolution, as well as the multiplicity and complexity of causal connections.

An account of structural transformations made in merely economic and technological terms would have left, in the Western European case, a number of questions unanswered, particularly with respect to the timing of those structural transformations. I have shown, indeed, that a large-scale process of structural transformation had already been in progress in the 1950s in Western Europe, well before the economic and technological environment had started to change in that part of the world. Economic and technological conditions truly began to evolve in Western Europe in the 1960s and 1970s, following redefinition of the economic space.[3] Undeniably, changes in economic and technological conditions had an impact on Western European systems of industrial production but only at a second stage, starting in the 1960s. This second stage—interpreted in Western Europe as indicative of an 'American challenge'—merely reinforced a restructuring that had already been in progress for some time.

The 'American challenge' was characterized by the strong presence of private American economic actors, throughout the late 1960s and the 1970s, in Western Europe. Political stabilization in that part of the world and the promise of growth that seemed to lie behind the creation of a European Economic Community led large numbers of private American economic actors to the old continent. American multinational companies, investors, or consult- ing firms, until then quite prudent, started rushing to the new Western European frontier. They brought along their technologies, modes of production, methods of management, and organizational structures.[4] It is possible to argue convin- cingly, however, by the end of this book, that the contribution of those private actors merely reinforced and stimulated a large-scale, cross-national transfer process already well under way. The transfer process of the early postwar years had been in the main structural, as demonstrated above, and it had been monitored from within the public sphere. This postwar structural transfer process, which had been coordinated both on a national and on a cross-national level, had in fact prepared the way for the large-scale transfer of technologies, 'models of management', or knowledge that reached a peak in the 1960s and 1970s, this time mostly under the impulse of private economic actors.

Multiple Models and the Relative Character of 'Efficiency'

An important consequence, I have argued, of the large-scale, cross-national transfer process documented in this book was the unmistakable convergence of a number of structural features across Western European industries. Differences and peculiarities have nevertheless persisted, clearly setting Western European systems of industrial production apart from each other and distinguishing them also from the American model. That differences and peculiarities have remained in spite of a convergence of economic and technological conditions, starting in the 1960s, would tend to invalidate existing arguments pointing to a relationship of causality between those conditions and industrial structures (Chandler, 1962, 1977, 1990). For the very same reason, the idea of a superior and most efficient model of industrial organization had to be called into question.

Of the Western European countries under study, Italy—and more particularly the north-eastern and central parts of the country—has unmistakably provided the clearest illustration of a relative decoupling of economic and technological conditions on the one hand and structural transformations on the other. Starting in the 1960s, the Italian economic and technological environment was subjected to globalizing and homogenizing trends, as elsewhere in Western Europe. However, that particular country has quite successfully managed to resist a large-scale transfer of the American structural model. During the postwar years and to this day, Italians have developed and nurtured their own path to industrialization. Particularly in the north-east and center of the country, dense networks of small and medium-sized family firms have been extremely dynamic and efficient, relying on institutional frameworks set up and maintained by local communist or Christian Democratic governments. Those regions of Italy, with their specific system of industrial production traced back in this book to prewar traditions and legacies, are today amongst the richest and most prosperous in Europe.[5]

This leads us to a few important remarks. First of all, the ultimate objective behind this book was not to make any kind of comparisons nor draw any conclusions with respect to the efficiency, performance, or, on the contrary, relative weakness, in economic terms, of different systems of industrial production. The main focus was the genesis and evolution through time of those systems. The working hypothesis was that increased efficiency was not the necessary mainspring of structural evolution but a potential and relative consequence of this evolution. I believe many elements have been brought forward, throughout this book, to validate such an hypothesis.

The second remark is closely related to the first. Not only are efficiency and performance often mere consequences and not necessary causes, they are also relative—and in no case absolute—dimensions. It can indeed be safely concluded, by the end of this book, that given economic and technological conditions are compatible with different systems of industrial production.

Efficiency and performance can characterize at the very same time different types of structural arrangements, within relatively similar economic and technological environments. In the postwar Western European common market, for example, the system of industrial production characteristic of north-eastern and central Italy proved to be at least as efficient—albeit naturally in a different way—as its French or West German counterparts.

It seems important to emphasize, finally, particularly in light of the Italian case, that an analysis at the level of the nation-state has its limits. With respect to systems of industrial production and their evolution, the Italian case has indeed shown that key differences may be found across regions within the same country. A more systematic study of those cross-regional differences could certainly be contemplated to follow up the work presented in this book. It can be argued, more generally, that the relevant unit of analysis for similar types of studies might not always be the nation-state. Sub-national or supranational entities may sometimes have to be considered.

Lessons for Cross-National Programs of Economic Assistance

On a practical note, the comparative analysis presented in this book can lead to a series of conclusions with respect to transnational programs of assistance and their administration. Those conclusions are certainly worth pondering in a number of contemporary situations. They have particular relevance for the debate around Eastern European reconstruction and for discussions on the role of foreign aid. The overall success of the Marshall plan, in its financial, material, and technical dimensions, was apparently the direct consequence of two of its main features. First, the administrative agencies in charge of managing this large-scale program of assistance developed powerful means of control that reached down to the country and even to the project level. These sophisticated mechanisms of control combined with clear projects which were generally translated into detailed and concrete objectives.

Our empirical comparison has shown, on the other hand, that the success of the Marshall plan as a program of assistance had also depended on the capacity of the donor country—in this case the United States—to work with or co-opt local or national groups sympathetic to its projects and objectives. These groups did not need to have a large base of support locally as long as they were institutionally powerful, controlling key positions within the national institutional framework. The ability to set up solid and closely-knit cross-national networks, working in close synergy across national borders, has thus appeared to be a key factor of the relative success of the aid program. Those claims and conclusions could be worth taking into consideration in more contemporary situations.

Embeddedness and Role of the State

I have proposed, in this book, a reinterpretation of key developments in post Second World War Western European industries, in order to fit the timing and to reflect the complexities of historical events. My objectives, however, were not merely descriptive. There were also theoretical ambitions and the systematic comparison of national cases was expected to provide theoretical leverage. Naturally, both the objects studied and the methodology selected had an impact on the type of theory construction that could be contemplated. Due to the nature of the project, it was obvious from the very beginning that the extent of legitimate ambitions would be grounded on middle-range theory making. The result, naturally, was not a system but sets of theoretical tools or guidelines. Those tools could potentially be used to understand, generalize about, or even anticipate evolutions in other contexts, provided that in each case specific conditions were taken into account and integrated.

A number of theoretical guidelines emerging from the comparative analysis presented above merely reinforce already existing theoretical claims. The idea of the embeddedness of the economic sphere, for example, has undeniably and repeatedly been validated throughout this book (Polanyi, 1944; Granovetter, 1985). From the emergence of the corporate system of industrial production in the USA to its postwar transfer to Western Europe without forgetting the creation of a new Western European economic space after 1950, economic and industrial histories have been shown to be closely connected to evolutions in legal, political, or cultural spheres and to be dependent upon developments in geopolitical or institutional environments.

The systematic confrontation of the three empirical cases has made it possible to go one step further and to propose that political institutions and states are key actors with regard to large-scale, macro transformations in economic or industrial spheres. Structural changes in those spheres can take place, naturally, without the direct intervention of political institutions and state actors. But the systematic and large-scale disruption of a national system of industrial production will be very unlikely unless this process receives political and legal legitimization. Furthermore, such a systematic disruption of the *status quo* is bound to clash with vested interests in the economic and industrial spheres. If this is indeed the case, the impulse, support, or direction provided by political institutions and state actors to such a process can prove to be essential. Naturally, the greater the infrastructural power of political actors and their capacity to reach down into and intervene in economic and industrial spheres, the more they will be able—if such is their intention—to impose and generalize transformations, to fight off opposition and vested interests. Those conclusions on the key role of political institutions and state actors were illustrated in this book, both positively and negatively, through the historical cases that have been studied.

Conclusions of that sort are naturally valid on a much more general level and they certainly are lessons worth pondering, for example, with regard to the situation in post-communist Eastern Europe. Building on what was learnt in the case of postwar Western Europe, it is possible to argue that, in the context of radical transition and institutional reconstruction still characteristic today of most countries within the Eastern European region, state actors should not yet withdraw completely, quite the contrary. History also tells us that the characteristics and the objectives of those state actors are bound to have a significant impact on the process of transformation itself and on the direction it can take. Their control of key institutions and their influence over civil society will partly determine the success of the transformation. So will the strength and the capacity of opposition groups to organize and mobilize. One more key lesson to draw from history is that, to a significant extent, the geopolitical environment shapes processes of structural transformation in a particular country and guides the search for models in that same country. The complex patterns of geopolitical relationships that have emerged as a direct consequence of the historical developments described above would therefore have to be taken into account in a study of the recent transformations taking place on the Eastern European economic and industrial scene.

By the end of the 1940s, the world was a relatively simple place, and within the Western sphere of influence the American system of industrial production was the only possible or available model. The fall of the Berlin wall, however, has taken place in a context where models for economic and industrial reconstruction turned out to be multiple and competing and included not only the American but also the German, or the French. The origins of such a diversity—not incompatible, I have argued, with a degree of convergence— have been tracked down in this book and it appears that the current multiplicity of models for Eastern Europe is an indirect and partly unexpected outcome of processes described above. Furthermore, new cross-national actors and organizations have emerged since the 1950s. The emergence and institutionalization of these new actors and organizations have also been part of the story told here. The World Bank, the International Monetary Fund, or the European Union amongst others had, by the late 1980s, become full blown actors with a potentially significant impact on systems of industrial production at a cross-national, a national, or a regional level. They play a significant role on the geopolitical scene today and they would have to be integrated systematically into the analysis, for example, of contemporary transformations in Eastern Europe.

One important conclusion reached at the end of this book is therefore that political institutions and state actors have a major role to play in shaping national systems of industrial production, particularly with respect to large-scale transformations and radical evolution in situations of crisis or transition. This does not imply, however, that a significant and systematic involvement of state actors within the national economy and industry is always necessary or positive. In the empirical cases that were studied, public actors had fostered and monitored radical transformation with open markets, increased competition, less state intervention, and more private initiative as their ultimate objectives. The impulse initially came from the public sphere but this was to be short term and temporary. At one point or another, it was believed that state intervention would give way to private undertakings and leadership.

With respect to this last objective, West Germany has proved more successful in the long run than France. In a country where, from the very beginning, state intervention was less overt, less systematic, and less institutionalized, political and administrative actors knew how to step back. When the time came, they increasingly withdrew from the economic and industrial sphere, leaving private actors freer rein. This was much more difficult in France where state intervention was deeply institutionalized from the late 1940s. State actors and public institutions were instrumental in bringing about, in postwar France, rapid and significant transformations, steering along in particular a radical redefinition of the national industry. Nevertheless, while they were, in the early postwar years, a source of change, initiative, and renewal, they became fossilized through time and are by now greatly responsible for the rigidity of French social and economic arrangements. The civil service school, in particular—the ENA—which produced the second generation of French modernizers has contributed, in the longer term, to create a 'new class', a cast of public administrators who also took over a significant proportion of the French private sector. Far from being a source of change, this group is now, above anything else, intent on preserving its vested interests. It tends to resist any divesting of its own power while such was precisely the ultimate logic behind the large-scale transformation process launched in France in the immediate postwar period.

Combining Structural Constraints with Partly Independent Action

Highlighting the significance of legacies, path-dependencies, and institutional embeddedness amounted in fact to pointing towards sets of powerful constraints, which *a priori* structure and limit the sphere of individual action. Empirical cases, however, have attested to the possibility of change and what is more of radical change. There was a need, as a consequence, to reconcile theoretically a system of constraints with the possibility of change. This was done, throughout this book, in essentially three ways. First, the argument has allowed for historical accidents and unexpected occurrences, for the unpredictable synergy between the projects of different groups, for example, or for a chance encounter between a particular problem and a given solution.[6]

Then, the argument has brought the individual back in, with his (or her) personal convictions, value-orientations, and interests, not always entirely determined by the constraining socio-economic or institutional system in which he or she is situated. It turns out that the individual—or more often in our empirical cases sets of individuals belonging to closely-knit networks—

could be a source of change to the point of disrupting and redefining preexisting institutional constraints.

Finally, the very possibility of change has also been traced to transnational relationships. Such relationships can naturally disrupt the political and military balance of a given country; they can also have an impact on its social and economic make-up. The source of change, in this case, is external and transformations may thus be fairly radical, representing a significant and partly unpredictable departure from national legacies and local constraints. Those lessons from history are naturally valid in more contemporary situations and apply particularly in the case of Eastern Europe.

Cross-National Transfer: Building a Theoretical Framework

We finally come to the most original theoretical contribution of this book which bears on processes of transfer or diffusion. That such processes are at work in the realm of knowledge, values, or ideas has been argued and documented by others (Rogers, 1982; Latour, 1987; Hall, 1989; Guillén, 1994; Soysal, 1994; and Valdès, 1995). I have shown, in this book, that processes of transfer and diffusion can also play a significant role with respect to the transformation of structures, of organizational patterns, and of institutional frameworks. The demonstration carried particular weight because it bore on economic and industrial structures, on national systems of industrial production, which have generally been treated as operating and evolving in an essentially autonomous manner. The argument presented here is not about global or universal trends—whether of an economic, technological, or institutional nature—having an impact on national economies and industries in a parallel but unrelated fashion. It differs in that from evolutionary theories, whether in their 'efficiency' or 'rationalization' variants (Chandler, 1962, 1977, 1990; Williamson, 1975, 1985; Scott, Meyer *et al.*, 1994).

Processes of cross-national transfer or diffusion have been shown in this book to have precise historical or geographical origins. The logic underlying these processes, on the other hand, has emerged as being neither always nor necessarily a quest for economic efficiency or a competitive race towards technological innovation. Mechanisms of cross-national transfer or diffusion have turned out, as a consequence, to be quite diverse. They are not necessarily articulated, in particular, at a microeconomic level and they cannot be reduced to bilateral relationships between individual economic actors. Subsidiaries of multinational companies, consulting firms, investment banks, or professional associations can naturally all play their part in a cross-national transfer. This book has shown, however, that processes of cross-national transfer or diffusion can be articulated at a macro level and take place, as a consequence, on a much larger scale. In this case, other actors and mechanisms are involved and political institutions or government administrations play a key role.

The historical and comparative work presented here has precisely focused on large-scale macro processes of cross-national transfer, essentially of a structural kind. The emerging set of theoretical tools could still apply, however, with some marginal adaptation, to transfer processes more limited in their scale and not of a structural kind. This set of theoretical tools, which was presented in greater detail in previous chapters and will only be summarized here, can be divided into three main subsets each corresponding to a stage in the cross-national transfer process. Brought together in Figure 10, these subsets are respectively: (i) the conditions or origins of the transfer process; (ii) the process itself and its main mechanisms; and finally (iii) its reception and more particularly the obstacles it might encounter.

The comparative and historical study has shown that a number of conditions should be met simultaneously in order for a large-scale, cross-national transfer process to be possible, to be contemplated, and eventually to be launched. First of all, a traumatic disruption should bring, at the national level, an acute sense of crisis and a questioning of the legitimacy of preexisting institutional and structural arrangements. Then a redefinition of the geopolitical environment and, in particular, the emergence of relationships of asymmetrical dependence, should turn a foreign system of industrial production into an available model, in other words one which is both familiar and perceived to be superior. Finally a cross-national network of actors, sharing similar and compatible if not common objectives should bridge the gap between both countries. These 'modernizing' individuals may be only a small minority within their respective national environments. They should nevertheless hold and control key positions of power both within cross-national institutional channels and in those national institutions located at the articulation of state and economy in

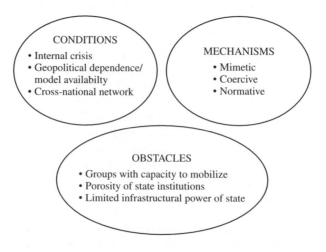

Figure 10. Stages of a cross-national transfer process

the receiving country, which are bound to play an essential role in the transfer process. This set of three conditions, it has been proposed, will significantly increase the likelihood that a large-scale, cross-national transfer process be considered and eventually launched in a given situation.

Then, the concrete implementation of such a large-scale, cross-national transfer process will require that a number of transfer mechanisms be not only elaborated but also operated. Three main types of transfer mechanisms have been identified. Using DiMaggio and Powell's (1983) terminology, they have been labeled respectively 'mimetic', 'coercive', and 'normative'. Varying degrees of geopolitical dependence account for differences in the mix of transfer mechanisms. The nature of this mix, on the other hand, is bound to have an impact on the transfer process, for example on its speed and on the extent of the 'translation' or adaptation of the original model. It may also influence national reactions, and in particular the degree of local resistance and the violence of opposition movements.

Indeed, the comparative and historical work presented in this book has emphasized that the concrete operating of those various transfer mechanisms was not likely to run smoothly. Obstacles could naturally stem from the existence of powerful and organized groups with a significant capacity to mobilize, and intent on resisting the transfer process. The porosity of state institutions apparently increased further the ability of these groups to impose their own views and thus to successfully resist the transfer process, while limiting at the same time the autonomy of political or administrative actors. Furthermore, notwithstanding the degree of resistance and the impact of opposition groups, a large-scale cross-national transfer process may be considerably slowed down, if not brought to a halt, because of the limited infrastructural power of political institutions and state actors, and in particular because of their limited leverage over the national economy and industry.

We might end with one final and key remark. Cross-national processes of transfer or diffusion cannot be uncoupled from a parallel process of diffraction, partial reinterpretation, or 'translation' of the original model to be transferred. The combination, in theoretical terms, of those two indissociable processes has required the crossbreeding of two main strains of 'institutional' or 'neo-institutional' theory. On the one hand, the tradition of organizational neo-institutionalism (DiMaggio and Powell, 1991) has been used to account for processes of transfer or diffusion themselves, their origins and mechanisms. On the other hand, the associated processes of reinterpretation or 'translation' have turned out to fit much better with the paradigms developed by the second tradition, which could be labeled historical or political neo-institutionalism (Skocpol, 1979; Evans *et al.*, 1985; Fligstein, 1990). The cross-fertilization between these two traditions, which has led in part to the originality of the theoretical argument proposed in this book, has undeniable implications for the thriving but multifaceted 'institutional' or 'neo-institutional' school in economic sociology. It clearly points to a number of fruitful research paths, both at an empirical and at a theoretical level, and the main conclusions bring along new questions. Opportunities to build upon this work are thus quite numerous but for now they must remain another story.

Notes

1. Quoted in Berghahn (1986: 332).
2. *Le Défi américain* was the title of a book published by Jean-Jacques Servan-Schreiber in 1967 which had a significant impact in France at the time. Servan-Schreiber was essentially arguing that Western European industrial firms would never stand up to the American challenge if they did not increasingly come to resemble their American counterparts, adopting American structural arrangements, organizational patterns, and modes of management.
3. I have argued earlier that this redefined economic space was itself an institutional creation prompted essentially by geopolitical and political considerations.
4. See McKenna (1997) for an interesting case study focusing on the McKinsey consulting firm and its role in this second wave of transfer.
5. 'Les désillusions politiques du Nord, région la plus riche d'Europe', *Le Monde* (April 11, 1996).
6. Cohen *et al.* (1972). The episode in American business history when the business community takes hold of the holding company device to bypass the antitrust legislation is clearly an example of a chance encounter between problem and solution.

BIBLIOGRAPHY

THEORY AND METHODS

Bendix, R. (1956), *Work and Authority in Industry* (John Wiley: NY).

Berger, S. and M. Piore (1980), *Dualism and Discontinuity in Industrial Societies* (CUP: NY).

Campbell, J. (1994), 'Recent Trends in Institutional Analysis: Bringing Culture Back Into Political Economy', unpublished paper presented at the Stanford Center for Organizations Research (Stanford University).

Campbell, J. and L. Lindberg (1990), 'Property Rights and the Organization of Economic Activity by the State', *American Sociological Review* (55).

Campbell, J., R. Hollingsworth, and L. Lindberg, eds. (1991), *Governance of the American Economy* (CUP: NY).

Chandler, A. (1962), *Strategy and Structure* (MIT Press: Cambridge, MA).

—— (1977), *The Visible Hand* (HUP: Cambridge, MA).

—— (1982), 'The M-Form: Industrial Groups, American Style', *European Economic Review* (19).

—— (1990), *Scale and Scope* (HUP: Cambridge, MA).

Coase, R. (1937), 'The Nature of the Firm', *Economica* (4).

Cohen, M., J. March, and J. Olsen (1972), 'A Garbage Can Model of Organizational Choice', *Administrative Science Quarterly* (17).

Crozier, M. (1963), *Le Phénomène Bureaucratique* (Seuil: Paris).

D'Iribarne, P. (1989), *La Logique de l'Honneur* (Seuil: Paris).

DiMaggio, P. and W. Powell (1983), 'The Iron Cage Revisited: Institutional Isomorphism', *American Sociological Review* (48).

Dobbin, F. (1994), *Forging Industrial Policy* (CUP: NY).

Drucker, P. (1946), *The Concept of the Corporation* (New American Library: NY).

DuBoff, R. and E. Herman (1980), 'Alfred Chandler's New Business History: A Review', *Politics and Society* (10: 1).

Edwards, R. (1979), *Contested Terrain* (Basic Books: NY).

Evans, P., D. Rueschmeyer, and T. Skocpol, eds. (1985), *Bringing the State Back In* (CUP: NY).

Fligstein, N. (1985), 'The Spread of the Multidivisional Form among Large Firms, 1919–1979', *American Sociological Review* (50: 3).

—— (1990), *The Transformation of Corporate Control* (HUP: Cambridge, MA).

Geertz, C. (1973), *The Interpretation of Cultures: Selected Essays* (Basic Books: NY).

Gerschenkron, A. (1962), *Economic Backwardness in Historical Perspective* (HUP: Cambridge, MA).

Glaser, B. and A. Strauss (1967), *The Discovery of Grounded Theory* (Aldine: Chicago).

Granovetter, M. (1985), 'Economic Action and Social Structure: The Problem of Embeddedness', *American Journal of Sociology* (91).

—— (1994), 'Business Groups', in Smelser and Swedberg, eds., *Handbook of Economic Sociology* (Princeton University Press: Princeton).

Guillén, M. (1994), *Models of Management* (University of Chicago Press: Chicago).

Hall, P., ed. (1989), *The Political Power of Economic Ideas* (Princeton University Press: Princeton).

Hamilton, G. and N. Biggart (1988), 'Market, Culture and Authority: Comparative Analysis of Management and Organization in the Far East', *American Journal of Sociology* (94: suppl.).

Hofstede, G. (1980), *Culture's Consequences* (Sage: Newbury Park).

—— (1993), 'Intercultural Conflict and Synergy in Europe', in Hickson, ed., *Management in Western Europe* (Walter de Gruyter: Berlin).

Kogut, B. and D. Parkinson (1994), The Diffusion of American Principles to Europe', in Kogut, ed., *Country Competition: Technology and the Organizing of Work* (OUP: NY).

Latour, B. (1987), *Science in Action* (HUP: Cambridge, MA).

Mann, M. (1986), *The Sources of Social Power,* vol.i. (CUP: NY).

Meyer, J. and B. Rowan (1977), 'Institutionalized Organizations: Formal Structure as Myth and Ceremony', *American Journal of Sociology* (83:2).

Mill, J. S. (1843), *A System of Logic, Ratiocinative and Inductive* (John Parker: West Strand).

Moore, B. (1966), *Social Origins of Dictatorship and Democracy* (Beacon Press: Boston).

North, D. (1981), *Structure and Change in Economic History* (Norton: NY).

—— (1990), *Institutions, Institutional Change and Economic Performance* (CUP: NY).

Perrow, C. (1981), 'Markets, Hierarchies and Hegemony: A Critique of Chandler and Williamson', in Van de Ven and Joyce, eds., *Perspectives on Organization Design and Behavior* (John Wiley: NY).

Piore, M. and C. Sabel (1984), *The Second Industrial Divide* (Basic Books: NY).

Polanyi, K. (1944), *The Great Transformation* (Beacon Press: Boston).

Polanyi, K., C. Arensberg, and H. Pearson (1957), *Trade and Market in the Early Empires: Economies in History and Theory* (Henry Regnery: Chicago).

Powell, W. and P. DiMaggio, eds. (1991), *The New Institutionalism in Organizational Analysis* (University of Chicago Press: Chicago).

Ragin, C. (1987), *The Comparative Method* (University of California Press: Berkeley).

Rogers, E. (1982), *Diffusion of Innovations* (Free Press: Detroit).

Roy, W. (1990), 'Functional and Historical Logics in Explaining the Rise of the American Industrial Corporation', *Comparative Social Research* (12).

—— (1991), 'The Rise of Large American Industrial Corporations: Efficiency and Power Explanations', unpublished paper.

Rumelt, R. (1974), *Strategy, Structure and Economic Performance* (Harvard Business School Press: Boston).

Schumpeter, J. (1942), *Capitalism, Socialism and Democracy* (Harper & Brothers: NY).

—— (1954), *History of Economic Analysis* (George Allen and Unwin: London).

Scott, R., J. Meyer *et al.* (1994), *Institutional Environments and Organizations* (Sage: Newbury Park).

Skocpol, T. (1979), *States and Social Revolutions* (CUP: NY).

—— ed. (1984), *Vision and Method in Historical Sociology* (CUP: NY).

—— (1992), *Protecting Soldiers and Mothers* (HUP: Cambridge, MA).

Skocpol, T. and M. Somers (1980), 'The Uses of Comparative History in Macrosocial Inquiry', *Comparative Studies in Society and History* (22).

Smelser, N. and R. Swedberg, eds. (1994), *The Handbook of Economic Sociology* (Princeton University Press: Princeton).

Soysal, Y. (1994), *Limits of Citizenship* (University of Chicago Press: Chicago).

Strang, D. and J. Meyer (1993), 'Institutional Conditions for Diffusion', *Theory and Society* (22).

Tolbert, P. and L. Zucker (1983), 'Institutional Sources of Change in the Formal Structure of Organizations', *Administrative Science Quarterly* (28).

Valdès, J. G. (1995), *Pinochet's Economists: The Chicago School in Chile* (CUP: NY).

Veblen, T. (1904), *The Theory of Business Enterprise* (C. Scribner's Sons: NY).

Weber, M. (1949), *The Methodology of the Social Sciences* (Free Press: NY).

—— (1958), *The Protestant Ethic and the Spirit of Capitalism* (C. Scribner's Sons: NY).

—— (1959), *Le Savant et le Politique* (Plon: Paris).

—— (1978), *Economy and Society* (University of California Press: Berkeley).

—— (1996), *Sociologie des religions* (Gallimard: Paris)

Weiss, L. (1988), *Creating Capitalism* (Basil Blackwell: NY).

Westney, E. (1987), *Imitation and Innovation* (HUP: Cambridge, MA).

Williamson, O. (1975), *Markets and Hierarchies* (Free Press: NY).

—— (1981), 'The Modern Corporation: Origins, Evolutions, Attributes', *Journal of Economic Literature* (XIX): 1537–68.

—— (1985), *The Economic Institutions of Capitalism* (Free Press: NY).

COMPARISON OF SEVERAL COUNTRIES

Becker, J. and F. Knipping, eds. (1986), *Power in Europe?* (Walter de Gruyter: Berlin).

Blackmer, D. and S. Tarrow, eds. (1975), *Communism in Italy and in France* (Princeton University Press: Princeton).

Burns, P. and J. Dewhurst, eds. (1986), *Small Business in Europe* (Macmillan: Basingstoke).

Cameron, R. (1989), *A Concise Economic History of the World* (OUP: NY).

Carew, A. (1987), *Labour under the Marshall Plan* (Wayne State University Press: Detroit).

Cassis, Y. (1997), *Big Business* (OUP: Oxford).

Chamberlin, E., ed. (1954), *Monopoly and Competition and their Regulation* (Macmillan: London).

Chandler, A. and H. Daems, eds. (1980), *Managerial Hierarchies* (HUP: Cambridge, MA).

Clapham, J. (1968), *Economic Development of France and Germany, 1815–1914* (CUP: Cambridge).

Devinat, P. (1927), *Scientific Management in Europe* (International Labor Office: Geneva).

Dyas, G. and H. Thanheiser (1976), *The Emerging European Enterprise* (Westview: Boulder).

Esposito, C. (1994), *America's Feeble Weapon: Funding the Marshall Plan in France and Italy, 1948–1950* (Greenwood: Westport).

Franko, L. (1974), 'The Move towards a Multidivisional Structure in European Organizations', *Administrative Science Quarterly* (19:4).

Fridenson, P. (1978), 'The Coming of the Assembly Line to Europe', in Krohn, Layton and Weingart, eds., *Dynamics of Science and Technology* (D. Reidel: Dordrecht).

Gillingham, J. (1991), *Coal, Steel and the Rebirth of Europe* (CUP: NY).

Harbison, F. and E. Burgess (1954), 'Modern Management in Western Europe', *American Journal of Sociology* (60).

Harbison, F. and C. Myers (1959), *Management in the Industrial World* (McGraw Hill: NY).

Hickson, D., ed. (1993), *Management in Western Europe* (Walter de Gruyter: Berlin).

Horn, N. and J. Kocka, eds. (1979), *Law and the Formation of the Big Enterprises in the 19th and Early 20th Centuries* (Vandenhoeck and Ruprecht: Göttingen, Germany).

Kerr, C., J. Dunlop, F. Harbison, and C. Myers (1960), *Industrialism and Industrial Man* (HUP: Cambridge, MA).

Kindleberger, C. (1984), *A Financial History of Western Europe* (Allen and Unwin: London).

Krippendorf, E., ed. (1981), *The Role of the USA in the Reconstruction of Italy and West Germany, 1943–1949* (Materialen 16: Berlin).

League of Nations (1945), *Industrialization and Foreign Trade* (Geneva).

Leo XIII (1891), 'On the Conditions of Workers—Rerum Novarum', in *Two Basic Encyclicals* (1943) (Catholic University of America Press: Washington).

Léon, P. (1978), *Histoire Economique et Sociale du Monde* (Armand Colin: Paris).

Locke, R. (1989), *Management and Higher Education since 1940* (CUP: Cambridge).

McKenna, C. (1997), 'The American Challenge: McKinsey & Company's Role in the Transfer of Decentralization to Europe, 1957–1975', *Academy of Management Proceedings* (Boston).

Maddison, A. (1991), *Dynamic Forces in Capitalist Development* (OUP: NY).

Maier, C. (1970), 'Between Taylorism and Technocracy: European Ideologies and the Vision of Industrial Productivity in the 1920s', *Journal of Contemporary History* (5:2).

—— (1975), *Recasting Bourgeois Europe* (Princeton University Press: Princeton).

—— (1981), 'The Two Postwar Eras and the Conditions for Stability in Twentieth Century Western Europe', *American Historical Review* (86: 1).

Maurice, M., A. Sorge, and M. Warner (1980), 'Societal Differences in Organizing Manufacturing Units', *Organization Studies* (1: 1).

Maxeiner, J. (1986), *Policy and Methods in German and American Antitrust Law* (Praeger: NY).

Milward, A. (1984), *The Reconstruction of Western Europe: 1945–1951* (University of California Press: Berkeley).

OECE (1954), *Les Problèmes de Gestion des Entreprises: Opinions Américaines, Opinions Européennes* (Paris).

Pius XI (1931), 'Forty Years after on Reconstructing Social Order—Quadragesimo Anno', in *Two Basic Encyclicals* (1943) (Catholic University of America Press: Washington).

Storey, D., ed. (1983), *The Small Firm: An International Survey* (St Martin's Press: NY).

Whitley, R., ed. (1992), *European Business Systems* (Sage: London).

Whitley, R. (1994), 'Dominant Forms of Economic Organization in Market Economies', *Organization Studies* (15: 2).

Whittington, R., M. Mayer, and F. Curto (1997), 'The Progress of the Amercian Multidivisional: Explaining Change and Resistance in France, Germany, and the United Kingdom, 1950–1993', paper presented at the EGOS Colloquium (Budapest).

UNITED STATES

Primary Sources

Foreign Relations of the United States—FRUS (1945: vol. iv; 1946: vol. v; 1947: vol. ii and vol. iii; 1948: vol. iii; 1949: vol. iv; 1950: vol. iii; 1951: vol. iv).

US Department of Commerce—Bureau of the Census (1951, 1971), *Statistical Abstract of the US.*

Memoirs and Texts Contemporary with the Events

Acheson, D. (1950), *Present at the Creation* (Norton: NY).

Ball, G. (1982), *The Past has another Pattern* (Norton: NY).

Hoffman, P. (1951), *Peace can be Won* (Doubleday: NY).

Kennan, G. (1967), *Memoirs: 1925–1950* (Little Brown: Boston).

Lewis, S. (1920), *Main Street* (Harcourt Brace: NY).

—— (1922), *Babbit* (Harcourt Brace: NY).

Sloan, A. (1963), *My Years with General Motors* (Doubleday: NY).

Taft, W. (1911), 'On the Antitrust Statute', *Message of the President of the USA to the Houses of Congress—December 5, 1911* (Washington).

Taylor, F. (1911), *The Principles of Scientific Management* (Harper: NY).

Vandenberg, A. ed. (1952), *The Private Papers of Senator Vandenberg* (Houghton Mifflin: Boston).

Secondary Sources

Arkes, H. (1972), *Bureaucracy, the Marshall Plan and the National Interest* (Princeton University Press: Princeton).

Berle, A. and G. Means (1932), *Modern Corporation and Private Property* (Macmillan: NY).

Bittlingmayer, G. (1985), 'Did Antitrust Policy Cause the Great Merger Wave?', *Journal of Law and Economics* (28).

Bork, R. (1966), 'Legislative Intent and the Policy of the Sherman Act', *Journal of Law and Economics* (9).

Burnham, J. (1941), *The Managerial Revolution* (John Day: NY).

Chayes, A. (1969), 'The Modern Corporation and the Rule of Law', in Mason and Edward, eds., *The Corporation in Modern Society* (Atheneum: NY).

Chernow, R. (1990), *The House of Morgan* (Atlantic Monthly: NY).

Clark, J. (1940), 'Toward a Concept of Workable Competition', *American Economic Review* (XXX: 2).

Collins, R. (1981), *The Business Response to Keynes, 1929–1964* (Columbia University Press: NY).

Creighton, A. (1990), 'The Emergence of Incorporation as a Legal Form for Organizations', Ph.D. thesis (Stanford University).

Gardner, L. (1970), *Architects of Illusion: Men and Ideas in American Foreign Policy, 1941–1949* (Quadrangle Books: Chicago).

Goodwyn, L. (1976), *Democratic Promise: The Populist Movement in America* (OUP: NY).

Gordon, J. S. (1988), *The Scarlett Woman of Wall Street* (Weidenfeld & Nicholson: NY).

Hogan, M. (1984), 'Paths to Plenty: Marshall Planners and the Debate over European Integration, 1947–1948', *Pacific Historical Review* (53: 3).

—— (1985), 'American Marshall Planners and the Search for a European Neo-Capitalism', *American Historical Review* (90: 1).

—— (1987), *The Marshall Plan: America, Britain and the Reconstruction of Western Europe, 1947–1952* (CUP: NY).

Hounshell, D. (1984), *From the American System to Mass Production, 1800–1932* (Johns Hopkins University Press: Baltimore).

Jones, B. (1972), 'The Role of Keynesians in Wartime Policy and Postwar Planning, 1940–1946', *American Economic Review* (62: May).

Josephson, M. (1932), *The Robber Barons* (Harcourt, Brace and World: NY).

Kaspi, A. (1986), *Les Américains* (Seuil: Paris).

Katzenstein, P., ed. (1978), *Between Power and Plenty* (University of Wisconsin Press: Madison).

Kolko, G. (1963), *The Triumph of Conservatism* (Free Press: NY).

Kolko, J. and G. Kolko (1972), *The Limits of Power: The World and United States Foreign Policy, 1945–1954* (Harper & Row: NY).

Lamoreaux, N. (1985), *The Great Merger Movement in American Business, 1895–1904* (CUP: NY).

Livermore, S. (1935), 'Success of Industrial Mergers', *Quarterly Journal of Economics* (50).

Lloyd, H. (1894), *Wealth against Commonwealth* (Harper & Brothers: NY).

McCraw, T. (1984), *Prophets of Regulation* (Belknap of HUP: Cambridge, MA).

Maier, C. (1978), 'The Politics of Productivity: Foundations of American International Economic Policy after World War II', in Katzenstein, ed., *Between Power and Plenty* (University of Wisconsin Press: Madison).

Mason, E. (1958), 'The Apologetics of Managerialism', *The Journal of Business* (31).

Mayo, E. (1933), *The Human Problems of an Industrial Civilization* (Macmillan: NY).

Milward, A. (1989), 'Was the Marshall Plan Necessary?', *Diplomatic History* (13).

Moody, J. (1904), *The Truth about the Trusts* (Moody Publishing Company).

Nelson, R. (1959), *Merger Movements in American Industry, 1895–1956* (Princeton University Press: Princeton).

Parker, R. (1994), 'The Subnational State and Economic Organization', Ph.D. thesis (UCLA).

Parker-Gwin, R. and W. Roy (1996), 'Corporation Law and the Organization of Property in the United States: The Origin and Institutionalization of New Jersey Corporation Law, 1888–1903', *Politics and Society* (24: 2).

Price, H. (1955), *The Marshall Plan and its Meaning* (Cornell University Press: Ithaca, NY).

Roetschlisberger, F. and W. Dickson (1939), *Management and the Worker* (HUP: Cambridge, MA).

Roy, W. (1991), 'Statutory Corporate Law and American Corporations, 1880–1913', paper presented at the SSHA Meetings (New Orleans).

Rupert, M. (1995), *Producing Hegemony* (CUP: NY).

Salant, W. (1989), 'The Spread of Keynesian Doctrines and Practices in the United States', in Hall, ed., *The Political Power of Economic Ideas* (Princeton University Press: Princeton).

Schriftgiesser, K. (1967), *Business and Public Policy: The Role of the Committee for Economic Development, 1942–1967* (Prentice Hall: Englewood Cliffs).

Sklar, M. (1988), *Corporate Reconstruction of American Capitalism, 1890–1916* (CUP: NY).

Skocpol, T. and M. Weir (1985), 'State Structures and the Possibilities for "Keynesian" Responses to the Great Depression in Sweden, Britain and the USA', in Evans, Rueschmeyer, and Skocpol, eds., *Bringing the State Back In* (CUP: NY).

Steel, R. (1980), *Walter Lippmann and the American Century* (Random House: NY).

Sutton F. *et al.* (1956), *The American Business Creed* (HUP: Cambridge, MA).

Sweezy, A. (1972), 'The Keynesians and Government Policy, 1933–1939', *American Economic Review* (62: May).

Thorelli, H. (1954), *The Federal Antitrust Policy: Origination of an American Tradition* (Johns Hopkins University Press: Baltimore).

Van der Pijl, K. (1984), *The Making of an Atlantic Ruling Class* (Verso: London).

Zunz, O. (1990), *Making America Corporate* (University of Chicago Press: Chicago).

FRANCE

Primary Sources

Archives Nationales, Paris, France:

80AJ—Commissariat au Plan: 80AJ/1; 80AJ/2; 80AJ/7; 80AJ/11; 80AJ/13; 80AJ/17; 80AJ/19; 80AJ/20; 80AJ/21; 80AJ/25; 80AJ/77; 80AJ/80; 80AJ/276; 80AJ/277

81AJ—Institutions de Productivité: 81AJ/42–94; 81AJ/132; 81AJ/176; 81AJ/177; 81AJ/178; 81AJ/179; 81AJ/180; 81AJ181; 81AJ/197; 81AJ/198; 81AJ/204–213; 81AJ/215

130AQ—Archives de Compagnies Privées

F12/9966—Concentrations Industrielles

F60bis and F60ter—Secrétariat Général du Comité Interministériel pour les Questions de Coopération Economique Européenne (SGCI): F60bis/517; F60bis/518; F60ter/378; F60ter/381; F60ter/383; F60ter/392; F60ter/393; F60ter/394; F60ter/468; F60ter/522

Fondation Jean Monnet pour l'Europe, Lausanne, Switzerland:

AME—Fonds 'Seconde Guerre Mondiale': vol. ii; vol. iii; vol. iv

AMF—Fonds 'Plan de Modernisation et d'Equipement de la France, 1945–1950'

AMG—Fonds 'Plan Schuman, 1950–1952'

AMH—Fonds 'Communauté Européenne pour le Charbon et l'Acier (CECA), 1952–1955'

Interviews conducted by and for the Monnet Foundation: George Ball, July 15, 1981; Robert Marjolin, November 24, 1981; Robert Nathan, December 18, 1981; Eugene Rostow, November 12, 1987; Pierre Uri, October 13, 1981

Published Documents:

AFAP (1953), *Productivité aux Etats-Unis—Rapport de la Cinquième Mission Française aux Etats-Unis, du 1er Mars au 20 Septembre 1952* (Paris).

Comité National de la Productivité (1953), *Actions et Problèmes de Productivité: 1950–53* (Paris).

Commissariat Général du Plan (1946), *Rapport Général sur le Premier Plan de Modernisation et d'Equipement, Octobre* (Paris).

Commissariat Général à la Productivité (1956), 'Programmes de Formation Professionnelle', in *Objectifs et Réalisations, 1955–1956* (Paris).

Documentation Française (1947), 'La Politique Economique Américaine et l'Aide à la France', *Notes et Etudes Documentaires* (726) (Paris).

Documentation Française (1950), 'Recueil de Documents sur la Productivité', *Notes et Etudes Documentaires* (1296) (Paris).

Documentation Française (1953), 'L'Aide Economique des Etats-Unis à la France', *Notes et Etudes Documentaires* (1819) (Paris).

Documentation Française (1959), 'L'Agence Européenne de Productivité', *Notes et Etudes Documentaires* (2604) (Paris).

French Embassy (1956), *Productivity in France: Abstract of the First Report of the French National Productivity Committee* (Washington).

IFOP (1953), 'Les Etats-Unis, les Américains et la France', in *Sondages* (2) (Paris).

Imprimerie Nationale (1961), *Annuaire Statistique de la France—Rétrospectif* (Paris).

INSEE (1952), *Bulletin Mensuel de Statistique* (Supplément Avril–Juin) (Paris).

INSEE (1953), 'Etude Spéciale sur l'Industrie Française', in *Etudes et Conjoncture* (Paris).

INSEE (1956), *Les Etablissements Industriels et Commerciaux en France en 1954* (Paris).

INSEE (1974), *Les Entreprises et Etablissements Industriels et Commerciaux en 1966* (Paris).

Journal Officiel (February 1, 1919), *Débats Parlementaires* (Paris).

Journal Officiel (June 22/23, 1945), *Débats de l'Assemblée Consultative Provisoire* (Paris).

SADEP (1953), *Aux Sources de la Productivité Américaine: Premier Bilan des Missions Françaises* (Paris).

Newspapers:

L'Express (weekly). 1953–1955.
Le Nouvel Observateur (weekly). 1950–1953.

Memoirs and Texts Contemporary with the Events

Barbas, J. C., ed. (1989), *Pétain: discours aux Français* (Albin Michel: Paris).
Beigel, E. (1947), 'France and National Planning', *Political Science Quarterly* (62: 3).
Bloch-Lainé, F. (1976), *Profession: fonctionnaire* (Seuil: Paris).
Bloch-Lainé, F. and J. Bouvier (1986), *La France restaurée* (Fayard: Paris).
Boris, G. (1933), *La révolution Roosevelt* (Gallimard: Paris).
De Gaulle, C. (1964), *Complete War Memories of de Gaulle* (Simon and Schuster: NY).

—— (1970), *Discours et messages, 1940–1946* (Plon: Paris).

Duhamel, G. (1930), *Scènes de la vie future* (Mercure de France: Paris).

Fourquet, F., ed. (1980), *Les Comptes de la puissance* (Encres: Paris).

Gravier, J. F. (1953), '18, rue Martignac: le cerveau du plan', *Preuves* (December).

Langer, W. (1947), *Our Vichy Gamble* (A.A. Knopf: NY).

Lefaucheux, P. (1945), 'Passage au socialisme', *Cahiers Politiques* (March/April).

Michel, H. and B. Mirkine-Guetzevitch eds. (1954), *Les Idées politiques et sociales de la Résistance* (Presses Universitaires de France: Paris).

Monnet, J. (1976), *Mémoires* (Fayard: Paris).

Monnet, J. and R. Schuman (1986), *Correspondance: 1947–53* (Fondation Monnet: Lausanne).

Saint-Jean, C. (1947), 'Philosophie du Plan Monnet', *Revue Politique et Parlementaire* (55).

Siegfried, A. (1927), *America Comes of Age* (Harcourt Brace: NY).

Villiers, G.(1978), *Témoignages* (France-Empire: Paris).

Secondary Sources

Autin, J. (1984), *Les Frères Péreire* (Perrin: Paris).

Azéma, J. P. (1979), *De Munich à la Libération* (Seuil: Paris).

Azéma, J. P. et F. Bédarida, eds. (1992), *Vichy et les Français* (Fayard: Paris).

Balzac (de) H. (1930), *César Birroteau* (Garnier Frères: Paris).

Bauer, M. (1985), *Les Grandes manoeuvres industrielles* (Belfond: Paris).

Bédarida, F. and J. P. Rioux, eds. (1985), *Mendès-France et le Mendésisme* (Fayard: Paris).

Boltanski, L. (1981), 'America, America . . . Le Plan Marshall et l'importation du management', *Actes de la Recherche en Sciences Sociales* (38).

—— (1982), *Les Cadres* (Editions de Minuit: Paris).

Bossuat, G. (1984), 'Le Poids de l'aide américaine sur la politique économique et financière de la France en 1948', *Relations Internationales* (37).

—— (1986), 'L'Aide américaine à la France après la seconde guerre mondiale', *Vingtième Siècle* (9).

—— (1992), *La France, l'aide américaine et la construction européenne: 1944–1954* (Ministère des Finances: Paris).

—— (1993), 'La Contre-valeur de l'aide américaine à la France et à ses territoires d'outre-mer', in *Le Plan Marshall et le relèvement économique de l'Europe* (Ministère des Finances: Paris).

Bouvier, J. (1992), *Les Rothschild—histoire d'un capitalisme familial* (Complexe: Paris).

Brochier, H. (1965), 'La Planification comme processus de décision', *Cahiers de la Fondation Nationale des Sciences Politiques* (140).

Burgess, E. (1959), 'Management in France', in Harbison and Myers, eds., *Management and the Industrial World: An International Analysis* (McGraw Hill: NY).

Bustarret, H. (1962), 'L'Industrie sidérurgique et le plan', in *Le Plan français* (Ministère de la Coopération: Paris).

Cameron, R. and C. Freedeman (1983), 'French Economic Growth: A Radical Revision', *Social Science History* (7).

Caron, F. (1981), *Histoire économique de la France—19e, 20e siècles* (Armand Colin: Paris).

Clough, S. (1946), 'Retardative Factors in French Economic Development in the 19th and 20th Centuries', *Journal of Economic History*.

Cohen, S. (1969), *Modern Capitalist Planning: The French Model* (HUP: Cambridge, MA).

Comte, A. (1907), *Cours de philosophie politique* (Schleicher Frères: Paris).

—— (1943), *Oeuvres choisies* (Aubier: Paris).

Djelic, M. L. (1996), 'Genèse et fondements du plan Monnet: l'inspiration américaine', *Revue Française d'Etudes Américaines* (68).

Dreyfus, M. (1995), *Histoire de la CGT* (Complexe: Paris).

Duchêne, F. (1994), *Jean Monnet* (Norton: NY).

Dussauze, E. (1938), *L'Etat et les ententes industrielles* (Librairie Technique et Economique: Paris).

Ehrmann, H. (1957), *Organized Business in France* (Princeton University Press: Princeton).

Fourastié, J. (1953), 'Towards Higher Labor Productivity in the Countries of Western Europe', *International Labour Review* (April).

Frank, R. (1986), 'The French Dilemma: Modernization with Dependence or Independence and Decline', in Becker and Knipping, eds., *Power in Europe?* (Walter de Gruyter: Berlin).

Girard, L. (1952), *La Politique des travaux publics du Second Empire* (Armand Colin: Paris).

Girault, R. (1986), 'The French Decision Makers and their Perception of French Power in 1948', in Becker and Knipping, eds., *Power in Europe?* (Walter de Gruyter: Berlin).

Gonod, P. (1962), 'La Contribution des actions de productivité à l'exécution des plans', in *Le Plan français* (Ministère de la Coopération: Paris).

Guibert, B. (1975), 'La Mutation industrielle de la France', *Collections de l'INSEE* (série E-173/174).

Hall, P. (1986), *Governing the Economy* (OUP: NY).

Hayward, J. (1986), *The State and the Market Economy* (New York University Press: NY).

Hoffmann, S. (1962), 'The Effects of World War II on French Society and Politics', *French Historical Studies* (62).

—— ed. (1963), *In Search of France* (HUP: Cambridge, MA).

IFRI (1992), *Rapport RAMSES* (Dunod: Paris).

Jeanneney, J. N. (1980), 'Hommes d'affaires au piquet, septembre 1944–janvier 1946', *Revue Historique* (January–March).

—— (1981), *L'Argent-caché* (Fayard: Paris).

Jenny, F. and A. P. Weber (1974), *Concentration et politique des structures industrielles* (Documentation Française: Paris).

Kaspi, A. (1971), *La Mission Jean Monnet à Alger: mars–octobre 1943* (Publications de la Sorbonne: Paris).

Kesler, J. F. (1964), 'Les Anciens de l'ENA', *Revue Française de Sciences Politiques* (April).

—— (1985), *L'ENA, la société, l'état* (Berger-Levrault: Paris).

Kindleberger, C. (1963), 'The Postwar Resurgence of the French Economy', in Hoffmann, ed., *In Search of France* (HUP: Cambridge, MA).

—— (1976), 'Technical Education and the French Entrepreneur', in Carter, Foster, Moody, eds., *Enterprise and Entrepreneurs in 19th and 20th Century France* (Johns Hopkins University Press: Baltimore).

Kuisel, R. (1981), *Capitalism and the State in Modern France* (CUP: NY).

—— (1988), 'L'American "Way of Life" et les Missions Françaises de Productivité', *Vingtième Siècle* (88).

—— (1993), *Seducing the French* (University of California Press: Berkeley).

Lacorne, D., J. Rupnik, and M.F. Toinet, eds. (1990), *The Rise and Fall of Anti-Americanism* (St Martin's Press: NY).

Lacouture, J. (1981), *Mendès-France* (Seuil: Paris).

Landes, D. (1949), 'French Entrepreneurship and Industrial Growth in the 19th Century', *Journal of Economic History* (IX).

—— (1964), 'French Business and the Businessman: A Social and Cultural Analysis' in Earle, ed., *Modern France* (Russel and Russel: NY).

Lauber, V. (1981), 'The Gaullist Model of Economic Modernization', in Hoffmann and Andrews, eds., *The Fifth Republic at Twenty* (State University of New York Press: Albany).

Lavau, G. (1955), 'Notes sur un "Pressure Group" Français, La CGPME', *Revue Française de Sciences Politiques* (V: 2).

Lévy-Leboyer, M. (1974), 'Le Patronat français a-t-il été malthusien?', *Mouvement Social* (88).

—— (1976), 'Innovation and Business Strategies', in Carter, Foster, and Moody, eds., *Enterprise and Entrepreneurs in 19th and 20th Century France* (Johns Hopkins University Press: Baltimore).

Magondeaux (de), O. (1937), *Ententes industrielles en France* (Librairie Générale de Droit et de Jurisprudence: Paris).

Margairaz, M. (1982), 'Autour des accords Blum-Byrnes, Jean Monnet entre le consensus national et le consensus atlantique', *Histoire, Economie, Société* (3).

—— (1993), 'Les Finances, le plan Monnet et le plan Marshall', in *Le Plan Marshall et le relèvement économique de l'Europe* (Ministère des Finances: Paris).

Milza, P. (1979), *De Versailles à Berlin: 1919–1945* (Masson: Paris).

Mioche, P. (1981), 'Aux origines du plan Monnet', *Revue Historique* (295: 2).

—— (1987), *Le Plan Monnet, genèse et élaboration, 1941–1947* (Publications de la Sorbonne: Paris).

Morvan, Y. (1972), *La Concentration de l'industrie en France* (Armand Colin: Paris).

Moutet, A. (1975), 'Origines du système de Taylor en France', *Mouvement Social* (93).

Nye, J. V. (1987), 'Firm Size and Economic Backwardness: A New Look at the French Industrialization Debate', *Journal of Economic History* (47: 3).

O'Brien, P. and C. Keyder (1978), *Economic Growth in Britain and France 1780–1914: Two Paths to the Twentieth Century* (Allen and Unwin: London).

Oppetit, B. (1972), *Les Structures juridiques de l'entreprise* (Librairies Techniques: Paris).

Paxton, R. (1973), *La France de Vichy, 1940–1944* (Seuil: Paris).

Péan, P. (1994), *Une jeunesse française: François Mitterrand, 1934–1947* (Fayard: Paris).

Plessis, A. (1973), *De la fête impériale au mur des fédérés, 1852–1871* (Seuil: Paris).

Quignard, P. (1994), *L'Occupation américaine* (Seuil: Paris).

Rémond, R. (1982), *Les Droites en France* (Aubier Montaigne: Paris).

Rioux, J. P. (1980), *La France de la quatrième république, 1944–52* (Seuil: Paris).

—— (1983), *La France de la quatrième république, 1952–1958* (Seuil: Paris).

Rochebrune, R. and J. C. Hazéra (1995), *Les Patrons sous l'occupation* (Odile Jacob: Paris).

Roehl, R. (1976), 'French Industrialization: A Reconsideration', *Explorations in Economic History*—2nd Series (13).

Rosanvallon, P. (1989), 'The Development of Keynesianism in France' in Hall, ed., *The Political Power of Economic Ideas* (Princeton University Press: Princeton).

Roussel, E. (1996), *Jean Monnet* (Fayard: Paris).

Rowley, A. (1982), *Evolution économique de la France du milieu du 19e Siècle à 1914* (SEDES: Paris).

Sawyer, J. (1952), 'The Entrepreneur and the Social Order', in Miller, ed., *Men in Business* (HUP: Cambridge, MA).

Sée, H. (1942), *Histoire économique de la France* (Armand Colin: Paris).

Sélinsky, V. (1979), *L'Entente prohibée* (Librairies Techniques: Paris).

Servan-Schreiber, J. J. (1967), *Le Défi américain* (Denoël: Paris).

Siritzky, S. and F. Roth (1979), *Le Roman de 'L'Express'* (Atelier Marcel Jullian: Paris).

Strauss, D. (1978), *Menace in the West* (Greenwood Press: Westport).

Trotignon, Y. (1976), *La France au 20e Siècle—Tome I* (Bordas Etudes: Paris).

Venturini, V. (1971), *Monopolies and Restrictive Trade Practices in France* (Sijthoff: Leyden).

Vinen, R. (1991), *Politics of French Business: 1936–45* (CUP: NY).

Wall, I. (1991), *The United States and the Making of Postwar France: 1945–54* (CUP: NY).

Weber, H. (1986), *Le Parti des patrons—Le CNPF, 1946–90* (Seuil: Paris).

Zysman, J. (1977), *Political Strategies for Industrial Order* (University of California Press: Berkeley).

—— (1983), *Governments, Markets and Growth* (Cornell University Press: Ithaca).

GERMANY

Primary Sources

Bundesarchiv, Koblenz, Germany:

Z45F—OMGUS Records: Bd17—Control Office Historical Branch; Bd18—Bipartite Control Office, Economics Division and Decartelization Branch; Bd20—Bipartite Control Office, ERP Secretariat; Bd26—Bipartite Control Office, Finance Group; Bd27 and Bd28—Bipartite Control Office, Commerce and Industry Group; Bd29—Bipartite Control Office, Coal Control Group; Bd39–Bd42—Economics Division; Bd64 and Bd65—Office of the Political Adviser

Bestand Z3—Wirtschaftsrat des Vereigniten Wirtschaftsgebietes

Bestand Z8—Verwaltung für Wirtschaft des Vereigniten Wirtschaftsgebietes

Bestand Z14—Der Berater für den Marshallplan beim Vorsitzer des Verwaltungsrates
des Vereigniten Wirtschaftsgebietes
Bestand B102—Bundesministerium für Wirtschaft
Bestand B140—Gesellschaft zur Förderung des deutsch-amerikanischen Handels
Bestand B146—Bundesministerium für den Marshallplan

Published Documents:

Merritt, A. and R., eds. (1970), *OMGUS Surveys—Public Opinion in Occupied Germany
1945–1949* (University of Illinois Press: Urbana).
Office of the Historian, US Department of State (1986), *Documents on Germany, 1944–
85* (Washington).
OMGUS Manpower Division (1949), 'The Development of Management Associations
in Germany—Dillard Bird', *Visiting Expert Series* (#12) (Frankfurt, Germany).
Ruhm von Oppen, B., ed. (1955), *Documents on Germany under Occupation: 1945–54*
(OUP: Oxford).
Statistisches Bundesamt (1953, 1954, 1973, 1974), *Statistisches Jahrbuch für die
Bundesrepublik Deutschlands* (Wiesbaden, Germany).

Memoirs and Texts Contemporary with the Events

Adenauer, K. (1966), *Memoirs: 1949–1953* (Henry Regnery: Chicago).
Borkin, J. and C. Welsch (1943), *Germany's Master Plan: The Story of Industrial
Offensive* (Duell, Sloan, and Pearce: NY).
Clay, L. (1950), *Decision in Germany* (Doubleday: NY).
—— (1984), 'Proconsul of a People, by another People, for both Peoples', in Wolfe,
ed., *Americans as Proconsuls, 1944–1952* (Southern Illinois University Press:
Carbondale and Edwardsville).
Erhard, L. (1958), *Prosperity through Competition* (Frederick Praeger: NY).
—— (1963), *The Economics of Success* (Van Nostrand: Princeton).
Martin, J. (1950), *All Honorable Men* (Little Brown: Boston).
Wolfe, R., ed. (1984), *Americans as Proconsuls, 1944–1952* (Southern Illinois Uni-
versity Press: Carbondale and Edwardsville).
Zink, H. (1957), *The USA in Germany* (Van Nostrand: Princeton).

Secondary Sources

Abelshauser, W. (1993), 'La Reconstruction de l'Allemagne de l'Ouest', in *Le Plan
Marshall et le Relèvement Economique de l'Europe* (Ministère des Finances: Paris).
Allen, C. (1989), 'The Underdevelopment of Keynesianism in the Federal Republic of
Germany', in Hall, ed., *The Political Power of Economic Ideas* (Princeton University
Press: Princeton).
Backer, J. (1971), *Priming the German Economy* (Duke University Press: Durham).
Bark, D. and D. Gress (1992), *Histoire de l'Allemagne depuis 1945* (Robert Laffond:
Paris).
Berghahn, V. (1984), 'Ideas into Politics: the Case of Ludwig Erhard', in Bullen, Von
Strandmann, and Polonsky, eds., *Ideas into Politics* (Croom Helm: London).

—— (1986), *The Americanization of West German Industry* (CUP: Cambridge).

Bowen, R. (1950), 'The Roles of Government and Private Enterprise in German Industrial Growth, 1870–1914', *Journal of Economic History* (Supplement X).

Braunthal, G. (1965), *The Federation of German Industry in Politics* (Cornell University Press: Ithaca).

Cable, J. (1979), 'Merger Development and Policy in West Germany since 1958', *Warwick Economic Research Papers* (150).

Cable, J. and M. Dirrheimer (1983), 'Hierarchies and Markets', *International Journal of Industrial Organization* (1).

Damm, W. (1958), 'National and International Factors Influencing Cartel Legislation in Germany', Ph.D. thesis (University of Chicago).

Dorn, W. (1957), 'The Debate over American Occupation in Germany in 1944–45', *Political Science Quarterly* (72: 4).

Droz, J. (1970), *La Formation de l'Unité Allemande, 1789–1871* (Hatier Université: Paris).

Edinger, L. (1960), 'Post-Totalitarian Leadership: Elites in the German Federal Republic', *American Political Science Review* (54: 1).

Gatzke, H. (1980), *Germany and the United States: A ' Special Relationship'?* (HUP: Cambridge, MA).

Gimbel, J. (1968*a*), *The American Occupation of Germany* (Stanford University Press: Stanford).

—— (1968*b*), 'American Military Government and the Education of a New German Leadership', *Political Science Quarterly* (83: 2).

Grosser (1985), *L'Allemagne en Occident* (Fayard: Paris).

Hardach, G. (1993), L'Intégration internationale de l'économie allemande', in *Le Plan Marshall et le relèvement économique de l'Europe* (Ministère des Finances: Paris).

Hardach, K. (1980), *The Political Economy of West Germany in the Twentieth Century* (University of California Press: Berkeley).

Hayes, P. (1987), *Industry and Ideology: I. G. Farben in the Nazi Era* (CUP: NY).

Kocka, J. (1971), 'Family and Bureaucracy in German Industrial Management, 1850–1914', *Business History Review* (45: 2).

—— (1978), 'Entrepreneurs and Managers in German Industrialization', in Mathias and Postan, eds., *The Cambridge Economic History of Europe*, vol. vii (CUP: Cambridge).

Lawrence, P. (1980), *Managers and Management in West Germany* (St Martin's Press: NY).

Levy, H. (1966), *Industrial Germany: A Study of its Monopoly Organizations and their Control by the State* (Frank Cass: London).

Liefmann, R. (1938), *Cartels, Concerns and Trusts* (Dutton: NY).

Link, W. (1991), 'Building Coalitions: Non-Governmental German-American Linkages', in Maier and Bischof, eds., *The Marshall Plan and Germany* (Berg: NY).

Maier, C. and G. Bischof, eds. (1991), *The Marshall Plan and Germany* (Berg: NY).

Marburg, T. (1964), 'Government and Business in Germany: Public Policy towards Cartels', *Business History Review* (38).

Mayer, H. (1969), *German Recovery and the Marshall Plan* (Atlantic Forum: Bonn).

Michels, R. (1928), *Cartels, Combines and Trusts in Postwar Germany* (Columbia University Press: NY).

Morgan, R. (1974), *The United States and West Germany, 1945–1973* (OUP: NY).

Nicholls, A. (1984), 'The Other Germany, the Neo-Liberals', in Bullen, Von Strandmann, and Polonsky, eds., *Ideas into Politics* (Croom Helm: London).

Owen-Smith, E. (1983), *The West German Economy* (St Martin's Press: NY).

Peacock, A. and H. Willgerodt, eds. (1989), *Germany's Social Market Economy: Origins and Evolution* (St Martin's Press: NY).

Peterson, E. (1977), *The American Occupation of Germany: Retreat to Victory* (Wayne State University Press: Detroit).

Pietri, N. (1982), *Evolution Economique de l'Allemagne du Milieu du 19e Siècle à 1914* (SEDES: Paris).

Pohl, H. (1993), 'Die Westdeutsche Währungsreform von 1948 und ihre Wirtschaftlichen Folgen', in *Le Plan Marshall et le relèvement économique de l'Europe* (Ministère des Finances: Paris).

Schwartz, T. (1991*a*), *America's Germany* (HUP: Cambridge, MA).

—— (1991*b*), 'European Integration and the 'Special Relationship': Implementing the Marshall Plan in the Federal Republic', in Maier and Bischof, eds., *The Marshall Plan and Germany* (Berg: NY)

Shirer, W. (1959), *The Rise and Fall of the Third Reich* (Simon and Schuster: NY).

Stokes, R. (1988), *Divide and Prosper* (University of California Press: Berkeley).

Taylor, G. (1979), 'The Rise and Fall of Antitrust in Occupied Germany', *Prologue* (11).

Tilly, R. (1982), 'Mergers, External Growth and Finance in the Development of Large Scale Enterprise in Germany, 1880–1913', *Journal of Economic History* (42: 3).

Vogl, F. (1973), *German Business after the Economic Revival* (Macmillan: London).

Wallich, H. (1955), *Mainsprings of German Revival* (Yale University Press: New Haven).

ITALY

Allen, K. and A. Stevenson (1974), *An Introduction to the Italian Economy* (Martin Robertson: London).

Blim, M. (1990), *Made in Italy* (Praeger: NY).

Brusco, S. (1982), 'The Emilian Model: Productive Decentralization and Social Integration', *Cambridge Journal of Economics* (6).

Clough, S. (1964), *The Economic History of Modern Italy* (Columbia University Press: NY).

D'Attore, P. P. (1981), 'The European Recovery Program in Italy: Research Problems', in Krippendorf, ed., *The Role of the United States in the Reconstruction of Italy and West Germany, 1943–49* (Materialen 16: Berlin).

De Cecco, M. (1972), 'Economic Policy in the Reconstruction Period, 1945–1951', in Woolf, ed., *The Rebirth of Italy, 1943–50* (Longman).

—— (1989), 'Keynes and Italian Economics', in Hall, ed., *The Political Power of Economic Ideas* (Princeton University Press: Princeton).

Goodman, E. and J. Bamford, eds. (1989), *Small Firms and Industrial Districts in Italy* (Routledge: London).

Grinrod, M. (1955), *The Rebuilding of Italy: Politics and Economics, 1945–55* (Royal Institute for Economic Affairs: London).

Harper, J. L. (1986), *America and the Reconstruction of Italy, 1945–48* (CUP: NY).

Hildebrand, G. (1965), *Growth and Structure in the Economy of Modern Italy* (HUP: Cambridge, MA).

Hughes, S. (1965), *The United States and Italy* (HUP: Cambridge, MA).

Istituto Centrale di Statistica (1955), *Censimento Generale dell'Industria e del Commercio, 1951* (Rome).

Istituto Centrale di Statistica (1976), *Censimento Generale dell'Industria e del Commercio, 1971* (Rome).

Miller, J. E. (1981), 'The Politics of Relief: the Roosevelt Administration and the Reconstruction of Italy, 1943–44', *Prologue* (Fall).

—— (1986), *The United States and Italy, 1940–1950* (University of North Carolina Press: Chapel Hill).

Orrù, M. (1991), 'The Institutional Logic of Small-Firm Economies in Italy and Taiwan', *Studies in Comparative International Development* (26: 1).

Pavan, R. (1976), 'Strategy and Structure: The Italian Experience', *Journal of Economics and Business* (28).

Romano, S. (1977), *Histoire de l'Italie du Risorgimento à nos Jours* (Seuil: Paris).

Vigezzi, B. (1986), 'Italy: The End of a Great Power and the Birth of a Democratic Power', in Becker and Knipping, eds., *Power in Europe?* (Walter de Gruyter: Berlin).

Weiss, L. (1984), 'The Italian State and Small Business', *European Journal of Sociology* (25).

Wiskemann, E. (1971), *Italy since 1945* (St Martin's Press: London).

Woolf, S. (1972), *The Rebirth of Italy, 1943–50* (Humanities: NY).

Zamagni, V. (1986), 'Betting on the Future: The Reconstruction of Italian Industry, 1946–52', in Becker and Knipping, eds., *Power in Europe?* (Walter de Gruyter: Berlin).

INDEX